MICROECONOMICS FOR MANAGERIAL DECISION MAKING

McGRAW-HILL BOOK COMPANY

New York | St. Louis | San Francisco
Auckland | Bogotá | Hamburg
Johannesburg | London | Madrid
Mexico | Montreal | New Delhi | Panama
Paris | São Paulo | Singapore
Sydney | Tokyo | Toronto

ROGER D. BLAIR
LAWRENCE W. KENNY

Professors of Economics
College of Business Administration
University of Florida

MICRO-
ECONOMICS
FOR
MANAGERIAL
DECISION
MAKING

MICROECONOMICS
FOR
MANAGERIAL
DECISION
MAKING

234567890   DODO   898765432

ISBN 0-07-005800-8

This book was set in Palatino by A Graphic Method Inc.
The editors were Bonnie E. Lieberman and James B. Armstrong;
the designer was Nicholas Krenitsky;
the production supervisor was Dominick Petrellese.
The drawings were done by Fine Line Illustrations, Inc.
R. R. Donnelley & Sons Company was printer and binder.

Library of Congress Cataloging in Publication Data

Blair, Roger D.
    Microeconomics for managerial decision making.

    Includes index.
    1. Microeconomics.   2. Managerial economics.
I. Kenny, Lawrence W.   II. Title.
HB172.B54   338.5'024658   81-11748
ISBN 0-07-005800-8   AACR2

To those who have helped us the most:
CHAU,
CHRIS,
DAVID,
and **DON**

CONTENTS

PREFACE

In teaching intermediate microeconomic theory for undergraduate business majors and for M.B.A. candidates, we have been made painfully aware of the fact that the traditional treatment goes unappreciated. Since the standard intermediate theory textbook was written primarily for economics majors, one should not be surprised to discover that such textbooks prove to be unpopular among business students. The most common complaints among students focus on the arcane or esoteric nature of pure theory. Moreover, students often fail to see how economic reasoning can usefully be applied to their major interest. Many a student has asked, "Why do I have to take microeconomic theory? I am an accounting [substitute "marketing," "management," "finance," "real estate"] major."

We have tried to anticipate this complaint in our text. Rather than merely put a few examples and/or applied problems in our text, we have attempted to teach economic principles and reasoning through repeated application. Our text covers the essential topics that are customarily taught in intermediate-level price theory courses. In addition, we have included a large variety of novel topics germane to business students. We begin by developing the core economic theory and principles that will be used throughout the text and then apply these principles repeatedly to numerous business decisions. Students learn not only how to apply price theory to the specific business decisions that we address but also how to apply the principles of price theory to just about any problem they will come across. In the process, students also end up learning the principles of price theory. There are additional benefits to this approach. When students discover that they can use microeconomics in making business decisions, they are happier and the course is more fun to teach.

Having a large number of applications in the textbook makes it possible to accomplish several goals. We are able to examine several business decisions that are of particular interest to *any* business major. For example, in the marketing chapter (Chapter 13), we consider advertising, private brands, and the allocation of sales personnel. Topics that are of special interest to accounting, insurance, finance, and management majors are found in other sections of the book. We also are able to include a large number of topics that are not found in the standard textbook. For example, we have developed the following: the choice of products and product quality, location decisions of the firm, investment decisions (under certainty and uncertainty), compensating wage differentials, optimal inventory (under certainty and uncertainty), joint products, peak-load pricing, spot markets, product survival, and transfer pricing. By including topics such as these, we hope to show students how robust and useful a command of microeconomics can be.

A great amount of material is covered in our text, and some additional material is found in the teacher's manual. This gives the instructor considerable flexibility. The instructor can concentrate on the core theory chapters, concentrate on the applications chapters, or allocate time evenly between the two.

The treatment of several topics found in other textbooks is novel. Chapter 3 is devoted to estimating demand functions. In this chapter, we do not concentrate on extensively developing the statistical theory behind regressions, an almost impossible task for one chapter. Instead, we emphasize the manager's role in deciding what variables (e.g., income, price of car batteries) should be included in a study of demand in his or her industry. We also describe in some detail the process of estimating a demand function. Furthermore, the appendix following Chapter 5 deals with the derived demand for inputs. In almost every treatment of derived demand, the magnitude of the output effect accompanying a change in a factor price is unspecified. On the other hand, in our development of derived demand, the uncertainty surrounding the output effect is removed, for the magnitude of the output effect depends on the change in the quantity of industry output that is demanded.

Much of the teaching in the textbook is done through rhetorical questions which are followed by answers. In this way, we try to demonstrate how economic reasoning is done. Furthermore, it helps to guide students in answering the questions found at the end of each chapter.

Finally, to convince the skeptic that microeconomic analysis is useful, we have included a number of anecdotes drawn from actual experience.

We, like all authors, had to face the question of how to refer to managers, customers, and so on. Our solution was to refer to the manager as "she" in roughly half the sections and as "he" in the rest of the sections.

This textbook owes a great deal to many people. Our students at the University of Florida have played a large part in this text. It was written to a large extent because we could not find a text that properly teaches microeconomics to business students. We also owe much to several classes at the University of Florida who endured early drafts of this book. The following people reviewed the entire manuscript and offered many useful suggestions during the development of the manuscript: Bruce Allen, Lee Benham, Donald Bumpass, Edward Deak, Damodar Gujarati, Harold Phillips, Mark Schaefer, Charles Stokes, Daniel Strang, and Daniel Williamson. We would also like to thank our colleagues Rashad Abdel-Kalik, James Adams, Dipankar Chakravarti, Douglas Diamond, and James Tipton for their perceptive comments on parts of the manuscript. Ella Carl provided a large number of helpful suggestions. Mary Jo Hancock and Dian Studstill diligently typed numerous drafts of this manuscript. Finally, we owe a very great debt to our families for their patience and support over the past two years.

ROGER D. BLAIR
LAWRENCE W. KENNY

MICROECONOMICS FOR MANAGERIAL DECISION MAKING

ONE

INTRODUCTION

1

FIRMS, MANAGERS, AND ECONOMICS

The term "managerial economics" means different things to different people. For us, however, managerial economics is simply the application of microeconomic principles to business problems by the manager of a firm. Whenever a manager makes a business decision on behalf of his firm, there are microeconomic principles that can assist him in making the best decision.

For a better appreciation of what this means, we shall discuss the nature of the firm and what its goals are. This provides a framework for describing the manager's role in the firm.

1.1

DEFINITION OF A FIRM

We observe firms all around us. From the humble hot dog stand and local 7-Eleven to the mighty General Motors and IBM, firms are pervasive in our economy. In a sense, we all know what a firm is. Nonetheless, it is helpful to have an explicit conception of the firm, reasons for its existence, and the role of the manager within the firm.

To this end, we may conceive of a firm as an organization that converts inputs into goods and services that it can sell. In a sole proprietorship, the owner-employee may buy or lease the necessary inputs and sell the output himself. There are many examples of such simple firms: an owner-operator of a taxi, a farmer, a lawyer who is a sole practitioner, and the owner of a small retail store. The owner of a taxi has to buy the goods and services necessary to keep his taxi operational—maintenance service, tires, batteries, gasoline, and so on. He also organizes his own labor services but has minimal supervisory duties. Other firms can be substantially more complicated. For example, an owner who does not perform all the labor has employees to supervise, and as we shall see, this is a very important factor. Additional complications may arise that are associated with coordinating a vast array of inputs in the production of a variety of outputs. The theme that is central to all firms, however, is that inputs are purchased and outputs are produced. The firm is an intermediary between the input and output markets.

1.2

WHY FIRMS EXIST

Firms are not really necessary *in principle*. All productive activities could be organized by relying on the price mechanism.[1] One could imagine separate contracts for each function

[1]Much of this discussion depends heavily upon Ronald H. Coase, "The Nature of the Firm," *Economica*, vol. 4, November 1937, pp. 386–405.

performed by firms as we know them. For example, knife blades could be made by an expert, as could the knife handles. An assembler could contract for the delivery of a specific number of handles and blades for assembly. The completed knives could be marketed by another specialist and finally delivered to the ultimate consumer. Any janitorial services could be purchased separately as needed. Independent accountants could keep the books. And so on.

Generally, however, we do not see production and distribution being organized through a series of market transactions requiring narrowly specified contracts. Instead, the entrepreneur gathers an array of inputs and directs production, distribution, and a host of other functions within a single firm. The entrepreneur, through managerial discretion, replaces market transactions with commands.

There are two reasons why production and distribution are organized through firms rather than through a series of individual contracts. First, there are costs associated with using the market. Second, output can be expanded by the use of group production.

TRANSACTIONS COSTS   When the market is used in each phase of the production of a product, various costs are incurred. For example, information is often costly. This means that each time an exchange is contemplated, the entrepreneur must ascertain a reasonable price for the transaction. Costs are also incurred in negotiating separate contracts for each exchange. When production is organized within the firm rather than through the marketplace, however, a large fraction of these costs is eliminated; because most inputs are owned, the entrepreneur can direct and redirect them as she pleases.[2] Furthermore, because it is costlier to make a series of extremely short-run contracts than a single contract of longer duration, firms, by eliminating the need to rely upon short-run contracts, facilitate planning. Production activity is also more concentrated geographically, with obvious savings in transportation costs, when production is organized within a firm than it is when production occurs through the marketplace. Finally, the government often treats market transactions differently from identical internal exchanges. The most obvious cases of this bias involve sales taxes and price controls. For example, if a sales tax is levied on each transaction, one pays taxes on the tax component of the price. The integration of some transactions under the umbrella of the firm can prevent this.

GROUP PRODUCTION   Another reason for the existence of firms is the organization of production by teams or groups.[3] If the output of a team exceeds the sum of the output that could be produced individually, there are benefits

---

[2]Workers do not agree to unconditionally obey the entrepreneur's directions. Nevertheless, within the agreed-upon limits, the entrepreneur has considerable flexibility in just how her workers are employed.

[3]The importance of group production was developed most fully by Armen Alchian and Harold Demsetz in "Production, Information Costs, and Economic Organization," *American Economic Review*, vol. 62, December 1972, pp. 777–795.

to organizing production by teams. Group production, however, is also costly because of the incentives inherent in group production for shirking.

When inputs are employed in a group effort, it is often difficult to assess the separate contribution of each member simply by observing the total output. We have often seen instances where an athletic team flounders when a seemingly ordinary team member is absent. This can also be true in a production setting. The difficulty of measuring the separate contributions causes a serious problem: there is an incentive for each worker to shirk that would not exist otherwise. In other words, each employee can reduce his effort in the hope that the others will maintain their efforts. Output will, of course, be reduced, but the shirker will enjoy greater leisure and the consequences of reduced production will be spread over the entire group. As a result, specialists are hired to monitor the efforts of each worker. The ultimate monitor in any firm is the entrepreneur, who organizes the firm and bears the business risks. Her compensation is in the form of a residual—the amount of money left after all payments to hired factors are made. Since she has title to the residual, she has no incentive to shirk herself and has an incentive to reduce the shirking of all other workers.

In summary, because of higher productivity of group production and the elimination of the additional transactions costs associated with individual production, firms come into existence. In particular, firms offer a superior organization of production if the dollar value of the extra output is at least as large as the total costs of organizing, monitoring, metering, and enforcing contracts with employees minus the additional transactions costs of individual production.[4]

1.3

GOALS OF THE FIRM

There are many goals that have been suggested as characterizing the motivation of the firm and its managers. These include profit maximization, staff maximization, sales revenue maximization, and growth maximization. While a number of these goals may have some appeal, the question of how real firms behave is a factual question.

Because of the weight of the evidence, we adopt in this book the convention that the goal of the firm is profit maximization. In Chapter 15, we will fully examine the implications of adopting a number of other assumptions about the goals of the firm. To appreciate the significance of the assumption of profit maximization, we first have to understand what is meant by the term "profit."

DEFINITION ▶   Profit Π is the difference between total revenue (TR) and total cost (TC):

$$\Pi = TR - TC$$

---

[4]This conclusion is found in Roger Leroy Miller, *Intermediate Microeconomics*, New York: McGraw-Hill Book Company, 1978.

Total revenue is a rather simple concept because the words generally mean the same thing to economists, accountants, and businesspersons. It is merely the firm's total receipts from the sale of its goods and services. In contrast, total cost does not mean the same thing to everyone. When economists use the term "cost," they mean both *explicit* and *implicit* costs. Explicit costs are the out-of-pocket expenditures that a firm makes to purchase resources. Implicit costs are incurred when the entrepreneur invests his own time and resources in the firm. These implicit costs are measured by the market value of the entrepreneur's time and resources. For example, if a firm's total revenue is $10,000 in one week and the explicit costs are $9,500, one may be tempted to claim a profit of $500. But from that $500, one must subtract the market value of the entrepreneur's efforts, say, $400. This leaves a profit of $100 unless there are other resources that have been neglected. Perhaps the business is conducted in a building owned by the entrepreneur. If so, the rental value of the building must also be deducted. Only by a careful accounting of all implicit as well as explicit costs can we accurately measure the firm's profit.

There are a number of reasons for assuming that firms maximize profit. An entrepreneur who maximizes her firm's profit can spend that profit on whatever she wishes. If the entrepreneur takes other considerations (e.g., the race of her employees or her firm's share of the market) into account when she makes her business decisions, her firm's profit, and thereby her personal consumption of goods and services, will fall. Moreover, competition from profit-maximizing firms may force a firm that does not maximize its profit out of business. For these reasons, we assume that the firm's owner wishes to maximize the firm's profits. Accordingly, when the manager is also the entrepreneur, there is ample reason to suppose that decisions will be made that tend to maximize the residual which we call profit. There is no conflict of interest.

In a more general setting, however, there may be some conflict of interest due to the fact that many managers are not entrepreneurs. Managers are interested in enhancing their own well-being, and it is clear that this will not always be consistent with the interests of the entrepreneur. For instance, managers who feel that their prestige depends on their firm's total revenue or on the number of staff members working under them will either try to bring in more total revenue than maximizes profit or try to hire too many staff members. Other managers may be interested in hiring their own children or in discriminating against certain groups of workers. Each of these actions costs the owners lost profits.

The firm's owners often respond to this problem by making it very costly for the manager not to maximize profit. Executive stock options, bonuses, and raises are used to give managers an incentive to maximize profit. As we shall see in Chapter 15, the empirical evidence suggests that managers are rewarded for profit maximization, not revenue maximization. Moreover, a great many predictions about firm behavior that are based on profit maximization have been verified. For these reasons, we shall assume that the manager makes economic decisions in an effort to maximize profits.

1.4

PROFIT MAXIMIZATION
OVER TIME

Very few businesses are in existence for only a year. Firms with a more extended lifetime have a stream of profits and losses over time. The sums that are paid to owners when firms are purchased reflect the value of expected future profits.

Entrepreneurs are interested not in maximizing the profit in any given year but in maximizing the value of the stream of profits and losses over time. As a result, losses are incurred today in order to make higher profits in future years. Plants are built, advertising campaigns are run, and training programs are established—all because the value of the expected future profits more than covers current costs. Banks recognize this when they lend money to firms.

For the manager to maximize the value of the stream of profits and losses over time, each future dollar of profit or loss must be made comparable to a dollar of profit or loss today. This is not a trivial task because $1 can be invested today and consequently can increase in value over time as it earns interest.

FUTURE VALUES Suppose a lender can earn 12 percent interest on an annual basis. In deciding how to invest her firm's funds, the manager must recognize that lending is a viable alternative. If she lends $100 at 12 percent interest, the firm will have $112 at the end of the first year:

$$\$100(1 + r) = \$100(1.12) = \$112$$

where r equals the interest rate. At the end of 2 years, the firm would have $125.44 because of the compounding of interest:

$$\begin{aligned}
\$100(1 + r)(1 + r) &= \$100(1 + r)^2 \\
&= \$100(1.12)^2 \\
&= \$100(1.2544) \\
&= \$125.44
\end{aligned}$$

We can see that the firm does not receive just another $12 in interest in the second year. Instead, it receives $13.44. The additional $1.44 results from earning interest on the first year's interest: 12 percent of $12 is $1.44.

As a general proposition, the future value (FV) of $1 at an interest rate of r per year in n years can be written as

$$FV = \$1(1 + r)^n$$

Once this is computed, the future value of, say, $547 in n years can be found by multiplying the future value of $1 by 547.

Needless to say, the arithmetic involved in calculating the future value of

$1 at 8 percent interest in, say, 14 years would be quite cumbersome if it is done by hand:

$$FV = \$1(1.08)^{14}$$

Fortunately, it is seldom necessary to perform such calculations by hand. There are inexpensive pocket calculators that handle the job quite nicely. In addition, there are tables that provide the future value of $1 in various years at a variety of interest rates.

Table 1 at the end of the book provides the future value of $1 for up to 25 years at different interest rates. For example, if we want to find the future value of $1 at 8 percent interest in 12 years, we look at the entry in the table in row (12) and the column headed 8 percent. This value is 2.518. If we want to know the future value of $500 invested at 8 percent interest for 12 years, we multiply the future value of $1 by 500:

$$FV (\$500) = \$500(2.518) = \$1,259.$$

PRESENT VALUES   Almost everyone knows that $1 to be received at some point in the future is worth less than $1 today. This is not entirely due to inflation, because it is equally true when the rate of inflation is zero. Rather, it is a reflection of the fact that $1 today can be invested and over time will earn interest until some point in the future. Suppose that $1 invested today could earn 10 percent over the course of a year. At the end of the year, the investor would have $1.10:

$$\$1.00(1 + 0.10) = \$1.10$$

We can see that $1 at the end of the year is worth less than $1 now. To find out how much less, we must ask the question, "What sum earning a 10 percent return will be worth $1 in a year?" The answer is

$$\$X(1 + 0.10) = \$1.00$$
$$\$X = \frac{\$1.00}{1.10}$$
$$= \$0.91$$

Accordingly, $1 a year from now is worth $0.91 today if the interest rate is 10 percent.

What happens if the manager must wait for 2 years in order to receive the $1? In that case, we have to calculate the interest factor for 2 years:

$$\$X(1 + 0.10)(1 + 0.10) = \$1.00$$
$$\$X = \frac{\$1.00}{(1.10)^2}$$
$$\$X = \$0.83$$

That is, the present value of a dollar 2 years from now is $0.83 cents if the interest rate is 10 percent. This procedure generalizes quite nicely. The present value of $1 in n years is

$$PV = \frac{\$1.00}{(1 + r)^n}$$

There are present-value tables that make our calculations a bit easier. Table 2 at the end of the book provides the present value of $1 to be received at various years in the future at various interest rates. For example, the present value of $1 to be received 8 years from now when the interest rate is 9 percent can be found in the table in the eighth row and the column headed 9 percent. The value is $0.502, which rounds to $0.50. In order to find the present value of $100 to be received 8 years from now at 9 percent interest, we simply multiply the table value of 0.502 by $100: $50.20.

Question   On his sixteenth birthday, John Jones is left a $5,000 bequest by his rich aunt. The money is to be paid in full on John's twenty-first birthday. What is the present value of $5,000 if the appropriate interest rate is 8 percent?

Answer   First, we must determine the present value of $1 to be collected in 5 years:

$$PV = \frac{\$1.00}{(1.08)^5}$$
$$= \$0.681$$

This can be calculated quite easily on a pocket calculator. Alternatively, it can be found in Table 2 at the intersection of row (5) and the column labeled 8 percent. To find the present value of $5,000, we simply multiply $5,000 by 0.681:

$$\$5,000(0.681) = \$3,405$$

Thus, the present value of the bequest is $3,405.

VALUING A STREAM OF PROFITS   As we have noted, most managers expect that their firms will receive profits over several years. If the manager wants to determine the present value of a stream of profits, all she has to do is calculate the separate present values and add them up. For example, if the firm's profit in the current year equals Π_0, the firm's profit 1 year in the future equals Π_1, profit 2 years hence equals Π_2, and so on, the present value of a profit stream running 4 years into the future equals

$$PV = \Pi_0 + \frac{\Pi_1}{1 + r} + \frac{\Pi_2}{(1 + r)^2} + \frac{\Pi_3}{(1 + r)^3} + \frac{\Pi_4}{(1 + r)^4}$$

Question   The manager of the firm XYZ has negotiated a government contract that runs for 4 years. It is expected to yield profits of $1,000 one year from now, $3,000 two years from now, $8,000 three years hence, and $5,000 in four years. For firm XYZ, the appropriate interest rate is 12 percent. What is the present value of the contract?

Answer   The manager of XYZ first has to note that the government contract yields zero profits in the current year (i.e., $\Pi_0 = 0$). Then she uses the information, given together with the above equation, to calculate the present value:

$$PV = \frac{\$1,000}{1.12} + \frac{\$3,000}{(1.12)^2} + \frac{\$8,000}{(1.12)^3} + \frac{\$5,000}{(1.12)^4}$$

$$= \$892.86 + 2,391.58 + 5,694.36 + 3,177.63$$

$$= \$12,156.43$$

This value is considerably less than the simple sum of yearly profits, which is equal to $17,000.

Firms that are in business for more than 1 year are assumed to maximize the present value of profits:

$$\Pi_0 + \frac{\Pi_1}{1+r} + \frac{\Pi_2}{(1+r)^2} + \cdots$$

In doing this, the value today of all current and future profits is maximized. In subsequent chapters, we shall see exactly what this implies for managerial policies.

1.5

ROLE OF THE MANAGER

Over time, more and more production activities have taken place within the firm. Correspondingly, market transactions are being used less and less to produce and distribute goods and services. As a noted economic historian has remarked, "the visible hand of management replaced what Adam Smith referred to as the invisible hand of market forces."[5] Consequently, management has a much more important function today than it did two centuries ago.

In today's firm, there is a myriad of tasks that managers perform. At a very general level, managers set production levels, obtain inputs, and may even choose a price at which to sell. Because of the complications present in the real world, managers handle many more specific tasks. For instance, they are called upon to predict demand, locate plants, choose product lines, set inventory levels, decide how much job safety to provide, and allocate funds to research and development. Financial decisions also must be made about the

---

[5] A fascinating historical account of this development is provided by Alfred D. Chandler, Jr., *The Visible Hand: The Managerial Revolution in American Business*, Cambridge, Mass.: Harvard University Press, 1977.

firm's appropriate debt structure, the composition of its portfolio, and the extent and nature of its insurance coverage. Accounting decisions regarding LIFO (last in first out) versus FIFO (first in first out) treatment of inventories, selecting the appropriate sample size for an audit, and picking a depreciation method are important to the firm's performance. Furthermore, marketing decisions about the allocation of sales representatives, the adoption of private brands, and advertising can make or break a firm. Every functional area within the firm provides opportunities for a manager to help or hurt his firm with the quality of his decision.

As we shall see in the coming chapters, managers fortunately can deal with most of these decisions by relying on one of several economic principles.

There are benefits and costs associated with undertaking almost any activity. We shall see that profits are maximized when the additional benefit from expanding the activity equals the additional cost associated with expanding the activity. This principle helps the manager decide how much to produce, what price to charge, how many cashiers to hire, how many plants to build, how much to advertise, what inventory levels to set, and so on. In each instance, the manager first has to identify the relevant benefits and costs.

Managers often have a number of options in the production, sale, or purchase of a commodity. Production can occur in any one of several plants. The product can be sold in any of many markets. Inputs can be purchased from several sources. The economic principle is clear: select the option that yields the greatest profit. Sell in the market that adds the most to the firm's total revenue and produce in the plant with the lowest cost of production. Furthermore, buy from the cheapest seller of a given product. Thus, because buyers search for the lowest prices, it may be difficult for the manager to charge different prices for the same product.

People get utility or happiness from many things. Because of this, consumers are willing to pay a higher price for a better commodity and workers are willing to receive a lower wage in exchange for a more enjoyable job. Recognition of this fact enables managers to make better decisions about product quality, plant location, and provision of job safety and fringe benefits.

In many respects, we are fortunate to not be living in a 1984 world where our every action is monitored. The inability to monitor every action poses some problems, however, for the firm. Employees can loaf on the job and steal from the firm. Foremen can promote unproductive employees in exchange for favors. Cartel members can secretly violate collusive agreements. Even managers can attempt to further their own interests at the expense of the firm's profit. Managers and owners must recognize the costs that imperfect knowledge imposes on the firm. These costs can be reduced by allocating resources toward the detection and punishment of inappropriate behavior.

AN EXAMPLE OF SUCCESSFUL MANAGERIAL
DECISIONS*

When a market is expanding generally, it is not a great feat to move in and ride along with the rest of the industry. Chesebrough-Pond, Inc., however, has been buying firms in mature or even declining markets and turning them into growth assets. This remarkable feat has been accomplished by perceptive managerial decisions.

While most of the major food processors were diversifying out of the food industry because of its low growth rate, Chesebrough bought the Ragú Packing Co. At the time, there was no spaghetti sauce that was being marketed nationally. As Chesebrough began its nationwide promotion of Ragú, soaring meat prices made spaghetti and noodles an attractive substitute for meat. Ragú now accounts for 62.8 percent of its market.

In the early 1970s, Health-tex was a very popular brand of children's wear. Due to limited production capacity, its owner had to allocate production and refused to open new accounts. In spite of a declining birthrate that would limit the growth potential in children's wear, Chesebrough bought Health-tex. By increasing productive capacity by 50 percent, Health-tex became the top selling national marketer of children's clothes.

A similar story can be told about Chesebrough's acquisition of G. H. Bass & Co., which made the popular Weejuns. In an industry that is being swamped by imports, many U.S. shoe producers have left the industry. Bass, however, was a profitable firm that was refusing new customers because of its limited production capacity. After Chesebrough acquired Bass, it expanded its facilities by 30 percent. There are plans to expand an additional 20 percent per year for the next 3 years. Chesebrough now is able to completely satisfy the demand for its product by shoe stores. Moreover, it has begun selling through large department stores rather than just through specialty stores. In addition, it has expanded the product offering from 200 styles and sizes to over 500.

By anticipating a surge in demand for spaghetti products and by recognizing two situations where production capacity was inadequate, the Chesebrough management was able to make profitable acquisitions.

*Source: "Chesebrough: Finding Strong Brands to Revitalize Mature Markets," Business Week, Nov. 10, 1980, pp. 73, 75–76.

These are some of the principles that we will use in Chapters 7–15 to analyze business decisions. The foundation for these and other principles is found in Chapters 2–6.

1.6 SUMMARY

In this chapter, we have examined the nature of firms, their goals, and the role of managers within firms. We saw that firms transform inputs into output and that production is organized around firms because this reduces transactions costs and because group production may be greater. A number of reasons were given for assuming that firms maximize profits. We also concluded that in an intertemporal setting, owners may be willing to experience lower profits this year in order to obtain higher profits in future years if the present value of profits is increased. Finally, we saw that the modern firm is quite complex and that consequently the manager has a very important role in determining the success or failure of the firm.

IMPORTANT NEW TERMS

Managerial economics

Firm

Manager

Transactions costs

Group (or team) production

Total revenue

Total cost

Profit

Explicit costs

Implicit costs

Profit maximization

Present value

PROBLEMS

1.1 A local furniture dealer once remarked, "I can always beat the price that Sears charges for identical merchandise." Upon some gentle probing, he revealed that this was possible because "Sears must pay rent on its store while I own my building and have no rent to pay." Does this owner-manager have a problem with his economic logic?

1.2 Calculate the present value of the 4-year government contract where the anticipated profits are $8,000 one year hence, $5,000 two years hence, $3,000 three years hence, and $1,000 four years hence.

1.3 Some garment workers are paid on a piece-rate basis, i.e.; their pay depends upon their output. A bricklayer is rarely paid on this basis. What explains the difference?

1.4 Suppose a manager is told to maximize profits. In her first year, she does fine. In her second year, a serious machine breakdown occurs because she had decided not to spend any money on maintenance in her first year. What mistake did she make?

REFERENCES

Alchian, Armen, and Harold Demsetz: "Production, Information Costs, and Economic Organization," *American Economic Review*, vol. 62, December 1972, pp. 777–795.

Chandler, Alfred D.: *The Visible Hand: The Managerial Revolution in American Business,* Cambridge, Mass.: Harvard University Press, 1977.

Coase, Ronald H.: "The Nature of the Firm," *Economica,* vol. 4, November 1937, pp. 386–405.

Kirzner, Israel M.: *Competition and Entrepreneurship,* Chicago: University of Chicago Press, 1973.

Levy, Haim, and Marshall Sarnat: "A Pedagogical Note on Alternative Formulations of the Goal of the Firm," *Journal of Business,* October 1977.

McEachern, W. A.: "A Review of Alternative Theories of the Firm," in *Managerial Control and Performance,* Lexington Books, 1975, chaps. 1 and 2.

Miller, Roger Leroy: *Intermediate Microeconomics.* New York: McGraw-Hill Book Company, 1978.

Stigler, George J.: "The Division of Labor Is Limited by the Extent of the Market," *Journal of Political Economy,* vol. 59, June 1951, pp. 185–193.

TWO

TOOLS FOR MANAGERIAL DECISION MAKING

2 CONSUMER-DEMAND THEORY

The successful economic activity of firms must ultimately satisfy the demands of consumers. Firms exist to provide something that consumers want. This is apparent for the retailer of consumer goods and for the manufacturer of final goods (e.g., cars, light bulbs) because the link between the consumer and the firm is rather obvious. But it is equally true for the producer of intermediate goods such as steel and cotton. This is because these goods are produced to supply manufacturers of final goods with some of the inputs that they require. Consequently, intermediate-goods producers are affected by the wants of final-goods consumers. For example, the coal producer who supplies an electric utility or the steel producer who manufactures I beams does so in indirect response to consumer demands. If individuals did not want electricity or the additional goods produced by new factories, the electric utility would have no need for the coal and builders would have no need for the I beams. Thus, the coal producer exists to provide indirectly something that consumers want; it is the same with the steel producer.

Managers must learn the determinants of individual demand and market demand. By understanding what determines demand, managers will be able, for example, to select the appropriate advertising media for promoting the commodities produced by the firm, to establish the optimal price to charge, and to make plans for the future array of product offerings.

This chapter will provide an understanding of consumer demand. The theory of consumer demand begins with the preferences of consumers for the various commodities available for consumption. First, we will find a way of representing consumer preferences among various commodities. At this stage, we will not be concerned about prices. Subsequently, we will introduce the fact that consumers will have to pay for the commodities they prefer. This, of course, will force consumers to choose among all the commodities. From this choice process, we will be able to derive the individual's demand curve for a particular commodity. Once we derive the demand curve for a single individual, we will use that to obtain the demand curve for the entire market, or the market-demand curve.

2.1

CONSUMER PREFERENCES

A consumer's preferences for various commodities may be a result of many factors: heritage, social environment, geographic environment, race, religion, sex, marital status, education, and so on. We are, however, unable to explain why one person's preferences or tastes are different from those of another person. Such an explanation would be extremely valuable to a manager who wants to sell a product, but we have no explanation to offer. What we do propose to do is take the consumer's preferences as given and proceed to represent them in an analytically convenient way.

Each consumer is assumed to be able to order bundles of commodities according to their relative worth to him. For example, suppose we have two market baskets each filled with goods and services; one is labeled A and the other is labeled B. The contents of these two baskets are as follows:

A	B
toothbrush	hamburger
pizza	comb
Playboy	*Business Week*
six-pack of beer	pair of Levi's
10 gallons of gasoline	football

We assume that each consumer is able to examine the two market baskets and decide whether A is preferred to B, B is preferred to A, or A and B are equally preferred. If a consumer can do this for any two market baskets, then he can rank all market baskets according to his preferences.

We are going to impose a restriction upon the consumer's preference ordering. In particular, we are going to insist that if the consumer prefers basket A to basket B and prefers basket B to basket C, then he must prefer basket A to basket C. This restriction is known as *transitivity*. In most circumstances, it would seem quite silly to have preferences that were not transitive. For example, if a consumer prefers a hamburger to a tuna sandwich and a tuna sandwich to a ham sandwich, most of us would find it a bit strange for that consumer then to express a preference for ham sandwiches over hamburgers. Finally, we shall assume that a consumer prefers more to less. This is known as the *nonsatiation* assumption, and it means that if one commodity bundle is larger than another, then the consumer will prefer the larger bundle. For example, let us examine the following bundles:

A	B
three oranges	three oranges
haircut	haircut
two hamburgers	one hamburger
Business Week	*Business Week*

It is clear that bundle A is larger than bundle B. Under the assumption that more is preferred to less, a consumer must prefer A to B.

We will proceed to develop the theory of individual demand and market demand as though we were living in a world where there are only two commodities available for consumption. The sole purpose of this abstraction from reality is to make it possible to show the theory graphically. But whatever we say about the two-commodity world can be extended to the real world, which has n commodities. A more general, albeit mathematical, treatment of consumer theory is contained in the appendix to this chapter.

Consider panel (a) of Figure 2.1. The distance from the origin along the horizontal axis represents the number of units of food. Similarly, the distance along the vertical axis from the origin represents the number of units of clothing. Each point in panel (a) represents a particular combination of food and clothing. Thus, market basket A contains 8 units of food and 4 units of clothing.

If this consumer's consumption of food fell from 8 units to 4 units while the clothing component remained fixed at 4 units, he would move from point

FIGURE 2.1   The concept of an indifference curve—all combinations of commodities that yield equal satisfaction.

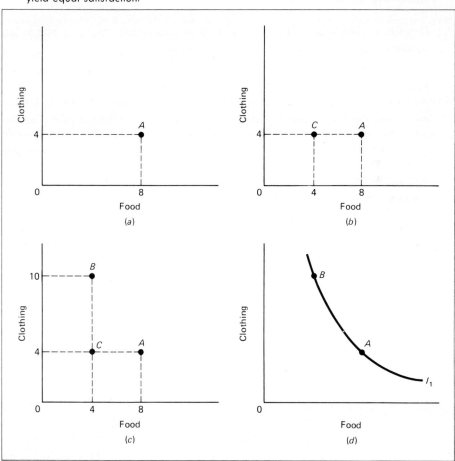

A to point *C* in panel (*b*). This consumer must be worse off because we have assumed that more is preferred to less. In this case, more food is preferred to less food.

Only if his consumption of clothing increases *sufficiently* to compensate him for his reduced food consumption, can he be as happy as he was at *A*. Suppose that at point *B* [panel (*c*)] the increase in clothing from 4 units to 10 units is just sufficient to fully compensate him for the decrease in food from 8 units to 4 units. What this means is that *A* and *B* are equally preferred. We say that the consumer is *indifferent* between *A* and *B*.

In a similar fashion, other points may be found that are as preferred as *A* and *B*. The set of these points—called an "indifference curve"—is given in panel (*d*) by the curve labeled I_1. The consumer would be as happy at any point on I_1 as at any other point on I_1.

DEFINITION ▶   An *indifference curve* is a locus of points representing various combinations of commodities that provide a consumer with the same level of satisfaction.

Question   The indifference curve in panel (*d*) has a negative slope. Do all indifference curves have a negative slope?

Answer   Yes, all indifference curves must be negatively sloped. This follows from the definition of an indifference curve and the assumption that more is preferred to less. Consider point *A* in Figure 2.2. If an indifference curve is not negatively sloped, it could be positively sloped. Then a point like *B* would be on the same indifference curve as *A*. But market basket *B* has more food *and* more clothing than basket *A*. Thus, it must be

FIGURE 2.2 Commodity bundles B, C, and D are larger than bundle A and must be preferred to A.

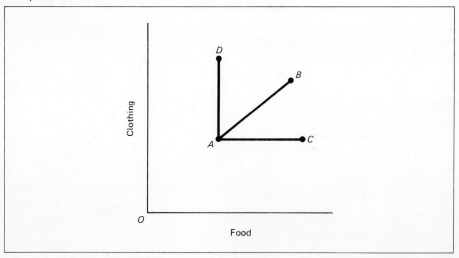

preferred to A. If it is preferred to A, it cannot be on the same indifference curve as A. (You should work out a similar argument for points C and D.)

Let us select another combination of food and clothing, say, point G in Figure 2.3. Point G must be preferred to point A. This is because at point G the consumer has both more food and more clothing than he has at point A, and our consumer always prefers more to less. Using the same procedure as before, we can identify all the commodity combinations that are equally preferred to G, thereby constructing another indifference curve. We have labeled the indifference curve through G as I_2.

We have seen that point G on indifference curve I_2 is preferred to point A on indifference curve I_1. In fact, any point on indifference I_2 is preferred to any point on indifference I_1. In particular, market basket K on I_2 produces greater satisfaction than market basket H on I_1. Can you show this? More generally, movements to the northeast place the consumer on indifference curves that yield successively higher levels of utility or satisfaction.

UTILITY FUNCTIONS   It is sometimes convenient to assign numbers to describe the amount of happiness or satisfaction associated with each indifference curve. A utility function does this. An example of a utility function is

$$U = XY$$

where the amount of utility U is the product of the quantities of commodity X and commodity Y. If $X = 1$ and $Y = 1$, then the level of satisfaction or utility is also 1: $U = XY = 1 \cdot 1 = 1$. If $X = 2$ and $Y = 2$, then the level of utility is 4: $U = XY = 2 \cdot 2 = 4$.

FIGURE 2.3   Indifference curves make it easy to compare market baskets like H and K: K is preferred to H.

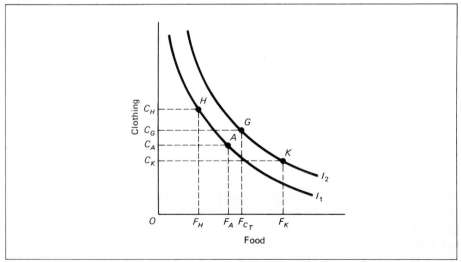

A utility function, in order to adequately describe behavior, must convey all the information found in the consumer's indifference curves. If consumption bundle C is preferred to consumption bundle A, then the utility number assigned to C must exceed the utility number assigned to A. If this is not true, then the utility function is not doing its job, which is to represent the consumer's preferences.

2.2

CONSUMER'S BUDGET CONSTRAINT

Consumers simply cannot have everything they want. They cannot have everything they want because they have limited money incomes. For each consumer, limited money income imposes a budget constraint upon the level of satisfaction he can achieve. This forces the consumer to choose among the goods and services available to him and limits the quantities that can be consumed. The fundamental assumption of consumer behavior is that each consumer selects among the various commodities so as to get the maximum utility that his limited income will allow. In order to understand what this implies about consumer behavior, we first have to thoroughly understand exactly how a consumer's choices are restricted by having a limited income.

We are going to proceed as though the consumer has selected his occupation and has decided how many hours he will be working. This means that his money income is fixed. Obviously, the sum of all his expenditures on various commodities cannot exceed his fixed money income M. This requirement is called his "budget constraint," which may be expressed algebraically in the two-commodity case as

$$P_X X + P_Y Y = M \qquad (2.1)$$

where X and Y are the quantities of the two commodities; P_X and P_Y are the prices of X and Y, respectively; and M is the consumer's fixed money income.

Equation (2.1) can easily be modified to handle more than two commodities. In fact, if we wanted to include saving, it would appear as a commodity, just like any other commodity, although with a price of \$1. Consequently, even a consumer who saves will always be constrained by his fixed income.

By dividing every term in equation (2.1) by P_Y and moving the term containing X to the right-hand side, the budget line can be written in the slope-intercept form for a straight line:

$$Y = \frac{M}{P_y} - \frac{P_x}{P_y} X \qquad (2.2)$$

where M/P_y is the intercept and $-P_x/P_y$ is the slope. This budget line is plotted in Figure 2.4. The line separates all combinations of these two commodities into two groups: those that this consumer can afford and those that he cannot afford. All market baskets on the budget line or in the shaded area are attainable by this consumer with income M. Those market baskets that lie above the budget line cost more than M dollars and, therefore, are financially unattainable.

The budget line in equation (2.2) describes the consumer's opportunities and the limits on his opportunities. In particular, if our consumer purchases no X, then he can purchase M/P_y units of Y. A consumer with an income of $21,000, for example, can purchase 5,600 units of Y if each unit of Y costs $3.75 and if he purchases nothing else. This allocation is represented by the Y intercept of the budget line. For the same reasons, M/P_x units of X are consumed at the X intercept of the budget line. Can you show this?

There is a cost to buying 1 unit of X. Since income is fixed, 1 unit of X is bought at the loss of P_x/P_y units of Y. This is the cost of X in terms of the units of Y which are foregone. Consider the following example. Suppose that the price of 1 unit of X is $15, while the price of Y is $3.75. In order for the consumer to *purchase 1 unit* of X at a cost of $15, he must reduce his expenditures on Y by $15. This means that he must give up

$$\frac{\$15}{\$3.75} = 4$$

units of Y. To get a second unit of X, 4 more units of Y must be sacrificed. Another way of saying this is that the slope of this particular consumer's budget line equals

$$-\frac{P_x}{P_y} = -\frac{15.00}{3.75} = -4$$

CHANGES IN INCOME OR PRICES   We can examine the effects of changes in income or prices. First, let's see what happens when income changes and

FIGURE 2.4   The budget line separates the available commodity combinations into those that are attainable and those that are unattainable.

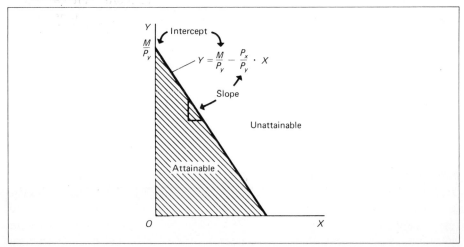

prices remain the same. Suppose that our consumer gets promoted and re-ceives a 33 percent raise in salary; that is, M increases by 33 percent but prices P_x and P_y remain at their original values. In panel (a) of Figure 2.5, we see that this increase in income causes both intercepts of the budget line to increase in value and has no effect on the slope of the budget line ($-P_x/P_y$). The new budget line accordingly is parallel to and above the old budget line. This, of course, is precisely what we should have anticipated. With a higher money income, a greater number of the available market baskets are attainable. Moreover, the slope of the budget line remains unchanged because a change in income has no effect on commodity prices, which determine the cost of X in terms of Y.

Now let's see what happens when income is fixed and one of the prices changes.

In panel (b) of Figure 2.5, we can see the effects of a change in the price of X. Suppose the price of X were to fall by 25 percent. We see that the Y in-tercept term (M/P_y) is not affected because income and the price of Y are unchanged. The slope of the line, however, is changed from $-P_x/P_y$ to $-0.75P_x/P_y$. This causes the budget line to rotate outward. As a result of the price decrease, X becomes cheaper and more commodity combinations become attainable. Similarly, a 30 percent increase in the price of X causes the budget line to rotate about the Y intercept toward the origin. Again, the Y intercept remains the same, but the slope changes from $-P_x/P_y$ to $-1.3P_x/P_y$, which makes the budget line steeper.

FIGURE 2.5   (a) The effect of a change in income and (b) the effect of a change in price on the budget line.

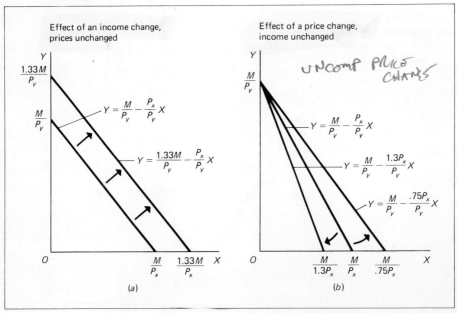

(a)

(b)

Question What happens to the budget line if the price of Y doubles?

Answer Since the price of Y appears in both the Y intercept term and in the slope, both will change. Interestingly, the intercept on the X axis does not change. (Can you see why?) If the consumer were to spend nothing on X, the maximum amount of Y that he could buy would be reduced by one-half. What this means is that the Y intercept falls from M/P_y to $M/2P_y$. The slope changes from $-P_x/P_y$ to $-P_x/2P_y$, resulting in a flatter budget line. These effects can be seen in Figure 2.6.

2.3

UTILITY MAXIMIZATION

The consumer's problem is to get the highest level of utility possible from her fixed income. This is not an easy task, for there are thousands of commodities to choose from. Indeed, many of these commodities will not be purchased by any one consumer. To take one example, most consumers purchase no more than two or three kinds of the breakfast cereals that are available. Nevertheless, consumers do not appear to have any difficulty in allocating their income to maximize their happiness. Even children can decide how to spend their limited funds. Let's now see what's involved in maximizing utility subject to a budget constraint.

A consumer's indifference curves describe her preferences about goods and services. The consumer's budget constraint tells us exactly which combinations of goods and services are attainable. Our task is to put these together.

Suppose that we plot all the consumer's indifference curves in the positive quadrant of the XY plane. Since every point in this quadrant represents a bundle of X and Y, an indifference curve will go through each point.

FIGURE 2.6 The effect of doubling the price of Y is to make the budget line flatter.

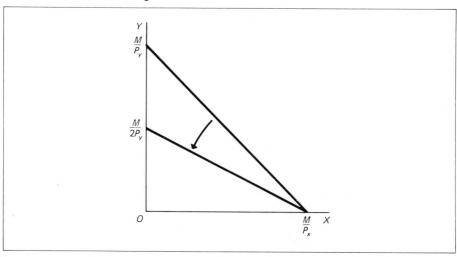

Consequently, the indifference curves will fill the entire quadrant and we will not be able to see very much.

Now take the budget line from Figure 2.4 and superimpose it on these indifference curves. Clearly, in order to learn which indifference curves are attainable, we must focus our attention on a few indifference curves.

In panel (a) of Figure 2.7, we have highlighted indifference curve I_3 out of the thousands and thousands that are on that plane. The budget line is also drawn in this panel. Since our consumer is interested in maximizing utility, I_3 would have some appeal. Unfortunately, none of the points on I_3 is attainable because all the points on I_3 lie above the budget line. Although the consumer would like to be on indifference curve I_3, she simply cannot manage it. She does not have the income necessary to enable her to buy any of the combinations of commodities on I_3.

Let's now consider indifference curve I_1 in panel (b) of Figure 2.7. Since I_1

FIGURE 2.7 Utility maximization occurs at a tangency between an indifference curve and the budget line.

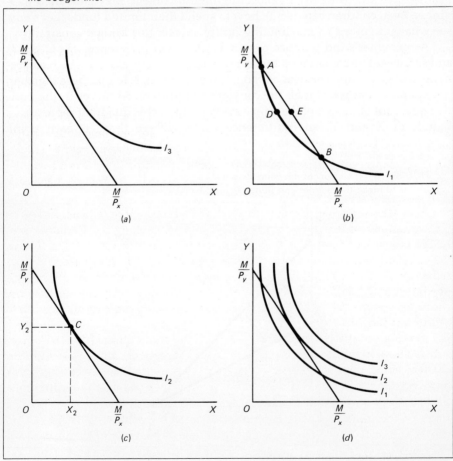

intersects the budget line at points A and B, we know that the consumer can afford at least two of the commodity bundles on I_1. In fact, the consumer can buy A or B or any bundle on indifference curve I_1 between A and B. None of these bundles, however, will maximize the consumer's utility. Consider bundle D, which is on I_1 and therefore is equivalent in utility terms to A and B. The bundle at point E contains more X than the bundle at point D. Consequently, bundle E must be preferred to bundle D. This means that E lies on a higher indifference curve than D, A, or B. Furthermore, since E is on the budget line, it is attainable. Thus, because a more desirable combination of commodities than bundles A or B can be purchased by the consumer, neither A nor B can maximize this consumer's utility.

Finally, let's examine indifference curve I_2 in panel (c) of Figure 2.7. We can see that I_2 is just tangent to the budget line at point C. Higher indifference curves are associated with higher levels of utility, but higher indifference curves are like I_3—they are unattainable. We can also see that any other attainable bundles of commodities will be like A and B—they will be on lower indifference curves. Consequently, such bundles will yield lower utility. Thus, the best that the consumer can do is the utility level associated with indifference curve I_2. The utility-maximizing combination of X and Y is X_2 and Y_2.

The optimal allocation of the consumer's income at point C represents an *equilibrium* for her. What this means is that the consumer has no incentive to choose another attainable allocation. This is because all other attainable combinations of commodities are less desirable. Now, let us investigate the nature of the consumer's equilibrium.

At the point of tangency, the slope of the budget line is equal to the slope of the indifference curve. Recall that the slope of the budget line is $-P_x/P_y$. This tells us the rate at which the market will allow the consumer to substitute one commodity for another. For example, if the price of X is \$2 and the price of Y is \$10, then any consumer can buy an extra 5 units of X for each unit of Y he does not buy.

Now let's see what the slope of the indifference curve tells us. In Figure 2.8, we can examine a move from point A to point B along indifference curve I_0. The movement from A to B entails a substitution of X for Y. In particular, the consumer must have an increase in X equal to ΔX to compensate for the reduction in Y of ΔY; ΔY is a negative number. The slope of the chord connecting A and B is $\Delta Y/\Delta X$. For the movement from A to B, the slope of the chord tells us the rate at which X must be substituted for Y in order to leave utility unchanged.

Moving point B closer to A, the slope of the chord still tells us the rate of substitution. In panel (a) of Figure 2.9, we can see that the rate of substitution changes along the indifference curve by examining the slopes of the chords from A to points B, B', and B''. When the movement along the indifference curve is very small (infinitesimal), the rate of substitution is given by the slope of the tangent to the indifference curve at point A. This tangent is shown in panel (b) of Figure 2.9. But the slope of the tangent to the indifference curve at A is equal to the slope of the indifference curve at A. Thus, the

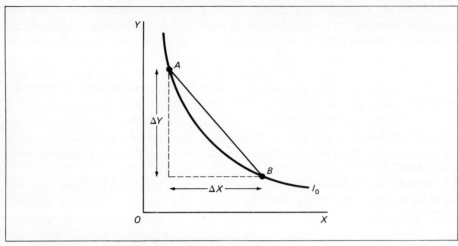

FIGURE 2.8   The slope of the chord
connecting A and B shows the rate of
substitution between X and Y that leaves
utility unchanged.

slope of the indifference curve measures the rate at which the consumer is
willing to substitute a very small quantity of X for Y without changing utility.
This concept is important enough to warrant a special name: the marginal
rate of substitution.

DEFINITION ◗   The *marginal rate of substitution* (MRS_{YX}) is the
maximum rate at which a consumer is willing to substitute one commodity
for another while maintaining a constant level of satisfaction or utility. We

FIGURE 2.9   As the movement along I_0
becomes smaller, the slope of the chord
approaches the slope of the tangent to I_0
at A.

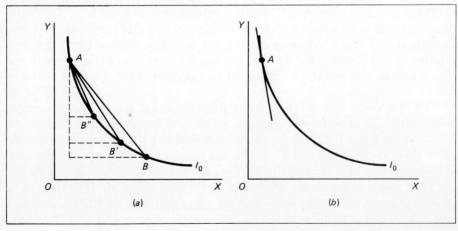

can write this symbolically as

$$-\frac{\Delta Y}{\Delta X} = MRS_{YX}$$

In equilibrium the slope of the budget line $(-P_X/P_Y)$ is equal to the slope of the indifference curve. Consequently, we have

$$MRS_{YX} = \frac{P_x}{P_y} \tag{2.3}$$

This means that in equilibrium the rate at which the consumer is willing to substitute X for Y (MRS_{YX}) is equal to the rate at which the market will allow the consumer to substitute X for Y while keeping total expenditure constant.

The importance of this can be seen by considering point A in Figure 2.10. At point A, the MRS_{XY} exceeds the ratio of prices. Suppose, for example, that the absolute value of the slope of indifference curve I_1 is $^5/_2$ at point A while the price of X is \$2 and the price of Y is \$1. Substituting these values into equation (2.3), we see that $^5/_2$ is greater than $^2/_1$. A marginal rate of substitution of $^5/_2$ means that the consumer is willing to sacrifice 5 units of Y to gain 2 units of X. But for a sacrifice of 5 units of Y the market will give the consumer \$5, which is enough to buy more than 2 units of X. Consequently, the consumer can be better off, that is, can increase her utility, by moving away from point A. Thus, she moves away from A and toward point C. Can you develop a similar argument to show why the consumer would move from point B toward point C?

So far, the indifference curves have all been drawn so that they become

FIGURE 2.10 The consumer can increase her utility by moving to C when the MRS_{XY} exceeds the price ratio (point A) and when the MRS_{XY} is less than the price ratio (point B).

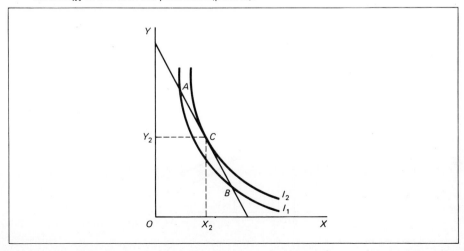

flatter as X increases. Indifference curves with this property are said to be convex.

Convexity offers a plausible description of preferences. To see this, consider Figure 2.11. Starting at point A, the individual has a lot of Y and not much X. Consequently, she is willing to accept only $X_2 - X_1$ units of X for $Y_1 - Y_2$ units of Y. If she were at point B, however, she would already have a lot of X and not much Y. In order for her to be willing to part with the same amount of Y, she would have to receive $X_4 - X_3$ units of X. Although the sacrifices in Y are equal, the amount of X required as compensation to leave her equally satisfied is much larger at B than at A.

What would happen if indifference curves became *steeper* as X increased? Indifference curves with this property, called concavity, are shown in Figure 2.12. A consumer with concave indifference curves who faces budget constraint AB does not maximize her utility by consuming at point C, where the budget line is tangent to indifference curve I_1. She can move to a higher indifference curve by moving along the budget constraint toward points A or B. This process would continue until she ended up at either point A or point B; the point on the highest indifference curve would be chosen. In this particular diagram, point A maximizes the consumer's utility. At point A, no X is consumed. The consumer spends all her money on Y. Utility maximization under concave indifference curves always results in a corner solution where one of the goods is not consumed. If we observe that positive quantities of both X and Y are being consumed, then we can infer that the indifference curves are convex. Since we do not often observe consumers spending all their money on any one commodity (e.g., oranges), we can be pretty sure that indifference curves are convex.

FIGURE 2.11 The changes in Y are the same: $Y_1 - Y_2 = Y_3 - Y_4$. But the amount of X required to leave utility unchanged has increased: $X_4 - X_3 > X_2 - X_1$.

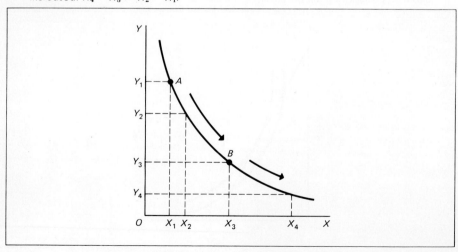

2.4

EFFECTS OF A CHANGE IN INCOME

We have seen that the quantities of X and Y that the consumer purchases are the outcome of utility maximization subject to a budget constraint. If the consumer's budget line shifts, the combinations of X and Y that are available to him change, and this leads him to alter the quantities of X and Y that he purchases.

Suppose that his income increased and that prices remained constant. We know from our earlier discussion that the budget line shifts outward. In panel (*a*) of Figure 2.13, we see the original consumer equilibrium quantities X_1 and Y_1. After an increase in income, the budget line shifts from AB to CD. Since prices have not changed, AB is parallel to CD. Although the marginal rate of substitution of X for Y at the point (X_1, Y_1) is equal to the slope of the new budget line, the point (X_1, Y_1) is no longer an equilibrium point because it does not exhaust the new, higher budget. The new equilibrium is found where indifference curve I_2 is tangent to new budget line CD. We can see that the new equilibrium involves greater quantities of both goods: X_2 is greater than X_1, and Y_2 is greater than Y_1. In this case, both X and Y are said to be normal goods.

DEFINITION ▶ A *normal* good is one whose consumption increases as income rises.

As we can see in panel (*b*) of Figure 2.13, not every good need be a normal good. In this instance, the new equilibrium involves a greater quantity of Y but a smaller quantity of X. When this occurs, X is said to be inferior.

FIGURE 2.12 Concave indifference curves lead to specialization in consumption.

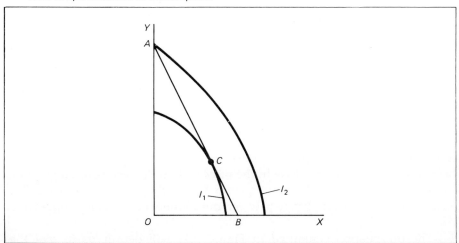

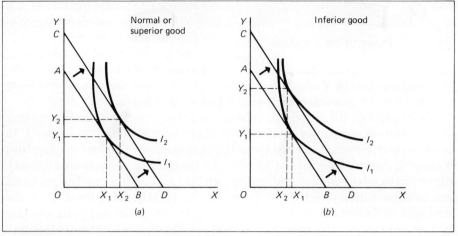

FIGURE 2.13 As income increases and prices are unchanged, the budget line shifts outward. Consumption of normal or superior goods increases [panel (a)], while consumption of inferior goods declines [panel (b)].

DEFINITION ▶ An *inferior* good is one whose consumption falls as income rises.

Question Is it possible for every good to be an inferior good?

Answer No. Remember that savings can be considered to be a good. If every good were inferior, then total expenditure would fall as the consumer's income rose; the consumer would not be spending all his income.

2.5

CONSUMER DEMAND

We can also consider the effect of a change in one price when income is fixed and the other price remains constant. Our discussion of Figure 2.5 indicated that a change in the price of X would cause the budget line to rotate about the intercept on the y axis.

Suppose that the price of Y is fixed at $\overline{P}_y$ and that income is fixed at M. Let us begin with a price of X equal to P_{X1}. In Figure 2.14, we have plotted appropriate budget line AB. The equilibrium quantity of X is X_1. As the price of X declines to P_{X2}, the budget line rotates to AC and the optimal quantity of X becomes X_2. A further decrease in the price of X to P_{X3} results in budget line AD and an optimal quantity of X equal to X_3. Finally, at the lowest price, P_{X4}, X_4 is consumed at the tangency between indifference curve I_4 and budget line AE.

The information contained in Figure 2.14 will permit us to plot the consumer's demand curve. In particular, we plot equilibrium quantities X_1, X_2, X_3, and X_4 against corresponding prices P_{X1}, P_{X2}, P_{X3}, and P_{X4}. When all such pairs are plotted, we have the consumer's demand curve.

DEFINITION ▶   The consumer's *demand curve* relates the optimal quantities purchased by the individual to the various market prices of the commodity. Money income and the prices of other goods are held constant.

An example of a consumer-demand curve is presented in Figure 2.15 and is based upon the information contained in Figure 2.14. Note that we are measuring the price of X on the vertical axis and the quantity of X on the horizontal axis. Usually, we shall find demand curves for each individual consumer to be negatively sloped, which simply means that as the price of the product falls, the consumer will buy more of that product when income and other prices remain constant.

There are two reasons why demand curves usually are negatively sloped.

First, when the price of a product (say, apples) falls, the additional happiness obtained from spending $1 more on apples rises relative to the marginal happiness from $1 spent on other goods because $1 now buys more apples. This will lead consumers to increase their consumption of apples and to decrease their consumption of other goods until $1 brings about the same increase in happiness for each good.

FIGURE 2.14   As the price of X falls, the quantity of X consumed increases. As the price of X falls from P_{x1} to P_{x2}, the quantity consumed increased from X_1 to X_2. Similarly, X_3 and X_4 are consumed at P_{x3} and P_{x4}.

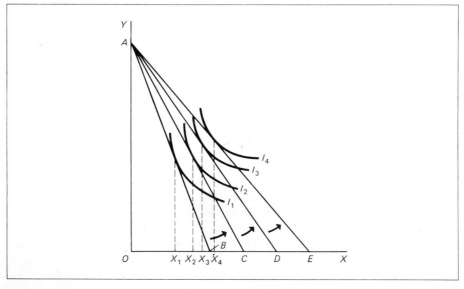

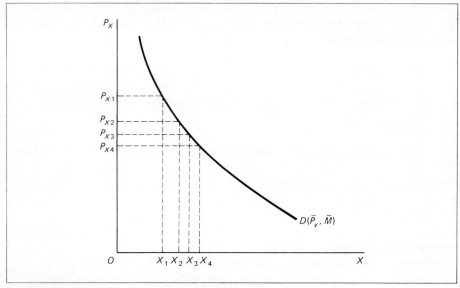

FIGURE 2.15 The demand curve for X holds the price of Y fixed at $\bar{P}_y$ and money income fixed at $\bar{M}$. It shows the maximum quantity of X that a consumer will buy for any particular price of X.

Second, when the price of apples falls, consumers are better off. They are now able to purchase more of all goods and will tend to increase their consumption of particular goods.

We should emphasize the distinction between a "change in demand" and a "change in the quantity demanded." Any time there is a change in the quantity demanded, we are talking about a movement along the demand curve. For example, if the price of X falls from P_{X1} to P_{X3}, then the demand curve in panel (a) of Figure 2.16 indicates that quantity demanded will increase from X_1 to X_3.

In contrast, when we say that there has been a change in demand, we really should say that there has been a change in the demand schedule. In other words, the curve in panel (b) of Figure 2.16 has shifted to a new location. This shift cannot be caused by a change in the price of X. A change in anything else, however, can cause a shift in the demand curve. For example, the label on the demand curve indicates that the price of Y and the consumer's income are constant. If either of these were to change, the demand curve would shift. If X is normal, then, as we saw in panel (a) of Figure 2.13, an increase in income at any price of X would cause the optimal quantity of X to increase. That is, an increase in income would cause the demand curve to shift to the right. In panel (b) of Figure 2.16, we have shown demand-curve shifts that result from increasing income from M to M'' and from decreasing income from M to M'. Demand-curve shifts also can result from changes in the prices of other goods and services.

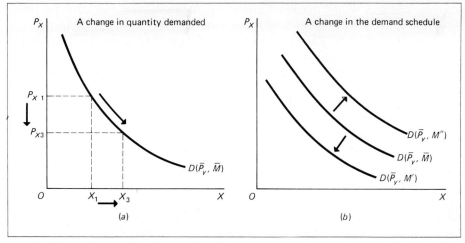

FIGURE 2.16   The distinction between (a) a change in the quantity demanded and (b) a change in the demand schedule.

2.6

MARKET DEMAND

Individual consumers do not often buy enough of any one product to interest a firm. The firm is more interested in the collective demands of all individuals, which is the market demand. Market demand is the horizontal summation of all the individual demand curves.

In Figure 2.17, we show a simplified world composed of two individuals and how the market demand is derived from their individual demand

FIGURE 2.17   Market demand is the aggregation of individual market demand curves..

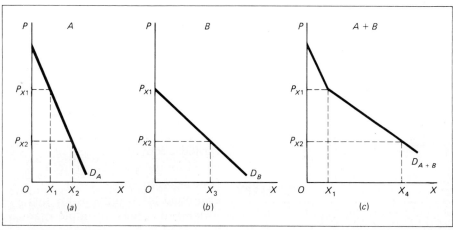

curves. The real-world market-demand aggregation works exactly the same way for a market composed of thousands or even millions of individual consumers' demands. Panels (*a*) and (*b*) in Figure 2.17 depict individual demand curves for individuals *A* and *B*. For all prices equal to P_{X1} or higher, individual *B* demands no *X* at all. Thus, the market demand at these prices is the same as individual A's own demand at these prices. For prices below P_{X1}, we have to add the relevant quantities from the two individual demand curves. For example, at a price of P_{X2}, *A* will demand X_2 units of *X* and *B* will want X_3 units. The market-demand curve must be constructed so that the total market demand X_4 is equal to X_2 plus X_3. If this is done for all prices, we will construct the market demand labeled D_{A+B}.

In the case of two or just a few individuals, the market demand will have a noticeable kink or kinks. In Figure 2.17, this occurs at price P_{X1}, where individual *B* begins to consume positive quantities. If there were a few individuals in the market, this would happen a few times. For markets with many consumers, however, the market-demand curve will be smooth because the significance of any single individual is reduced.

The responsiveness of quantity demanded to changes in the product's price nevertheless will reflect both how responsive individual demand is to changes in price and the frequency with which individual consumers enter the market as the price falls. If a large number of individuals begin to consume a good when the price falls by a small amount, the market-demand curve will be quite responsive to changes in price. A manager therefore must be aware not only of the typical consumer's response to price changes but also of how many new consumers will enter a market as price falls.

Before we leave this section, let us recall, for reasons that have already been discussed, that it is extremely likely (although not necessary) that demand curves are negatively sloped. Despite the theoretical possibility of a positively sloped demand curve, no economist has ever found one. It seems reasonable therefore to conclude that when the price of just about any good rises, the quantity demanded of that good will fall.

Question   Answer true, false, or uncertain: Economics predicts that per capita consumption of wine will be higher in France than in Sweden.

Answer   True. Wine is produced in France. The Swedes must import wine from other countries. The cost of transporting the wine to Sweden causes the relative price of wine to be higher in Sweden than in France. As a result, the average Swede will consume less wine than the average Frenchman.

2.7

SUMMARY

The manager of a firm must be concerned about the nature of the demand for the good or service that his firm sells. In this chapter, we have examined the origins of the market-demand curve. We found that the market-demand curve is a simple aggregation of individual-demand curves. In turn, the individual-demand curve is a result of consumer preferences for products. We have seen how to derive the consumer's demand curve from his preferences by using a graphical representation of these preferences and information about his financial ability to consume.

In the next chapter, we shall see how a manager can obtain more specific information about the market-demand curve for his product.

IMPORTANT NEW TERMS

Indifference curve

Utility

Budget line

Normal good

Inferior good

Demand curve

Marginal rate of substitution

PROBLEMS

2.1 Show that indifference curves cannot cross.

2.2 What happens to the consumption of pork chops when money income and all prices double?

2.3 The *Wall Street Journal* reports that we are headed for a serious recession. You are the manager of a firm that produces Starcho Lunch, which is an inferior good. What should your short-run production plans be?

2.4 Suppose that the individual is examining combinations of risk and return. If the person does not like risk but does like return, what will her indifference curves look like?

2.5 One of our basic assumptions in analyzing consumer demand is that the consumer prefers more to less. But we see consumers making charitable donations. Since this reduces consumption, we have empirical proof that more is *not* preferred to less. Do you agree?

2.6 A consumer buys 100 gallons of gasoline at current prices. The President levies an additional tax of $0.10 per gallon. Not wanting to hurt the consumer, he then gives the consumer a $10 rebate (100 · $0.10). The consumer finds that he is better off. Why? The manager of the gasoline station finds that she sells less gasoline than before both the tax and the rebate. Why?

2.7 The XYZ Corporation has recently entered the synthetic leather field and hopes to make shoe leather obsolete. If XYZ is successful, the manager of a grocery store will find that the price of lamb rises. Why?

2.8 Suppose that Lushly consumes only low-quality Scotch and high-quality Scotch. Answer true, false, or uncertain: a $0.50 per quart tax on Scotch will cause Lushly to substitute low-quality Scotch for high-quality Scotch.

MATHEMATICAL APPENDIX

2A.1

UTILITY MAXIMIZATION

In mathematical form, the consumer is assumed to maximize his utility

$$U = U(x_1, x_2, \ldots, x_n) \qquad \text{(A2.1)}$$

where x_i denotes the quantity of the ith good or service, subject to his budget constraint

$$\sum_{i=1}^{n} P_i x_i = M \qquad \text{(A2.2)}$$

where M represents the consumer's fixed money income and P_i is the price of the ith commodity.

In order to solve this optimization problem, we form a Lagrange expression

$$L = U(x_1, \ldots, x_n) + \lambda \left(M - \sum_{i=1}^{n} P_i x_i \right) \qquad \text{(A2.3)}$$

where λ is a Lagrange multiplier. The optimum allocation of the given money income M is obtained by setting the first partial derivatives of L equal to zero:

$$\frac{\partial L}{\partial x_i} = \frac{\partial U}{\partial x_i} - \lambda P_i = 0 \qquad i = 1, 2, \ldots, n$$

$$\frac{\partial L}{\partial \lambda} = M - \sum_{i=1}^{n} P_i x_i = 0 \qquad \text{(A2.4)}$$

These first-order conditions must be solved for the optimal quantities of the commodities. This will give us the individual-demand functions for each good as functions of income M and all the prices. The last equation in (A2.4) simply ensures that all the consumer's income is spent. Since the first n equations in (A2.4) can be written as

$$\frac{\partial U / \partial x_i}{P_i} = \lambda$$

and λ is a constant, we may conclude that optimality requires that

$$\frac{\partial U/\partial x_1}{P_1} = \frac{\partial U/\partial x_2}{P_2} = \cdots = \frac{\partial U/\partial x_n}{P_n} \qquad \text{(A2.5)}$$

$\partial U/\partial x_i$ can be interpreted as the increase in total utility resulting from 1 more unit of X_i. Thus, optimality requires an allocation of income such that the last \$1 spent on each commodity yields equal returns in terms of satisfaction.

2A.2

INDIFFERENCE CURVES

The indifference curve developed in the text is simply the solutions to

$$U^\circ = U(x_1, ..., x_n) \qquad \text{(A2-6)}$$

where U° is a fixed level of utility.

2A.3

MARGINAL RATE OF SUBSTITUTION

The marginal rate of substitution is found by totally differentiating the utility function. For example, start with utility function $U = U(x_1, x_2)$. Since utility does not change along an indifference curve, we set the total differential equal to zero:

$$dU = \frac{\partial U}{\partial x_1} dx_1 + \frac{\partial U}{\partial x_2} dx_2 = 0$$

Algebraic manipulation yields

$$-\frac{dx_2}{dx_1} = \frac{\partial U/\partial x_1}{\partial U/\partial x_2}$$

which is defined to be the marginal rate of substitution.

3

MARKET DEMAND: CHARACTER-ISTICS AND ESTIMATION

The demand for a firm's product is crucially important to the survival of the firm. Many important decisions depend upon the manager's having specific knowledge about the determinants of the demand for the firm's product. As an example, predictions about the future demand for the firm's product help the manager make many current production decisions. This knowledge is particularly useful in guiding the manager's decisions about acquiring "fixed" inputs such as capital equipment and relatively skilled labor.[1] Boeing Aircraft Company, for instance, would be ill-advised to incur the expense of hiring many new engineers just before the beginning of a long slump in the demand for airlines. Reasonably accurate predictions of future demand are based upon a solid understanding of the historical determinants of demand. Consequently, a manager must acquire an appreciation for these determinants if he is to predict demand.

Prediction is not the only reason for understanding the firm's demand. For those managers of firms who are able to affect the price paid for their product, a knowledge of the determinants of demand is essential to choosing a price that will maximize the firm's profit.

Recent advances in computer technology have made it quite inexpensive to estimate demand functions if the appropriate data are available. Calculators are available for $40 which estimate a simple relationship between price and quantity demanded. There are also calculators selling for under $200 that are able to estimate quantity demanded as a function of several variables. With these calculators, all the manager essentially has to do is to enter the data (e.g., prices and quantities) into the calculator. The calculator, which has been programmed appropriately, then performs the necessary calculations and gives the manager the numbers defining the estimated relationship. Since the estimation of demand functions is so easy and cheap, there is little reason not to use this valuable tool. There are, however, some pitfalls in demand estimation; as we shall see, these can easily be avoided.

This chapter is a completely self-contained treatment of the estimation of demand. Accordingly, we will first summarize the theory of consumer demand, which is more fully developed in Chapter 2. The concept of price elasticity then will be developed, and the remainder of the chapter will be concerned with specific issues in the estimation of demand functions.

---

[1] In Section 9.7, which begins on page 255, we discuss why capital equipment and skilled labor are called fixed inputs.

3.1

A SUMMARY OF DEMAND THEORY

Consumers get satisfaction, or utility, by consuming goods and services. Some commodities provide more satisfaction than others to a specific consumer. This is reflected in that consumer's preferences for the thousands of goods and services in the marketplace. Each consumer faces a budget constraint that prevents her unlimited consumption. Consequently, there are some combinations of commodities that she can afford and many others that she cannot afford. Thus, she must confine her ultimate choice to those affordable combinations.

In deciding upon a consumption plan, the consumer will attempt to choose the combination of goods and services that maximizes her satisfaction or utility subject to her budget constraint. In other words, the consumer will choose the most preferred bundle of goods from those that she can afford. A change in a price or a change in her income will alter the set of bundles that are available to her and therefore will result in a new optimum bundle. The quantity chosen of each good is a function of the consumer's income (M) and the prices that she faces ($P_1, P_2, \ldots, P_n$):

$$Q_1 = f(P_1, P_2, \ldots, P_n, M)$$
$$Q_2 = g(P_1, P_2, \ldots, P_n, M)$$
$$\cdots\cdots\cdots\cdots\cdots\cdots\cdots\cdots\cdots \qquad (3.1)$$
$$Q_n = z(P_1, P_2, \ldots, P_n, M)$$

The first equation in (3.1) says that the quantity of good 1 demanded depends on the price of good 1, the prices of all other goods, and income. The other equations in (3.1) have a similar interpretation. We call the functions $f(\ ), g(\ ), \ldots, z(\ )$ demand functions, which reflect the consumer's preferences.

DEFINITION ▶   A *demand function* is a function that expresses the relationship between the quantity demanded of a specific good and income and various prices.

The demand function for, say, typewriters might look like the following:

$$Q_2 = 101{,}371 - 1.27P_1 - 301.76P_2 - 0.70P_3 + \cdots + 0.02P_n + 1.12M \quad (3.2)$$

where P_1 is the price of paper, P_2 is the typewriter price, P_3 is the price of ribbons, P_n is the price of pencils, and M is income.

When the price of a good rises, the cost of consuming that good relative to the cost of other goods increases. This, in general, causes consumers to shift their consumption away from the now more expensive good and toward other goods, which have become relatively less expensive. In our typewriter demand equation (3.2), we can see that the coefficient on the price of typewriters is negative. This means that an increase in the price of typewriters will reduce the number of typewriters demanded.

While there is a tendency for the quantity demanded of other goods to increase in response to an increase in the price of a typewriter, there are individual exceptions to this general tendency. These exceptions are goods for which a typewriter is a complement.

> **DEFINITION ▶**   Two goods are said to be *complements* when, other things being equal, a rise in the relative price of one good leads to a fall in the consumption of the other good.

In our typewriter example, we see that paper and typewriter ribbons are complements for typewriters. If the price of paper (P_1) or the price of typewriter ribbons (P_3) rises, then the quantity of typewriters demanded will fall.

In contrast, the coefficient on the price of pencils is positive. This means an increase in the price of pencils will cause an increase in the quantity of typewriters demanded. These two goods are substitutes.

> **DEFINITION ▶**   Two goods are said to be *substitutes* when, other things being equal, a rise in the relative price of one good leads to an increase in the consumption of the other good.

When income rises, expenditures on all goods together increases. Thus, there is a tendency for the quantity demanded of individual goods to increase as income rises. The demand function for typewriters in equation (3.2) shows this tendency; the positive coefficient on M indicates that an increase in income, other things equal, leads to an increase in the consumption of typewriters. Although for a great many goods consumption increases in response to an increase in income, the consumption of some goods, called inferior goods, decreases as income rises.

> **DEFINITION ▶**   A good is said to be *normal* if its consumption increases when income increases, other things being equal.

> **DEFINITION ▶**   A good is said to be *inferior* if its consumption decreases when income increases, other things being equal.

There are several examples of inferior goods. An increase in income is associated with a decrease in quantity of fish consumed.[2] Black-and-white television sets provide another example of an inferior good. When income rises, consumers purchase higher quality television sets, such as color television

---

[2]There are, of course, individual species of fish which are not inferior, but the "average" fish is an inferior good.

sets; the increase in demand for high-quality television sets is accompanied by a decrease in demand for low-quality television sets.

3.2

THE ELASTICITY OF DEMAND

The elasticity of demand is a useful measure of the responsiveness of the quantity demanded to changes in price. Although the elasticity of demand (defined later in this section) is related to the slope, it is not quite the same. Let's see why the slope itself does not provide a satisfactory measure.

When other prices and income are held constant, there is a negative relationship between the price of any good and the quantity demanded of that good. For example, suppose that a 1-cent increase in the price of a pencil causes the quantity of pencils demanded each month to fall by 75,744 pencils. The slope of the demand curve is $\Delta P/\Delta Q = -1/75{,}744$. If the slope is used as a measure of price sensitivity, the demand for pencils appears to be highly responsive to price changes.

Now let's measure pencil demand in terms of gross of pencils rather than in terms of pencils. A gross of pencils equals 144 pencils. A 1-cent increase in the price of a pencil now results in a fall in quantity demanded equal to

$$\frac{75{,}744}{144} = 526$$

Now the slope of the demand curve is $\Delta P/\Delta Q = -1/526$. Thus when pencil consumption is measured in terms of gross of pencils, the demand for pencils does not appear to be very responsive to price changes. Consequently, a disturbing feature of using the slope of the demand curve as a measure of the responsiveness of quantity demanded to price changes is that it varies with the units in which consumption is measured.

One measure of the responsiveness of the quantity demanded to price changes that is not affected by the units in which consumption is measured is the elasticity of demand.

DEFINITION ▶   The *elasticity of demand*, or *price elasticity* ϵ, equals minus the percentage change in the quantity demanded divided by the percentage change in the price of that product. The elasticity of demand for a product is written as

$$\epsilon = -\frac{\Delta Q/Q}{\Delta P/P}$$

Since price and quantity changes move in opposite directions, the minus sign makes the price elasticity positive.

Question A 2 percent increase in the price of steel is associated with a 1 percent decrease in the quantity of steel demanded. Find the price elasticity.

Answer

$$\epsilon = -\frac{-1\%}{2\%} = .5$$

The elasticity of demand also yields valuable information about the effect of a change in price on total revenue.

DEFINITION ▶   A firm's or industry's *total revenue* (TR) equals the total income received by the firm or industry in payment for its product. We can write this as

TR = PQ

where P and Q are the price and quantity, respectively.

We know that $P_A Q_A$ equals the expenditure by consumers on apples. This also equals the total revenue received by the producers of apples. Suppose that price P_A falls by 1 percent. If the price elasticity (ϵ_A) equals 1, this change in price will cause the quantity demanded to rise by 1 percent, leaving total revenue ($P_A Q_A$) unchanged. In this case, the increase in total revenue associated with the increase in quantity is exactly offset by the decrease in total revenue associated with the fall in price. In contrast, if the price elasticity is less than 1, quantity demanded rises by less than 1 percent when price falls by 1 percent; the increase in total revenue associated with the rise in quantity is overwhelmed by the decrease in total revenue associated with the fall in price, and consequently total revenue falls. Finally, it is easy to see that a 1 percent fall in price leads to an increase in total revenue if the price elasticity is greater than 1 (e.g., 2). The scenarios associated with each of these cases are outlined in Table 3.1.

The ambiguity in whether a fall in price causes total revenue to increase or decrease may also be seen graphically. In Figure 3.1, Q_0 units are demanded at the price P_0. When the price drops to P_1, Q_1 units are demanded. Total revenue changes from $P_0 Q_0$ to $P_1 Q_1$. A smaller price is now received on the first Q_0 units sold, resulting in a reduction in total revenue of $(P_0 - P_1)Q_0$. But $Q_1 - Q_0$ more units are sold at price P_1 than were sold at

TABLE 3.1
EFFECT OF A 1 PERCENT DECREASE
IN PRICE ON TOTAL REVENUE

PRICE ELASTICITY (ϵ)	CHANGE IN PRICE (P_A)	CHANGE IN QUANTITY (Q_A)	CHANGE IN TOTAL REVENUE ($P_A Q_A$)
1	Falls 1%	Rises 1%	No change
Less than 1	Falls 1%	Rises less than 1%	Falls
More than 1	Falls 1%	Rises more than 1%	Rises

price P_0 and as a result total revenue rises by $P_1(Q_1 - Q_0)$. Whether the gain in total revenue outweighs the loss in total revenue depends on the magnitude of the price elasticity, for the area labeled "gain" becomes larger as the price elasticity gets bigger.

Suppose we rearrange the elasticity expression as follows:

$$\epsilon = -\frac{\Delta Q/Q}{\Delta P/P} = -\frac{\Delta Q}{Q} \cdot \frac{P}{\Delta P} = -\frac{\Delta Q}{\Delta P} \cdot \frac{P}{Q}$$

Since $\Delta P/\Delta Q$ is the slope of the demand curve, we should recognize $\Delta Q/\Delta P$ as 1 divided by the slope. Now we can see the relationship between the slope of the demand curve and the elasticity of demand. The slope is not unrelated to the elasticity at a point.

Question Two linear demand curves, D and D', intersect at $P = P_1$ and $Q = Q_1$ in Figure 3.2. Which demand curve is more elastic?

Answer Demand curve D is more elastic than demand curve D'. This can be seen by substituting into the elasticity formula:

$$\epsilon = -\frac{\Delta Q}{\Delta P} \cdot \frac{P}{Q}$$

For both demand curves, $P = P_1$ and $Q = Q_1$. Minus the slope of demand curve D is $-\Delta P/\Delta Q = -(P_1 - A)/(Q_1 - 0) = (A - P_1)/Q_1$, while minus the slope of D' is $-\Delta P/\Delta Q = (B - P_1)/Q_1$. As a result, we can see from the fact that $B - P_1$ is greater than $A - P_1$ that

$$\frac{Q_1}{A - P_1} > \frac{Q_1}{B - P_1}$$

FIGURE 3.1 The effect of a fall in price from P_0 to P_1 on total revenue.

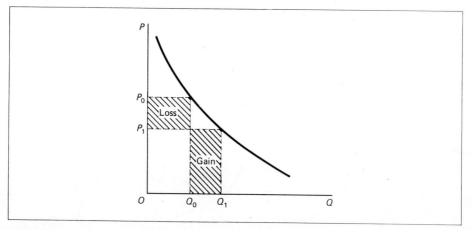

Consequently,

$$\frac{Q_1}{A - P_1} \cdot \frac{P_1}{Q_1} > \frac{Q_1}{B - P_1} \cdot \frac{P_1}{Q_1}$$

The left-hand side of the inequality is the price elasticity of D, and the right-hand side is the price elasticity of D'.

In subsequent chapters, we will be interested in comparing the change in total revenue that comes from selling 1 more unit with the increase in total cost that comes from producing 1 more unit. Interestingly, the change in total revenue associated with selling 1 more unit is related to the price elasticity. Consider what happens when the price is lowered sufficiently to sell 1 more unit.

DEFINITION ▶   The *marginal revenue* (MR) is defined to be the change in total revenue that results when 1 more unit is sold:

$$MR = \frac{\Delta TR}{\Delta Q}$$

In the first paragraph of the mathematical appendix, we show that

$$MR = P\left(1 - \frac{1}{\epsilon}\right) \tag{3.3}$$

If the price elasticity (ϵ) equals 1, then $MR = 0$ and total revenue does not change as quantity increases. If the price elasticity is greater than 1, then it's easy to see that the marginal revenue is positive. (For example, plug in 3 for ϵ, and you will find that $MR = {}^2/_3 P$.) What this means is that total revenue is in-

FIGURE 3.2   When two linear demand curves intersect, the flatter one (D) is more elastic than the steeper one (D') at the point of intersection.

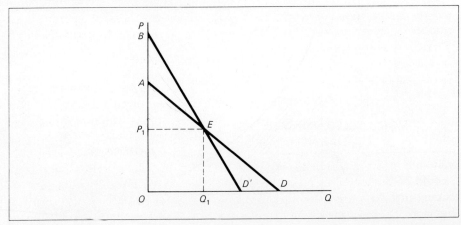

creasing as the quantity demanded rises (in response to a fall in price). Accordingly, equation (3.3) is just another way of categorizing the ambiguity in the change in total revenue accompanying a move down the demand curve.

3.3
THE STATISTICAL NATURE OF EMPIRICAL DEMAND FUNCTIONS

Each consumer purchases thousands of different goods during his life. A properly specified demand function would specify the quantity demanded of a particular good as some function of the prices of *all* goods consumed and of the consumer's income. Neither economists nor managers know precisely the prices of all the goods. Moreover, it is very costly to use *all* the data that statisticians have accumulated. For these reasons, the manager must be content to use a small number of prices to explain the variation in the demand for her product.

Which prices should be chosen for this purpose? Just as an increase in some prices will cause the demand for the firm's product to rise and an increase in other prices will cause the demand for the firm's product to decrease, changes in still other prices will have a negligible impact on the quantity demanded of the firm's product. When estimating a demand function for her product, the manager therefore should include as explanatory variables (1) the price of the product, (2) consumer income, and (3) other prices which have a sizable impact on the demand for the product. Thus, the quantity of butter demanded might be estimated as a function of the price of butter, consumer income, the price of margarine, and the price of bread. In principle, the price of lubricating oil should be included, but it is unlikely to have a large effect on the demand for butter.

By focusing on some prices and ignoring others, we are neglecting some of the determinants of the quantity demanded. Moreover, some of the variables, such as income, may be imperfectly measured. This introduces an element of error into the estimation and very naturally leads us into statistics. An understanding of some basic statistical theory should enable managers to confidently estimate routine demand functions and to know when to call upon a statistician or an econometrician, specialists in this area. It is often not necessary, however, for the manager of a business to spend a vast amount of time studying the theory of statistics in order to successfully estimate a demand function.

3.4
MODEL SELECTION AND THE GATHERING OF DATA

Many decisions that are made in the course of estimating a demand function require an intimate knowledge of the market being investigated; a manager's expertise is especially valuable in these decisions. We just concluded that the quantity demanded should be estimated as a function of the price of the product, consumer income, and the other prices which have a sizable impact on the quantity demanded. Thus, one of the more important decisions that a manager must make when estimating a demand function involves choosing a set of prices that have a big effect on the quantity demanded. This process of settling on a set of variables to use in empirical work is called selecting a model.

Question   How does a manager know *which* prices have a large effect on the demand for his product?

Answer   There is, unfortunately, no magic formula which picks goods whose prices should be included in a demand function. Goods that are closely related to the firm's product are likely candidates. Thus, the quantity of records demanded is probably closely tied to the prices of stereo equipment, televisions, home video recorders, and concert tickets. Nevertheless, other variables often have an important impact on the quantity demanded, and a good intuition about the market and an intimate knowledge of the market are often extremely useful in determining which prices have a large impact on the demand for the firm's product.

Sometimes insight about which variables have an important effect on the quantity demanded can be gained by first noting that what is really demanded is a more abstract concept than what is purchased.[3] To make this discussion more concrete let's assume that when consumers buy movie tickets, they want to see a movie and have no special interest in the movie ticket itself. To see a movie at a movie theater, consumers must go to the theatre, buy a ticket, spend time watching the movie, and return from the theater. The cost of seeing a movie therefore is related to the cost of the ticket, the cost of getting to and from the theater, and the value of the consumer's time. An increase in any of these three components of the cost of seeing a movie will cause the demand for movies to fall.

Casual observation provides some support for these predictions. As a result of the gasoline shortage in the summer of 1979, movie attendance fell markedly. One reason why per capita movie theater attendance is higher in urban areas than in rural areas is that theaters are closer to consumers in urban areas than in rural areas. Furthermore, differences in the value of time can explain why younger consumers attend movies more frequently. The opportunity cost of their time is lower than it is for adults. This framework also suggests that with the advent of large video screens, video disks, and cable television, the experience of going out to a movie can now be closely approximated at home. As these substitutes fall in price, the demand for movie tickets undoubtedly will fall.

Economics thus provides a framework which explains how the demand for movie tickets is related to age, urbanization, the availability of gasoline, and the prices of products which offer a similar experience. More generally, the quantity demanded of a particular product will be related to the component costs that are associated with using the product and to the prices of other products that offer a similar experience.

---

[3]This idea is developed more fully in Chapter 7.

Once the manager has selected a model, he must gather data to estimate the demand function. The government publishes a wealth of information. Among its more useful publications for estimating demand functions are the following:

U.S. Department of Labor, Bureau of Labor Statistics, *Handbook of Labor Statistics*

U.S. Department of Labor, Bureau of Labor Statistics, *Monthly Labor Review*

U.S. Department of Commerce, Bureau of the Census, *Statistical Abstract of the United States*

U.S. Department of Commerce, Bureau of the Census, *Historical Statistics of the United States, Colonial Times to 1970*

U.S. Department of Commerce, Social and Economic Statistics Administration, *Long Term Economic Growth 1860–1970*

The manager can obtain additional data from industry publications or from the firm's own records.

The whole process associated with estimating a demand function will become much clearer if we follow the steps involved in estimating a particular demand function. Consider a corporate executive working in a large oil firm who is charged with estimating the demand function for motor fuel in the United States. She has determined that income, the price of automobiles, and the price of gasoline are likely to have a sizable effect on fuel consumption. A more complete study might consider some additional variables, but for purposes of illustration, we will concentrate on these.

Modifications often have to be made to published data before they can be used. For example, the consumption of some products will increase over time simply because the population grows over time. But our executive does not want the data on fuel consumption to reflect population growth. Accordingly, she gathers data on total motor-fuel consumption and on the U.S. population from various editions of the *Statistical Abstract of the United States*. These data, for the years 1953 to 1977, are shown in columns (1) and (2) of Table 3.2. Per capita motor-fuel consumption, found in column (3), is obtained by dividing total motor-fuel consumption by the population.[4] The table shows that total fuel consumption has more than doubled since 1953. But per capita fuel consumption has less than doubled over the same period. Thus, to distinguish increases in demand due to other factors from increases in demand caused by population growth, it is important to adjust the data for population growth.

Fuel consumption should be related to consumer income. Over time, however, consumer income changes because of both increases in productiv-

---

[4]Virtually every statistical computer program can perform data transformations such as this one.

ity and inflation. For example, the average weekly earnings of production workers rose from about $100 in 1967 to about $200 in 1979, yet consumers were not twice as well off in 1979 as they were in 1967. This is because the cost of living increased over this period; a dollar did not buy as many goods in 1979 as it did in 1967. Consequently, the manager will want a measure of consumer income that has been adjusted for inflation.

It is not difficult to adjust nominal income for inflation. To see how this is

TABLE 3.2

FUEL AND INCOME DATA

YEAR	TOTAL MOTOR-FUEL CONSUMPTION (BILLION GALLONS) (1)	POPULATION (MILLIONS) (2)	PER CAPITA MOTOR-FUEL CONSUMPTION (GALLONS) (3)	GROSS REAL WEEKLY EARNINGS (1967 DOLLARS) (4)
1953	47.9	160.184	299.0	79.6
1954	49.6	163.026	304.2	80.2
1955	53.1	165.931	320.0	84.4
1956	55.7	168.903	329.8	86.9
1957	57.4	171.984	333.8	87.0
1958	59.1	174.882	337.9	86.7
1959	62.2	177.830	349.8	90.2
1960	63.7	180.671	352.6	91.0
1961	65.0	183.691	353.9	92.1
1962	66.6	186.538	357.0	94.8
1963	64.5	189.242	340.8	96.5
1964	67.9	191.889	353.9	98.3
1965	71.1	194.303	365.9	100.6
1966	74.6	196.560	379.5	101.7
1967	77.7	198.712	391.0	101.8
1968	82.9	200.706	413.0	103.4
1969	88.1	202.677	434.7	104.4
1970	92.3	204.875	450.5	102.7
1971	97.6	207.045	471.4	104.9
1972	105.1	208.842	503.3	108.7
1973	110.5	210.396	525.2	109.3
1974	106.3	211.899	501.7	104.6
1975	109.0	213.597	510.3	101.7
1976	115.7	215.252	537.5	103.4
1977	119.6	216.921	551.4	104.4

done, suppose that the "average item" costs $1 in 1967. An income of $10,000 could purchase 10,000 "average items" in 1967. If the price of the "average item" rose to $1.50 in 1975, an income of $10,000 could purchase only

$$\frac{10,000}{1.50} = 6,666$$

"average items" in 1975. Thus, the real income or purchasing power of the consumer's income fell to $6,666 by 1975. As a general rule, dividing actual current income by a measure of the current price of the "average item" provides a measure of the purchasing power of consumer income. This is often called real income, as opposed to nominal income.

The government produces several data series that measure real income. Our executive has chosen to use a series on the average gross real weekly earnings of production and nonsupervisory workers on private nonagricultural payrolls from the *Handbook of Labor Statistics*. These data are found in column (4) of Table 3.2. As we can see, there were significant increases in real income in the 1950s and 1960s. But consumers were not much better off in 1977 than they were in 1970.

To simplify the discussion, we will be relating fuel consumption in any year to real earnings in that year. This specification ignores the fact that consumers save and borrow to reallocate their consumption over time. Because of large fluctuations from year to year in the price of food, the income of many farmers also fluctuates considerably from year to year. There is also a great deal of variability in the income of individuals in several other occupations (e.g., stockbrokers, real estate agents). The consumption of individuals in these occupations, however, does not vary nearly as much as their income varies from year to year. Part of the income in plentiful years is put aside for leaner years. For similar reasons, students going into lucrative professions such as business, law, or medicine consume more in their student years than students going into occupations with low incomes.

What this suggests is that an individual's present and future wealth is one factor affecting his consumption over his lifetime. Because a large part of this wealth comes from the stream of income flowing to an individual over his lifetime, the more sophisticated demand studies use a weighted average of current and past real income levels to measure wealth. Furthermore, some wealth is held in the housing, bond, and equity markets. It is easy to see that a plunge in the stock market will result in a drop in consumer wealth and consequently will cause the demand for many goods to fall. Demand functions for consumer durables have been estimated with more precision when variables measuring the fortunes of the stock market are included.

The U.S. Bureau of Labor Statistics publishes very detailed information on prices in the *Handbook of Labor Statistics* and in the *Monthly Labor Review*. Once again, some manipulation is required before the data are usable. Suppose that between 1975 and 1976 prices rose by 7 percent on average. That is, the rate of inflation equaled 7 percent. If tire prices increased 7 percent between 1975 and 1976, then tire prices were no more expensive in 1976 *compared to other goods* than they were in 1975. Tire prices and the prices of other goods increased at the same rate. This means that the relative price of tires did not change between 1975 and 1976. Consequently, if nominal income also rose by 7 percent, consumers would have no incentive to alter their consumption between 1975 and 1976.

It is easy to manipulate the Bureau of Labor Statistics data to obtain a measure of relative prices. Let's see why this manipulation makes sense. The Bureau of Labor Statistics price data are published in the form of price indexes. For example, the consumer price index (CPI) value (in terms of 1967) of

TABLE 3.3

RELATIVE PRICES

YEAR	CPI: ALL ITEMS (1967 = 100) (1)	CPI: GASOLINE (1967 = 100) (2)	RELATIVE PRICE OF GASOLINE (3)
1953	80.1	80.3	1.003
1954	80.5	82.5	1.025
1955	80.2	83.6	1.042
1956	81.4	86.5	1.063
1957	84.3	90.0	1.068
1958	86.6	88.8	1.025
1959	87.3	89.9	1.030
1960	88.7	92.5	1.042
1961	89.6	91.4	1.020
1962	90.6	91.9	1.014
1963	91.7	91.8	1.001
1964	92.9	91.4	.984
1965	94.5	94.5	1.004
1966	97.2	97.0	.998
1967	100.0	100.0	1.000
1968	104.2	101.4	.973
1969	109.8	104.7	.954
1970	116.3	105.6	.908
1971	121.3	106.3	.876
1972	125.3	107.6	.859
1973	133.1	118.1	.887
1974	147.7	159.9	1.083
1975	161.2	170.8	1.060
1976	170.5	177.9	1.043
1977	181.5	188.2	1.037

the cost of all items in year t equals

$$CPI_{a,t} = \frac{\text{Price of all items in year } t}{\text{Price of all items in 1967}} \cdot 100$$

This index is shown in column (1) of Table 3.3. We can see that prices generally increased very little during the 1950s and 1960s. In other words, the rate of inflation was very low during this period. On the other hand, the rate of inflation has been much higher in the 1970s. Similarly, the consumer price

RATIONING DUMMY (4)	CPI: NEW CAR (1967 = 100) (5)	CPI: USED CAR (1967 = 100) (6)	RELATIVE PRICE OF CAR (7)
0	95.8	89.2	1.122
0	94.8	75.9	.966
0	90.8	71.8	.919
0	93.5	69.1	.879
0	98.4	77.4	.943
0	101.5	80.2	.951
0	105.9	89.5	1.044
0	104.5	83.6	.966
0	104.5	86.9	.990
0	104.1	94.8	1.057
0	103.5	95.9	1.054
0	103.2	100.1	1.081
0	100.9	99.4	1.053
0	99.1	96.9	.999
0	100.0	100.0	1.000
0	102.7	102.1	.980
0	104.4	103.1	.940
0	107.6	104.3	.900
0	112.0	110.2	.910
0	110.0	110.5	.881
0	111.1	117.6	.877
1	117.5	122.6	.827
0	127.6	146.4	.897
0	135.7	167.9	.966
0	142.9	182.8	.985

index value (in terms of 1967) of the price of gasoline in year t equals

$$CPI_{g,t} = \frac{\text{Price of gasoline in year } t}{\text{Price of gasoline in 1967}} \cdot 100$$

If we divide the index value for the price of gasoline in year t by the index value for the price of all items in year t, we get

$$P_{g,t} = \frac{CPI_{g,t}}{CPI_{a,t}} = \frac{\text{Price of gasoline in year } t}{\text{Price of all items in year } t} \cdot \frac{\text{Price of all items in 1967}}{\text{Price of gasoline in 1967}}$$

As can be seen, $P_{g,t}$ equals the relative price of gasoline in year t divided by the relative price of gasoline in 1967. If, as we move through time, gasoline becomes relatively more expensive, $P_{g,t}$ will increase. Consequently, $P_{g,t}$ is a measure of the *relative* price of gasoline.

Our executive has decided to use $P_{g,t}$ to measure variations over time in the relative price of gasoline. We show values for $P_{g,t}$ in column (3) of Table 3.3. The data show that the relative price of gasoline fell almost steadily from 1957 to 1973. The formation of OPEC resulted in a sharp increase in the relative price of gasoline in 1974, but the relative price of gasoline subsequently fell. In fact, in half the years in the period 1953–1960, gasoline was relatively more expensive than in 1977.

Often, a lot is gained from thinking carefully about a market before doing empirical work. The market for motor fuel was seriously affected by the price controls which were placed on motor fuel in 1974. As we shall see in Chapter 11, the long lines that resulted are a common outcome of price controls. Waiting in line makes gasoline costlier than it would have been with no lines because time is valuable and accordingly leads to a fall in the quantity of gasoline demanded. To capture the increase in the total price of gasoline that accompanied the price ceiling of 1974, a so-called dummy variable has been created, which equals 1 in 1974 and 0 in all other years. The interpretation of this variable will become clear later on.

The quantity of motor fuel demanded should also be affected by the relative price of cars. The Bureau of Labor Statistics published indexes on new car prices and on used car prices. These are given in columns (5) and (6) of Table 3.3. Since approximately 90 percent of the cars on the road are used cars, our executive has created the following variable, which measures the relative price of cars:

$$P_{a,t} = \frac{.1CPI_{n,t} + .9CPI_{u,t}}{CPI_{a,t}}$$

where $CPI_{n,t}$ = consumer price index value for new cars
 $CPI_{u,t}$ = consumer price index value for used cars

Let's summarize what we have seen so far. After examining the market for the commodity in question, our petroleum executive decided upon the following model: the quantity of gasoline demanded over time is a function of the following:

1 The relative price of gasoline

2 Real income

3 The relative price of automobiles

4 The presence of price controls

Before we estimate this demand function, let's examine a simple case.

3.5
BIVARIATE REGRESSIONS: THEIR MEANING AND INTERPRETATION

By focusing our attention on the simple relationship between price and quantity, we shall be able to get a feel for demand estimation. Because this is a relationship between two variables, it is called a bivariate relationship. Since the problem is two-dimensional, we can use some graphs to develop some intuition about estimation. The more general treatment in the next section should follow naturally from the present development.

Consider the scatter of price and quantity combinations found in panel (a) of Figure 3.3. These data need to be summarized to be useful to managers who are interested in knowing what quantity of this product will be demanded at a particular price. We would like to find a linear demand curve that provides a reasonable approximation to the group of points in panel (a) of Figure 3.3. Line AB in panel (b) does not fit the data well at all. This line indicates that very little will be demanded at low prices and that a great deal will be demanded at high prices. In fact, a negative relationship between price and quantity is observed rather than the positive one implied by line AB. Consequently, a line with a negative slope may approximate the data more closely than a line with a positive slope. But not all negatively sloped lines fit the data equally well. Line CD in panel (c) of Figure 3.3 fits the data better than line AB, but line CD tells us that at very low prices less is demanded than is actually demanded and that at very high prices more is demanded than is actually demanded. We should be able to find a line that avoids these systematic errors. Line EF in panel (d) of Figure 3.3 is one such line. It fits the data better than either line AB or line CD.

So far, we have been "eyeballing" the data and guessing at the location of a demand curve that approximates the observations. This is a tedious and imprecise way of proceeding. The manager's task would be simplified if she could use a systematic rule for finding the best line to approximate a scatter of points.

Any line describing a relationship between price and quantity can be written in the form

$$\hat{Q} = a + bP$$

where $\hat{Q}$ is the quantity demanded that is predicted by the line. In panel (a) of Figure 3.4, line CD is represented as

$$\hat{Q} = a_0 + b_0 P$$

Notice that we have adopted the mathematical convention of putting the independent variable P on the horizontal axis and the dependent variable Q on the vertical axis. For each of the n data points in panel (a), the *actual* quantity demanded Q_i is equal to the quantity demanded that is predicted by line $\hat{Q}_i$ plus the error of the prediction e_i. That is,

$$Q_i = \hat{Q}_i + e_i = a_0 + b_0 P_i + e_i \qquad i = 1, 2, \ldots, n$$

This is called a regression equation of quantity on price.

In panel (a) of Figure 3.4, the errors are given by the vertical lines extending from line CD to the data points. For example, line CD, which is only an approximation, implies that Q_A will be demanded when the price equals P_2. But, in fact, Q_2 was demanded at this price according to actual data. The error $(Q_2 - Q_A)$ is represented by the vertical line going from Q_A to Q_2 at price P_2.

FIGURE 3.3   Fitting a demand curve to a scatter of price-quantity combinations.

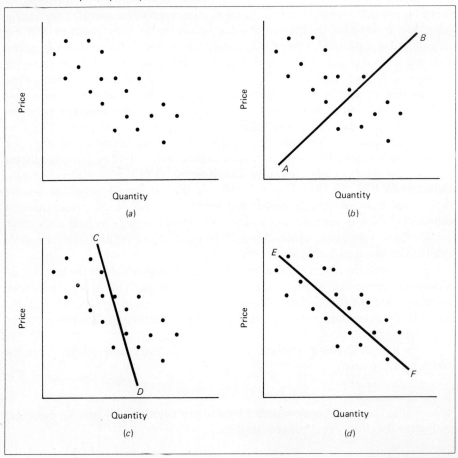

(a)

(b)

(c)

(d)

One widely adopted rule for finding the best line to describe a relationship is to find the values for a and b that minimize the sum of the squared vertical distances between the line and the data points. That is,

$$e_1^2 + e_2^2 + \cdots + e_n^2$$

is minimized.[5] The values of a and b that minimize the summed squared errors will be called $\hat{a}$ and $\hat{b}$, and the regression line associated with these values is called the ordinary least squares regression line. Line EF in panel (b) of Figure 3.4 is an ordinary least squares regression line. Notice how the errors associated with this line tend to be smaller than the errors associated with line CD. In particular, line EF estimates that Q_B will be demanded at P_2. Actually, Q_2 is demanded. The error here $(Q_2 - Q_B)$ is less than the error associated with line $CD(Q_2 - Q_A)$.

The coefficients $\hat{a}$ and $\hat{b}$ have an economic interpretation. First, $\hat{a}$ is the intercept of the regression line. It equals the quantity, estimated by the regression line, that would be purchased if the price were zero. Next, $\hat{b}$ is the slope of the regression line. It gives the change in quantity, estimated

---

[5]We will not show in this text exactly how this is done. For the somewhat tedious derivation of the ordinary least squares regression line, the student can refer to any econometrics textbook and to a great many statistics textbooks.

FIGURE 3.4   The least-squares regression line is closer to the observations than any other line.

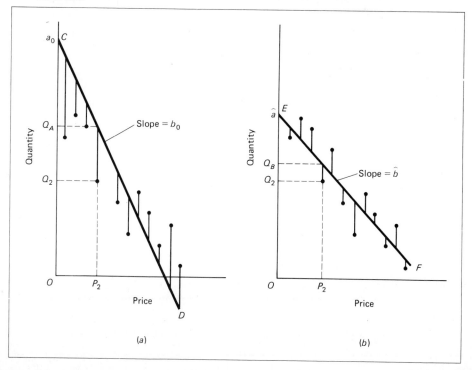

(a)   (b)

by the regression line, that results when the price increases by 1 unit. Because the regression line in panel (b) of Figure 3.4 implies that the quantity demanded *decreases* as the price rises, the regression coefficient $\hat{b}$ that is associated with this line is negative.

Some scatters of data can be closely approximated by regression lines. For example, the regression line in panel (a) of Figure 3.5 lies very close to every data point. Other scatters of data, however, can not be closely approximated by regression lines. In these cases, the ordinary least squares regression line will not come very close to many of the data points. An example of this is the regression line in panel (b) of Figure 3.5.

One popular measure of the closeness with which the regression line approximates a scatter of points is R^2. Before we define this measure, however, a few terms need to be defined.

DEFINITION ▶ The *mean* of a variable is its average value. For example, the mean value of the quantity demanded equals

$$\mu_Q = \frac{1}{n}\sum_{i=1}^{n} Q_i$$

DEFINITION ▶ The *variance* of a variable is equal to its average squared deviation from its mean. As an example, the variance in the quantity demanded is defined to be

$$\sigma_Q^2 = \frac{1}{n}\sum_{i=1}^{n} (Q_i - \mu_Q)^2$$

This variance measures the average variation in the quantity demanded.

FIGURE 3.5 There can be large differences in how closely regression lines will approximate the data.

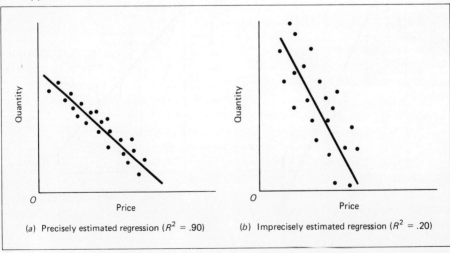

(a) Precisely estimated regression ($R^2 = .90$) (b) Imprecisely estimated regression ($R^2 = .20$)

DEFINITION ▶   The *coefficient of determination* (R^2) measures the proportion of the variation in quantity demanded that is explained by the variation in the price. It can be calculated as

$$R^2 = 1 - \frac{\frac{1}{n}\sum_{i=1}^{n} e_i^2}{\sigma_Q^2}$$

The R^2 tells us how closely the regression line fits the observed data. For example, if *all* data points lay along a straight line, that line would explain all the variation in the quantity demanded. There would be no variation in quantity demanded left unexplained by the line (i.e., each e_i equals 0), and the R^2 would equal 1. The R^2 will be close to 1 in value when the regression line very closely approximates the scatter of data points, as in panel (*a*) in Figure 3.5. In contrast, the R^2 will be close to 0 when the regression line is a very poor approximation of the scatter of data points, as in panel (*b*) of Figure 3.5.

One of the principal reasons for estimating demand functions is to determine the effects of an increase in price on the quantity demanded. The regression estimates that a 1-unit increase in price brings about a $\hat{b}$-unit change in the quantity demanded. But our limited model of demand contains some inherent imprecision. Thus, we must wonder how confident we can be that the quantity demanded will change by $\hat{b}$ units when the price increases by 1 unit. In order to resolve this issue, first we need to define the standard deviation.

DEFINITION ▶   The *standard deviation* of a variable equals the square root of its variance.

A rough rule of thumb is that if there are enough observations on prices and quantities, then there is less than a 5 percent probability that the "true" trade-off between price and quantity lies outside the interval

$$\hat{b} - 2\sigma_{\hat{b}} < b < \hat{b} + 2\sigma_{\hat{b}}$$

where $\sigma_{\hat{b}}$ is the standard error of $\hat{b}$. A full explanation of just what the standard error represents is provided in elementary econometrics texts. In order to avoid an extended discussion of statistics, we shall simply note that the standard error is the standard deviation of the estimator. As such, it provides some feeling for the precision of the estimator $\hat{b}$. In any case, computer regression programs produce estimates of the standard error of $\hat{a}$ and of the standard error of $\hat{b}$. These are denoted as $\sigma_{\hat{a}}$ and $\sigma_{\hat{b}}$, respectively.

To put all these results together, let's now return to our corporate executive in the large oil campany who was charged with estimating the demand function for motor fuel. The first thing she did was to plot the actual relationship between the per capita consumption of motor fuel ($Q_{g,t}$) and the relative price of gasoline ($P_{g,t}$). The data are found in Tables 3.2 and 3.3. Her plot is reproduced in Figure 3.6.

She specified her regression model as

$$Q_{g,t} = a + bP_{g,t} + e_t$$

The regression procedure employed the observed values for quantity demanded and prices paid to estimate values for a and b. The regression that was estimated from the data plotted in Figure 3.6 was

$$Q_{g,t} = 840.688 - 437.981P_{g,t}$$
$$(261.027)\ (260.577) \qquad R^2 = .11$$

This regression line is also drawn in Figure 3.6. The numbers in parentheses are the standard errors of the coefficients. Apparently, there are other important determinants of motor-fuel demand besides the relative price of gasoline, for the $R^2 = .11$ means that the regression line explains only 11 percent of the variance in the demand for motor fuel. In a time-series study such as this one, this is not a good fit.

The regression estimates that if the relative price of gasoline ($P_{g,t}$) were zero, then per capita consumption of motor fuel would equal 840.688 gallons per year, nearly double current consumption levels. Furthermore, we can be approximately 95 percent sure that the true intercept falls in the interval

$$840.688 - 2 \cdot 261.027 < a < 840.688 + 2 \cdot 261.027$$
$$318.634 < a < 1362.742$$

The coefficient on the relative price of gasoline ($P_{g,t}$) means that an increase in the relative price of gasoline from 1.0 to 2.0 is estimated to cause the per capita demand for motor fuel to fall by 437.981 gallons per year; this

FIGURE 3.6 The demand curve for gasoline estimated by ordinary least squares.

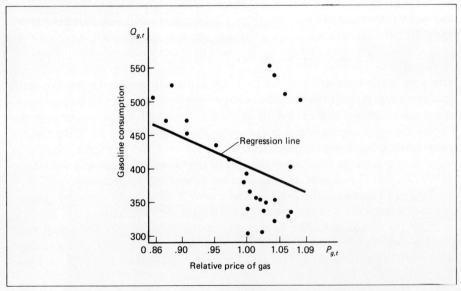

fall in motor-fuel consumption is equal to the total motor-fuel consumption in 1969. A more typical increase in the relative price of motor fuel from 1.0 to 1.1 is estimated to bring about a drop in the demand for motor fuel of 43.798 gallons per year. This, however, is not a very precise estimate. We can be approximately 95 percent certain that the true slope coefficient falls in the interval

$$-437.981 - 2 \cdot 260.577 < b < -437.981 + 2 \cdot 260.577$$
$$-959.135 < b < 83.173$$

Apparently, we cannot be very certain that the coefficient is not zero: the value zero lies in this 95 percent interval. When this occurs, the variable (the relative price of gasoline in this instance) is said to be statistically insignificant. Equivalently, we cannot say with 95 percent confidence that an increase in the relative price of gasoline has *any* effect on motor-fuel consumption.

Perhaps our petroleum executive did not do very well with this model because it was too limited. There were too many things left out. But the exercise was instructive because it provided an understanding of bivariate regressions. This understanding will make it easier to interpret regressions with many variables. Since she cannot be satisfied with the performance of this simple model, our executive will have to add other variables.

3.6

MULTIVARIATE REGRESSIONS

It is very easy to graph a relationship between the quantity demanded of a firm's product and the product's price. It is impossible to graph a more complicated relationship between quantity demanded and the price of the product, the price of related goods, and income. For this reason, multivariate regressions which describe these more complicated relationships are often viewed with much more apprehension than they deserve. Multivariate regressions really are very simple extensions of the bivariate regressions we just discussed. The coefficients are chosen so as to minimize the sum of the squared errors, and the coefficients of the variables once again can be interpreted as slopes.

The oil company manager expanded her demand model to

$$Q_{g,t} = a + b_1 P_{g,t} + b_2 \text{RATION}_t + b_3 \text{EARN}_t + b_4 P_{c,t} + b_5 \text{SURPRISE}_t + e_t$$

where RATION_t = rationing dummy variable [Table 3.3 column (4)]
EARN_t = gross real weekly earnings [Table 3.2 column (4)]
$P_{c,t}$ = relative price of autos [Table 3.3 column (7)]

The final variable, SURPRISE, shows why inspecting the data can be very fruitful.

Our executive was very astute and noticed that there were four data points in the upper-right-hand corner of Figure 3.6 that seemed far removed from other data points. Upon further investigation, she learned that these data points corresponded to the years 1974–1977. She pondered what would make consumption greater than expected at these high price levels. Noting that gasoline was very cheap in the years immediately preceding the formation of OPEC (the Organization of Petroleum Exporting Countries) and that 90 percent of the cars on the road are used cars, she reasoned that motor-fuel consumption in the period 1974–1977 was unexpectedly high because most of the cars on the road in those years had been bought prior to the formation of OPEC when low gas prices were anticipated for future years. To capture the phenomenon of consumers being stuck with fuel-inefficient cars immediately after the formation of OPEC she created a variable called SURPRISE. This variable equals zero in the years prior to the formation of OPEC. In the years after OPEC was formed, it equals the number of cars per capita still in existence which were bought prior to the formation of OPEC. The values for SURPRISE are given in Table 3.4.

Now let's see how the expanded model performs. The oil company executive obtained the following results, using data for the years 1953–1977:

$$Q_{g,t} = 731.026 - 488.144\,P_{g,t} - 62.303\,\text{RATION}_t + 3.360\,\text{EARN}_t$$
$$\quad\ (150.496)\quad (100.041)\qquad (20.703)\qquad\qquad (.638)$$

$$- 193.777\,P_{c,t} + 327.765\,\text{SURPRISE} \qquad R^2 = .968$$
$$\quad (53.131)\qquad (31.589)$$

The regression line fits the data extremely well. The value for R^2 indicates that 96.8 percent of the variance of the demand for gasoline is explained by the regression line. We can see that bringing in additional variables sometimes can improve the fit tremendously.

TABLE 3.4
VALUES OF THE VARIABLE SURPRISE

YEAR	SURPRISE	YEAR	SURPRISE
1953	0	1966	0
1954	0	1967	0
1955	0	1968	0
1956	0	1969	0
1957	0	1970	0
1958	0	1971	0
1959	0	1972	0
1960	0	1973	0
1961	0	1974	.519
1962	0	1975	.485
1963	0	1976	.459
1964	0	1977	.418
1965	0		

Once again, the estimated value for the intercept (731.026) is the implied consumption level when *all* the variables equal zero. That is, when $EARN_t = P_{g,t} = P_{c,t} = RATION_t = SURPRISE_t = 0$, then the annual quantity of gasoline demanded is estimated to equal 731 gallons per capita.

As before, the coefficient of the relative price of gasoline ($P_{g,t}$) equals the estimated change in the quantity of motor fuel demanded that would accompany a 1-unit increase in the relative price of gasoline. This coefficient implies that an increase in the relative price of gasoline from 1.0 to 1.1 would bring a fall in per capita motor-fuel consumption of about 48.8 gallons per year.

The coefficient of the relative price of gasoline is estimated much more precisely in the multivariate regression than in the bivariate regression. In the multivariate regression, we can be approximately 95 percent certain that the gasoline price coefficient falls in the interval

$$-488.144 - 2 \cdot 100.041 < b < -488.144 + 2 \cdot 100.041$$
$$-688.226 < b < -288.062$$

This means there is a 95 precent probability that a 1-unit increase in the relative price of gasoline will cause the quantity of gasoline demanded to fall by 288 to 688 gallons. In this case, the relative price of gasoline is said to exert a significant and negative impact on the quantity of gasoline demanded. You might try to show that each of the other variables also exerts a significant influence on the quantity of gasoline demanded.

The rationing dummy variable RATION equals 1 in 1974 and 0 in every other year. The coefficient of -62.303 means that the per capita quantity of motor fuel demanded was 62 gallons less in the year in which RATION equaled 1 in value (1974) than in the years in which RATION equaled 0 in value (all other years), other things being equal. We have noted that 1974 was the only year in the period 1953–1977 in which there were gas lines. A reasonable inference, therefore, is that gas lines brought about a 62-gallon fall in fuel demand.

Question   How much higher would the relative price of gasoline have to have been in 1974 to have accomplished the same result as the gas line?

Answer   The effect of a change in the relative price of gasoline ($\Delta P_{g,t}$) on the quantity of gasoline demanded equals

$$-488.144 \cdot \Delta P_{g,t}$$

For this to equal the effect of gas lines,

$$-488.144 \cdot \Delta P_{g,t} = -62.303$$
$$\Delta P_{g,t} = .128$$

That is, the relative price of gasoline would have to have been .128 higher than it was in 1974. In fact, the relative price of gasoline rose by .20 between 1973 and 1974. This analysis suggests that it would have to have risen by .33 between 1973 and 1974 if gas lines were to be avoided.

The regression estimated that a $1 increase in the real weekly earnings of workers results in a 3.36-gallon increase per year in fuel demand. Income has a very small effect on the quantity of gasoline demanded. From 1953 to 1977, *real* weekly earnings increased by $25. This is estimated to result in an increase in per capita fuel demand of 84 (=25 · 3.36) gallons a year.

Motor-fuel demand also is relatively unresponsive to changes in the relative price of automobiles $(P_{c,t})$. An increase in the relative price of automobiles from 1.0 to 1.1 is estimated to lead to a 19-gallon-a-year decrease in the quantity of motor fuel demanded per capita.

Finally, the coefficient of SURPRISE is 327.765. From Table 3.4, we can see that the variable SURPRISE equals 0 in the years 1953–1973 and ranges in value from .519 to .418 in the years 1974–1977. Remember that SURPRISE is the number of cars per capita that were acquired prior to the formation of OPEC. The coefficient of SURPRISE implies that consumers in 1974 demanded 170 (=327.765 · .519) more gallons per capita than they would have had they not owned .519 (low mileage) cars per capita which were bought prior to the formation of OPEC. With the passage of time, cars age and eventually are scrapped. By 1977, there were only .418 cars per capita that had been bought prior to the formation of OPEC, and in 1977 the surprise associated with the formation of OPEC is estimated to result in 137 (= 327.765 · .418) more gallons per capita demand than would have been demanded if the high fuel prices had been anticipated.

The oil company executive was quite pleased with the outcome of her work. She was able to explain almost all the variation in the quantity demanded since her R^2 was .968. Furthermore, all the variables had the expected effects on the quantity demanded and all had a significant impact on demand. In addition, she learned which variables were responsible for the major changes over time in the quantity of motor fuel demanded. She learned that real earnings and the relative price of automobiles had a comparatively small effect on gasoline demand and that variables related to the relative price of gasoline had sizable effects on the quantity of gasoline demanded.

3.7

FUNCTIONAL FORM

There is nothing in economic theory which compels a linear relationship between a price and quantity or between income and quantity. Using prices and income in a linear regression to explain variation in quantity demanded usually results in a good fit. Sometimes, however, a better fit can be obtained if income squared or the logarithm of income is substituted into the linear regression for income or if price squared or the logarithm of price is substituted into the linear regression for some price. Other functional forms are also available for managers to try. Finding the best functional form usually requires some experimentation.

The oil company executive was not content with her multivariate regression results. She wanted to be sure other functional forms would not fit the data better. The plot of the relative price of gasoline against the quantity demanded in Figure 3.6 revealed a fairly linear relationship between these two variables. A plot of the relative price of cars against the quantity of gasoline demanded also revealed no glaring nonlinear relationship between the relative price of cars and the quantity demanded. A plot of real earnings against the quantity of motor fuel demanded, however, showed that the relationship between fuel consumption and real earnings is not linear. This plot is reproduced in panel (*a*) of Figure 3.7. It is clear that regression line *AB* in panel (*a*) predicts that at low real earnings levels fuel consumption is lower than it actually is and that at middle real earnings levels fuel consumption is higher than it actually is.

Because the plot of points in panel (*a*) in Figure 3.7 resembled half of a parabola, the executive thought that she might get a better fit if she used earnings squared rather than earnings, in her regression. The relationship between earnings squared and fuel consumption is plotted in panel (*b*) of Figure 3.7. Bivariate regression line *CD* in panel (*b*) appears to fit the data better than does regression line *AB* in panel (*a*). She also estimated the following multivariate regression:

$$Q_{g,t} = \hat{a} + \hat{b}_1 P_{g,t} + \hat{b}_2 \text{RATION}_t + \hat{b}_3 (\text{EARN}_t)^2 + \hat{b}_4 P_{c,t} + \hat{b}_5 \text{SURPRISE}_t + e_t$$

In other words, she replaced earnings with earnings squared.

The results for the new regression were quite good:

$$Q_{g,t} = 846.898 - 457.160 P_{g,t} - 63.482 \text{RATION}_t$$
$$(127.527) \quad (101.934) \qquad (20.349)$$

$$+ .019(\text{EARN}_t)^2 - 101.541 P_{c,t} + 321.216 \text{SURPRISE}_t \qquad R^2 = .969$$
$$(.003) \qquad\qquad (52.148) \qquad (31.645)$$

FIGURE 3.7   Using different functional forms can improve the estimated relationship.

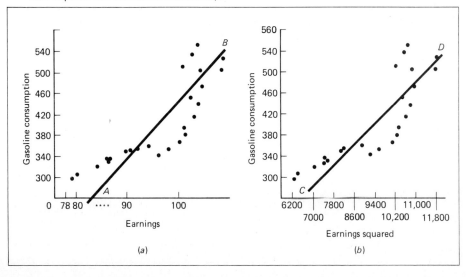

(a)   (b)

If this regression is compared with the regression reported in the previous section, it can be seen that she got a slightly better fit using earnings squared than she did using earnings; the R^2 was higher when earnings squared was used. The coefficient on earnings squared implies that the quantity demanded rises by .019 gallons when earnings squared increases by $1. Replacing earnings with earnings squared in the regression had very little impact on the other coefficients. Continued experimentation (e.g., using earnings cubed instead of earnings squared) could improve her results still further.

3.8

THE IDENTIFICATION PROBLEM

In Chapter 5, we will show that the prices and quantities found in competitive markets occur at the intersections of demand curves and supply curves. Price and quantity change when the demand curve shifts, when the supply curve shifts, or when both curves shift. To give some interpretation to a set of price-quantity points, it is necessary, therefore, to understand what caused the point of intersection between the supply curve and the demand curve to move.

In many markets, particularly in agriculture, the demand curve is stable and the supply curve fluctuates from year to year. Fluctuations in the supply of corn, for instance, are the inevitable by-product of variations in the weather. Similarly, the supply of fuel oil shifted as new oil fields were discovered, as new technologies for drilling for oil were developed, and as OPEC emerged. A market with these characteristics is depicted in panel (a) of Figure 3.8. As the supply curve shifts, the points where the supply curve and

FIGURE 3.8   Regressing quantity on price estimates a demand curve when supply is unstable [panel (a)] but estimates a supply curve when demand is unstable [panel (b)].

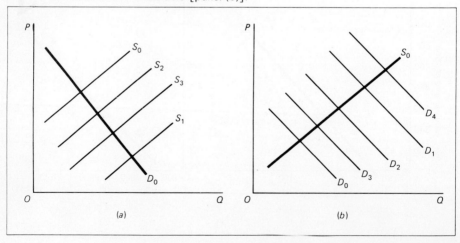

(a)   (b)

the demand curve intersect trace out the demand curve. In a market such as this, the manager who fits a line through the equilibrium points and estimates

$$Q = a + bP$$

is estimating demand function D_0 for his product.

In other markets, it is the supply curve which is relatively stable. Virtually all of the fluctuations occur in the demand curve. In durable-goods industries, fluctuations in the demand for durable goods follow the business cycle. When consumers are going through financially difficult times, they reduce their expenditures, in part, by cutting back on their purchases of durable goods such as cars, houses, and refrigerators. A market dominated by fluctuations in demand is shown in panel (b) of Figure 3.8. In this instance, a manager who fits a regression relating quantity to price will be estimating the supply curve! Some variation in the supply curve is obviously necessary for there to be any possibility of estimating the demand curve.

In still other markets, changes in price and quantity are the result of shifts in both demand and supply curves. As can be seen from Figure 3.9, fitting a line like AB through the set of equilibrium points will estimate neither a demand curve nor a supply curve. To disentangle the demand curves from the supply curves, additional knowledge of econometrics is necessary. At this point, it would be best to call on a firm like B & K Consultants, which will provide an econometrician, a specialist in the statistics of economic relationships.

FIGURE 3.9   If both supply and demand are unstable, regressing quantity on price provides an estimate of neither supply nor demand.

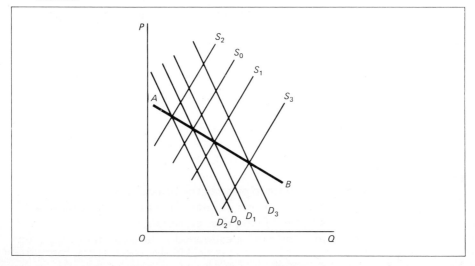

3.9

**EXPERIMENTAL AND
NONEXPERIMENTAL METHODS**

There are four principal methods of estimating demand functions. We will now examine each of these in turn.

First, the firm can conduct a survey in which consumers are asked how much of the firm's product they will purchase at different prices. This is very expensive, but more important, consumers do not always do what they say they are going to do. Consumer answers are unreliable for a number of reasons. It is difficult for consumers to quickly assess how much they would demand at various prices. A consumer may also try to please the interviewer by giving him answers he thinks the interviewer would like to hear or vice versa. Survey answers consequently must be used cautiously. At the very least, some understanding of how survey answers correspond to actual demand is necessary.

Another experimental method involves selecting several markets which are thought to be representative of the national market and then setting a different price in each of the chosen markets. A demand curve can be estimated by fitting a regression line through the price-quantity points. For this method to work, the firm must first have some control over the price of its product. For example, a box manufacturer in a competitive market would lose virtually all its customers if it raised the price of its boxes above the competitively determined price (see Chapter 5). Because of their cost, these experiments are often of short duration, and the result can sometimes be marred by the time it takes consumers to find out about the firm's new price and by local events such as layoffs, strikes, and snowstorms. Longer experiments also have their problems. For one thing, they make it easier for individuals in the markets where the firm's product is inexpensively priced to purchase the product and resell it in the markets where the product is relatively expensive.

For these reasons, most demand functions are not estimated from experimental data even though information from test markets can be useful for other purposes. The third estimation procedure is to use cross-sectional data. But very few demand functions are estimated by comparing the consumption levels of different households at a specific time. The reason is that for many products, there is little or no variation in price from consumer to consumer. This is largely the result of competition among producers and of little geographic variation in production costs. For other commodities it may cost more to produce the good in one area than in other areas. In competitive markets, the local prices will reflect these cost differences. But because of transportation costs, there may be no incentive to reduce the geographical variation in price by buying in the inexpensive markets and slightly undercutting the price in the expensive markets. For instance, partly because of geographic variation in the wages that must be paid restaurant workers, there is some variation from place to place in the price of a restaurant meal of a certain quality. Consumers, however, do not drive from New York City to the Connecticut suburbs to get a better deal on restaurant meals. In markets such as this, demand functions can be estimated if suitable information on price is available. The U.S. Bureau of the Census publishes a great deal of cross-sectional data on population characteristics and constitutes a valuable data source.

Finally, we may consider the use of time-series data. For the reasons just given, the vast majority of demand functions are estimated from time-series data on income, prices, and quantity. The demand function for motor fuel, which was discussed earlier in this chapter, was estimated from time-series data.

There are a number of refinements that were not discussed in the gasoline example that are sometimes used when doing empirical work using time-series data. If quarterly data are used, seasonal variation in demand can be picked up by using dummy variables. If we were interested in estimating the demand function for vacations in the Bahamas, a dummy variable could be created which equals 1 during the tourist season and which equals 0 during the off-season. The coefficient of this variable would estimate the increase in demand between the off-season and the peak season. Additional variables may also be needed because it sometimes takes time for consumers to find out about and respond to price changes. Some consumers, therefore, are responding to last period's price when they choose how much to purchase today. By using the current price and prices lagged one or more periods, we can deal with this problem.

The use of time-series data makes it easier for the firm to forecast future demand. If the manager knows how the quantity demanded depends on real income and relative prices, then predictions about the future course of real income and of relative prices will enable the manager to forecast the quantity that will be demanded of his product. Some of the data required for these forecasts are generated by firms such as Data Resources, Inc., which operate econometric models of the economy. The manager's forecast, of course, is only as good as the estimates of his demand function and the predictions about real income and relative prices. A forecast based on the best information available is nevertheless better than no forecast. In Chapter 6, we shall consider the value of forecasting in more detail.

3.10

SUMMARY

We have seen that the quantity demanded of a particular product is related to real income and relative prices. A statistical problem arises when demand curves are estimated at least partially because some prices are being omitted from the estimation. There often is a sizable payoff to careful thought about which variables should be included in a regression. Economic theory sometimes, but not always, provides guidance in this decision. Some attention is also necessary to ensure that the variables included in a regression are measuring *real* income and *relative* prices.

Estimating a bivariate regression simply amounts to finding the line that best describes a scatter of points. A multivariate regression is a slightly more complicated regression. In either type of regression, the coefficients of the variables correspond to slopes. There are statistics that indicate how accurately the regression line fits a scatter of points and with what precision the variable coefficients are estimated. Sometimes, spending some time experimenting with different functional forms improves the fit. We must always be alert to the fact that regression relating price to quantity may not always be estimating a demand function.

IMPORTANT NEW TERMS

Demand function

Normal good

Inferior good

Complement

Substitute

Elasticity of demand or price elasticity

Marginal revenue

Bivariate regression

Multivariate regression

Mean

Variance

Standard deviation

R^2

Cross-sectional data

Time-series data

PROBLEMS

3.1 You have just bought a resort in the mountains. Show how you would estimate the demand function for vacations at that resort.

3.2 Interpret the coefficients of the following demand function:

Number of ABC pens $= 31{,}473 - 1{,}376$ price of ABC pens
        (7,165)   (701)

                    $+ 685$ price of Cheapo pens $R^2 = .786$
                    (135)

Standard errors are in parentheses.

3.3 Answer true, false, or uncertain: If the price elasticity for hamburgers equals .8, then an increase in the price of hamburgers will result in more money being spent on hamburgers.

3.4 In the past year, the price of color TV sets rose 3 percent. Evaluate: Consequently, color TV sets have become relatively more expensive in the past year.

3.5 Suppose your boss shows you the following announcement: "All government price supports for corn will be abandoned." He then remarks "But I don't care about corn, I want to know what will happen to soybean prices." What should your response be?

3.6 Draw two linear demand curves that intersect on the price axis. Prove that at a given price both demand curves have the same elasticity.

3.7 Answer true, false, or uncertain: A proposal by the ABC Consulting Company to estimate the price elasticity of demand for refrigerators using 1980 data on refrigerator purchases in 165 large cities should be viewed with some caution.

REFERENCES

Johnston, J.: *Econometric Methods*, 2d ed., New York: McGraw-Hill Book Company, 1972.

Maddala, G. S.: *Econometrics*, New York: McGraw-Hill Book Company, 1977.

MATHEMATICAL APPENDIX

3A.1
THE RELATION BETWEEN MARGINAL REVENUE AND PRICE ELASTICITY

$$MR = \frac{d\,TR}{dQ}$$

$$= \frac{dPQ}{dQ}$$

$$= P\frac{dQ}{dQ} + Q\frac{dP}{dQ}$$

$$= P + Q\frac{dP}{dQ}\frac{P}{P}$$

$$= P\left[1 - \left(-\frac{QdP}{PdQ}\right)\right]$$

$$= P\left(1 - \frac{1}{\epsilon}\right)$$

PRODUCTION AND COSTS

The wants, needs, and preferences of consumers are represented by the market-demand function. Successful business firms must ultimately satisfy these consumer demands. In so doing, the firm must supply a commodity to the consumer. Whether the commodity in question is a tangible good or a service, the firm must produce something, and how much the firm produces depends upon the costs incurred in producing various quantities of output. These costs depend, in turn, upon the production function of the firm. Consequently, in this chapter, we shall begin with a formal analysis of the production function of the firm. Subsequently, we shall develop the firm's cost curves, which will provide the analytical foundation for the manager's supply decisions. This material also gives us a framework for subsequent applications. For example, we shall use these concepts to analyze the manager's supply response when there is technological change, when the government imposes various types of taxes, and when input prices change.

The development and discussion in this chapter will proceed as though the output is a tangible product rather than a service. This is solely for expositional convenience. Modifying the discussion to pertain to services usually would require only a minor change of wording.

A final caveat is in order. The discussion that follows suggests that a manager knows precisely what his production function is. Unfortunately for all of us, there is no manual that carefully details the production function of each product. In fact, a manager starts off with only a vague idea of the production function that he actually employs. Often, he finds the best way to organize his inputs for producing the specific product he sells through a trial-and-error procedure. This involves some groping to find the most efficient way of doing things. The reason that the exposition adopts the fiction that production functions are known precisely is that the language is less cumbersome. We should keep in mind, however, that this convention is merely for expositional convenience.

4.1

PRODUCTION FUNCTION

In producing a commodity, the manager combines inputs or factors of production according to some recipe. By "inputs," we mean the services of labor, raw materials (e.g., iron ore), intermediate goods (e.g., sheet steel), and capital equipment (e.g., a lathe). The recipe that is followed is more formally termed a "production function." Specifically, the production function describes the relationship between any specific collection of inputs and the maximum amount of output that can be produced from that collection. Of course, the current state of knowledge is embodied in the form of the production function.

The general form of the production function can be written as

$$Q = f(X_1, X_2, \ldots, X_n) \tag{4.1}$$

where Q represents the quantity of output, X_i denotes the quantity of the ith input, and f is the rule that translates the inputs into output. In this case, there are n inputs and one output, which means that we need $n + 1$ dimensions in order to graphically portray this relationship. Since this is not possible if n exceeds 2, we shall simplify the problem to some degree for the sole purpose of providing a graphical analysis. All of what follows can be generalized quite easily to the production function in equation (4.1). But the generalization cannot be made graphically. Nonetheless, we shall indicate these generalizations as we proceed. For now, let us consider a two-input production function

$$Q = q(L, K) \tag{4.2}$$

where Q is the firm's output, L and K denote quantities of labor services and capital, respectively, and q relates the inputs to the output.[1]

SHORT-RUN PRODUCTION   Within a given period of time, it is more difficult to acquire additional units of some inputs than of others. For instance, General Motors would find it very expensive, if not impossible, to build another automobile plant in the space of a week relative to the cost if General Motors had 2 years to build the extra plant. During that same week, however, General Motors could hire an additional assembly line worker with very little additional cost. On the basis of these considerations, the *short run* is defined as a period of time during which the manager does not vary at least one input because of the expense associated with such alteration. For ease of exposition, let us assume that capital is not varied on a day-to-day basis while the quantity of labor can be varied daily. Under this constraint, the short-run production function can be written as

$$Q = q(L, \bar{K}) \tag{4.3}$$

where the bar over K signifies that the quantity of capital is fixed.

We can get some feeling for this short-run production function by examining the data in Table 4.1. The size of MacDavid's hamburger stand has already been determined. The manager wants to determine the relationship between the number of hamburgers produced and the number of employees. He experiments by starting with one employee and adding an extra one each hour for 8 hours. His findings are reproduced in Table 4.1 and are plotted in

---

[1] An example of a production function that has been estimated empirically is the Cobb-Douglas production function:

$$Q = AL^\alpha K^{1-\alpha} \qquad 0 < \alpha < 1$$

In this production function, A is a technological efficiency parameter and α and $1-\alpha$ measure the responsiveness of output to changes in the quantities of the inputs.

TABLE 4.1
OUTPUT OF HAMBURGERS WITH VARIOUS
QUANTITIES OF LABOR

NUMBER OF EMPLOYEES	NUMBER OF HAMBURGERS
1	20
2	70
3	130
4	180
5	220
6	250
7	250
8	220

Figure 4.1, where the number of employees is measured on the horizontal axis and the number of hamburgers on the vertical axis. When these points are connected, we have a very crude total product curve. After the output began to decline with the eighth worker, the manager lost interest in any further experimentation.

The short-run production function expressed in equation (4.3) could take on many forms. One reasonable short-run production function is plotted in Figure 4.2. Here, we have described output as a function of the fixed quantity of capital and varying quantities of labor services. We see that for small quantities of labor, output responds rather dramatically to changes in labor.

FIGURE 4.1   The production function for
hamburgers at MacDavid's hamburger stand.

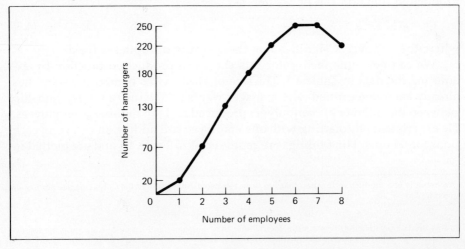

This is because the fixed quantity of capital is large relative to the number of workers. One could envision two or three workers scurrying around a large factory. As the manager adds a few more workers, less time is wasted in moving from one place to another. In addition, greater specialization of labor is possible, which also increases efficiency. These efficiencies cause the firm's output to increase greatly when more labor is used. Subsequently, output will increase more slowly in response to equal increases in the amount of labor hired. This is because the opportunity for additional gains from the specialization and more efficient use of labor diminishes as more labor is used. Eventually, as more and more workers are added, the congestion of workers will be so severe that a maximum output will be reached. Any further additions to the work force will actually decrease the quantity of output.

LONG-RUN PRODUCTION The *long run* is defined as a period of time during which the quantities of all inputs are adjusted (if necessary). A two-input, long-run production function can be written as in equation (4.2). Even though the production function described by equation (4.2) is a simplification of equation (4.1) to the case of only two inputs, the graphical representation of the two-input production functions is rather cumbersome. This is because the production function in (4.2) generates a surface in three dimensions. Although we are able to deal with three-dimensional geometry, it is very awkward.

Fortunately, it is possible to represent in only two dimensions the production opportunities that exist when there are two variable inputs. To do this, we begin with the labor-capital plane in panel (*a*) of Figure 4.3. Each point in the plane specifies a particular combination of labor and capital. These combinations can usefully be grouped according to how much output each combination will yield. For example, suppose that the manager discov-

FIGURE 4.2 The short-run production function $Q = q(L, \bar{K})$ relates the quantity of the variable input to the resulting output.

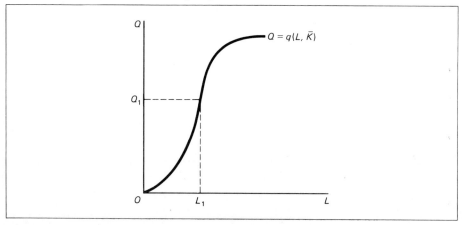

ers that he can produce 237 hammers with the following combinations of capital and labor:

UNITS OF CAPITAL	NUMBER OF WORKERS
15	2
11	3
8	5
5	9
4	13

These points are plotted in panel (*a*). By connecting them we can get a feel for other combinations of capital and labor that will also produce 237 hammers.

If the manager had an algebraic expression for his production function, he could get his computer department to find all the combinations of capital and labor that would produce, say, 250 hammers. If these combinations were plotted, he would have a curve such as the one labeled $Q = 250$ in panel (*b*) of Figure 4.3. This curve is called an isoquant.

DEFINITION▶   An *isoquant* is a curve that shows all the combinations of inputs that will produce a specific level of output according to a particular production function.

Each combination of capital and labor lies on an isoquant. In Figure 4.4, we show three isoquants labeled Q_1, Q_2, and Q_3. These isoquants have three

FIGURE 4.3   (*a*) An approximation of an isoquant from several specific points. (*b*) An isoquant showing all combinations of capital and labor that will produce 250 hammers.

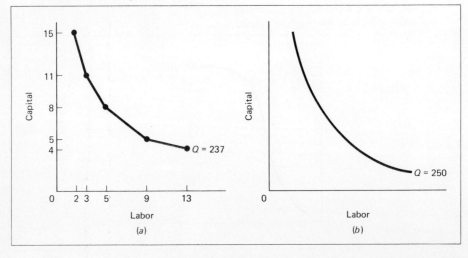

properties that are of some interest: (1) the isoquants are negatively sloped, (2) a movement in the northeasterly direction moves the firm to an isoquant representing greater output, and (3) the isoquants are convex.

NEGATIVE SLOPE   To see why an isoquant should have a negative slope, it will be convenient to consider the following definition.

DEFINITION ▸   The *marginal product* (MP) of an input is the change in output that results from increasing the employment of that input by 1 unit. We can write the marginal product of, say, labor as

$$MP_L = \frac{\Delta Q}{\Delta L}$$

We will show later in this chapter why a firm will never combine inputs in such a way that any marginal product is negative. Consequently, we shall proceed on the assumption that the marginal product of labor and the marginal product of capital are positive. Starting from point A, suppose that the amount of labor used by the firm is increased by 1 unit from L_1 to L_2. Since the marginal product of labor is positive, the firm's output must increase. In particular, it will increase by the marginal product of labor. In order for output to remain at Q_1, capital must decrease. Specifically, capital must decrease just enough for the decrease in output from reducing capital to equal the increase in output from increasing labor. In Figure 4.4, capital falls from K_1 to K_2 as labor rises from L_1 to L_2 when the firm moves from A to B along isoquant Q_1, producing the observed negative slope.

FIGURE 4.4   Three isoquants on an isoquant map. Slope is negative because marginal products of capital and labor are positive.

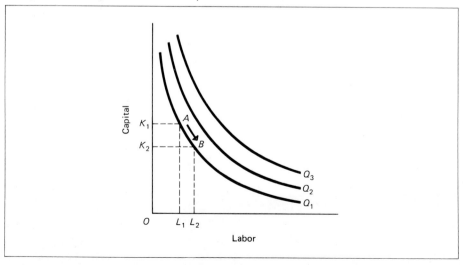

MOVEMENTS IN A NORTHEASTERLY DIRECTION   In Figure 4.5, we have selected two isoquants from the isoquant map and highlighted them. Let's compare point A on Q_1 with point B on Q_2. The manager is using more labor *and* more capital at point B than at point A. With more of both inputs, we should expect to produce more output. In fact, that is always the case whenever the marginal products are positive. Consequently, Q_2 must be larger than Q_1. Thus, as the manager moves from one isoquant to another in a northeasterly direction, he is moving to larger quantities of output.

CONVEXITY   Finally, we might note that the typical isoquant has a convex shape; that is, the isoquant becomes flatter as labor increases. What this means is that as the manager reduces his employment of capital, **the increase in labor necessary to compensate for a given decrease in capital rises.** For example, the movement along the Q_1 isoquant in Figure 4.6 from A to B and from C to D involves equal decreases in capital. The quantity of labor required to compensate for the decrease in capital is much larger for the movement from C to D than for the movement from A to B. It is clear that $L_2 - L_1$ is smaller than $L_4 - L_3$ although $K_1 - K_2$ is precisely equal to $K_3 - K_4$.

4.2

INPUT SUBSTITUTION

As the manager alters the input proportions by moving from point to point along an isoquant, she is obviously substituting one input for the other. The marginal rate of technical substitution of capital for labor measures the degree of input substitutability along an isoquant. In particular, it measures the rate at which the

FIGURE 4.5   Movement in a northeasterly direction results in greater output: $Q_2 > Q_1$.

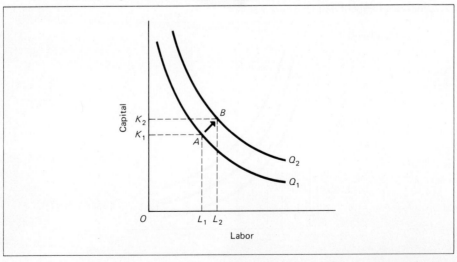

manager may substitute one input for another while holding output constant, that is, while sliding along an isoquant.

DEFINITION ▶ The *marginal rate of technical substitution* (MRTS) of capital for labor is the decrease in capital that results from a 1-unit increase in labor, when output is held constant. This can be written compactly as

$$\text{MRTS}_{KL} = -\frac{\Delta K}{\Delta L}$$

Thus, the MRTS_{KL} at any point on an isoquant is given by minus the slope of the isoquant at that point. We can relate this to the marginal products of capital and labor.

Consider Figure 4.7. Suppose the manager has been producing Q_1 by employing the combination of capital and labor at point A. Suppose that she decides to move to point B. By itself, the decrease in capital, ΔK, would cause output to fall to Q_2. Referring back to the definition of marginal product, we can see that this change in output is equal to the marginal product of capital times the change in the quantity of capital:

$$\Delta Q = Q_2 - Q_1 = \text{MP}_K \cdot \Delta K$$

The increase in labor, ΔL, by itself must increase output from Q_2 to Q_1. This change in output is equal to the marginal product of labor times the change

FIGURE 4.6 The convexity of the isoquant means that as capital is decreased successively, the increase in labor necessary to hold output constant rises: $K_1 - K_2 = K_3 - K_4$, but $L_4 - L_3 > L_3 - L_1$.

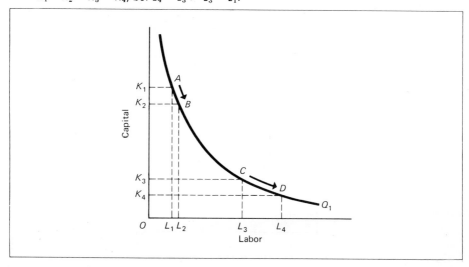

in the quantity of labor:

$$\Delta Q = Q_1 - Q_2 = MP_L \cdot \Delta L$$

Since A and B are both on isoquant Q_1, the changes in output must sum to zero:

$$MP_K \cdot \Delta K + MP_L \cdot \Delta L = 0$$

Algebraic rearrangement yields

$$-\frac{\Delta K}{\Delta L} = \frac{MP_L}{MP_K}$$

When points A and B are very close together, this also measures the slope of the isoquant. Thus,

$$-\frac{\Delta K}{\Delta L} = MRTS_{KL} = \frac{MP_L}{MP_K}$$

4.3

COST MINIMIZATION

An isoquant describes all the input combinations that are sufficient to produce a specific quantity of output. There is nothing, however, in our analysis of isoquants thus far that recommends one input combination over another along an isoquant, for all combinations of inputs on an isoquant yield the same output. Consequently, solely on the basis of production considerations, each input combination on an isoquant is just as good as any other input combination on that isoquant.

FIGURE 4.7 Decomposing the movement from A to B reveals that the slope of the isoquant can be expressed as the ratio of marginal products: $-\Delta K/\Delta L = MP_L/MP_K$.

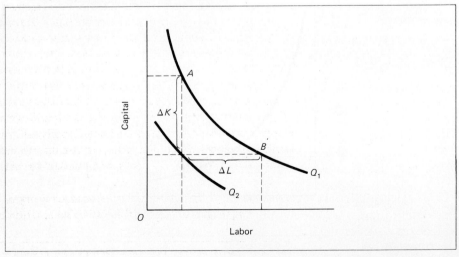

But firms have to pay for the inputs that are employed. As a result, some input combinations are superior to others because they cost less. We shall assume, in fact, that the manager wants to minimize the cost of producing any particular output that he elects to produce. This objective is consistent with many managerial goals and, in particular, is consistent with the maximization of profit.

The costs incurred by the firm are equal to the sum of the amounts paid for the inputs used in production. For a given number of dollars, there is a whole array of input combinations that can be purchased by the manager. These alternatives are described by the cost equation:

$$C = wL + sK \qquad (4.4)$$

where C represents the number of dollars, L and K are the quantities of labor and capital, respectively, and w and s are the prices of labor and capital. Thus, wL represents the manager's expenditures on labor and sK represents his expenditures on capital. For the time being, we shall assume that the input prices are determined by the market and are accepted as given by the manager. This enables us to rearrange the cost equation (4.4) into the slope-intercept form for a straight line:

$$K = \frac{C}{s} - \frac{w}{s} L \qquad (4.5)$$

When the quantity of labor is zero, K equals C/s. Thus, C/s is the intercept on the K axis. By definition, $-w/s$ is the slope of the line. Slope $-w/s$ equals the reduction in capital that must accompany a 1-unit increase in labor if total cost C is to remain constant. For example, suppose each worker costs the firm $4 per hour and 1 unit of capital costs $16 per hour. Then, if the manager increases his employment of labor by one person per 8-hour day, he must also reduce his employment of 1 unit of capital by 2 hours per day to keep costs the same.

> **DEFINITION ▸**   An *isocost* is a line that describes the combinations of inputs that can be purchased for a given sum of money.

Several isocosts are shown in Figure 4.8. Each of these isocosts is drawn for the same input prices. Since the ratio of input prices determines the slope of the isocost line, all three isocosts have the same slope. Accordingly, the lines are parallel to one another. The differences among these isocosts are due to a different amount of money being associated with each one. Of course, C_1 is greater than C_2. (How do we know?)

COST-MINIMIZING INPUT COMBINATION   Now we have a convenient way of determining the cost-minimizing combination of inputs. Suppose the manager wants to minimize the cost of producing 200 bicycle wheels. First, we want to see the isoquant that represents 200 bicycle wheels. This is shown in panel (*a*) of Figure 4.9. Any combination of capital and labor on the 200 isoquant will produce 200 bicycle wheels. The manager's job is to find the least expensive combination on this isoquant.

Suppose he tries spending C_1 dollars on inputs. In panel (*b*), an expenditure of C_1 dollars will produce 200 bicycle wheels at point Z, where the C_1 isocost intersects the 200 isoquant. But Z and Y cost the same amount since they are on the same isocost. And combination X must cost less than combination Y because it contains the same amount of capital and less labor. Thus, X must cost less than Z. Furthermore, X is on the 200 isoquant. Consequently, it is cheaper to produce 200 bicycle wheels using combination X than using combination Z which costs C_1 dollars.

Suppose the manager reduces her expenditure to C_2. In panel (*c*), we can see that the C_2 isocost lies entirely below the 200 isoquant. Thus, C_2 dollars will not purchase any input combination that is large enough to produce 200 bicycle wheels.

Rather than jump around with large changes in the expenditure on inputs, the manager can start from C_2 and simply add $1 at a time until she finds an isocost that will buy some input combination that is adequate for producing 200 bicycle wheels. In panel (*d*), we see that C_3 dollars will do the trick. The input combination of L_0 units of labor and K_0 units of capital will produce 200 bicycle wheels since this point is on the 200 isoquant. Any other labor-capital combination on the 200 isoquant will cost more than C_3 dollars, and any combination of labor and capital that lies on a lower isocost line will prove to be inadequate to produce 200 bicycle wheels.

According to our present objective of minimizing the cost of producing 200 units of output, the input combination L_0 and K_0 is optimal. We notice that the optimal input combination is found where the isoquant associated

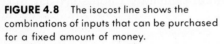

FIGURE 4.8 The isocost line shows the combinations of inputs that can be purchased for a fixed amount of money.

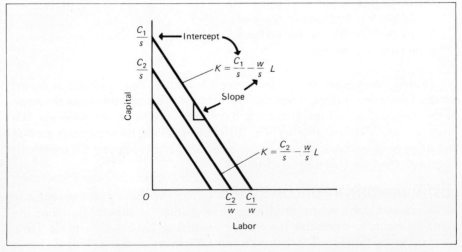

with the designated output level is just tangent to an isocost. At the point of tangency, the slopes of the isoquant and the isocost are equal. Thus, for an optimal input combination, the marginal rate of technical substitution (minus the slope of the isoquant) equals the input price ratio (minus the slope of the isocost). In other words, the rate at which the manager must substitute capital for labor to keep output constant at 200 is just equal to the rate at which the market allows the manager to substitute capital for labor to keep costs constant at C_3. Consequently, we may write

$$\text{MRTS}_{KL} = \frac{\text{MP}_L}{\text{MP}_K} = \frac{w}{s} \tag{4.6}$$

In other words, when costs have been minimized, the ratio of marginal products of the inputs will be equal to the input price ratio.

FIGURE 4.9   The cost-minimizing combination of inputs is found where the specified isoquant is tangent to an isocost line.

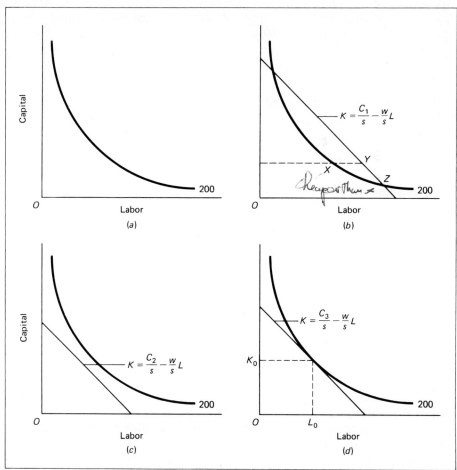

This last result (4.6) can be rearranged algebraically into a more convenient form:

$$\frac{MP_L}{w} = \frac{MP_K}{s} \tag{4.7}$$

Thus, when labor and capital are employed properly, their marginal product-price ratios will be equal. For example, suppose the manager employs 83 workers and 14 units of capital to produce a certain quantity of output. If the wage rate is $4 per hour and labor's marginal product is 20, then this ratio is 5. Now suppose that the price of capital services is $10. If the marginal product of capital is 50, then this combination will be optimal:

$$\frac{20}{\$4.00} = \frac{50}{\$10.00} = 5$$

Now let's see what happens when the ratios are not equal. Suppose in this example that the marginal product of capital is only 40. The combination of 83 workers and 14 units of capital will not minimize costs. If the manager reduces his use of capital by 1 unit, he reduces output by 40 units and saves $10. He can restore this lost output by adding two workers because labor's marginal product is 20. The cost of this additional labor will be $8. Thus he saves the firm $2, and the original combination did not minimize cost.

For costs to be minimized, the increase in output from the last $1 spent on an input must be the same for all factors of production. This version of the optimality conditions can be generalized to as many inputs as we please:

$$\frac{MP_1}{P_1} = \frac{MP_2}{P_2} = \cdots = \frac{MP_n}{P_n} \tag{4.8}$$

where P_i is the price of the ith input. If any of the equalities in (4.8) do not hold, the manager can reduce the costs of producing that output level by changing the input proportions.

EFFECTS OF A CHANGE IN AN INPUT PRICE   When the price of an input changes, the manager generally will have to react if he is to continue minimizing the cost of producing a given output. Suppose that the manager has minimized costs and is operating where

$$\frac{MP_{L_0}}{w_0} = \frac{MP_{K_0}}{s_0}$$

If the wage rate increases from w_0 to w_1, then

$$\frac{MP_{L_0}}{w_1} < \frac{MP_{k_0}}{s_0}$$

at the initial cost-minimizing position. That is, an increase in the wage rate causes the additional output resulting from spending $1 more on labor to be less than the additional output resulting from spending $1 more on capital. This gives the manager an incentive to substitute away from labor and toward capital.

This can also be seen graphically. In Figure 4.10, the firm initially minimized the cost of producing Q_0 by using L_0 units of labor and K_0 units of capital on isocost AB. An increase in the wage rate makes isocosts steeper. If expenditures on inputs stay at the same level C_0, the intercept of the isocost on the capital axis (C_0/s) would be unchanged. An increase in the wage rate of labor from w_0 to w_1 thus would rotate the isocost about its capital intercept from AB to AD. As can be seen, fewer inputs can now be purchased as a result of the increase in labor's price. In fact, none of the input combinations along AD are sufficient to produce Q_0. The manager will simply have to spend more money if production is to be maintained at the Q_0 level.

Any additional expenditures on inputs entail moving to a higher isocost that is parallel to the AD isocost. In Figure 4.11, we can see that the manager will have to spend C_2 dollars on isocost EF is he elects to produce Q_0 with the old combination of inputs, L_0 and K_0. Unfortunately, this old combination of inputs no longer minimizes costs. The new cost-minimizing combination is K_1 and L_1, which is found where isocost GH is tangent to the Q_0 isoquant. Thus, we can see that the wage increase caused the manager to substitute away from labor and toward capital in the production of Q_0 units of output. In this case, $K_1 - K_0$ units of capital are substituted for $L_0 - L_1$ units of labor.

Question   In Figure 4.11, isocosts AD, EF, and GH are parallel. Why?

Answer   For each of these isocosts, the wage rate is w_1 and the price of capital is s_0. Therefore, the slope of each of these isocosts is $-w_1/s_0$.

EXPANSION PATH   When the manager of a firm elects to expand output, he must move from one isoquant to another. If we continue to assume that he

FIGURE 4.10   The effects of an increase in the wage rate on the isocost when total costs are held constant.

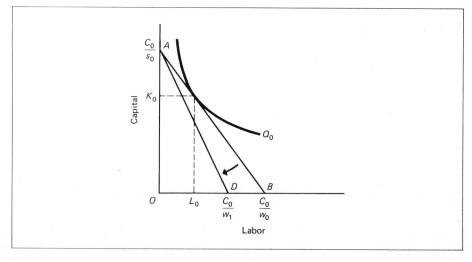

wants to minimize the cost of whatever output is produced, we see that the manager is faced with finding a new optimal combination of inputs. The solution to this problem is shown in Figure 4.12. We see the cost-minimizing input combinations for four different output levels. If the manager elects to produce output Q_1, he will hire L_1 units of labor and K_1 units of capital. In contrast, if he decided on output Q_3, he would want L_3 units of labor and K_3 units of capital. Thus, as the firm's output is expanded, the manager spends just enough more on inputs to move the isocost to a point of tangency with the new isoquant. By connecting all of the points of tangency, we obtain the firm's expansion path.

DEFINITION ▶   For any given input prices, the firm's *expansion path* is the locus of all cost-minimizing combinations of inputs.

SHORT RUN   Cost minimization in the short run is quite simple in the model we have been examining. Since there are only two inputs and one of them is fixed, the only way for the manager to alter the quantity of output is by moving along the total product curve in Figure 4.2. Given the fixed quantity of capital, the optimal input combination for producing Q_1 units of out-

FIGURE 4.11   An increase in the wage rate from w_0 to w_1 causes the manager to reduce his use of labor from L_0 to L_1 and to increase his use of capital from K_0 to K_1 in the production of Q_0.

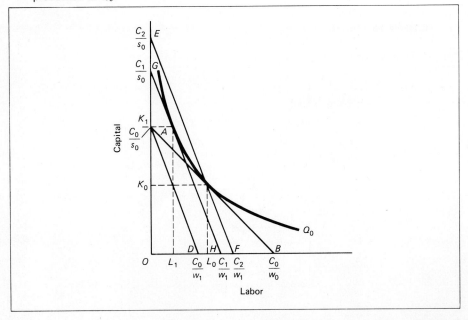

put is $\bar{K}$ units of capital and L_1 units of labor services. The cost of the fixed capital must be incurred in any event, so cost minimization in this setting merely requires selecting the appropriate quantity of labor. If a manager is charged with producing Q_1, the cost-minimizing quantity of labor is L_1. We should note that the wage rate of labor did not affect this short-run choice. In the long run, the wage rate affects the combination of capital and labor selected. Accordingly, the selection of $\bar{K}$ units of capital was a function of labor's wage rate. But once the firm is committed to $\bar{K}$, the optimal quantity of labor will not be sensitive to changes in the wage rate.

4.4

THE SPECIAL CASE OF FIXED PROPORTIONS

In the production functions that we have examined so far, the manager minimized cost by substituting away from labor and toward capital as labor became relatively more expensive. But there is a class of production functions in which costs are minimized by *not* substituting between capital and labor when input prices change. These production functions are called "fixed proportions production functions" because the ratio of capital to labor that is chosen by the manager does not depend on the price of labor or the price of capital.

Consider the following fixed proportions production function:

$$Q = \min(\beta_L L, \beta_K K)$$

where β_L and β_K are constants measuring the productivity of labor and the

FIGURE 4.12 The firm's expansion path is the locus of cost minimizing input combinations.

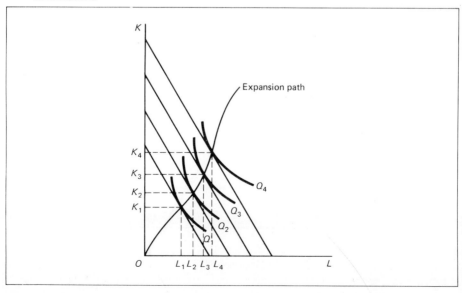

productivity of capital, respectively. This production function says that the quantity that is produced is the minimum of $\beta_L L$ and $\beta_K K$. For example, seven buttons (B) *and* one yard of cloth (C) are required to produce one shirt. Thus, the number of shirts S that can be produced from a pile of buttons and cloth is

$$S = \min\left[\left(\frac{1}{7}\right)B, \left(\frac{1}{1}\right)C\right]$$

In this case, β_B equals $1/7$ and β_C equals 1. Suppose we have 70 buttons and 12 yards of cloth. Substitution of these values tells us that the number of shirts is 10,

$$S = \min\left(\frac{70}{7}, \frac{12}{1}\right) = 10$$

even though there is enough cloth for a dozen shirts. The extra cloth is simply redundant because it cannot be used without the necessary number of buttons.

ISOQUANTS   Let's see what the isoquants look like for a fixed proportions production function. First, we shall examine the isoquant for $Q = 1$. Suppose that $L = 1/\beta_L$ and $K = 1/\beta_K$. This is point A in Figure 4.13. At point A, $\beta_L L = \beta_L(1/\beta_L) = 1$ and $\beta_K K = \beta_K(1/\beta_K) = 1$. Consequently,

$$Q = \min(\beta_L L, \beta_K K) = \min(1, 1)$$

Thus, at A, 1 unit of output is produced.

Now suppose that the manager holds the quantity of capital constant at $1/\beta_K$ and consider employment levels of labor greater than $1/\beta_L$. For example,

FIGURE 4.13   A fixed proportions production function has right-angled isoquants.

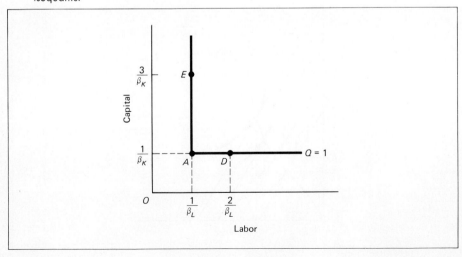

suppose $L = 2/\beta_L$. Then

$$Q = \min(2, 1) = 1$$

Thus at point D in Figure 4.13, 1 unit of output is produced. Similarly, 1 unit of output will be produced at any point directly to the right of point A.

The same logic applies to the set of points directly above A. If labor is held constant at $1/\beta_L$ while capital is increased to, say, $3/\beta_K$, then

$$Q = \min(1, 3) = 1$$

Thus, at point E in Figure 4.13, 1 unit of output is produced. In fact, 1 unit of output is produced at any point directly above A.

The isoquant for $Q = 1$ is graphed in Figure 4.13. It is right-angled, with a corner at $L = 1/\beta_L$ and $K = 1/\beta_K$.

A good example of a fixed proportions production function is ditchdigging. Suppose that it takes 1 hour for one man with one shovel to dig a regulation-sized hole. Ignore any complications related to fatigue. Clearly, giving this man two shovels will not enable him to dig any more holes. Similarly, two men with one shovel will not be able to dig any more holes in 1 hour than one man with one shovel; the second man has nothing to do but watch the first man dig.

What happens if the labor and capital associated with point A in Figure 4.13 are each doubled? At this new point (point G in Figure 4.14), we see that

$$Q = \min\left[\beta_L \left(\frac{2}{\beta_L}\right), \beta_K \left(\frac{2}{\beta_K}\right)\right] = 2$$

Thus, a doubling of the two inputs will double the total output. You should be able to show that the isoquant for $Q = 2$ is right-angled, with a corner at

FIGURE 4.14 A doubling of both inputs will double the output with a fixed proportions production function.

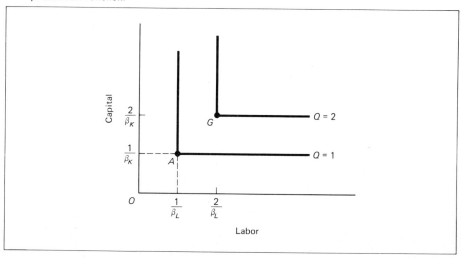

point G. Can you also show that any other isoquant will have its corner on the line that goes through the origin and point A?

COST MINIMIZATION Suppose the manager is responsible for producing Q_1 units of output. We can see in Figure 4.15 that no matter what the relative input prices are, she will minimize her costs by using L_1 units of labor and K_1 units of capital. Irrespective of whether labor is relatively expensive, as in isocost AB, or relatively cheap, as in isocost CD, her cost of producing Q_1 is minimized by producing at the corner of the Q_1 isoquant. If she chose to produce at any other point on the isoquant, she would be using more of one of the inputs without any compensating reduction in the use of the other input. To return to the ditchdigging example, a manager would be foolhardy to send one man with two shovels out to dig a ditch when it only takes one man and one shovel to dig the ditch. No matter what the wage rate or the price of shovels is, the second shovel is redundant.

Although input prices do not affect the quantities of labor and capital that are chosen to produce a given level of output, input prices do affect the cost of production. Once again, suppose that the manager wants to produce Q_1 units of output. When the wage rate equals w_1 and the price of capital equals s_1, the cost of producing Q_1 is minimized by producing at point A on isocost BD in Figure 4.16. Here, K_1 units of capital and L_1 units of labor are employed at a cost of C_1 dollars. If the wage rate rises from w_1 to w_2 and the cost of production remains at C_1, then the isocost rotates about point B from BD to BE. To produce Q_1, the manager must increase her expenditure on inputs to C_2. The isocost FG that is associated with this total cost intersects the Q_1 isocost at point $\hat{A}$. In contrast to the variable proportions case, we see

FIGURE 4.15 The manager will employ L_1 units of labor and K_1 units of capital to produce Q_1 units of output no matter what the relative input prices are. This is due to fixed proportions.

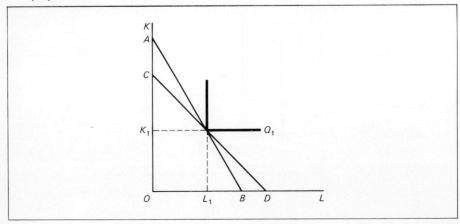

in Figure 4.16 that the cost-minimizing combination of capital and labor continues to be the original L_1 and K_1; there is no substitution away from labor to capital. Any other combination of labor and capital will either be insufficient for producing Q_1 or cost more than L_1 and K_1.

Exercise Starting with the original isocost BD in Figure 4.16, trace the manager's adustment to a decrease in the price of capital.

4.5

COST CURVES OF THE FIRM

LONG RUN The expansion path of the firm is a handy device for deriving the firm's cost curves. In fact, the cost curves of the firm are simply a rearrangement of the information contained in the expansion path diagram. To see this, consider the definition of long-run total cost.

DEFINITION ▸ The firm's *long-run total cost curve* shows the minimum total cost of producing every possible level of output.

It is clear from this definition that we can derive the firm's total cost curve by plotting the cost of each optimal input combination against the quantity of output that it will generate. For example, suppose workers earn $4 per hour and units of capital cost $10. Various outputs, input combina-

FIGURE 4.16 An increase in the wage rate from w_0 to w_1 increases the cost of producing Q_1 units of output but does not affect the use of inputs in producing Q_1.

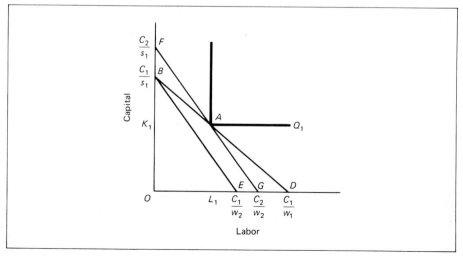

tions, and total costs are shown in Table 4.2. As output increases, the input combinations shown are taken from the expansion path. Long-run total costs (LTC) are shown in column (4). For instance, the total cost of 100 units of output is $82. Similarly, the total cost of 125 units is $100. Total cost curves have proved cumbersome to use for analysis. Instead, we usually prefer to use average cost curves, which are also obtained easily from the expansion path.

DEFINITION ▶   *Long-run average cost* (LAC) is the minimum per unit cost of output. It is usually written as

$$LAC = \frac{LTC}{Q}$$

In column (5) of Table 4.2, we show the long-run average cost of producing the various outputs in column (1). From the definition of long-run average cost, it is clear that each entry in column (5) is obtained by dividing column (4) by column (1). By plotting these output values along the horizontal axis and the average costs along the vertical axis, we can construct the firm's average cost curve. This is shown in panel (*a*) of Figure 4.17. We have joined the points with straight-line segments to give a rough idea of the curve's shape. In panel (*b*), we have drawn a smooth U-shaped average cost curve labeled LAC. Of course, not every average cost curve is U-shaped. In Chapter 5, we show that firms with declining average cost curves tend to become monopolies. Other firms have horizontal average cost curves, and in Chapter 5, we learn that we cannot determine how much a firm with a horizontal average cost curve will produce in a competitive industry. For these reasons, the exposition is often easier if U-shaped average cost curves are used.

Marginal cost is an extremely important concept for economic analysis. As any economic activity is extended or contracted, marginal cost measures the change in total cost that results.

TABLE 4.2
LONG-RUN TOTAL COSTS OF PRODUCTION
(w = $4.00 and s = $10.00)

OUTPUT (1)	LABOR (2)	CAPITAL (3)	LTC (4)	LAC (5)
25	3	2	$32	$1.28
50	4	3	46	.92
75	6	4	64	.85
100	8	5	82	.82
125	10	6	100	.80
150	11	8	124	.83
175	13	10	152	.87

DEFINITION ▶ *Marginal cost* is the change in total cost that accompanies a 1-unit increase in output. Alternatively, we may express marginal cost as

$$MC = \frac{\Delta TC}{\Delta Q}$$

The marginal cost curve can also be derived from the firm's expansion path. To determine the marginal cost of expanding output from, say, Q_3 to $Q_3 + 1$, we first determine the optimal quantities of the inputs. In Figure 4.18, we see that the manager will use L_3 units of labor and K_3 units of capital to produce Q_3 and will employ L_5 and K_5 to produce $Q_3 + 1$. The total cost of producing Q_3 units of output is $wL_3 + sK_3$, while the total cost of producing $Q_3 + 1$ unit of output is $wL_5 + sK_5$. Consequently, the change in total cost that results from producing the $Q_3 + 1$th unit is

$$\Delta TC = w(L_5 - L_3) + s(K_5 - K_3)$$

According to our definition, this is the marginal cost of the $Q_3 + 1$th unit.

If we were to do this for all values of output, we would have the long-run marginal cost curve labeled LMC in Figure 4.19. We can see that the marginal cost curve lies below the average cost curve to the left of the minimum point of LAC. To the right of the minimum point, LMC is above LAC, and at the minimum point of the LAC curve, LMC is equal to LAC. This graph was not drawn this way by accident. In fact, the relationship between marginal cost and average cost is characteristic of all marginal-average relationships. One of the more familiar of these relationships is between marginal tem-

FIGURE 4.17 (a) The hypothetical data from Table 4.2. (b) A smooth U-shaped long-run average cost curve.

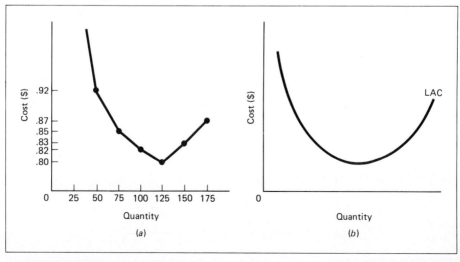

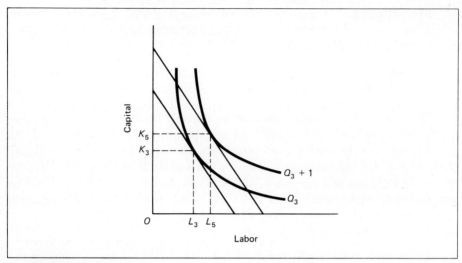

FIGURE 4.18 The marginal cost of
increasing production by 1 unit from Q_3 to
$Q_3 + 1$ is equal to the difference in the total
cost of producing Q_3 and $Q_3 + 1$.

perature and average temperature. When hot water (the marginal temperature) is added to a tub of warm water, the average temperature of the water in
the tub rises. Similarly, the addition of cold water (the marginal temperature)
to a tub of warm water will lower the average temperature of water in the tub.
To return to costs, the average cost increases as output expands if marginal
cost exceeds average cost and is thus "pulling" average cost up. Analogously,
average cost falls when marginal cost is below average cost and thereby pulls
it down.

FIGURE 4.19 The relationship between
long-run average cost (LAC) and long-run
marginal cost (LMC).

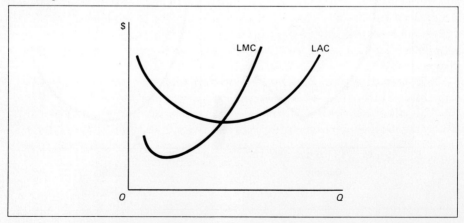

Question   It takes one man 2 hours with one shovel to dig one "regula-tion-sized" hole. Additional shovels, unless accompanied by additional men, do not increase output, and additional men without additional shov-els do not lead to greater production. (a) If the wage rate is $4 per hour and the rental rate on shovels is $1 per hour, what is the marginal cost of one regulation-sized hole? (b) How is marginal cost related to output? (c) Suppose the wage rate rises to $5. What is the new marginal cost?

Answer   (a) The expenditures on labor equal the wage rate ($4) times the number of hours spent digging each hole (2), or $8. The expenditure on shovels for each hole equals the rental rate ($1) times the number of hours a shovel is used in digging one hole (2), or $2. The marginal cost is thus $8 + 2 = 10$. (b) From the information given, the marginal cost of a hole is $10 no matter how many holes are dug. Consequently, in this ex-ample the marginal cost curve is horizontal. (c) Shovel expenditures per hole remain at $2. Labor expenditures rise to $5 \cdot 2 = \$10$, and the new marginal cost equals $10 + 2 = \$12$.

SHORT RUN   As we have seen, the total cost of producing any output in the short run equals the fixed cost of the capital input (TFC) plus the variable cost of the labor input (TVC):

$$TC = TFC + TVC \qquad (4.9)$$

These total curves can be plotted from the information contained in Figure 4.2 plus the input prices. First, we see that there are $\bar{K}$ units of capital. No matter what level of output is selected by the manager, the quantity of capital will remain the same. Consequently, the total fixed cost will be constant:

$$TFC = s\bar{K}$$

Graphically, the TFC curve is a horizontal line in Figure 4.20. The height of the TFC curve is determined by the price of capital s and quantity $\bar{K}$.

In contrast, the total variable costs depend upon the output level selected by the manager because the quantity of labor employed is a function of the desired output. Consequently, when we plot total variable costs against out-put, the shape of the function depends very much upon the shape of the total product curve. Based upon the total product curve in Figure 4.2, the TVC curve will resemble that in Figure 4.20. The total cost curve (TC) will be the simple *vertical* sum of the total fixed cost (TFC) and total variable cost (TVC) curves.

For analytical purposes, these short-run total cost curves are cumber-some. It is much easier to use average and marginal cost curves.

The short-run average cost curves are easily obtained. From the disaggregation of total cost into its fixed and variable components, we see that short-run average cost (AC) is composed of average fixed cost (AFC) and average variable cost (AVC). To be more specific, we find that

$$AC = AFC + AVC$$

if we divide both sides of equation (4.9) by quantity Q.

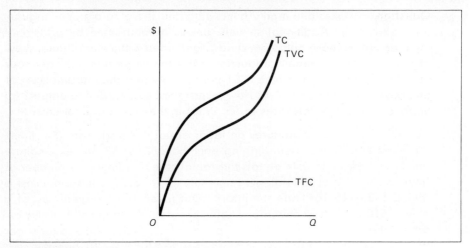

FIGURE 4.20   The total cost (TC), total variable cost (TVC), and total fixed cost (TFC) curves can be derived from the total product curve plus information on input prices.

The average fixed cost, which is equal to a constant (TFC) divided by quantity, obviously decreases as output rises. An average fixed cost curve is shown in Figure 4.21. At point B, Q_1 units are produced at an average fixed cost of AFC_1. By definition, the product of Q_1 and AFC_1 is the total fixed cost. This product is represented by the area of $ABCO$. Similarly, the area of $DEFO$ equals the same total fixed cost. A curve with the property that the product of the coordinates of any point on the curve equals a constant is called a rectan-

FIGURE 4.21   Average fixed cost curves are rectangular hyperbolas.

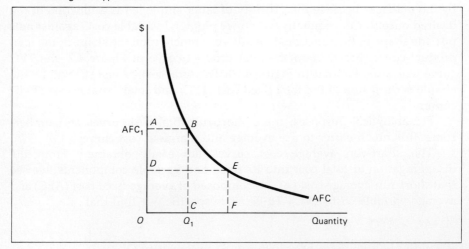

gular hyperbola. Thus, all average fixed cost curves are rectangular hyperbolas.

The shape of the AVC curve, however, is not so easy to ascertain. In panel (a) of Figure 4.22, we present a graphical approach to determining the shape of AVC. Since AVC is equal to TVC divided by Q, the numerical value of AVC is equal to the slope of a straight line from the origin to the TVC curve. For example, the straight line to point Z has a slope equal to TVC_1 divided by Q_1. TVC_1 is the total variable cost necessary for producing the output Q_1. Consequently, the slope of line OZ measures the average variable cost (AVC). As output expands to Q_2, we see that the ray from the origin to the TVC curve is flatter. This indicates that the AVC at an output equal to Q_2 is less than AVC at Q_1. As output expands further, the ray from the origin is even flatter than OW. Thus, the AVC at Q_3 is lower than AVC at Q_2. In fact, the AVC at Q_3 is as low as it can get. Any ray from the origin that is flatter than OY, which is tangent to the TVC curve, will not touch the TVC curve. Moving to output Q_4, we see that AVC has risen again. Interestingly, the AVC at Q_2 is equal to the AVC of Q_4 This is because the total variable cost at both of these outputs lies on ray OWW'. It is clear from these limited examples that the TVC curve in panel (a) of Figure 4.22 generates a U-shaped AVC curve.

Derivation of the marginal cost curve proceeds a bit differently. In the short run, marginal cost equals the increase in total variable cost that results from producing one more unit of output. This means that marginal cost is given by the *slope* of the TVC curve, which in turn is measured by the slope

FIGURE 4.22 (a) The derivation of average variable cost requires measuring the slope of a ray from the origin to TVC curve.
(b) Marginal cost is given by the slopes of the tangents to the TVC curve.

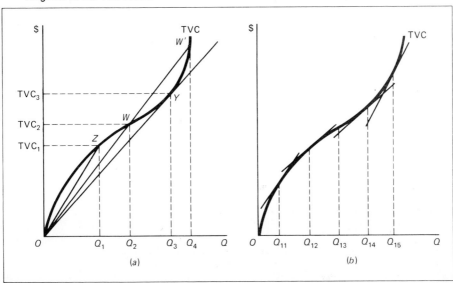

of the line that is tangent to the TVC curve. In panel (b) of Figure 4.22, as we move from Q_{11} to the higher levels of output, we see that the TVC curve gets flatter initially, reaches a minimum at Q_{13}, and begins to rise after that. It is clear, for example, that the tangent to TVC at Q_{11} is steeper than the tangent at Q_{12}. At Q_{13}, we encounter an inflection point, which is where the slope of the TVC curve stops falling and starts rising. Again, what all this indicates is that the marginal cost curve is U-shaped.

We know from our earlier discussion of Figure 4.19 that the short-run marginal cost curve should intersect the AVC curve at its minimum point. This can also be seen in panel (a) of Figure 4.22. At Q_3, the slope of the ray from the origin and through Y measures AVC. But in its role as a tangent, it measures MC. Consequently, MC and AVC are equal at Q_3 in panel (a).

These curves are shown in Figure 4.23. Since AFC equals AC − AVC, we can omit the AFC curve from this diagram.

Question   Show the total fixed cost incurred by the firm in Figure 4.23.

Answer

$$TC = TVC + TFC$$

or

$$TFC = TC - TVC$$

$$= AC \cdot Q - AVC \cdot Q$$

since

$$AC = \frac{TC}{Q} \quad \text{and} \quad AVC = \frac{TVC}{Q}$$

FIGURE 4.23   Short-run cost curves of the firm: average cost (AC), average variable cost (AVC), and marginal cost (MC).

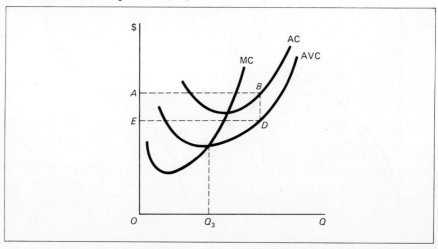

But AC · Q is the area of a rectangle with height AC and width Q. Similarly AVC · Q is the area of a rectangle with height AVC and width Q. Thus, total fixed cost is the area of a rectangle with height AC − AVC and width Q. For any given Q, TFC is obtained by forming a rectangle by drawing lines from AC and AVC to the cost axis and from AC to AVC. One such rectangle is *ABDE* in Figure 4.23. The area of the rectangle equals total fixed cost.

4.6

RELATIONSHIP BETWEEN LONG-RUN AND SHORT-RUN COST CURVES

When the manager adjusts output as a long-run strategy, she will move the firm along the expansion path. In the short run, however, she does not do this. For example, if the manager decides to reduce the firm's output by 10 percent tomorrow, she will not reduce all her inputs. Because of the expense of altering the quantities of some inputs in the short run, these inputs will be fixed for a while. The effect of the great cost associated with varying some inputs in the short run is to reduce the production flexibility available to the manager. Since she adjusts only the variable inputs, the input proportions will not be optimal from the perspective of the long run. Common sense therefore suggests that the per unit cost of production will be higher in the short run than in the long run. In fact, this suggestion is correct as we shall see in Figure 4.24.

Suppose the manager had been producing Q_2 and employing L_2 units of labor and K_2 units of capital in doing so. If she reduces output to Q_1, in the short run she must slide along the horizontal line $K = K_2$ until she reaches the

FIGURE 4.24   The short-run costs of producing either Q_1 or Q_3 are higher than the long-run costs since there is less flexibility in the short run than in the long run.

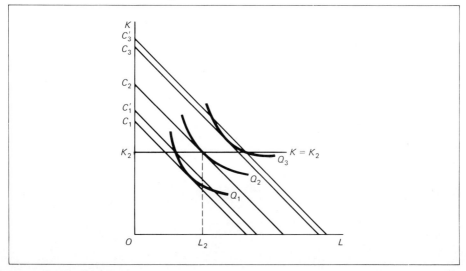

Q_1 isoquant. We can see that this is not at the point of tangency between the Q_1 isoquant and the isocost labeled C_1. Instead, it is at the intersection of the C_1' isocost and the isoquant. As a result, the total costs of producing Q_1 in the short run exceed the long-run total costs of producing Q_1. This is because the manager who reduces her output in the short run is saddled with too much capital. Consequently, the short run average cost (SAC) exceeds the long-run average cost (LAC) for a decrease in output from Q_2.

A similar result holds for increases in output. For example, if the manager expands output to Q_3, the only way that this can be accomplished in the short run is to move along the horizontal line $K = K_2$ until the Q_3 isoquant is reached. Again, we find that this occurs at a point of intersection between the isocost labeled C_3' and the Q_3 isoquant rather than at the point of tangency between isocost C_3 and isoquant Q_3. In this case, the manager, who is attempting to expand production in the short run, does not have enough capital to produce efficiently. Consequently, the short-run average cost (SAC) of Q_3 exceeds the long-run average cost (LAC).

By fixing capital at K_2, a short-run average cost can be derived as in the preceding section. If it is plotted on the same diagram as the long-run average cost curve, we shall see that it lies above the LAC curve except at the output level that corresponds to Q_2 in Figure 4.24. At that output, the SAC curve is just tangent to the LAC curve because the input combination of L_2 and K_2 is on the firm's expansion path. Similarly, starting with other points along the firm's expansion path, other short-run average cost curves may be derived. Thus, we show the relationship between the firm's LAC and three SAC curves in Figure 4.25. The reader should note that each SAC curve is

FIGURE 4.25   The long-run average cost curve is the envelope of the short-run average cost curves.

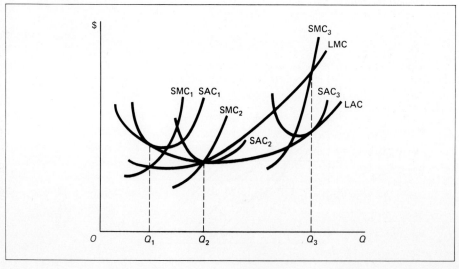

tangent to the LAC curve. For the production of Q_3, the plant size corresponding to SAC_3 is optimal. We can see, however, that for most SAC curves the point of tangency does not coincide with the minimum point of the SAC curve. This is not an optical illusion; rather, it is a property of the curves.

Associated with each SAC curve is a short-run marginal cost curve (SMC). This is constructed according to the procedures developed in the preceding section. For the long-run, there is only one point or one output level where each SAC curve is relevant. That occurs at the point of tangency between the short-run average cost and the long-run average cost. For example, SAC_1 is relevant in the long run only for output Q_1. Consequently, the only point on SMC_1 that has long-run relevance is the point that corresponds to Q_1. Thus, SMC_1 and LMC cross at that output level. We see that, in general, the SMC curve lies above LMC to the right of the intersection and below LMC to the left of the intersection.

4.7

SUMMARY

In this chapter, we have derived the firm's cost curves. In doing so, we covered a great deal of ground. First, we discussed the firm's production function, which transforms inputs into output. After finding a graphical representation for the production function, which is called an isoquant map, we showed how the manager can minimize the cost of producing various quantities of output. In developing these concepts, we examined measures of input substitutability and the notions of fixed and variable proportions.

Under the assumption that the manager's decisions do not affect input prices, we used the technical relations developed from the production function plus the given input prices to derive the firm's cost functions. In addition to the total cost curve, we also developed the average and marginal cost curves for the short run and the long run. Finally, we investigated the relationship between the long-run and short-run cost curves.

IMPORTANT NEW TERMS

Production function

Short run

Long run

Fixed input

Variable input

Isoquant

Isocost

Variable proportions

Fixed proportions

Marginal product

Marginal rate of technical substitution

Cost minimization

Average cost

Marginal cost

PROBLEMS

4.1 Answer true, false, or uncertain: Average cost is always less than marginal cost.

4.2 The wage rate of labor is $6, and the price of raw materials equals $2. The marginal product of labor is 16 while the marginal product of raw materials is 4. Evaluate: Can a firm operating under these conditions be maximizing profit?

4.3 Describe how you would go about estimating the marginal product of any input.

4.4 Answer true, false, or uncertain: A firm will never find it optimal to employ an input at a level where its marginal product is negative.

4.5 Explain why the short-run marginal cost curve lies above the long-run marginal cost curve to the right of the intersection and below the long-run marginal cost curve to the left of the intersection.

4.6 Suppose that the wage rate rises. Prove that the firm's average cost curve must rise.

4.7 Answer true, false, or uncertain: Suppose that the production of ABC, Inc.'s output requires only two inputs. If the input prices are equal, then cost minimization will lead the manager to employ equal quantities of the two inputs.

REFERENCES

Ferguson, C. E., and John P. Gould: *Microeconomic Theory*, Homewood, Illinois: Richard D. Irwin, Inc., 1975.

McConnell, Campbell: *Economics*, New York: McGraw-Hill Book Company, 1978.

Wonnacott, Paul, and Ronald Wonnacott: *Economics*, New York: McGraw-Hill Book Company, 1979.

MATHEMATICAL APPENDIX

A4.1

MARGINAL RATE OF TECHNICAL SUBSTITUTION

The marginal rate of technical substitution of capital for labor ($MRTS_{KL}$) is defined as minus the slope of an isoquant:

$$-\frac{dK}{dL} = MRTS_{KL}$$

For a production function,

$$Q = q(K, L)$$

we can take the total differential

$$dQ = \frac{\partial q(K, L)}{\partial L}\, dL + \frac{\partial q(K, L)}{\partial K}\, dK$$

For movements along an isoquant, the quantity does not change and, therefore, dQ must equal zero. Algebraic rearrangement yields:

$$-\frac{dK}{dL} = \frac{\partial q(K, L)/\partial L}{\partial q(K, L)/\partial K} = \frac{MP_L}{MP_K}$$

Thus, we find that $MRTS_{KL} = MP_L/MP_K$.

A4.2

COST MINIMIZATION

The manager wants to minimize the firm's costs, which are defined as

$$TC = p_1 x_1 + p_2 x_2 + \cdots + p_n x_n = \sum_{i=1}^{n} p_i x_i$$

subject to the constraint that total output be equal to a given quantity,

$$Q_0 = f(x_1, \ldots, x_n)$$

The lagrangian for this problem is

$$L = \sum_{i=1}^{n} p_i x_i + \lambda[Q_0 - f(x_1, \ldots, x_n)]$$

The total cost of producing Q_0 is minimized by setting each of the first partial derivatives equal to zero:

$$\frac{\partial L}{\partial x_i} = p_i - \lambda \frac{\partial f(x_1, \ldots, x_n)}{\partial x_i} = 0 \qquad i = 1, \ldots, n$$

$$\frac{\partial L}{\partial \lambda} = Q_0 - f(x_i, \ldots, x_n) = 0$$

Since $\partial f(x_1, \ldots, x_n)/\partial x_i$ is the marginal product of the ith input, we know that

$$\frac{p_i}{\mathrm{MP}_i} = \lambda \qquad i = 1, 2, \ldots, n$$

Consequently, we obtain the optimization rule found in the text:

$$\frac{\mathrm{MP}_1}{p_1} = \frac{\mathrm{MP}_2}{p_2} = \cdots = \frac{\mathrm{MP}_n}{p_n}$$

A4.3
RELATIONSHIP BETWEEN AVERAGE AND MARGINAL COST

The graphed relationship between average cost and marginal cost can be easily proved in a more formal fashion. Average cost can be written as TC/Q. The derivative of average cost gives the slope of the average cost curve. Of course, the sign of the derivative tells us whether the AC curve is increasing or decreasing. Now,

$$\frac{d(TC/Q)}{dQ} = \frac{Q\,dTC/dQ - TC}{Q^2}$$

$$= \frac{dTC/dQ - TC/Q}{Q}$$

$$= \frac{(MC - AC)}{Q}$$

Since quantity Q is positive, the slope of the average cost curve is negative when the term in parentheses is negative. This occurs when MC is less than AC. Similarly, the slope of AC is positive when MC is greater than AC. When AC equals MC, the slope of AC is zero, which occurs at its minimum point.

A4.4
HOW MANY MARGINAL COST CURVES?

One marginal cost curve suffices for the TC curve and for the TVC curve. This can be demonstrated quite easily. Since

$$TC = TVC + TFC$$

and

$$MC = \frac{dTC}{dQ}$$

we find that

$$MC = \frac{d(TVC + TFC)}{dQ}$$

$$= \frac{d\,TVC}{dQ} + \frac{d\,TFC}{dQ}$$

$$= \frac{d\,TVC}{dQ}$$

because TFC does not change with variation in output and, therefore, $dTFC/dQ$ is zero.

5

THEORY OF THE FIRM

In this chapter, we shall build upon the two preceding chapters in our development of the theory of the firm. Our analysis focuses on the polar models of the competitive firm and the monopolistic firm. In particular, we are interested in the manager's price and output decisions, his selection of inputs, and his decision on plant scale. Throughout this development, we shall assume that the manager's goal is to maximize profit subject to the constraints imposed by the demands of consumers and by the firm's cost conditions.

The purpose of this development is to provide a framework for subsequent analysis. Here, we treat the stylized models of the firm that will prove useful in subsequent applications of economic decision making. We begin with the competitive model and subsequently move to the monopoly model. We have purposely omitted the models of oligopoly and monopolistic competition. These models tend to be ad hoc in nature and not very useful in application. A model of collusive behavior, however, is found in Chapter 12. Finally, there is a fairly lengthy appendix to this chapter that deals with the derived demand for factors of production.

5.1 COMPETITION: ITS MEANING

We are concerned with competition as it describes a market structure. The essence of competition in the word's popular use is strong rivalry, as between football teams or tennis players. In contrast, the economist's conception of competition does not rely upon strong rivalry. Rather, economic competition is highly impersonal in nature and there is an absence of active rivalry. In fact, perfect competitors are often good friends and may be quite cooperative. The hallmark of economic competition is the absence of market power of one economic agent over another. We shall discuss the central characteristic of competitive markets and a few conditions that help to ensure an absence of market power.

PRICE-TAKING BEHAVIOR In perfectly competitive markets, all economic agents behave as price takers. Neither the buyer of a good nor the seller of the good behaves as if he can affect the price of the good being transacted. For example, if the market for tomatoes were competitive, then each buyer of tomatoes would be a price taker. The opening of one more pizza place by Pizza Hut would not alter the price that Pizza Hut pays for tomatoes. Similarly, a consumer would pay the competitive price for each pound of tomatoes whether he bought 1 pound, 3 pounds, or 6 pounds. The point is that the price of tomatoes would not rise as a result of his purchasing 6 pounds of tomatoes rather than 3 pounds of tomatoes. In a competitive tomato market, producers of tomatoes would also be price takers. A tomato farmer would not feel that planting an extra 50 acres of tomatoes has any effect on the price he receives for tomatoes.

The individual's inability to alter prices therefore characterizes competitive markets. Let us now briefly consider three conditions that are favorable to competition in markets.

1. Homogeneous Products The market must first be defined so that consumers have no preference for a particular firm's output. In other words, consumers must be indifferent as to the source of supply. For example, all granulated sugar is the same; thus consumers do not care which brand of sugar they buy. Similarly, firms that want sheet metal of a particular specification must be indifferent as to the source of supply. This requirement precludes a seller from having whatever market power would result from a preference for its output.

2. Large Number of Buyers and Sellers Typically, a consumer would feel like a price taker simply because his purchases of any single commodity are small relative to the total sales of that commodity. Similarly, if a firm accounts for a very small share of the total industry output, the manager is likely to feel that she cannot affect the price. An industry with a large number of similarly sized buyers and with a large number of similarly sized sellers is accordingly more likely to be competitive than an industry with few buyers and sellers. Of course, if buyers got together to boycott a commodity or if sellers got together to fix prices, the market would not be competitive. Boycotts can occur in industries with large numbers of buyers, and price fixing can occur in industries with large numbers of sellers. Neither occurrence is frequent, however, because of organizational costs.[1]

3. Perfect Information (Knowledge) Information also facilitates competition. Consumers who are aware of the price being offered by each firm in the industry will never willingly pay a higher price than the lowest price offered, other things being equal. Consequently, firms insisting on higher prices go out of business. If information is costly, consumers may be aware of the prices of only three or four firms. In this situation, a firm may raise its price without losing all of its customers. The lack of full information therefore would give each firm the ability to alter the price it charges. In later chapters, we will see how the lack of perfect information affects the firm's decisions.

5.2

**SHORT-RUN
PROFIT MAXIMIZATION**

The manager of a competitive firm will attempt to maximize the firm's profits. We want to find out what decisions she must make in order to maximize profit. In Chapter 1, profit

---

[1] In Chapter 12, we will show how other factors in addition to the number of buyers and sellers determine whether or not price fixing occurs in an industry.

Π was defined as the difference between total revenue (TR) and total cost (TC):

$$\Pi = \text{TR} - \text{TC}$$

$$= P \cdot Q - C(Q)$$

where P is price, Q is quantity, and $C(Q)$ is the total cost function.

The manager of a competitive firm feels that she can produce as much or as little as she wishes without affecting the market price. For example, she can sell 1 unit for P_1, 2 units for P_1 each, 3 units for P_1 each, and so on. The demand curve faced by the manager of a competitive firm is thus horizontal at price P_1; this demand curve is graphed in Figure 5.1. We see that the market price does not change no matter what output the manager produces. If the manager of a competitive firm increases output from Q_0 to $Q_0 + 1$, total revenue rises from $P_1 Q_0$ to $P_1(Q_0 + 1)$, an increase of P_1 dollars. Thus, the increase in total revenue from expanding output by 1 unit equals P_1, which is the competitive price. This competitive price is taken as given by the manager.

In Chapter 3, we defined the change in total revenue that resulted from a 1-unit increase in output to be the marginal revenue (MR).

$$MR = \frac{\Delta \text{TR}}{\Delta Q}$$

This is a very important concept to the manager, because it conveys what happens to total revenue when output expands. For the competitive firm, marginal revenue is constant and equal to the market price, as we have shown in Figure 5.1.

PROFIT MAXIMIZATION   By varying output, the manager can alter total revenue and total cost and thereby profit. She will expand and contract output

FIGURE 5.1   The demand curve for the competitive firm is a horizontal line: an expansion of output leaves price unchanged.

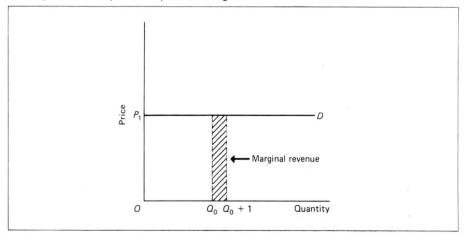

until she finds the point where the effect on profit of a small change in output is zero:

$$\frac{\Delta \Pi}{\Delta Q} = \frac{\Delta TR}{\Delta Q} - \frac{\Delta TC}{\Delta Q} = 0$$

We have just seen that $\Delta TR/\Delta Q$ is marginal revenue. In the last chapter, $\Delta TC/\Delta Q$ was defined as marginal cost. Thus, profit maximization requires that the manager select that output where marginal revenue equals marginal cost:

$$MR = MC$$

In a competitive industry, the marginal revenue equals the market price. Consequently, in a competitive industry, profit is maximized by producing where

$$P = MC \tag{5.1}$$

Let's try to see why this is true. In Figure 5.2, we have added the firm's marginal cost curve to the demand curve. Consider the situation at output Q_3. Profit is *not* maximized by producing Q_3 units of output. When 1 more unit is produced, total revenue rises by P_1, while total cost rises by the marginal cost, which equals C_3. Profit increases when output expands from Q_3 to $Q_3 + 1$ because total revenue increases more than total cost increases. To be precise, the increase in profit equals $P_1 - C_3$. As long as price exceeds marginal cost, the manager is able to bring about additional increases in the firm's profit by expanding production. The manager therefore will expand production until price equals marginal cost. In Figure 5.2, Q_2 is the output level that maximizes profit. At higher levels of output, say, Q_4, profit can be

FIGURE 5.2   Profit is maximized by producing quantity Q_2 where MC $=$ MR.

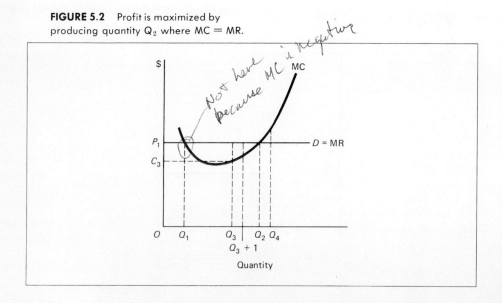

increased by reducing output. A reduction in output would reduce total revenue by less than the reduction in total cost and, accordingly, would increase profit.

Question   We know that the manager should produce where marginal cost equals marginal revenue. But how much profit does the firm make?

Answer   In order to find out how much profit the firm earns, we need to add the average cost curve to our diagram. In Figure 5.3, we have put in the demand and the average and marginal cost curves. At the optimal output Q_2, the firm's profit is equal to total revenue minus total cost. Total revenue equals price times quantity, which is measured by the area of rectangle P_1AQ_2O. Since the total cost is equal to average cost multipled by the quantity, total cost is equal to the area of rectangle C_2BQ_2O. Consequently, the firm's profit, which can be written as $(P_1 - C_2)Q_2$, equals the area of rectangle P_1ABC_2.

Question   If the manager should select the output where marginal cost equals marginal revenue, can she maximize profit by producing Q_1? Since MC equals MR at Q_1, if the answer is no, why not?

Answer   The answer is an unambiguous no. To see that this must be correct, examine the effect of a movement away from Q_1. An increase in output would leave marginal revenue above marginal cost. But this is a sign that output should be expanded, which produces a further movement away from Q_1. A decrease in output from Q_1 would result in marginal cost being above marginal revenue. Thus, the cost saving associated with a decrease in output would exceed the revenue forgone by reducing output. This means that output should be decreased still further. Again, this moves

FIGURE 5.3   Total profit is measured by rectangle P_1ABC_2, which is the difference between total revenue P_1AQ_2O and total cost C_2BQ_2O.

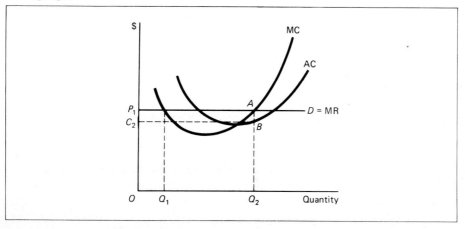

the firm away from Q_1. Accordingly, profit is lower at Q_1 than at output levels immediately around Q_1. In fact, profit is minimized at Q_1.

We have already seen that a manager who is not producing Q_2 can increase her firm's profit by moving toward production level Q_2. This means that profit is maximized by producing Q_2.

But price equals marginal cost at both Q_1 and Q_2. At Q_1, where profit is minimized, the marginal cost curve is falling. On the other hand, the marginal cost curve is rising at Q_2, where profit is maximized. Thus, a manager in a competitive industry will not maximize profit by producing where the slope of the marginal cost curve is negative.

5.3

SHORT-RUN SUPPLY CURVES

In Figure 5.3, the firm supplied Q_2 units of output in response to a price of P_1. In this section, we want to determine the manager's, and ultimately the industry's, supply response to various prices.

The firm's supply response to different prices is represented by the firm supply curve.

DEFINITION ▶   The *supply curve* of the firm shows the maximum amount that the firm will produce per unit time at different prices, all other things being equal.

DERIVATION OF THE FIRM'S SUPPLY CURVE   In Figure 5.4, we have drawn the average total cost, average variable cost, and marginal cost curves of the firm. Let us begin with a market price equal to P_1. At this price, profit is maximized by producing Q_1 units of output. Similarly, if the price falls to P_2, marginal cost is equal to price (or marginal revenue) at Q_2 units of output. In both instances, price exceeded average total cost so we could be confident that the firm's profits would be positive.

This is not the case, however, for price P_3. At a price of P_3, if the manager produces where marginal cost equals price, average total cost will be greater than the price. When per unit cost exceeds per unit revenue, losses occur. Interestingly, the manager will still elect to produce Q_3 units of output and sell them at a price of P_3. He does this because his losses are smallest this way.

If the manager decides to produce zero output, revenue obviously will be zero. Cost, however, will be equal to the total fixed costs, which are unavoidable. Thus, the firm's loss in that period will be equal to the total fixed costs. These fixed costs are measured in Figure 5.4 by the difference between average total cost (ATC) and average variable cost (AVC) at Q_3 times Q_3: $(\text{ATC}_3 - \text{AVC}_3)Q_3$. This is because the difference between average total cost and average variable cost equals average fixed cost (see Chapter 4).

If the manager elects to produce Q_3, where marginal cost is equal to P_3, then total revenue will be $P_3 \cdot Q_3$ and total cost will be equal to $\text{ATC}_3 \cdot Q_3$. The firm's loss will then be equal to $(\text{ATC}_3 - P_3)Q_3$, which is smaller than the loss at zero output: $(ATC_3 - AVC_3)Q_3$. Consequently, in the short run the manager minimizes the firm's loss by producing when the price equals P_3. This is because the revenue that the firm receives from selling Q_3 units of output is greater than the variable cost involved in producing Q_3 units of output.

Consider price P_4. At this price, variable costs are just covered by the total revenue generated by selling Q_4 units of output at P_4. Thus, the firm's losses are equal to total fixed costs whether the manager produces Q_4 or zero. He will have to base his output decision upon other considerations.

For all prices below P_4, the loss incurred by producing where marginal cost equals price is greater than the fixed costs. The price will not cover the per unit variable costs. Consequently, losses will be minimized by producing no output at all.

Exercise Construct a diagram like Figure 5.4. Draw a $D_5 = MR_5$ line below P_4. Show with appropriately drawn rectangles that the loss by producing where $MC = MR_5$ is larger than the loss associated with zero output.

All these results can now be put together to construct the firm's short-run supply curve. For all prices below the minimum point on the average variable cost curve, the manager maximizes the firm's profit by producing nothing. For all prices above the minimum point on the average cost curve, he maximizes profit by producing where price equals marginal cost. Thus, the relationship between the price offered and the quantity that the firm

FIGURE 5.4 The firm's short-run supply curve is identical to its marginal cost curve above the average variable cost curve.

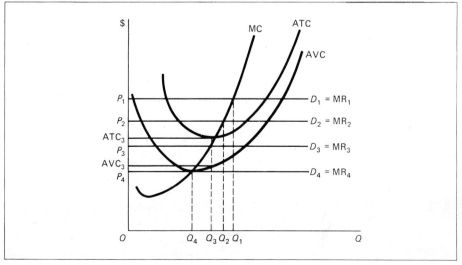

supplies is given by the marginal cost curve above the average variable cost curve. In other words, the firm's supply curve is its marginal cost curve above its average variable cost curve.

INDUSTRY SUPPLY CURVE UNDER CONSTANT INPUT PRICES   The industry supply curve represents the collective supply response of all firms in the industry to different prices. As we shall see, its derivation depends on whether input prices change when industry output rises or falls. Let us first consider the case where the prices of the inputs employed in a particular industry are unaffected by changes in the industry output. This is a plausible situation when the industry usage of inputs is small relative to the input market. For example, the manufacturers of mailboxes use inputs that can be employed in many other industries. As a result, the demands that these producers make on the input markets are very small relative to the size of these markets. Thus, if the output of mailboxes were to rise by, say, 20 percent, there would be an almost negligible (relative to the total quantity used) increase in the quantity demanded of these inputs by all the industries that use them. Consequently, the prices of the inputs used to produce mailboxes are unaffected by fluctuations in mailbox production.

If input prices do not respond to changes in industry output, we may simply add up the marginal cost curves of the various firms to obtain the industry supply curve. A small example of this is shown in Figure 5.5, where the supply curves associated with a two-firm industry are depicted. The industry supply curve in panel (c) is obtained by adding up the relevant sections of the marginal cost curves of firms A and B. At the price P_1, firm A supplies q_{1A} and firm B supplies q_{1B}. The quantity that is supplied by the in-

FIGURE 5.5   When input prices are unaffected by changes in industry output, industry supply is the horizontal summation of the firms' marginal cost curves.

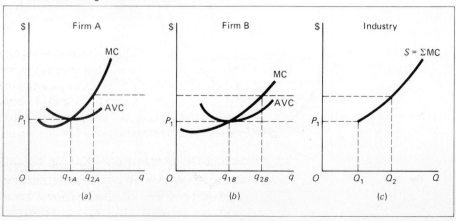

dustry at this price (Q_1) equals the sum of q_{1A} and q_{1B}. Similarly, q_{2A} plus q_{2B} equals Q_2. Of course, nothing would be forthcoming at any price below P_1. (Why?)

The industry supply curve need not be a simple continuous function. Differences among firms can cause "jumps" in the supply responses of existing and potential firms. An example of this is shown in Figure 5.6. As drawn, firm A has lower cost curves than firm B. Firm A is said to be a more efficient firm than firm B since firm A can profitably produce at lower prices than firm B can. This greater efficiency stems from firm A's having either better managerial resources or more productive inputs. For example, an oil company may happen to discover a particularly productive set of oil fields; others are not as

FIGURE 5.6 When there are firms of varying efficiency, the industry supply curve may be discontinuous.

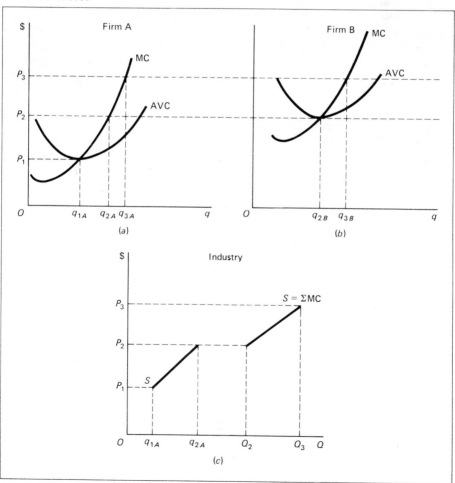

lucky. Similarly, some companies are blessed with more insightful owners or more creative managers than other companies.

At price P_1, firm A is the only firm producing in the industry. Thus, until firm B begins production at price P_2, the industry supply curve is firm A's marginal cost curve above average variable cost. The entry of firm B into the industry at price P_2 causes the supply curve to be discontinuous at P_2; the industry supply at $P_2(Q_2)$ equals the sum of the quantity supplied by firm A (q_{2A}) and of the quantity supplied by firm B(q_{2B}). Similarly, q_{3A} plus q_{3B} equals Q_3. Other points on the supply curve can be obtained in an analogous way. When there are a large number of firms in the industry, the jumps or gaps are small and the industry supply is fairly smooth.

INDUSTRY SUPPLY CURVE UNDER VARYING INPUT PRICES   When the industry accounts for a substantial share of the total market for an input, a change in industry output may have an impact upon the price of that input. The most likely effect would be for an increase in the demand for the input to push up its price. From our discussion in Chapter 4, it is clear that the firm's cost curves are constructed for given input prices. When input prices change, the cost curves will shift. In particular, if industry output expands, we should expect at least some input prices to rise and, as a result, the average and marginal cost curves for each firm will shift up. We can examine the effects of this in Figure 5.7.

Suppose that the firm in Figure 5.7 is supplying Q_1 units of output in response to a price of P_1. If the price were to rise to P_2, the firm would attempt to expand its output to Q_2. At that output, marginal cost MC_1 would equal the new price P_2 and profits would be maximized. But if all of the firms in the industry respond to the rise in the output price by increasing production, the

FIGURE 5.7   When input prices rise with increases in industry output, the firm's supply curve s is steeper than its marginal cost curve.

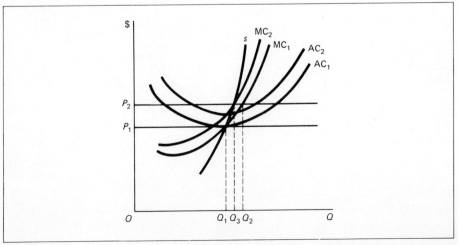

price of some inputs will rise and consequently the average and marginal cost curves will shift to, say, AC_2 and MC_2. Under these new input prices, the optimal output for this firm would be Q_3 rather than Q_2.

In this way, we can construct a firm supply curve that reflects the increases in input prices that occur as *industry* output rises. In Figure 5.7, we have labeled the firm's supply curve s. Note that the points (Q_1, P_1) and (Q_3, P_2) lie on the s curve. We can easily see that the firm supply curve is much steeper than any of its marginal cost curves.

When input prices depend on industry output, the industry supply curve is the horizontal summation of the short-run firm supply curves s. Graphically, the summation technique is the same one used in summing the marginal cost curves. Clearly, this industry supply curve is steeper than the corresponding industry supply curve associated with constant input prices.

5.4

LONG-RUN
PROFIT MAXIMIZATION

In the short run, the manager of a firm maximizes profit subject to the constraints imposed by having at least one input fixed. In the long run, however, all the manager's inputs are variable. Consequently, there may still be an incentive to alter the quantity of the fixed input in the long run even when the manager has maximized short-run profits. Unless all such incentives are absent, the manager will not have maximized long-run profits. Figure 5.8 illustrates these issues.

Suppose that the manager was producing Q_1 units of output and selling them at the market-determined price of P_1. If price increases to P_2, the man-

FIGURE 5.8 When price rises, the manager can maximize the short-run profits by using his fixed inputs more intensively. Long-run profit maximization however, requires a change in the quantity of the fixed input.

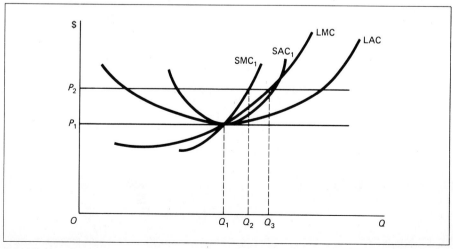

ager's immediate response will be to increase output to Q_2. At Q_2, the short-run marginal cost (SMC$_1$) is equal to the new price of P_2. We can see, however, that the firm's short-run average cost (SAC$_1$) exceeds the long-run average cost (LAC) at an output of Q_2. Consequently, the manager will recognize that her current plant is being utilized too intensively. Thus, at this price (P_2) she will want to increase the size of her plant to reduce the per unit costs of the output. This incentive will exist until the plant size is adjusted so that the firm produces where long-run marginal cost (LMC) equals price P_2. At that point, the new short-run average cost will be tangent to the long-run average cost at output Q_3. This is shown in Figure 5.9 where we can also see that the new short-run marginal cost curve equals price P_2 at output Q_3.

In summary, the conditions that must be satisfied for long-run profit maximization are

$$P = \text{LMC} = \text{SMC}$$

and

$$\text{SAC} = \text{LAC}$$

If these equalities do not hold, the manager has failed to maximize profit.

A manager in a competitive industry maximizes profit in the long run by operating on the long-run marginal cost curve (LMC). But once again, some points on the marginal cost curve will prove to be unacceptable. For example, in Figure 5.10, marginal revenue and marginal cost are equated at Q_1 units of output when P_1 is the price. At this level of output, however, total revenue

FIGURE 5.9 The adjustment to long-run profit maximizing output Q_3 requires a change in all inputs such that SAC$_2$ is tangent to LAC at Q_3.

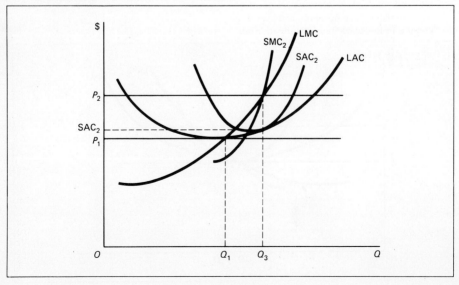

equals P_1Q_1 and total cost equals LAC_1Q_1. The firm's economic loss equals $(LAC_1 - P_1)Q_1$ and is given by the area of rectangle P_1LAC_1AB. In the long run, the firm will not choose to operate when it is making economic losses. Accordingly, any point on the long-run marginal cost curve below the long-run average cost curve is unacceptable to the firm, for these points represent economic losses. Thus, the firm's long-run supply curve is that part of the long-run marginal cost curve that is above the long-run average cost curve.

AN ALTERNATIVE FORMULATION There is another way of formulating the problem of maximizing profits that is of some interest. Instead of incorporating the constraint imposed by the production function into the cost function, we can substitute it directly into the profit function:

$$\Pi = PQ(L,K) - wL - sK$$

Now the manager will expand the employment of the two inputs until the marginal effect on profit is 0:

$$\frac{\Delta\Pi}{\Delta L} = P\frac{\Delta Q}{\Delta L} - w = 0$$

$$\frac{\Delta\Pi}{\Delta K} = P\frac{\Delta Q}{\Delta K} - s = 0$$

(5.2)

Remember that $\Delta Q/\Delta L$ is the marginal product of labor and $\Delta Q/\Delta K$ is the marginal product of capital. Thus, we see that profit maximization requires hiring labor and capital until

$$P \cdot MP_L = w$$

and

$$P \cdot MP_K = s$$

(5.3)

FIGURE 5.10 In the long run, the manager will produce the output where $P = LMC$ only if P is greater than or equal to LAC.

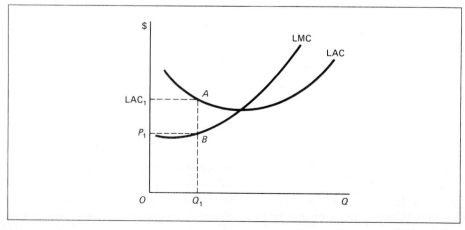

Let's see if these conditions make any sense. First, consider the employment decision for labor. By definition, when L increases by 1 unit, the firm's output rises by the marginal product of L, which is $\Delta Q/\Delta L$. Since with each additional unit of output total revenue rises by P dollars, using 1 more unit of L increases total revenue by $P \cdot \Delta Q/\Delta L$ dollars, which is appropriately called the value of the marginal product of L. But 1 more unit of L costs the firm w dollars. Consequently, the manager has an incentive to increase her use of L if the resultant increase in total revenue exceeds the increase in total cost. Only when $P \cdot \Delta Q/\Delta L$ equals w is profit maximized. A similar logic describes the determination of the optimal level of capital.

We can also solve the optimality conditions (5.3) for P and write them as:

$$P = \frac{w}{\mathrm{MP}_L}$$

and

$$P = \frac{s}{\mathrm{MP}_K}$$

Again consider the condition for labor: $1/\mathrm{MP}_L$ equals $\Delta L/\Delta Q$, which is the increase in labor that would be necessary to increase output by 1 unit. Thus, $w(1/\mathrm{MP}_L)$ is the expenditure on L that would be necessary to increase output by 1 unit by only increasing L. This is marginal cost. A similar argument can be made for capital. Once again, a necessary condition for profit maximization is that price be equal to marginal cost. Since all the inputs are variable, the marginal cost in question is long-run marginal cost.

Question Answer true, false, or uncertain: A competitive firm whose product sells for $10 maximizes profit by operating where the marginal product of raw materials equals 5 when the price of raw materials equals $2.

Answer False, This question requires a careful reading. At the firm's chosen position, the value of the marginal product of raw materials equals $10 \cdot 5 = \$50$. Because $50 exceeds the cost of raw materials ($2), the firm should increase its use of raw materials.

5.5

COMPETITIVE INDUSTRY EQUILIBRIUM

The situation depicted in Figure 5.9 is one of firm equilibrium but not necessarily of industry equilibrium. At an output of Q_3 and with a plant size denoted by SAC_2, the competitive firm is maximizing long-run profits. As a result it has no incentive to alter anything: it is in equilibrium. But we should note that P_2 exceeds SAC_2 at an output of Q_3. Consequently, the firm is enjoying economic profits equal to $(P_2 - \mathrm{SAC}_2)Q_2$. This represents a return that exceeds the next best alternative investment for the firm's assets. As a result, resources outside the industry will have an incentive to flow into this industry. The magnitude of this response is dependent upon the characteristics of potential firms. In the following analysis, we will assume first that there is an infinite number of potential firms with identical cost curves. Subsequently, we will alter this by assuming that some firms are more efficient than other firms.

CONSTANT INPUT PRICES WITH IDENTICAL FIRMS   In Figure 5.11, we consider the case where input prices remain constant to the industry and where there are an infinite number of potential firms with identical cost curves. In panel (a), industry supply and demand curves are depicted. In panel (b), we examine a competitive firm's reactions to price changes.

Initially, the market demand curve is D_1 and the short-run industry supply curve is S_1. Since we have assumed that input prices are constant, the industry short-run supply curve is the horizontal sum of the relevant sections of the short-run marginal cost curves of the n_1 firms that are producing in this industry. Q_1 units of output are produced at a price of P_1 at the intersection of D_1 and S_1. At this price, each firm elects to produce q_1 units of output, thereby earning a competitive return. Since no economic profit is made under this solution, firms have no incentive to leave or enter the industry.

Now suppose that the demand curve shifts from D_1 to D_2. The immediate impact will be for price to increase from P_1 to P_2. In response to the price rise, our firm in panel (b) has increased its output from q_1 to q_2. Since P_2 exceeds the firm's short-run average costs, profits will be positive and other firms will enter the industry. The effect of entry will be for the short-run industry supply curve to shift to the right. As it does so, the price will fall and the individual firm will move back along its short-run marginal cost curve. As long as the price exceeds P_1, the firms in the industry will enjoy economic profits. Consequently, still more firms will enter. The incentive for further entry

FIGURE 5.11   For a constant-cost industry with identical firms, the long-run supply (LRS) is horizontal. All firms produce q_1 in equilibrium, and industry output is changed by altering the number of firms producing.

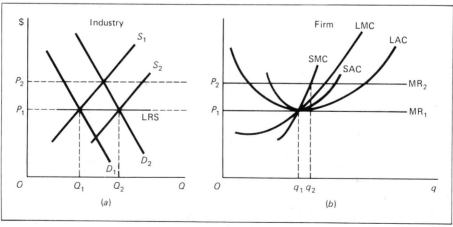

disappears only when the short-run industry supply function shifts to S_2 and price falls back to P_1. Now industry output will be Q_2 and the firm's output will be q_1, which is back where the firm began. The increase in the industry output of $Q_2 - Q_1$ is accomplished by having more firms in the industry; each firm's output is q_1. Although many firms may have been lured into the industry by the prospect of economic profits, entry continues until only a competitive rate of return is earned.

The *long-run industry supply curve* is made up of long-run equilibrium positions. In long-run equilibrium, firms have no incentive to enter or leave the industry. Thus, we see that the points (Q_1, P_1) and (Q_2, P_1) are long-run equilibrium points and, therefore, lie on the long-run supply curve. In Figure 5.11, we have labeled the long-run supply curve LRS. When input prices are constant, the long-run supply function is horizontal.

In summary, we can see from panel (*b*) of Figure 5.11 that if an industry made up of identical firms is in long-run equilibrium, then

$$P = \text{LMC} = \text{SMC} = \text{LAC} = \text{SAC}$$

If any of the equalities does not hold, either the manager has failed to maximize profit or the industry is not in equilibrium.

CONSTANT INPUT PRICES WITH DIFFERENCES IN FIRMS   We will now consider the case where input prices remain constant and where some firms are more efficient than other firms. The cost curves of three representative firms and the industry demand and supply curves are found in Figure 5.12. Firm A is a relatively efficient firm and enters the industry when the price equals P_0; this is called firm A's "entry price." At this price, firm A makes no economic profits. At higher prices, however, firm A makes positive economic profits, and other less efficient firms, which would have operated at a loss at lower prices, enter the industry. The entry of less efficient firms does *not* drive the price back to P_0 because these less efficient firms lose money at P_0. The long-

FIGURE 5.12   In an industry with constant costs but heterogeneous firms, the long-run supply (LRS) will be positively sloped due to successive entry.

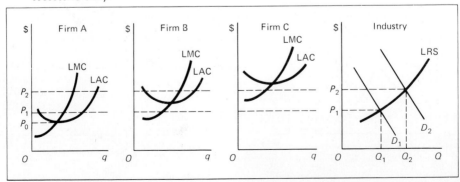

run supply curve (LRS) reflects the entry decisions of all potential firms; it is the horizontal sum of all long-run marginal cost curves above the minimum points on the long-run average cost curves.

If the industry demand curve is D_1, then the price equals P_1 and *all* firms with entry prices at or below P_1 are producing. The more efficient firms in the industry are making positive economic profits, and firms with an entry price of P_1 are making zero economic profits. The industry is in long-run equilibrium, despite the existence of economic profits in the industry, because no firm not already in the industry can enter the industry and make positive economic profits. Firms such as firms B and C would lose money at price P_1.

If the industry demand curve shifts out to D_2, the price rises to P_2. This leads each firm in the industry to produce more and attracts less efficient firms, such as firm B, into the industry. Industry price P_2 and quantity Q_2 represent a long-run equilibrium because no firm can enter the industry and make an economic profit. Firms such as firm C would lose money if they tried to produce at price P_2.

VARYING INPUT PRICES WITH IDENTICAL FIRMS   For expositional reasons, let us return to the assumption that there are an infinite number of identical potential firms. In many instances, input prices will rise as the industry expands its output. We deal with this in Figure 5.13. In panel (*a*) we have industry supply and demand, while in panel (*b*) we have a firm's long-run cost curves. The corresponding short-run cost curves have been deleted to reduce congestion.

Initially, the demand curve is D_1 and the industry short-run supply curve is S_1. The industry short-run supply curve is the horizontal sum of the n_1

FIGURE 5.13   In an industry facing rising input prices, the long-run supply curve is positively sloped.

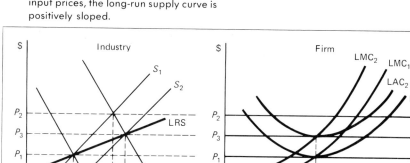

short-run firm supply curves. S_1 is constructed so that the effects of changes in the output of these n_1 firms on input prices are already incorporated into S_1. S_1 and D_1 intersect at price P_1 and quantity Q_1. When the industry is producing Q_1, each firm's cost curves are LAC_1 and LMC_1. Consequently, in this solution, each firm is making zero economic profits and there is no incentive for firms to enter or exit the industry.

Suppose that demand shifts to D_2. The immediate response by the n_1 firms in the industry is to increase output to Q_2 and price to P_2. But at this new price, price exceeds average cost and each firm consequently is earning economic profit. This brings new firms into the industry, and as industry output thus increases, input prices rise. As a result, the firm's cost curves rise. Entry continues until each firm in the industry earns a competitive return. In Figure 5.13, this occurs when the short-run supply curve has shifted to S_2 and LMC_2 and LAC_2 are each firm's cost curves. Thus, the increase in demand from D_1 to D_2 results in an expansion of output from Q_1 to Q_3 and an increase in price to P_3. Price does not return to the previous level because the expansion in output caused at least some input prices to rise.

It is not possible to say on a priori grounds just what happens to the firm's output. In Figure 5.13, we examined the special case where the minimum points on LAC_1 and LAC_2 occurred at the same output level. Under these circumstances, the firm's output remains the same, its costs rise, its total revenue rises, and its profits remain at the competitive level. This need not always be the case. Clearly, if the long-run average cost curve shifts up and to the right, then the firm would produce a higher output.

The long-run supply curve is made up of long-run equilibrium points such as (Q_1, P_1) and (Q_3, P_3) and is labeled LRS in panel (a) of Figure 5.13. It is positively sloped becaused input prices increase as industry output expands.[2]

5.6

MONOPOLY

The polar opposite of the perfectly competitive firm is the monopoly firm. A monopoly is said to exist when a single firm produces a commodity for which there are no close substitutes. This, of course, does not mean that substitution is absolutely impossible. It just means that the price of other commodities can change significantly without inducing much substitution away from the monopolized product.

SOURCES OF MONOPOLY In many contexts, it is simply assumed that a monopoly exists and the analysis proceeds as though that situation will persist indefinitely. It is of some interest to note, however, that there are two main theories concerning the source of monopoly power. First, some economists advance the *self-sufficiency* theory. This is a belief that a firm can produce monopoly power without any substantial assistance from anyone

---

[2]Since the analysis of the effects of increasing cost on an industry composed of firms of varying levels of efficiency is virtually identical to what was just discussed, we will not undertake that analysis.

else. Through creative genius, superior efficiency, or better foresight one firm comes to dominate an industry and no other firm is able to successfully copy its methods. In contrast, other economists believe that any self-sufficient monopoly power is transitory and fleeting. Sustained monopoly power requires the government's assistance. These economists endorse the *interventionist* theory of monopoly power.

Several specific sources of monopoly are identified in the following paragraphs. Readers should decide for themselves the extent to which the maintenance of monopoly depends upon goverment intervention and how prevalent monopoly is.

1. Control of an Essential Raw Material   The classic example of this is Alcoa's control of bauxite reserves in the 1930s and early 1940s. Alcoa was alleged to have preempted the available supplies of bauxite ore, which are absolutely necessary for the production of aluminum, through purchases or long-term contracts. As a result, in 1945 a circuit court of appeals found that Alcoa accounted for some 90 percent of aluminum production in the United States.

It should be noted that any company could have acquired the large quantity of bauxite reserves which Alcoa acquired. That is, nothing precluded others from competing with Alcoa in mineral rights acquisition. Indeed, competition for control of bauxite should drive up the price of the associated mineral rights. This competition would dissipate any monopoly profits stemming from the control of bauxite reserves.

2. Patents   When a firm has a patent, it is granted the exclusive right to produce a certain commodity or to use a specific production process for a limited time. Patents are offered as rewards to stimulate inventive or creative efforts, which advance knowledge and make information available. It is claimed that a person would have little incentive to invent a better mousetrap if he were not going to reap some reward for doing so.

The grant of a patent is supposed to ensure that no one will copy an invention during the life of the patent. Although the patent affords the inventor legal protection against blatant copying, it does not provide absolute protection. The monopoly power which comes from a patent is limited because patents are often narrowly defined. Other firms are thus allowed to closely approximate the patented process.

Once again, any firm has the opportunity to be the firm which creates the innovation. Competition for the patented process (e.g., six firms trying to be *the* firm which develops and patents nylon) will reduce the expected monopoly profits arising from the ownership of a patent.

3. Natural Monopoly   A natural monopoly exists when the forces of competition cause all firms but one to exit the industry. This is a result of the interaction between technological conditions that require large scale for efficient production and demand conditions that indicate that one plant of minimal efficient size is approximately sufficient to supply the entire market at a price that covers full cost. Public utilities provide the classic examples of natural monopoly.

4. Market Franchise   There are industries where entry is controlled by the

AN UNUSUAL SOURCE OF MONOPOLY*

For monopoly power to persist, there must be some way to prevent firms from entering the industry in response to positive profits. The airline industry provides an interesting example of how this can work. Prior to 1978, the airline industry was heavily regulated by the Civil Aeronautics Board (CAB). In particular, fares were regulated to prevent price competition. This resulted in excess profits, which would ordinarily induce entry, but entry by outsiders into profitable routes was foreclosed by the CAB. Thus, certain routes generated positive profits for a favored few without the threat of new entry.

In 1978, Congress decided to deregulate the airlines. In principle, this exposed the profitable routes to entry by outsiders. In fact, some entry has occurred but not as much as one might expect. The stumbling block is the need for ground facilities at the airport such as ticket counters and gates. The airlines that were originally serving the profitable routes generally have the ground facilities tied up through long-term contracts. To the extent that those who enjoyed positive profits can deny access to the routes by controlling access to the ground facilities, there will be no entry. This will serve to protect the interests of those with a monopoly position and thwart Congress's intention to have more competition.

*Source: "Finding Space for New Airlines" Business Week, Dec. 8, 1980, pp. 104 and 106.

government. Consequently, the government agency can confer monopoly power, at least locally, on a firm simply by precluding entry. Examples abound: banking, airline routes, TV and radio frequencies, hospitals, cable TV firms, and so on. Usually, some concessions are extracted in exchange for the protection. In many cases, firms must submit to some form of direct regulation regarding rates charged, quality of service, the scope of service, and the rate of return on investment.

5.7

DEMAND AND MARGINAL REVENUE UNDER MONOPOLY

For a monopolist, the demand function for the firm's output and the industry demand function are identical. This is because a monopolist, by definition, is the only firm in the industry. The manager can operate at any point on the demand curve for her product and will choose that position on the demand curve that maximizes the monopolist's profit.

The monopolist's profit can be increased or decreased by adjusting output. The benefit to the firm of producing 1 more unit of output is the resulting change in the total revenue that the firm receives, which is the firm's marginal revenue. Because a monopolist faces a downward sloping demand curve, the monopolist's marginal revenue is less than the price at which the product sells.

An example will help to show why this is the case. Suppose that the manager can sell 100 units of output at $500 apiece, generating a total revenue of $50,000. Because the monopolist's demand curve is negatively sloped, the manager can sell 101 units of output only if the price falls to, say, $498. The 101st unit of output brings $498 directly to the firm. But in order to sell 101 units of output, the manager is charging $2 less per unit, which costs the firm

$200 in lost revenue on the 100 units it was already able to sell. On net, the 101st unit of output adds

$$\$498 - 200 = \$298$$

to the firm's total revenue. Consequently, the marginal revenue at the 101st unit of output is $298 even though the product sells for $498.[3]

We could derive the marginal revenue that corresponds to each point on the demand curve. For a linear demand curve, there is a very simple relationship between the demand curve and the marginal revenue curve. Suppose that the demand curve can be written as

$$P = 500 - 2Q$$

which we have plotted in Figure 5.14. The intercept on the price axis is 500 and the slope of the demand curve is -2. The total revenue for the firm is

$$PQ = (500 - 2Q)Q$$

$$= 500Q - 2Q^2$$

By the definition of marginal revenue, we find that

$$MR = \frac{\Delta TR}{\Delta Q} = 500 - 4Q$$

---

[3]Recall that for the competitive firm, price and marginal revenue are identical. This is because the competitive firm's demand curve is horizontal.

FIGURE 5.14   The marginal revenue curve bisects the horizontal distance between the price axis and the demand curve.

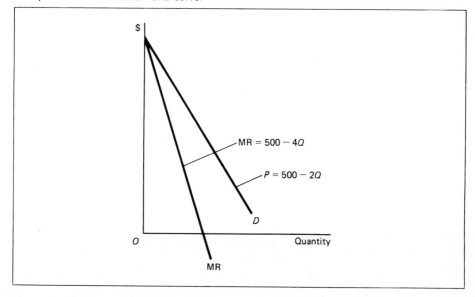

Notice that the intercept remains at 500, but the slope is twice as steep: -4 compared to -2.

We have plotted the marginal revenue curve in Figure 5.14 along with the demand curve. Since MR and D have the same intercept while MR is twice as steep as D, the marginal revenue curve will bisect the horizontal distance between the price axis and the demand curve.

We also notice that at very low prices, marginal revenue is negative. When the marginal revenue is negative, total revenue falls as output increases. The manager has little incentive to produce 1 more unit of output if total revenue falls as a result!

5.8

SHORT-RUN MONOPOLY PROFIT MAXIMIZATION

The manager of a monopolistic firm wants to do the same thing as the manager of a competitive firm: maximize profits. In order to do this, she must select that output where the difference between total revenue and total cost is largest. In Figure 5.15, we have graphed the demand D, marginal revenue (MR), average total cost (ATC), and marginal cost (MC) curves of a monopolist. Profits are maximized when the marginal impact on profit of a small change in output is zero. Since profit is defined as

$$\Pi = TR - TC$$

the marginal impact on profit of a small change in output is

FIGURE 5.15   Profit maximization requires producing where MC = MR. Price will be P_1 and profit equals the striped area.

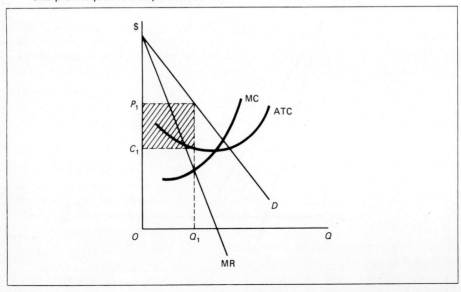

$$\frac{\Delta \Pi}{\Delta Q} = \frac{\Delta TR}{\Delta Q} - \frac{\Delta TC}{\Delta Q}$$

$$= MR - MC$$

If this is set equal to zero, we find that the manager of a monopolistic firm, as well as the manager of a competitive firm, maximizes profits where marginal revenue equals marginal cost: $MR = MC$. The difference between the competitive and monopolistic solutions is found in the marginal revenue curve. For the competitive firm, the marginal revenue curve is a horizontal line at the market price. On the other hand, the marginal revenue curve of the monopolistic firm is negatively sloping and lies below the demand curve. The manager in Figure 5.15 maximizes the monopolist's profits by producing Q_1 units of output, which will be sold at price P_1.

Question How can we be sure that profit is maximized when the manager produces where marginal cost and marginal revenue are equal?

Answer Consider points around Q_1. At an output less than Q_1, the manager could increase his profit by expanding output by 1 unit; this is because the increase in total revenue from selling 1 more unit (MR) exceeds the increase in total cost from producing 1 more unit (MC). Similarly, at an output level which exceeds Q_1, profit can be increased by contracting production. Consequently, Q_1 will be sold for the profit-maximizing price of P_1. Total revenue will be $P_1 \cdot Q_1$ while total cost will be $C_1 \cdot Q_1$. As a result, the monopoly's profit will be $(P_1 - C_1)Q_1$, which is equal to the striped rectangle in the diagram.

Question Is it true that monopolists all earn exorbitant profits?

Answer This is essentially an empirical question. At this point, however, we can say that there is no theoretical reason for believing the statement. Simply the fact that there is only one firm in an industry is no guarantee that the monopolist will make a profit. The output decision criteria are analogous for both the managers of monopolistic and the managers of competitive firms. Specifically, in the short run, the manager will maximize the firm's profits by producing where marginal cost equals marginal revenue as long as the resulting price is at least as large as the average variable costs.

We can see this in Figure 5.16. At output Q_1, the MR and MC curves intersect. The price on the industry demand curve that corresponds to output Q_1 is P_1. This price is less than the average total cost of Q_1, which is labeled C_1. But we can see that P_1 is greater than C_2 which is the average variable cost of output Q_1. In this case, the firm will lose the difference between total cost and total revenue by producing Q_1. This loss is $(C_1 - P_1)Q_1$. If the manager elected to produce zero output, the short-run loss would be equal to the total fixed costs. In Figure 5.16, we can measure the total fixed costs as $(C_1 - C_2)Q_1$. This loss is clearly larger than the loss associated with positive output Q_1.

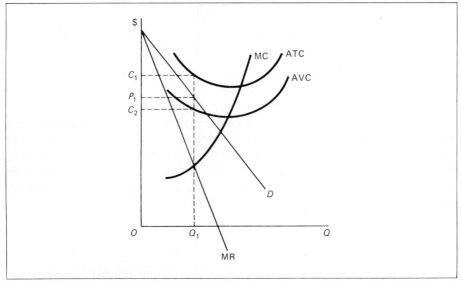

FIGURE 5.16   Profit maximization in the short run dictates that the manager should produce where MC = MR as long as $P \geq$ AVC.

In summary, the manager of a monopolistic firm will produce where marginal cost equals marginal revenue, provided that the corresponding price is at least as large as average variable cost. Thus, the short-run equilibrium conditions for the firm are

$$MC = MR$$

and

$$P \geq AVC$$

Otherwise, the firm will produce zero output. A manager who does not meet these conditions is failing to maximize profit.

MAXIMIZING PUBLISHING PROFITS*

Publishers of books usually have a property right in the privilege of publishing their books. This property right, which is called a *copyright*, protects against other publishers publishing the same material. In many instances, U.S. publishers will sell overseas publishing rights to foreign publishers. By selecting the appropriate price, the U.S. publisher can extract most (if not all) of the profit that can be earned in the foreign market.

For example, in Figure 5.17, D and MR represent demand and marginal revenue in the British market. The marginal cost of publishing and distributing the book in England is MC_1, while the marginal cost of publishing the book in the United States, transporting it to England, and distributing is MC_2. If the U.S. copyright holder publishes the book in the United States, the profit-maximizing price and output are P_2 and Q_2. Total profit would be $\Pi_2 = (P_2 - C_2)Q_2$. If the book is published in England, a larger profit is earned:

$\Pi_1 = (P_1 - C_1)Q_1$. The U.S. copyright holder would be willing to have the book published in England as long as its profit was at least Π_2. This means that the lump-sum fee for the publishing rights must be at least Π_2. A British publisher would be willing to publish the book as long as it did not lose money. This means that the lump-sum fee for the publishing rights cannot exceed Π_1. The fee for the publishing rights that is in fact chosen will depend upon the relative bargaining ability of the two sides.

Recently, some U.S. publishers have stopped selling their publishing rights to British publishers. The reason given was the high cost of publishing in Britain. To see why, let's change the labels in the figure. The demand and marginal revenue curves are unchanged, but MC_1 now represents the per unit cost of production in the United States plus the transportation cost to Britain, while MC_2 is the per unit cost of production in Britain. Now the U.S. copyright holder can earn profits of $(P_1 - C_1)Q_1$ by producing the books itself and shipping. British production will yield profits of only $(P_2 - C_2)Q_2$. Consequently, the U.S. publisher is now better off by retaining the publishing rights and proceeding on its own.

---

*Source: "Britain: U.S. Publishers Invade a Troubled Book Market," Business Week, Dec. 15, 1980, p. 45.

5.9

LONG-RUN MONOPOLY PROFIT MAXIMIZATION

Since there is only one firm in this industry by definition, when the firm is in long-run equilibrium, the industry is also in long-run equilibrium. Typically, we assume that no entry is possible in this industry. Consequently, positive profits are compatible with long-run industry equilibrium.[4] Thus, it is possible to have a situation like the one in Figure 5.18.

---

[4]This is in marked contrast to the competitive industry where the marginal firm will earn zero economic profits.

FIGURE 5.17 Publishing profits vary due to different production costs in the United States and Britain.

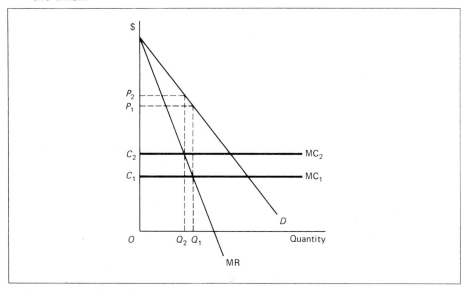

Long-run profit maximization for the monopoly firm requires that long-run marginal cost (LMC) be equal to marginal revenue (MR). When the firm produces Q_0 units of output, we see that long-run average cost is equal to short-run average cost. As a result, short-run marginal cost equals long-run marginal cost. In this case, the long-run monopoly profit is $(P_0 - C_0)Q_0$. Thus, we can see that the conditions for long-run profit maximization are

$$MR = LMC = SMC$$

$$SAC = LAC$$

$$P \geq LAC$$

The essence of long-run equilibrium is that the firm is producing where long-run marginal cost equals marginal revenue and the manager has no incentive to alter the size of his plant.

AN ALTERNATIVE FORMULATION   Once again, it is instructive to consider an alternative problem. We can write the monopolist's profit function as

$$\Pi = P \cdot Q(L,K) - wL - sK$$

The manager will want to hire labor and capital up to the point where the marginal impact on profit of any further increase is zero:

$$\frac{\Delta \Pi}{\Delta L} = MR \cdot MP_L - w = 0$$

FIGURE 5.18   Economic profits (striped area) are consistent with monopolistic long-run equilibrium.

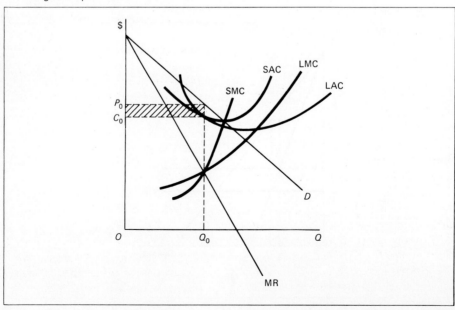

and

$$\frac{\Delta \Pi}{\Delta K} = \text{MR} \cdot \text{MP}_K - s = 0$$

Let's see if these conditions make any sense. Consider the purchasing decision for capital. An increase in K by 1 unit increases output by MP_K, and, because each unit increase in output increases total revenue by MR, the additional capital increases total revenue by $\text{MR} \cdot \text{MP}_K$. We call $\text{MR} \cdot \text{MP}_K$ the marginal revenue product of capital. When 1 more unit of K is employed, total cost rises by s. Profit maximization requires that the increase in total cost equal the increases in total revenue.

We have seen earlier that

$$\frac{s}{\text{MP}_K} = \text{MC}$$

Thus, these conditions for profit maximization can be written in a familiar form, namely, that $\text{MR} = \text{MC}$.

Question Answer true, false, or undecided: A monopolist whose product sells for $1 and who pays labor $4 per hour maximizes his profits by employing enough labor so that the marginal product of labor is 4 units of output per hour.

Answer False. The monopolist maximizes profit by equating the marginal revenue product of labor ($\text{MR} \cdot \text{MP}_L$) to the wage rate ($4).

$$\text{MR} \cdot \text{MP}_L = 4$$

Now since the product sells for $1, the monopolist's marginal revenue is less than $1, and the only way in which profit can be maximized is for the marginal product of labor to be greater than 4 units per hour.

5.10

SUMMARY

In this chapter, we have examined the theory of the firm from the polar opposites of pure competition and monopoly. We have focused on these models because our experience has been that most managerial decisions can be analyzed with one of these two models. If the firm has very little market power, the manager can use the competitive model for decision making. In contrast, if the firm has appreciable market power, the monopoly model is appropriate.

We shall see in the chapters that follow that many managerial decisions involve cost minimization. For the most part, market structure is not an important consideration in these cases.

The monopoly model provides some guidance in a number of other situations where the firm has or can obtain some market power. For example, we will use this model to help us make the appropriate price and output decisions when a new product is being introduced or when advertising expenditures are being planned.

IMPORTANT NEW TERMS

Competitive market

Supply curve

Monopoly

PROBLEMS

5.1 Answer true, false, or uncertain: Since all firms in a competitive industry have equal marginal costs, it is meaningless to talk about more efficient or less efficient firms.

5.2 A monopolist maximizes profit by selling at a price of $2 when his marginal cost is $1.50. The rental price of capital is $0.75. Is he maximizing profit if the marginal product of capital is 2?

5.3 Suppose that a copper monopoly faces the following demand curve:

$$P = 100 - .01Q$$

(a) What is marginal revenue? (b) If the monopolist's marginal cost is horizontal at $4, what is the profit-maximizing output?

5.4 Answer true, false, or uncertain: A competitive firm will never operate where marginal cost is less than average variable cost.

5.5 Answer true, false, or uncertain: A monopolist charges a price that exceeds marginal cost.

5.6 Suppose that the retail grocery industry is composed of identical firms. Is the long-run supply curve of groceries positively sloped? If so, why?

5.7 The owner of a monopoly observes that a 2 percent increase in price results in a 1 percent fall in the quantity of output demanded. Evaluate: The manager should be fired.

REFERENCES

Becker, Gary: *Economic Theory*, New York: Alfred A. Knopf, Inc., 1971.

Ferguson, C. E., and John P. Gould: *Microeconomic Theory*, Homewood, Illinois: Richard D. Irwin, Inc., 1975.

Friedman, Milton: *Price Theory*, Chicago: Aldine Publishing Company, 1976.

Silberberg, Eugene: *The Structure of Economics*, New York: McGraw-Hill Book Company, 1978.

Stigler, George J.: *The Organization of Industry*, Homewood, Illinois: Richard D. Irwin, Inc., 1968.

MATHEMATICAL APPENDIX

5A.1

COMPETITIVE PROFIT MAXIMIZATION

The manager wants to maximize

$$\Pi = PQ - C(Q) \tag{A5.1}$$

where Π is profit, P and Q represent the price and quantity of output, respectively, and $C(Q)$ is the total cost function. To find an extremum, we set the first derivative equal to zero:

$$\frac{d\Pi}{dQ} = P - \frac{dC(Q)}{dQ} = 0 \tag{A5.2}$$

Thus, we see that marginal revenue must equal marginal cost. To ensure that we have a maximum, we must have

$$\frac{d^2\Pi}{dQ^2} = -\frac{d^2C(Q)}{dQ^2} < 0 \tag{A5.3}$$

Since $dC(Q)/dQ$ is marginal cost, $d^2C(Q)/dQ^2$ is the slope of the marginal cost. Thus, for the competitive firm, the marginal cost curve must have a positive slope at the point where marginal cost and marginal revenue are equal.

Alternatively, we could write the profit function as

$$\Pi = P \cdot f(x_1, \ldots, x_n) - \sum_{i=1}^{n} w_i x_i \tag{A5.4}$$

where $f(x_1, \ldots, x_n)$ is the production function and x_i and w_i are the quantity and price of the ith input.

The necessary conditions for profit maximization are

$$\frac{\partial\Pi}{\partial x_i} = P\frac{\partial f}{\partial x_i} - w_i = 0 \qquad i = 1, \ldots, n \tag{A5.5}$$

Thus, optimality requires hiring inputs until the value of the marginal product ($P\,\partial f/\partial x_i$) equals the input price.

Finally, we could write the conditions in (A5.5) as

$$P = \frac{w_i}{\partial f/\partial x_i} \qquad i = 1, \ldots, n \tag{A5.6}$$

which means that price must equal marginal cost.

5A.2

MONOPOLISTIC PROFIT MAXIMIZATION

The manager of the monopolistic firm wants to maximize

$$\Pi = PQ - C(Q) \tag{A5.7}$$

where $C(Q)$ is the firm's total cost function. The first-order condition for an extremum is

$$\frac{d\Pi}{dQ} = \left(P + Q\frac{dP}{dQ}\right) - \frac{dC(Q)}{dQ} = 0 \tag{A5.8}$$

which simply requires the equality of marginal revenue and marginal cost. The second-order condition to ensure a maximum of profit rather than a minimum is

$$\frac{d^2\Pi}{dQ^2} = \frac{d\text{MR}(Q)}{dQ} - \frac{d\text{MC}(Q)}{dQ} < 0 \tag{A5.9}$$

This means that the slope of the marginal cost curve must be greater than that of the marginal revenue curve.

Once again, it is illuminating to give an alternative derivation of the conditions for profit maximization. We saw that the firm's profit could be written as

$$\Pi = P \cdot f(x_1, x_2, \ldots, x_n) - w_1 x_1 - w_2 x_2 - \cdots - w_n x_n \tag{A5.10}$$

For the monopolist, price depends on the quantity produced. The necessary conditions for profit maximization are

$$\frac{\partial \Pi}{\partial x_i} = P \frac{\partial f(\cdot)}{\partial x_i} + f(\cdot) \frac{dP}{dQ} \frac{\partial f(\cdot)}{\partial x_i} - w_i = 0 \qquad i = 1, 2, \ldots, n \tag{A5.11}$$

But, since

$$P + f(\cdot) \frac{dP}{dQ} = \text{MR}$$

these conditions can be restated as

$$\frac{\partial \Pi}{\partial x_i} = \text{MR} \frac{\partial f(\cdot)}{\partial x_i} - w_i = 0$$

In other words, the marginal revenue product, $\text{MR} \cdot \partial f / \partial x_i$, must be equal to the input's price.

We showed earlier that

$$\frac{w_i}{\partial f(\cdot)/\partial x_i} = \text{MC}$$

These conditions for profit maximization thus ensure that marginal revenue equals marginal cost.

APPENDIX: THE DERIVED DEMAND FOR INPUTS

Numerous firms produce intermediate goods which are used in other industries as inputs. The sheet metal produced by some firms is used to produce machines, automobiles, and so on. The managers of firms that produce these intermediate goods are quite interested in what determines the demand for their products. In this appendix, we will examine the determinants of an industry's demand for labor and nonlabor inputs. As a by-product of this analysis, we will also come to understand why goods such as computers have become relatively less expensive over time and why goods such as education have become relatively more expensive over time.*

The exposition that follows contains several equations, but the level of the mathematics is not very high. In fact, the mathematics is really very simple, so don't be scared off! The analysis is surprisingly intuitive.

A.1

FIXED PROPORTIONS

The easiest production function to work with is the fixed proportions production function

$$Q = \min(\beta_L L, \beta_K K) \qquad (A.1)$$

which was introduced in Chapter 4. With this production function we will be able to obtain most of the results on the derived demand for inputs. A more general production function will be used later in this appendix to bring substitution effects into the analysis.

You should recall that the isoquants for this production function are right-angled. In particular, the isoquant for $Q = 1$ is right-angled with a corner at $K = 1/\beta_K$ and $L = 1/\beta_L$. There are two things to note about this production function. First, if we start at the corner of the isoquant for $Q = 1$ and increase labor and capital each by some common percentage, then output will increase by the same percentage. For example, by tripling inputs, output becomes

$$Q = \min \left(\beta_L \frac{3}{\beta_L}, \beta_K \frac{3}{\beta_L} \right) = 3$$

By similarly starting at any other point on the isoquant for $Q = 1$ and increasing capital and labor by a common percentage, we will find that output will also increase by the same percentage. Such a production function is said to have constant returns to scale.

DEFINITION ▶ A production function is said to have *constant returns to scale* if a change in all inputs by a common percentage changes output by the same percentage.

---

*The material in this appendix draws heavily on H. Gregg Lewis's lectures at the University of Chicago on derived demand. We are grateful to him for allowing us to use this material.

Question   Answer true, false, or uncertain: The production function

$$Q = \min(L^2, K^2)$$

has constant returns to scale.

Answer   False. Suppose that $L = 1$ and $K = 1$. Then $Q = \min(1^2) = 1$. If labor and capital were to double to $L = 2$ and $K = 2$, then output would quadruple to $Q = \min(2^2, 2^2) = 4$. Clearly, a doubling of labor and capital has not doubled output; output has more than doubled. A production function with these characteristics is said to have increasing returns to scale.

The second thing to note about this production function is that the location of the isoquants depends on the efficiency or productivity of the inputs. If the efficiency parameter of labor (β_L) were to increase by 10 percent from β_L to $1.1\,\beta_L$ and the efficiency parameter of capital (β_K) were to increase 10 percent from β_K to $1.1\beta_K$, then the corner of the isoquant for $Q = 1$ would move toward the origin. This is seen in Figure A.1. Because labor and capital are more efficient, fewer units of labor and capital are required to produce 1 unit of output. To once again use our ditchdigging example, more efficient workers dig ditches faster than less efficient workers, and a well-designed shovel produces more holes from the labor of any given worker than a poorly designed shovel.

FEASIBLE INPUT COMBINATIONS   It is illuminating to present the isoquants somewhat differently. After dividing each term in equation (A.1) by Q, we have

FIGURE A.1   An increase in the efficiency of inputs will shift the isoquants closer to the origin. This indicates that fewer inputs are now necessary to produce each quantity of output.

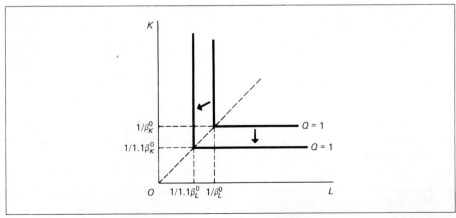

$$1 = \min\left(\beta_L \frac{L}{Q}, \ \beta_K \frac{K}{Q}\right)$$

What this means is that if the amount of labor used to produce each unit of output (L/Q) equals $1/\beta_L$, then $\beta_L\, L/Q = 1$ and $\beta_K\, K/Q$ must be greater than or equal to 1. In other words, the amount of capital used to produce each unit of output (K/Q) must be at least $1/\beta_K$. It is impossible to produce a unit of output with less than $1/\beta_K$ units of capital. Similarly, if the amount of capital used to produce each unit of output equals $1/\beta_K$, then no less than $1/\beta_L$ units of labor must be used to produce each unit of output. We have just verbally described a right-angled isoquant in L/Q and K/Q space with a corner at $L/Q = 1/\beta_L$ and $K/Q = 1/\beta_K$. This isoquant, which is graphed in Figure A.2, depicts the combinations of labor and capital that can be used to produce *each* unit of output. All points below and to the left of the isoquant are infeasible. This is just another way of saying that at least $1/\beta_K$ units of capital must be used to produce each unit of output and at least $1/\beta_L$ units of labor must be used to produce each unit of output.

COST MINIMIZATION The manager wants to minimize the cost of producing the firm's output. You may recall from Chapter 4 that total cost equals

$$C = wL + sK$$

By dividing through by Q,

$$AC = \frac{C}{Q} = w\frac{L}{Q} + s\frac{K}{Q} \tag{A.2}$$

After dividing each term in equation (A.2) by s and rearranging terms, we can write

FIGURE A.2   At least $1/B_L$ and $1/B_K$ units of labor and capital are necessary to produce a unit of output.

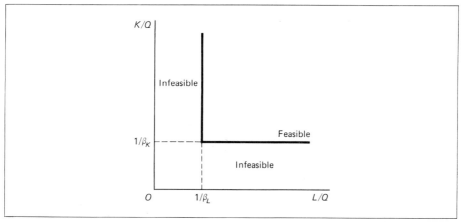

$$\frac{K}{Q} = \frac{AC}{s} - \frac{w}{s}\frac{L}{Q} \tag{A.3}$$

This is a straight line. We have plotted it in Figure A.3. The intercept on the vertical axis is AC/s, while $-w/s$ is the slope. This line gives the combinations of labor per unit output and of capital per unit output that are associated with the same average cost.

The manager minimizes costs by finding the lowest feasible average cost (AC). In Figure A.4, the manager could produce at an average cost of AC_0 by choosing the input-to-output ratios at points A or B. At point A, however, the manager is using more capital to produce each unit of output than he has to, and he can reduce the average cost of production by moving toward point C. Similarly, by moving from point B to point C, the firm can reduce its average cost by eliminating unnecessary expenditures on labor. Consequently, the manager minimizes the average cost by producing at the corner (point C), where average cost equals AC_1.

The firm will *always* minimize its cost by operating at the corner no matter what the factor prices are. Other feasible positions always involve unnecessary utilization of either labor or capital. At the corner C,

$$\frac{K}{Q} = \frac{1}{\beta_K}$$
$$\frac{L}{Q} = \frac{1}{\beta_L} \tag{A.4}$$

FIGURE A.3   Combinations of L/Q and K/Q that hold per unit cost constant.

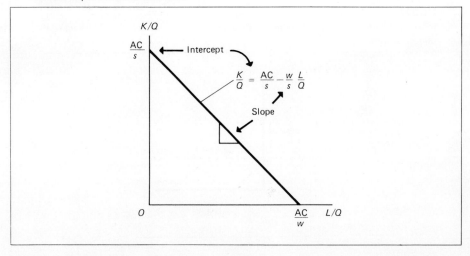

Equations (A.4) give the cost-minimizing input-to-output ratios for any set of factor efficiency parameters.

FIRM AND INDUSTRY SUPPLY CURVES We are now in a position to explicitly derive the firm's cost-minimizing average cost. Solving (A.4) for L and K and substituting into the cost equation, we have

$$C = wL + sK$$

$$= w\frac{Q}{\beta_L} + s\frac{Q}{\beta_K} \tag{A.5}$$

We obtain average cost by dividing equation (A.5) by Q:

$$AC = \frac{w}{\beta_L} + \frac{s}{\beta_K}$$

Let's assume that the firm is unable to affect the prices that it pays for labor and for capital. Then average cost is unrelated to output. This means that the average cost curve is horizontal. Since the average cost curve is horizontal, the marginal cost equals average cost. As a result,

$$MC = AC = \frac{w}{\beta_L} + \frac{s}{\beta_K} \tag{A.6}$$

and if the firm is in a competitive industry, then equation (A.6) gives this

FIGURE A.4   The manager will minimize the average cost of production by employing $1/B_L$ units of labor and $1/B_K$ units of capital per unit of output.

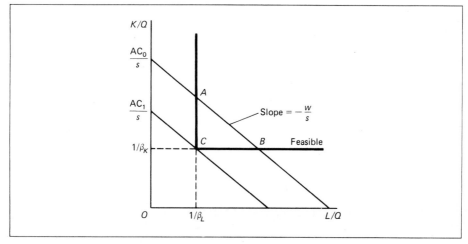

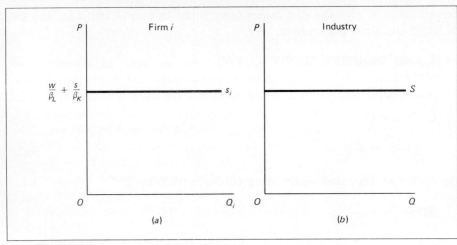

FIGURE A.5 Firm and industry supply curve:
are horizontal with constant returns to scale
production and unchanging input prices.

firm's supply curve, which is depicted in panel (*a*) of Figure A.5. If every firm
in the industry has the same production function and faces the same input
prices, then the industry supply curve is also horizontal at the price
$w/\beta_L + s/\beta_K$. The industry supply curve is graphed in panel (*b*) of Figure A.5.

FIGURE A.6   (a) The effects of movement
along a demand curve and (b) shifts of
the demand curve on the quantity sold.

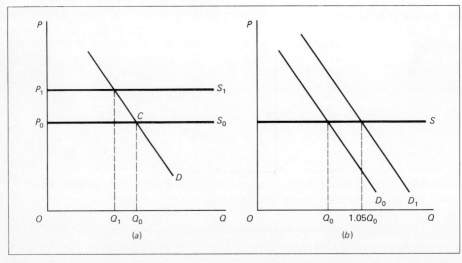

There is a demand curve for the product produced by this industry, and the equilibrium output is where the industry demand curve intersects the industry supply curve, as at point C in panel (*a*) of Figure A.6.

Question How many firms are there in this industry?

Answer The number of firms cannot be determined. The demand curve will intersect the supply curve at the price $w/\beta_L + s/\beta_K$. Consequently, the competitive firm's marginal revenue curve is a horizontal line at the price $w/\beta_L + s/\beta_K$. But the firm's marginal cost curve also is a horizontal line at that price. This means that marginal cost equals marginal revenue at every quantity. The firm's profits are the same whether the manager produces 1 unit of output or 100,000 units of output. Thus, we cannot determine how much any one firm will produce. And if we do not know how much each firm produces, we cannot know how many firms will be required to produce the total industry output. The total industry output of, say, 100,000 units could be produced by one firm or as many as 100,000 firms.

CHANGES IN QUANTITY DEMANDED As the supply curve shifts up and down, the equilibrium position moves along the demand curve. In order to understand how much industry output falls as the price rises, we therefore must turn to the demand curve. In Chapter 3, the price elasticity was defined to be

$$\epsilon = -\frac{dQ}{dP}\frac{P}{Q} = -\frac{dQ/Q}{dP/P}$$

It is minus the percentage change in quantity (dQ/Q) divided by the percentage change in price (dP/P). Because the notation for percentage changes is cumbersome, we will create a simpler notation for percentage changes, the · operator.

DEFINITION ▶ $\dot{a}$, for any a, is defined to be the percentage change in a; $\dot{a} = da/a$.

The definition of the price elasticity accordingly can be expressed as

$$\epsilon = -\frac{\dot{Q}}{\dot{P}}$$

where $\dot{Q}$ is the percentage change in quantity and $\dot{P}$ is the percentage change in price. This definition can be rewritten as

$$\dot{Q} = -\epsilon\dot{P} \tag{A.7}$$

All this means is that if the price elasticity is 1.5, a 1 percent rise in the price (that is $\dot{P} = 1$ percent) will cause the quantity demanded to change by

$$\dot{Q} = -1.5(1 \text{ percent}) = -1.5 \text{ percent}$$

The quantity demanded falls by 1.5 percent. Similarly, a 1 percent fall in the price will cause the quantity demanded to rise by 1.5 percent.

SHIFTS IN DEMAND   Our discussion thus far has centered on movements along a demand curve in response to changes in price. The quantity demanded can also change because the demand curve shifts. Equation (A.7) can be rewritten to accommodate shifts in the demand curve:

$$\dot{Q} = -\epsilon \dot{P} + \dot{D} \qquad (A.8)$$

where $\dot{D} = $ percentage change in quantity demand at a given price as the demand curve shifts.

The first term on the right-hand side of equation (A.8) represents movement along a demand curve, while the second term on the right-hand side represents movement from one demand curve to another at a given price. Suppose, for example, that price does not change ($\dot{P} = 0$) and that because of an increase in income the quantity demanded at the current price rises by 5 percent ($\dot{D} = 5$ percent).

$$\dot{Q} = \dot{D} = 5 \text{ percent}$$

Thus, the quantity demanded rises by 5 percent, as can be seen in panel (b) of Figure A.6. There are, of course, other reasons for demand curves to shift. Other prices change and tastes may change.

FUNDAMENTAL EQUATIONS OF DERIVED DEMAND: FIXED PROPORTIONS   The change in the quantity of output is consequently related to changes in price and to shifts in the demand curve. But since price equals marginal cost

$$P = \frac{w}{\beta_L} + \frac{s}{\beta_K}$$

changes in output are ultimately related to (1) changes in factor prices (w, s), (2) changes in the efficiency of inputs (β_L, β_K), and (3) shifts in the demand curve.

Suppose now that the firm used *only* labor to produce its output and that 3 hours of labor are required to produce each unit of output. At a wage rate of $5 per hour, the price will be $15. A 10 percent rise in the wage rate from $5 per hour to $5.50 per hour would cause the product's price to rise by 10 percent, from $15 to $16.50. A 10 percent rise in the price of capital would not have any effect on the product's price because capital is not used to produce this product. This example illustrates the proposition that the effect of an increase in the price of an input on the product's price is directly related to the importance of that input. In particular, it can be shown that

$$\dot{P} = \alpha \left(\frac{\dot{w}}{\beta_L}\right) + (1-\alpha) \left(\frac{\dot{s}}{\beta_K}\right)^* \tag{A.9}$$

where

$$\alpha = \frac{wL}{wL + sK} = \text{share of labor in total cost}$$

$$1 - \alpha = \frac{sK}{wL + sK} = \text{share of capital in total cost}$$

Thus, the greater the share of labor in total cost, the more price will increase in response to an increase in the price of labor or a decrease in the productivity of labor. Similarly, the effect of a change in the price of capital or in the efficiency of capital on the product's price will be larger when a greater share of total costs goes to capital.

Equation (A.9) illustrates the general rule that if

$$x = x_1 + x_2 + x_3$$

then

$$\dot{x} = \frac{x_1}{x}\dot{x}_1 + \frac{x_2}{x}\dot{x}_2 + \frac{x_3}{x}\dot{x}_3$$

There are two other useful rules governing percentage changes. According to the first rule, if

$$x = x_1 \cdot x_2$$

---

*
$$dP = d\frac{w}{\beta_L} + d\frac{s}{\beta_K}$$

$$\frac{dP}{P} = \frac{d(w/\beta_L)}{P} + \frac{d(s/\beta_K)}{P}$$

$$= \frac{w/\beta_L}{P}\frac{d(w/\beta_L)}{w/\beta_L} + \frac{s/\beta_K}{P}\frac{d(w/\beta_K)}{s/\beta_K}$$

Using the $\cdot$ operator,

$$\dot{P} = \frac{w/\beta_L}{P}\left(\frac{\dot{w}}{\beta_L}\right) + \frac{s/\beta_K}{P}\left(\frac{\dot{s}}{\beta_K}\right)$$

But $\dfrac{w/\beta_L}{P}$ has a simple interpretation. Substituting for P and multiplying by Q we get

$$\frac{w/\beta_L}{P} = \frac{(w/\beta_L)Q}{(w/\beta_L)Q + (s/\beta_K)Q}$$

$$= \frac{wL}{wL + sK}$$

since

$$Q = \beta_L L = \beta_K K$$

Therefore,

$$\dot{P} = \alpha \left(\frac{\dot{w}}{\beta_L}\right) + (1-\alpha) \left(\frac{\dot{s}}{\beta_K}\right)$$

then

$$\dot{x} = \dot{x}_1 + \dot{x}_2{}^*$$

The second rule states that if

$$x = \frac{x_1}{x_2}$$

then

$$\dot{x} = \dot{x}_1 - \dot{x}_2\dagger$$

Using this latter rule, equation (A.9) can be rewritten as

$$\dot{P} = \alpha\dot{w} + (1 - \alpha)\dot{s} - \alpha\dot{\beta}_L - (1 - \alpha)\dot{\beta}_K$$

This result can be substituted into equation (A.8) to yield

$$\dot{Q} = \dot{D} - \epsilon\alpha\dot{w} - \epsilon(1 - \alpha)\dot{s} + \epsilon\alpha\dot{\beta}_L + \epsilon(1 - \alpha)\dot{\beta}_K \qquad (A.10)$$

Finally, since

$$L = \frac{Q}{\beta_L}$$

and

$$K = \frac{Q}{\beta_K}$$

then

$$\dot{L} = \dot{Q} - \dot{\beta}_L$$
$$= \dot{D} - \epsilon\alpha\dot{w} - \epsilon(1 - \alpha)\dot{s} + (\epsilon\alpha - 1)\dot{\beta}_L + \epsilon(1 - \alpha)\dot{\beta}_K \qquad (A.11)$$

and

$$\dot{K} = \dot{Q} - \dot{\beta}_K$$
$$= \dot{D} - \epsilon\alpha\dot{w} - \epsilon(1 - \alpha)\dot{s} + \epsilon\alpha\dot{\beta}_L + [\epsilon(1 - \alpha) - 1]\dot{\beta}_K \qquad (A.12)$$

---

*We can prove this:

$$dx = x_2 dx_1 + x_1 dx_2$$
$$\frac{dx}{x} = \frac{x_2 dx_1}{x_2 x_1} + \frac{x_1 dx_2}{x_1 x_2}$$
$$= \frac{dx_1}{x_1} + \frac{dx_2}{x_2}$$

†This can also be proved:

$$dx = \frac{x_2 dx_1 - x_1 dx_2}{x_2^2}$$
$$\frac{dx}{x} = \frac{x_2}{x_1}\left(\frac{dx_1}{x_2} - \frac{x_1 dx_2}{x_2^2}\right)$$
$$= \frac{dx_1}{x_1} - \frac{dx_2}{x_2}$$

Equations (A.11) and (A.12) are the fundamental equations of derived demand under fixed proportions. These equations appear to be much too difficult to understand. Actually, they summarize some rather intuitive results. To see this, consider an industry where the price elasticity equals $^4/_3$ and where $^3/_5$ of total cost goes to labor. Thus, $\epsilon = {}^4/_3$, $\alpha = {}^3/_5$, and $(1 - \alpha) = {}^2/_5$.

Question Suppose that the quantity demanded at current prices rises by 5 percent and that w, s, β_L, and β_K do not change (that is, $\dot{w} = \dot{s} = \dot{\beta}_L = \dot{\beta}_K = 0$). What happens to the derived demand for L and K?

Answer By substituting into (A.11) and (A.12) we find that

$$\dot{L} = \dot{D} = 5 \text{ percent}$$

$$\dot{K} = \dot{D} = 5 \text{ percent}$$

Since 5 percent more output is demanded at current prices, 5 percent more output will be produced. To produce 5 percent more output, 5 percent more labor and 5 percent more capital are demanded by the industry.

Question Suppose that the wage rate rises by 5 percent and that D, s, β_L, and β_K do not change. What is the effect upon the derived demand for labor and capital?

Answer By substituting into (A.11) and and (A.12) we find that

$$\dot{L} = -\epsilon \alpha \dot{w} = -\frac{4}{3} \cdot \frac{3}{5} \cdot 5 \text{ percent} = -4 \text{ percent}$$

$$\dot{K} = -\epsilon \alpha \dot{w} = -\frac{4}{3} \cdot \frac{3}{5} \cdot 5 \text{ percent} = -4 \text{ percent}$$

When the price of labor rises by 5 percent, marginal cost rises by labor's share in total cost ($^3/_5$) times 5 percent, or 3 percent. This, in turn, causes the price to rise by 3 percent. When the price rises by 3 percent, the quantity demanded falls by the price elasticity ($^4/_3$) times 3 percent, or 4 percent. To produce 4 percent less output, 4 percent less capital and 4 percent less labor will be demanded.

Question The price of capital increases by 5 percent while D, w, β_L, and β_K are unchanged. What is the impact upon the derived demand for labor and capital?

Answer By substituting into equations (A.11) and (A.12), we find that

$$\dot{L} = -\epsilon(1 - \alpha)\dot{s} = -\frac{4}{3} \cdot \frac{2}{5} \cdot 5 \text{ percent} = -\frac{8}{3} \text{ percent}$$

$$\dot{K} = -\epsilon(1 - \alpha)\dot{s} = -\frac{4}{3} \cdot \frac{2}{5} \cdot 5 \text{ percent} = -\frac{8}{3} \text{ percent}$$

As capital becomes 5 percent more expensive, marginal cost increases by capital's share in total cost ($^2/_5$) times 5 percent, or 2 percent. As a result, price rises by the same 2 percent. The quantity of output demanded falls by the price elasticity ($^4/_3$) times 2 percent, or $^8/_3$ percent, owing to the 2 percent increase in output price. As output falls by $^8/_3$ percent, the quantity of labor demanded and the quantity of capital demanded also fall by $^8/_3$ percent.

Question Suppose that special training caused labor's efficiency to increase. In particular, let β_L increase by 5 percent. What effect will this have on the derived demand for labor and capital?

Answer Substitution into (A.11) and (A.12) reveals that

$$\dot{L} = (\epsilon\alpha - 1)\dot{\beta}_L = \left(\frac{4}{3} \cdot \frac{3}{5} - 1 \right) 5 \text{ percent} = -1 \text{ percent}$$

$$\dot{K} = \epsilon\alpha\dot{\beta}_L = \frac{4}{3} \cdot \frac{3}{5} \cdot 5 \text{ percent} = 4 \text{ percent}$$

An increase in β_L by 5 percent means that 5 percent less labor is required to produce each unit of output. Thus, at any output level, 5 percent less labor will be demanded. But there is a second effect associated with labor's increased efficiency. Because less labor is required to produce each unit of output, the marginal cost falls. In particular, it falls by the percentage fall in the amount of labor required (5 percent) times the share of labor in total cost ($^3/_5$), or 3 percent. This, in turn, causes the output price to fall by 3 percent. In response to this 3 percent fall in price, the quantity demanded increases by 4 percent, and to produce 4 percent more output, 4 percent more labor and 4 percent more capital are demanded. When the two effects are combined, the quantity of labor demanded falls by 1 percent (= 4 percent $-$ 5 percent) and the quantity of capital demanded rises by 4 percent. Less labor is demanded because the increase in labor which results from the fall in price is less than the decrease in labor required to produce the given level of output.

Question Are the effects of a change in the efficiency of capital the same?

Answer The effects of a 5 percent increase in β_K are quite similar. Substitution into (A.11) and (A.12) reveals that

$$\dot{L} = \epsilon(1 - \alpha)\dot{\beta}_K = \frac{4}{3} \cdot \frac{2}{5} \cdot 5 \text{ percent} = \frac{8}{3} \text{ percent}$$

$$\dot{K} = [\epsilon(1 - \alpha) - 1]\dot{\beta}_K = \left(\frac{4}{3} \cdot \frac{2}{5} - 1 \right) 5 \text{ percent} = -\frac{7}{3} \text{ percent}$$

With a 5 percent increase in the efficiency of capital, marginal cost falls by capital's share in total cost ($^2/_5$) times 5 percent, or 2 percent. Since this causes the output price to fall by 2 percent, the quantity of output demanded rises by $^8/_3$ percent, and as a result the quantity of labor demanded and the quantity of capital demand increase by $^8/_3$ percent. But at any output level, 5 percent less capital is now required. Consequently, on net the quantity of capital demanded falls by $^7/_3$ percent ($= ^8/_3$ percent $- 5$ percent) and the quantity of labor demanded rises by $^8/_3$ percent.

Question   What would happen if both labor and capital became 5 percent more efficient? In other words, what happens to the derived demand for labor and capital when

$$\dot{\beta}_L = \dot{\beta}_K = \dot{\beta} = 5 \text{ percent?}$$

Answer   Substitution into (A.11) and (A.12) yields the following results:

$$\dot{L} = (\epsilon\alpha - 1)\dot{\beta}_L + \epsilon(\alpha - 1)\dot{\beta}_K = (\epsilon - 1)\dot{\beta}$$

$$= \left(\frac{4}{3} - 1\right) 5 \text{ percent} = \frac{5}{3} \text{ percent}$$

(A.13)

$$\dot{K} = \epsilon\alpha\dot{\beta}_L + [\epsilon(\alpha - 1) - 1]\dot{\beta}_K = (\epsilon - 1)\dot{\beta}$$

$$= \left(\frac{4}{3} - 1\right) 5 \text{ percent} = \frac{5}{3} \text{ percent}$$

You should fill in an explanation of these effects.

Question   Answer true, false, or uncertain: Technological change in a particular industry throws workers in that industry out of work.

Answer   Uncertain. If both labor and capital become more productive at the same rate, then by equation (A.13) the quantity of labor demanded increases if the price elasticity exceeds one and decreases if the price elasticity is less than one. Only if the price elasticity exceeds one will the increase in demand for labor, because more output is demanded, exceed the decrease in the quantity of labor required to produce the given output.

A.2

VARIABLE PROPORTIONS

Until this point, we have been assuming that firms do not substitute between labor and capital. We will now introduce substitution between inputs and see how this modifies the fixed proportions results. We will again assume that production functions have constant returns to scale.

The firm's production function may be written as

$$\frac{Q}{\beta} = F(L, K)$$

(A.14)

where $\beta =$ a parameter of the efficiency of inputs.

Suppose that with L_0 and K_0 inputs, Q_0 output is produced. Since the production function has constant returns to scale, the output obtained when inputs are multiplied by a factor λ is equal to λ times the original output:

$$F(\lambda L_0, \lambda K_0) = \lambda Q_0 = \lambda F(L_0, K_0)$$

If we let

$$\lambda = \frac{\beta}{Q}$$

the property of constant returns to scale can be used in equation (A.14) to show that

$$1 = f\left(\frac{\beta L}{Q}, \frac{\beta K}{Q}\right)$$

Once again, we have a curve that depicts the feasible combinations of labor and capital for the production of each unit of output. The feasible combinations of $\beta L/Q$ and $\beta K/Q$ that are implied by equation (A.15) are shown by curve AB in Figure A.7. Any point below curve AB is not possible; too few inputs are being used to produce each unit of output.

COST MINIMIZATION   Once again, the manager wants to minimize the cost of producing each unit of output. When each term in equation (A.3) is multiplied by β, we have

$$\frac{\beta K}{Q} = \frac{\beta AC}{s} - \frac{w}{s}\frac{\beta L}{Q}$$

This line gives the combinations of $\beta K/Q$ and $\beta L/Q$ which are associated

FIGURE A.7   Minimizing the per unit cost of production leads to a familiar result: hiring inputs such that $w/s = MRTS_{KL}$.

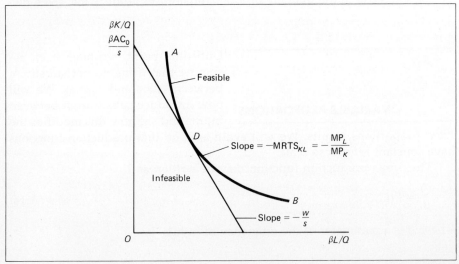

with the same average cost. Costs are minimized by finding the lowest such isoaverage cost line which is feasible. In Figure A.7, cost is minimized at point D, where the isoaverage cost line is tangent to the feasible curve AB. At point D, average cost equals AC_0. Any other feasible input combination is associated with higher average cost. It can be shown that the slope of the feasible curve is minus the marginal rate of technical substitution.* At the tangency, therefore, the usual cost-minimizing condition holds:

$$\frac{w}{s} = \frac{MP_L}{MP_K} = MRTS_{KL}$$

SUBSTITUTION BETWEEN INPUTS   As labor becomes more expensive relative to capital, w/s rises and the firm substitutes away from labor toward capital. In Figure A.8, an increase in the relative price of labor from $(w/s)_0$ to $(w/s)_1$ causes the optimum position to shift from point D to point E. There is an increase in the amount of capital used in the production of each unit of output (K/Q) and a decrease in the amount of labor used in the production of each unit of output (L/Q). This implies that the capital-labor ratio increases. In fact, the capital-labor ratio increases from the slope of line OD to the slope of line OE.

How responsive is the relative usage of capital (as measured by the capital-labor ratio) to changes in relative factor price?

DEFINITION ▶   The *elasticity of substitution* σ is defined to be the percentage change in the capital-labor ratio required to change the marginal rate of technical substitution by 1 percent.

$$\sigma = \frac{\dot{K}/L}{\dot{MRTS}_{KL}} = \frac{\dot{K}/L}{MP_L/MP_K}$$

The elasticity of substitution measures how easy it is to substitute between inputs. When isoquants are quite flat, it is very easy to substitute between inputs, and the elasticity of substitution is large. When isoquants have a great deal of curvature, input substitution is small. In the fixed proportions production function, the elasticity of substitution equals zero.

We are now in a position to quantify the substitution from labor to capital when labor becomes relatively expensive. Equation (A.14) can be rewritten as

$$Q = \beta F(L, K)$$

$$= \beta L \left(\frac{1}{L} F(L, K) \right) \tag{A.15}$$

$$= \beta L F(1, K/L)$$

$$\text{*} \qquad 0 = \frac{\partial F(L, K)}{\partial L} d \frac{\beta L}{Q} + \frac{\partial F(L, K)}{\partial K} d \frac{\beta K}{Q}$$

$$\frac{d(\beta K/Q)}{d(\beta L/Q)} = -\frac{\partial F(L, K)/\partial L}{\partial F(L, K)/\partial K} = -\frac{MP_L}{MP_K} = -MRTS_{KL}$$

The last result follows from the production function's having constant returns to scale. It is convenient to rewrite this as

$$Q = \beta L f(K/L) \tag{A.16}$$

where

$$f(K/L) = F(1, K/L)$$

Let us *define* $1 - \mu$ to equal $\dfrac{f(\dot{K}, L)}{(\dot{K}/L)}$. Equation (A.16) can be rewritten in terms of percentage changes as

$$\dot{Q} = \dot{\beta} + \dot{L} + \dot{f}(K/L)$$

$$= \dot{\beta} + \dot{L} + (1 - \mu)\left(\frac{\dot{K}}{L}\right) \tag{A.17}$$

By definition

$$\frac{\dot{K}}{L} = \sigma\left(\frac{MP_L}{MP_K}\right)$$

and since $w/s = MP_L/MP_K$ in equilibrium, we can write this as

FIGURE A.8 An increase in the relative price of labor (w/s) leads to a reduction in the amount of labor used in the production of each unit of output and to an increase in the amount of capital used n the production of each unit of output, thereby increasing the capital ratio.

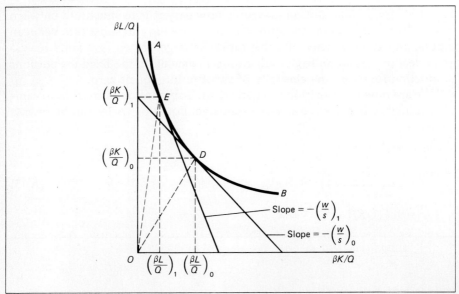

$$\frac{\dot{K}}{L} = \sigma\left(\frac{\dot{w}}{s}\right)$$ (A.18)

When equations (A.17) and (A.18) are combined

$$\frac{\dot{\beta}L}{Q} = -(1-\mu)\sigma\left(\frac{\dot{w}}{s}\right)$$

Finally, it can be shown that in equilibrium $\mu = \alpha$.* Therefore,

$$\frac{\dot{\beta}L}{Q} = -(1-\alpha)\sigma\left(\frac{\dot{w}}{s}\right)$$ (A.19)

Similarly, it can be shown that

$$\frac{\dot{\beta}K}{Q} = \alpha\sigma\left(\frac{\dot{w}}{s}\right)$$ (A.20)

FUNDAMENTAL EQUATIONS OF DERIVED-DEMAND: VARIABLE PROPOR-TIONS
If equations (A.19) and (A.20) are combined with equation (A.10) we have the following:

$$\dot{L} = \dot{D} - [\epsilon\alpha + (1-\alpha)\sigma]\dot{w} + (1-\alpha)(\sigma-\epsilon)\dot{s} + (\epsilon-1)\dot{\beta}$$ (A.21)

---

* $$C = wL + sK$$

$$AC = w\frac{L}{Q} + s\frac{K}{Q}$$

$$AC = \frac{w(\beta L/Q) + s(\beta K/Q)}{\beta}$$

$$\dot{AC} = \frac{w\beta L/Q}{\beta AC}\left(\frac{w\dot{\beta}L}{Q}\right) + \frac{s\beta K/Q}{\beta AC}\left(\frac{s\dot{\beta}K}{Q}\right) - \dot{\beta}$$

$$\frac{w\beta L/Q}{\beta AC} = \frac{wL/Q}{C/Q}$$

$$= \frac{wL}{C}$$

$$= \alpha$$

Therefore,

$$\dot{AC} = \alpha\left(\frac{w\dot{\beta}L}{Q}\right) + (1-\alpha)\left(\frac{s\dot{\beta}K}{Q}\right) - \dot{\beta}$$

$$= \alpha\dot{w} + (1-\alpha)\dot{s} + \alpha\frac{\dot{\beta}L}{Q} + (1-\alpha)\frac{\dot{\beta}K}{Q} - \dot{\beta}$$

$$= \alpha\dot{w} + (1-\alpha)\dot{s} - \dot{\beta} - \alpha(1-\mu)\left(\frac{\dot{K}}{L}\right) + (1-\alpha)\mu\left(\frac{\dot{K}}{L}\right)$$

$$= \alpha\dot{w} + (1-\alpha)\dot{s} - \dot{\beta} + (\mu-\alpha)\left(\frac{\dot{K}}{L}\right)$$

For given factor prices and input efficiency, long-run cost minimization implies that the average cost curve is horizontal. That is,

$$\dot{AC} = 0 = (\mu-\alpha)\left(\frac{\dot{K}}{L}\right)$$

For this to occur, μ must equal α.

$$\dot{K} = \dot{D} - [\epsilon(1-\alpha) + \alpha\sigma]\dot{s} + \alpha(\sigma - \epsilon)\dot{w} + (\epsilon - 1)\dot{\beta} \qquad (A.22)$$

These two equations describe the derived demand for labor and for capital in any competitive industry where there are constant returns to scale and where variations in the industry demand for factors do not affect factor prices. The fixed proportions results described in equations (A.11) and (A.12) are special cases of the above equations when the elasticity of substitution σ equals zero. Since the only new results found in equations (A.21) and (A.22) are associated with changes in factor prices, we will now turn to a discussion of the effects of changes in factor prices on the quantities of factors demanded.

EFFECT OF A WAGE RATE INCREASE   If the wage rate increases while everything remains constant, equations (A.21) and (A.22) become

$$\dot{L} = -[\epsilon\alpha + (1-\alpha)\sigma]\dot{w}$$
$$\dot{K} = \alpha(\sigma - \epsilon)\dot{w}$$

This results in an increase in marginal cost, and as the product's price rises, the quantity of output demanded falls. As production falls, the quantity of capital demanded and the quantity of labor demanded also fall. These output effects should be very familiar by now. If the firm can substitute between capital and labor (that is, if $\sigma > 0$), the firm responds to the increase in the relative price of labor by substituting away from labor and toward capital. This substitution effect reduces the quantity of labor demanded and increases the quantity of capital demanded. When output and substitution effects are combined, they bring about a fall in the quantity of labor demanded. The quantity of capital demanded increases if the substitution effect overcomes the output effect. More precisely, the quantity of capital demanded rises if the elasticity of substitution is greater than the price elasticity.

EFFECT OF AN INCREASE IN THE PRICE OF CAPITAL   If the price of capital increases while everything else remains constant, equations (A.21) and (A.22) become

$$\dot{L} = (1-\alpha)(\sigma - \epsilon)\dot{s}$$
$$\dot{K} = -[\epsilon(1-\alpha) + \alpha\sigma]\dot{s}$$

In the now familiar output effect, the quantities of labor and capital demanded fall because the increase in the cost of production causes the quantity of output demanded to decline. If the firm is able to substitute between capital and labor, then the firm substitutes away from capital and toward labor as capital becomes relatively expensive. When output and substitution effects are combined, the quantity of capital demanded unambiguously falls as the price of capital rises. The quantity of labor demanded increases if the substitution effect is greater than the output effect; this occurs when $\sigma > \epsilon$.

This general framework can be modified to accommodate the existence of a monopoly, supply curves that are not perfectly elastic, short-run behavior, and other changes. We will not pursue any of these modifications in this book. Instead, we hope that our discussion of the derived demand for inputs has provided some insight into this process. We will now use some of the derived-demand apparatus to explain changes over time in relative prices.

A.3
CHANGES OVER TIME IN RELATIVE PRICES

As we saw in Chapter 2, the quantity demanded of individual products is determined in part by *relative* prices. If industry supply curves are horizontal over a substantial range of output, then relative prices will be determined principally by supply conditions. We have shown that the change in marginal cost in an individual industry can be rewritten as

$$\dot{P}_i = \alpha_i \dot{w} + (1 - \alpha_i)\dot{s} - \dot{\beta}_i$$

where

α_i = share of labor in industry i
$\dot{\beta}_i$ = percentage change in the efficiency of inputs in industry i

To examine changes in relative price, we must compare the change in the specific industry's price to the average change in prices in the economy. The average change in price is

$$\dot{\bar{P}} = \bar{\alpha}\dot{w} + (1 - \bar{\alpha})\dot{s} - \dot{\bar{\beta}}$$

where

$\bar{\alpha}$ = average share of labor in economy
$\dot{\bar{\beta}}$ = average rate of change in the efficiency of inputs in the economy

The change in the relative price of good i ($P_i/\bar{P}$) is therefore

$$\left(\frac{\dot{P}_i}{\bar{P}}\right) = \dot{P}_i - \dot{\bar{P}}$$

$$= (\alpha_i - \bar{\alpha})\,\dot{w} + [\,(1 - \alpha_i) - (1 - \bar{\alpha})\,]\dot{s} + \dot{\bar{\beta}} - \dot{\beta}_i$$

$$= (\alpha_i - \bar{\alpha})\dot{w} + (\bar{\alpha} - \alpha_i)\dot{s} + \dot{\bar{\beta}} - \dot{\beta}_i \qquad (A.23)$$

If both input prices are rising or falling at the same rate (that is, $\dot{w} = \dot{s}$), then the change in relative prices is determined solely by the difference between the economy wide rate of technological change ($\dot{\bar{\beta}}$) and the industry's rate of technological change ($\dot{\beta}_i$).

$$\frac{\dot{P}_i}{\bar{P}} = \dot{\bar{\beta}} - \dot{\beta}_i$$

For instance, suppose that inputs in industry i become 2 percent more efficient per year; this will cause the price of good i to fall by 2 percent per year. But if inputs in the average industry become 5 percent more efficient per year, average prices will fall by 5 percent per year, and the *relative* price of good *i* will *rise* by 3 percent (= 5 percent − 2 percent) per year. Consequently, the relative price in an industry which is experiencing relatively rapid technological change falls over time, and the relative price in an industry which is experiencing relatively slow technological change rises over time. One of the reasons why computers and calculators are much more prevalent in our society than they once were is that their relative prices have fallen. Relative prices have fallen in the computer and calculator industries because there has been much more technological progress in these industries than in other industries.

Question Answer true, false, or uncertain: Over time, the time spent in prison for most crimes has fallen; this is because judges have "gone soft."

Answer Uncertain or false. While it is possible that judges have become more lenient, their decisions may also be responses to economic forces. There has been very little technological change in incarceration. Consequently, incarceration has become relatively expensive over time, and society has responded by demanding less incarceration.

If factor prices do not change at the same rate over time, there are other forces in addition to relative technological change which mold relative prices over time. Equation (A.23) implies that if labor becomes relatively more expensive over time, then industries which have a higher than average share of labor in total costs will become relatively more expensive. This is because industries in which labor is unimportant experience a very small change in marginal cost compared to industries in which labor is much more important.

IMPORTANT NEW TERMS

Constant returns to scale

Elasticity of substitution

PROBLEMS

A.1 Answer true, false, or uncertain: As the price of capital rises, the quantity of labor demanded in the precision-tool industry falls.

A.2 Answer true, false, or uncertain: The production function

$$Q = L + 2K$$

has constant returns to scale

A.3 Assume that it takes 8 units of labor *and* 4 units of raw material to produce a bookshelf (i.e., this a fixed proportions production function.)

The price of labor is $1 and the price of raw material is $3. The price elasticity of bookshelves is 1.5. (Give numerical answers.)

(a) What is the price of bookshelves? (Assume the industry to be competitive.) Suppose the price of raw materials rises to $3.15. (b) What is the new price of bookshelves? (c) What happens to the quantity of bookshelves demanded? (d) What happens to the quantity of labor demanded?

A.4 Answer true, false, or uncertain: The price of crude oil rises by 10 percent. Therefore, the marginal cost of producing gasoline will rise by 10 percent.

A.5 An engineer predicts that technological change in the calculator industry will increase marginal productivity by 10 percent over the next 2 years. Since the price elasticity facing the calculator industry is 1.5, the quantity of calculators purchased is predicted by the consulting firm XYZ to increase by 15 percent over the next 2 years. Does this prediction seem reasonable? How would you respond as the consultant?

6 DECISIONS UNDER UNCERTAINTY

Until this point, we have assumed implicitly that the manager knew with certainty all the relevant variables. Specifically, when he made, say, a production decision, we assumed that he knew with absolute certainty the prices and quantities of the inputs that he would be using and the price that the firm would receive for the output. As a moment's reflection will reveal, perfect certainty is hardly the order of the day in the business world. For example, the prices that commodities and inputs will command tomorrow cannot be known with certainty because of the vagaries of supply and demand. Moreover, employees sometimes fail to come to work as scheduled for various reasons, and machines break down on a random basis. The examples are almost endless. In this chapter, we shall develop a framework for making decisions under uncertainty. We shall then use this framework to investigate the value to the manager of more accurate information about the future and optimal production levels in the face of uncertainty. Elsewhere in this book we shall discuss the roles that inventories, long-term contracts, and insurance play in coping with randomness and the effects of uncertainty on decisions regarding the firm's capital structure, prices, wage rates, and long-term projects.

6.1 RISK VERSUS UNCERTAINTY

The literature on randomness and how a decision maker can cope with a lack of perfect certainty no longer draws a distinction between risk and uncertainty. Frank Knight's traditional distinction was based upon the existence of probabilities that could be assigned to the possible outcomes when randomness was present.[1] For Knight, *risk* signified situations where the possible outcomes of a random event could be specified and the probability of each outcome's occurrence was known. *Uncertainty*, on the other hand, was said to exist when only the possible outcomes were known, but not the probabilities. For example, suppose we knew that there were ten slips of paper in a jar and that five were marked with a red dot, three had a green dot, and two had a blue dot. If the random event is the color that one draws when a single slip is selected from the jar, we know that the relative frequencies (i.e., the probabilities) of red, green, and blue are $5/10$, $3/10$, and $2/10$, respectively. This situation would be characterized as one of *risk* by Knight. In contrast, if all we knew was that slips of paper marked with different colors were placed in a jar, then we

[1]Frank H. Knight, *Risk, Uncertainty, and Profit*, Boston: Houghton Mifflin Company, 1921.

would not know the probability of drawing a red, blue, or green slip of paper. This would constitute an *uncertain* situation according to Knight's dichotomy.

In many contexts, this distinction has been dropped. The Bayesian notion of subjective probabilities can be employed to convert any uncertain situation into one of risk. In this process, a decision maker assigns to each random event his best guess of the "true" probability of the event's occurrence. This subjectively determined probability is then used to aid in decision making. In this way, the use of Bayesian statistics converts uncertainty into risk. Following most of the economics literature, we shall use the terms risk and uncertainty interchangeably.[2]

A subjective probability is a decision maker's best guess of the true probability of the event's occurrence. The true probability is called the objective probability and can be learned only by repeated experience with the particular uncertain event. But many investment opportunities are one-shot deals. The same opportunities are never repeated. Consequently, it is not possible to determine the true probabilities through repeated sampling. For this reason, probability beliefs in many business situations are subjective. For example, consider the manager who must decide whether or not to authorize an investment of $10 million in a carburetor design project. The value of the new design will depend upon the resulting gas mileage increase, which is unknown at the time of the manager's decision. His decision will depend on the subjective probabilities that he assigns to possible mileage increases and their resulting market value.

6.2

MANAGEMENT'S OBJECTIVE FUNCTION

Let us consider a very simple situation that involves uncertainty. Suppose that the input prices and the firm's production function are known with certainty but that the demand function facing the firm is random. Further, suppose that the manager must specify the quantity of output *before* she observes the actual price that consumers will pay for the commodity. This is not an uncommon situation facing a manager: farmers face considerable uncertainty about the price they will receive in the fall for crops planted in the spring, and producers of new fashion lines and new model cars often must produce a considerable quantity before they get any consumer reaction to their products. For simplicity, we shall assume that the product is perishable so that the manager will sell all the output rather than store some of it for future sales. Now the manager must recognize that the firm's profit is a random variable,

$$\tilde{\Pi} = \tilde{P}Q - C(Q)$$

[2]For a helpful survey of the economics literature, see John J. McCall, "Probabilistic Microeconomics," *Bell Journal of Economics*, vol. 2, Autumn 1971, pp. 403–433. Since McCall's survey appeared, there has been a flood of articles on the subject, none of which distinguish between risk and uncertainty. One who persists in this distinction is William Baumol in his *Economic Theory and Operations Analysis*, Englewood Cliffs, N.J.: Prentice-Hall, Inc., 1977.

because the price is a random variable. The tildes over Π and P denote the fact that they are random.

Up to this point, we have been proceeding on the assumption that the manager would attempt to maximize the firm's profits. Now, however, this is no longer possible. Since there is some degree of randomness in the profit function, profit is not completely under the control of the manager. In the case under consideration, the demand curve for the firm's product is random. This means that the demand curve shifts up and down according to some random process. In Figure 6.1, the average or mean price is denoted by $\bar{P}$.[3] The actual price, however, is subject to a probability distribution. In Figure 6.1, the frequency with which a price occurs $[\Pr(P)]$ is given by the height of the continuous bell-shaped curve. Thus, on any given day the actual price can be almost anything, but the relative frequency of prices far away from $\bar{P}$ is less than the frequency of prices close to $\bar{P}$. As an example, we can consider the following discrete probability distribution of prices:

Price	$5	6	7	8	9	10	11	12
Probability	.08	.14	.18	.20	.18	.12	.08	.02

Although we cannot predict the actual price for tomorrow, we can calculate the expected price. To do this, we multiply each possible price by the proba-

---

[3]The mean was defined in Chapter 3. The average or mean value also is termed the "expected value." For example, the expected value on the roll of a die is

$$1(^1/_6) + 2(^1/_6) + 3(^1/_6) + 4(^1/_6) + 5(^1/_6) + 6(^1/_6) = 3.5$$

This is a weighted average where each possible outcome is weighted by the probability of its occurrence.

FIGURE 6.1 Random demand for a competitive firm.

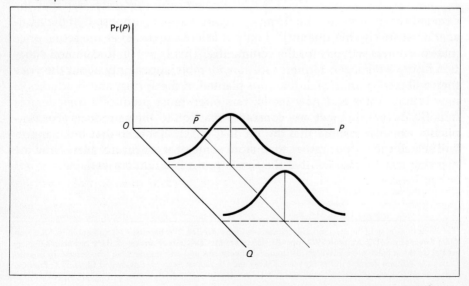

bility of its occurrence and add up the results:

$$\overline{P} = 5(.08) + 6(.14) + 7(.18) + 8(.20) + 9(.18) + 10(.12) + 11(.08) + 12(.02)$$
$$= \$8.04$$

Thus, the average (or expected) price is \$8.04.

When the relevant economic variables are *not* random, the manager of a competitive firm will produce that output where price equals marginal cost in order to maximize profits. In a world with random demand, she must select her output prior to knowing the actual price. The manager obviously cannot proceed as she did when demand was known with certainty. Since demand is random, profit is also random and it does not make sense to speak of maximizing a random variable. Consequently, we cannot speak of profit maximization. We must search for another objective function for the manager. Ideally, this objective function should take account of two factors: (1) the manager's attitude toward risk and (2) the manager's perceptions of the likelihood of various outcomes. Fortunately, the von Neumann–Morgenstern approach to decision problems under uncertainty accommodates both factors and provides a logical way to make decisions.[4] This is the theory of expected utility.

6.3

EXPECTED UTILITY THEORY

The idea that attitudes toward risk are important in evaluating risky outcomes is certainly not new. In the early 1700s, Nicolas Bernoulli examined a paradoxical situation where the expected value of a particular gamble was infinite, but no one would pay very much for the privilege of playing the game. The reason that was advanced at that time was that the value of money cannot be measured in proportion to its quantity but should be measured in proportion to the utility that individuals derive from it. Both Daniel Bernoulli and Gabriel Cramer recognized this and proposed specific functional forms for the utility function.[5] Over 200 years later, von Neumann and Morgenstern developed a set of axioms that describe preferences. If the axioms are accepted, then one is led to the proposition that individuals in risky situations will maximize the expected utility of wealth.

THE VON NEUMANN–MORGENSTERN AXIOMS Most textbook presentations of the axioms follow the particularly lucid presentation of Luce and Raiffa rather than the original treatment of von Neumann and Morgenstern.[6] We shall also follow the Luce and Raiffa treatment.

Axiom 1 An individual decision maker can compare any two risky alterna-

---

[4]John von Neumann and Oskar Morgenstern, *Theory of Games and Economic Behavior*, Princeton: Princeton University Press, 1944.

[5]Daniel Bernoulli, "Exposition of a New Theory on the Measurement of Risk" (1738), translated by Louise Sommer, *Econometrica*, vol. 22, January 1954, pp. 23–36.

[6]See R. Duncan Luce and Howard Raiffa, *Games and Decisions*, New York: John Wiley & Sons, Inc., 1957.

tives; i.e., he can determine whether he prefers alternative A to alternative B or is indifferent between them.

Axiom 2   An individual decision maker's preferences among risky alternatives are transitive. In other words, if A is preferred to B and B is preferred to C, then A must be preferred to C.

Axiom 3   Suppose that risky alternative A involves a payment of X or of Y and that the decision maker prefers X to Y. If risky alternative B contains the same payments, then the decision maker will prefer A to B if and only if the probability of receiving X is higher for alternative A.

Axiom 4   Suppose that there are three alternatives: A, B, and C such that A is preferred to B and B is preferred to C. It is possible to construct a risky alternative where A and C are outcomes such that the decision maker is indifferent between that risky alternative and the certain alternative B.

Axiom 5   If a risky alternative contains an outcome that is also risky, then the first alternative can be expressed in terms of the basic outcomes by using the usual method of combining probabilities. For example, suppose risky alternative A contains outcome Z_1 with probability p and Z_2 with probability $(1 - p)$. Alternative A can be expressed as

$$A = [pZ_1, (1 - p)Z_2]$$

Now let Z_1 be a risky alternative that yields W_1 with probability q and W_2 with probability $(1 - q)$. Let Z_2 yield W_1 with certainty. We can also express alternative A as

$$A = [PW_1, (1 - P)W_2]$$

where

$$P = pq + (1 - p) \qquad \text{and} \qquad 1 - P = p(1 - q)$$

Axiom 6   If the decision maker is indifferent between the riskless alternative B and the risky alternative $D = [pA, (1 - p)C]$, then he will not care which appears as a possible outcome in another risky alternative. In other words, the decision maker will be indifferent between

$$W = [qB, (1 - q)E]$$

and

$$Z = [qD, (1 - q)E]$$

This set of axioms has not escaped criticism, but if one accepts them, then it can be shown that the optimal decision is one that maximizes the expected utility.[7] In most individual decision contexts, we shall be concerned with the maximization of the expected utility of wealth. For firm situations, one often refers to the expected utility of profit. We will now see what it means to maximize expected utility.

---

[7]A fairly accessible proof is provided by Haim Levy and Marshall Sarnat, *Investment and Portfolio Analysis*, New York: John Wiley & Sons, Inc., 1972, pp. 226–227.

6.4

RISK PREFERENCES

Preferences for risk or attitudes toward risk typically are described in terms of the decision maker's attitude toward actuarially fair gambles. An actuarially fair gamble occurs when the expected value of the gamble is equal to the price of playing. For example, suppose a person were offered the privilege of the following gamble: she receives $5 if a tossed coin lands on heads, but must pay $5 if the coin lands on tails. Assuming that the probability of heads or tails is one-half, this is an actuarially fair gamble. The expected value of the gamble is

$$E(V) = \frac{1}{2}(\$5.00) + \frac{1}{2}(-\$5.00) = 0$$

which is the price charged for the gamble. In contrast, consider a raffle where a ticket costs $1, the prize is a $500 color television set, and there are 1,000 tickets sold. With 1,000 tickets, the probability of any ticket's winning is .001. The expected value of a ticket is

$$E(V) = .001(\$500) + .999(0)$$
$$= \$0.50$$

which is less than the price. As a result, the raffle is not actuarially fair.

If a person rejects all actuarially fair gambles, then she is said to be *risk-averse*. If a person prefers to take actuarially fair gambles, then she is a risk seeker, or a *risk lover*. A *risk-neutral* person is one who is indifferent regarding such gambles. The risk-averse person may also be viewed as someone who will pay a positive price to avoid risk. She will sacrifice something in exchange for a reduction in risk. On the other hand, the risk lover will pay something for the privilege of gambling. If someone were to open a gambling casino that offered actuarially fair games, risk lovers would pay for admission. Of course, risk averters would not enter the casino if the price of admission were zero. These attitudes toward risk are captured in the shape of the decision maker's utility function. We measure utility on the vertical axis and wealth on the horizontal axis in each panel of Figure 6.2. In panel (*a*) of Figure 6.2, we see a risk averter's concave utility function. Panel (*b*) contains the linear utility function of a risk-neutral decision maker. The convex utility function in panel (*c*) belongs to a risk seeker.

These utility functions can be used to gain a better appreciation for the various attitudes toward risk. Consider the risk-averse individual in panel (*a*) of Figure 6.3 that begins with wealth W_1 and enjoys a utility level of $U(W_1)$. Suppose she is offered a bet of $10 on the toss of a coin. If she accepts the bet, her new wealth level will be W_2 if she loses, where $W_2 = W_1 - \$10$, or it will be W_3 if she wins, where $W_3 = W_1 + \$10$. The individual is not concerned with the increments in wealth per se. Rather, she is concerned about the increments in utility. In Figure 6.3, we can see that the loss in utility if she gambles and loses, $U(W_1) - U(W_2)$, is greater than the gain in utility if she

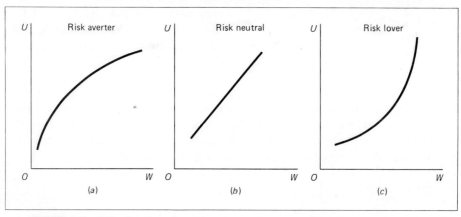

FIGURE 6.2   Utility functions for various attitudes toward risk.

gambles and wins, $U(W_3) - U(W_1)$. Suppose the gamble is actuarially fair in terms of money. In other words, the probability of losing $10 is equal to the probability of winning $10. But in terms of *utility*, the gamble is not "fair," because the size of the loss is greater than the size of the gain. Consequently, the risk-averse decision maker will reject the actuarially fair gamble. This, of course, does not mean that the risk averter will never gamble. It does mean, however, that the odds must be in her favor. Just how favorable the odds must be will depend upon the individual.

Compare this result to what happens when the same bet is offered to the risk-neutral decision maker or the risk seeker. In panel (b), we can see that · the changes in utility are equal for a $10 gain or for a $10 loss. Risk neutrality means that actuarially fair gambles in terms of money remain actuarially fair in terms of utility. Consequently, an actuarially fair bet makes a risk-neutral decision maker no better or no worse off. The risk seeker in panel (c) prefers risk, and we can see why. If she gambles and wins, the increase in utility,

FIGURE 6.3   Comparison of utility changes in a risky situation.

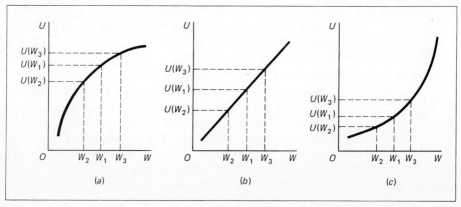

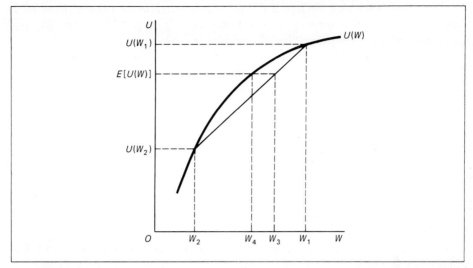

FIGURE 6.4   Expected utility and fire insurance for a risk averter.

$U(W_3) - U(W_1)$, is greater than the loss in utility, $U(W_1) - U(W_2)$, when she gambles and loses. This means that actuarially fair monetary gambles are actually in her favor in terms of utility.

The classic example of fire insurance serves to highlight these distinctions among risk preferences. First, let us examine the risk averter. In Figure 6.4, the risk-averse individual's concave utility function is labeled $U(W)$. Her wealth without any fire insurance will be W_1 if there is no fire and W_2 if there is a fire. For simplicity, we have assumed that a fire will do a specified amount of damage $(W_1 - W_2)$.[8] During any given time period, there is some probability p of a fire and, therefore, there is a probability p of the individual's actually experiencing wealth level W_2. Consequently, there is a probability $(1 - p)$ of no fire and a wealth level of W_1. The expected wealth level is W_3:

$$E(W) = pW_2 + (1 - p)W_1 = W_3$$

It is useful to be clear about one thing: the individual will *never* experience a wealth level of W_3. *Actual* wealth can only be W_1 or W_2. On average, the wealth will be W_3. The *actual* utility level will be either $U(W_1)$ or $U(W_2)$, but the expected utility will be

$$E[U(W)] = pU(W_2) + (1 - p)U(W_1)$$

As can be seen in Figure 6.4, the expected utility of wealth lies on the chord connecting the two possible points on the utility curve and is directly above the expected wealth level.[9]

---

[8]This is obviously a departure from reality, but it facilitates a graphical presentation. The more complicated case of multiple outcomes when there is a fire can be handled by the same principles.

[9]Levy and Sarnat, op. cit., offer a simple geometric proof of this proposition in their Appendix VI-2, pp. 228–229.

Fire insurance can remove the uncertainty surrounding the individual's wealth level. If one buys fire insurance, wealth is reduced from W_1 by the amount of the premium, but the resultant lower wealth is guaranteed by the insurance company. We know from our earlier discussion that the risk-averse decision maker prefers to avoid actuarially fair gambles. This indicates that she would be willing to pay more than the actuarially fair premium to avoid the financial risks of a fire. We can examine Figure 6.4 in an effort to find a *certain* wealth level that provides as much utility as the uncertain situation. The expected utility of the uncertain wealth is denoted as $E[U(W)]$ on the graph. We can see that the utility of wealth W_4 is precisely equal to the expected utility of wealth: $U(W_4) = E[U(W)]$. Thus, this particular individual would be indifferent between paying a fire insurance premium of $W_1 - W_4$ to guarantee a wealth level of W_4 and facing the uncertainty of a fire. If the insurance premium is less than $W_1 - W_4$, the utility level associated with purchasing fire insurance is greater than the expected utility level accompanying no insurance and she will maximize her utility by buying insurance. Try to show this.

In the fire insurance example, the actuarially fair premium would be $W_1 - W_3$ because this represents the expected loss in any time period. Thus, when the premium is $W_1 - W_3$, the insurance company expects to pay out as much money for claims as it takes in from premiums. Since our individual is risk-averse, she is willing to pay more than the actuarially fair premium to avoid risk. The difference between the actual premium and the actuarially fair premium is referred to as the "insurance loading." The loading part of the premium brings revenue to the firm to cover expenses other than casualty losses such as sales representatives' commissions, administrative expenses, and so on, and may also generate economic profit for the firm.

Question   Suppose that a particular individual's utility function can be written as

$$U = \sqrt{W}$$

Suppose that if there is a fire his wealth W equals 2,500 and that if there is no fire his wealth equals 40,000. There is a one-tenth probability of a fire. (a) Find the expected utility of his uncertain wealth. (b) What premium would he be willing to pay for the certain wealth level with the same utility? (c) Find the actuarially fair premium.

Answer

(a) The expected utility equals

$$\frac{1}{10}\sqrt{2{,}500} + \frac{9}{10}\sqrt{40{,}000} = \frac{1}{10}\cdot 50 + \frac{9}{10}\cdot 200 = 5 + 180 = 185$$

(b) The certain income associated with a utility level of 185 is $(185)^2$ or 34,225. He would be *willing* to pay

$$40{,}000 - 34{,}225 = 5{,}775$$

as a premium for a certain income of 34,225.

(c) The expected income equals

$$\frac{1}{10} \cdot 2{,}500 + \frac{9}{10} \cdot 40{,}000 = 250 + 36{,}000 = 36{,}250$$

Thus, the actuarially fair premium equals the difference between the no-fire income (40,000) and the expected income (36,250), which equals

$$40{,}000 - 36{,}250 = 3{,}750$$

Let's now turn to the risk lover. Since this optimistic person accepts all actuarially fair gambles, she may pose a problem for insurance companies. In Figure 6.5, we have drawn the risk lover's convex utility of wealth function. Additionally, we have put wealth levels W_1 (no fire and no insurance), W_2 (no insurance and a fire), and W_3 (the expected wealth level) on the wealth axis in the same place as in Figure 6.4. Owing to the convexity of the utility function, the chord joining the points on the function associated with W_1 and W_2 lies above the curve. As before, we can locate the expected utility of wealth $E[U(W)]$ at the point on the chord directly above the expected wealth W_3. This is what the individual experiences without fire insurance, i.e., by gambling. If we search for a certain wealth level such that the utility of the certain wealth is equal to the expected utility of the uncertain wealth, we find that W_4 fits the bill. For the risk lover, however, W_4 exceeds W_3. This means that the maximum fire insurance premium that will leave the decision maker as well off as without insurance is less than the actuarial value of the risk. Consequently, if insurance were provided to risk lovers, the average casualty loss would have to exceed the premium. This is not apt

FIGURE 6.5 Expected utility and fire insurance for a risk lover.

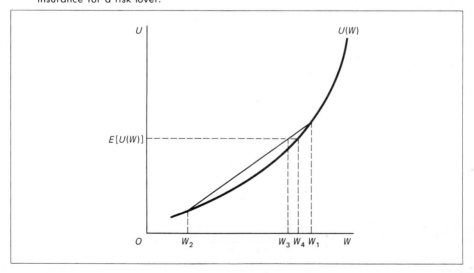

to interest many insurance companies since they would lose all of the other expenses associated with providing insurance in addition to the excess of the casualty losses over the premiums. Thus, insurance companies will not offer premiums which will be acceptable to risk lovers. *or people who are indifferent*

6.5

COMPARISON OF INVESTMENT OPTIONS

We can use these tools to compare several investment options in Figure 6.6. For example, suppose that option A will provide wealth levels W_1 or W_2 with probabilities p and $(1 - p)$, re-spectively. The expected wealth level $E(W)$ is calculated as $pW_1 + (1 - p)W_2$. Option B, on the other hand, offers a chance of a much greater gain W_3 but also exposes the individual to the chance of a much smaller payoff W_4. We can see that the difference between W_1 and W_2 is not very great compared to the difference between W_3 and W_4. We have constructed this example so that the expected values of the two options are identical. The decision maker will select the investment option that offers the highest expected utility. In this case, option A is obviously preferable: $E[U(W)]_A$ is greater than $E[U(W)]_B$. We can see that the dispersion of returns is greater for option B than for op-tion A. *For the risk-averse investor*, if two investment options have the same expected return, the one with the smaller dispersion will be preferred to the one with the larger dispersion.

Suppose a manager is faced with two R&D projects that each cost $1,000. In either case, the downside risk is the $1,000 expenditure that must be made initially. Project X offers a possible return of $3,000, while project Z may yield a $6,000 return. Let the probability of either outcome be one-half for project

FIGURE 6.6   Expected utility of two investment options.

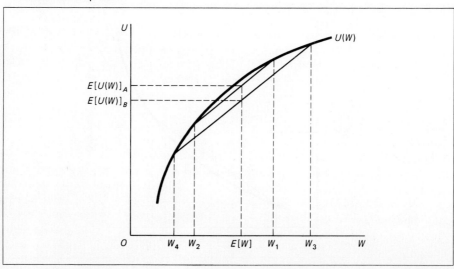

X. The expected value of the return is $1,000:

$$\frac{1}{2}(-\$1,000) + \frac{1}{2}(\$3,000) = \$1,000$$

In order for project Z to have the same expected value of $1,000, the probability of failure must be higher and the probability of success must be lower. In particular, project Z will have the identical expected value if p is equal to $^5/_7$:

$$\frac{5}{7}(-\$1,000) + \frac{2}{7}(\$6,000) = \$1,000$$

We can see in Figure 6.7 that a risk-averse project manager will select project X even though the downside risk is the same for X and Z and the maximum return is higher for Z. Again, this is the result of the return on project X having a smaller dispersion.

If two investment projects have the same dispersion but different expected values, the option with the highest expected value will provide the highest expected utility. This can be seen by examining the consequences of moving along a chord, such as AB in Figure 6.7. All readers should confirm this result for themselves.

6.6

MEAN-VARIANCE ANALYSIS

In the preceding section, we suggested the following decision rule:

Investment alternative A will be preferred to B if

FIGURE 6.7   Comparison of investment options.

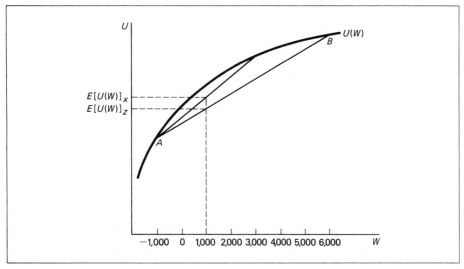

$$E(W)_A > E(W)_B \quad \text{and} \quad \text{var}(A) = \text{var}(B)$$

or

$$E(W)_A = E(W)_B \quad \text{and} \quad \text{var}(A) < \text{var}(B)$$

The variance was defined in Chapter 3. The variance of A measures the dispersion of A. This is the so-called mean-variance criterion developed by Harry Markowitz.[10] As a technical matter, the mean-variance criterion is strictly applicable only when decision makers are risk-averse and the random returns are subject to probability distributions with two parameters, which are independent functions of the mean and variance.[11] Under these assumptions, however, we can obtain a useful graphical interpretation that provides the basis for portfolio theory.

The mean and variance of every investment option can be calculated. Each option then can be represented by a single point on a mean–standard deviation diagram. In Figure 6.8, the expected return μ is on the vertical axis and the standard deviation of the return σ is on the horizontal axis. All points below the curve labeled EF represent investments or combinations of investments, while all points above the EF curve represent combinations of risk and return that do not exist. For example, point A may represent a single investment option or a combination of investment options with expected return μ_A and standard deviation of return σ_A. Point B, in contrast, represents a combination of risk and return that cannot be obtained from any single investment or from any combination of projects.

The EF curve is called the "efficiency frontier" because all points below the curve are dominated by at least one point on the curve. For example, if an individual is prepared to experience the risk associated with σ_A, he can obtain a much higher expected return than μ_A by moving to, say, point C on EF. Thus, C dominates A in the sense that it will be preferred to A. Similarly, if an individual is satisfied with an expected return of μ_A, he will not select A because a point like D will provide the same expected return, but involves a smaller standard deviation: $\sigma_D < \sigma_A$. Thus, A is not efficient, but points C and D are efficient. The efficiency frontier is analogous to a budget line; it separates attainable combinations of risk and return from unattainable combinations. A decision maker can select any point on the frontier according to his preferences for risk and return.

For risk-averse decision makers, return has positive value while risk has negative value. Thus, in order to induce a decision maker to accept a riskier combination of assets, one must increase the expected return on that combination of assets. Consequently, the indifference curves are positively sloped. In Figure 6.9 we have highlighted several indifference curves labeled U_1, U_2, U_3. Since higher returns are preferred to lower returns for the same risk, one increases utility by moving in a northwesterly direction. Given this individ-

---

[10]Harry M. Markowitz, "Portfolio Selection," *Journal of Finance*, vol. 7, March 1952, pp. 77–91.

[11]See Martin S. Feldstein, "Mean-Variance Analysis in the Theory of Liquidity Preference and Portfolio Selection," *Review of Economic Studies*, vol. 36, January 1969, pp. 5–12.

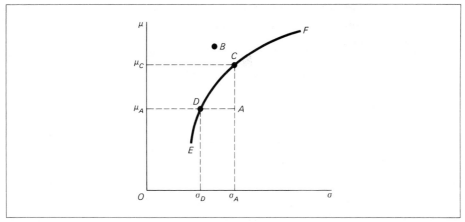

FIGURE 6.8   Efficiency frontier in portfolio analysis.

ual's preference function, the optimal combination of risk and return is σ^* and μ^* where U_2 is tangent to the efficiency frontier. The combination of risky assets that provides a return equal to μ^* for accepting risk σ^* is the optimal portfolio for this decision maker.

6.7

VALUE OF FORECASTING

It does not require remarkable insight to observe that the future is uncertain. And, as we shall see, this uncertainty imposes costs upon the firm. To the extent that the costs of uncertainty can be reduced by the manager, the firm's profits will be increased. Thus, the enlightened manager will attempt to mitigate the uncertainty that he faces. Nothing in this life is free, however. The manager must

FIGURE 6.9   Optimality in portfolio selection.

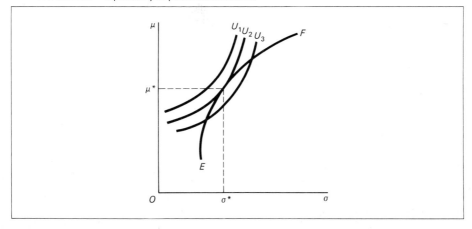

spend money to reduce the uncertainty that he faces. Accordingly, there is an optimal level of uncertainty. A simple example will make these general assertions a bit clearer.[12]

Consider a competitive firm that faces a random demand function. This means that the demand function is something like the one in Figure 6.1. We have plotted the *expected* price $E(P)$ for this firm in Figure 6.10. For simplicity, we have assumed a quadratic total cost curve, which yields a linear marginal cost MC curve like the one we have plotted. Since production is not instantaneous, the manager will have to select an output level prior to observing the price that the firm will receive for that output. As a result, the firm's profit is random. The least complicated case occurs when the manager acts in a risk-neutral fashion. This means that the utility function is linear and maximizing the expected utility of profit is equivalent to maximizing expected profit. It is clear that expected profit is maximized by producing where marginal cost equals expected price.[13] In Figure 6.10, we see that the manager will produce Q_0 in each period and sell it for whatever the actual price happens to be. Although this strategy maximizes *expected* profit, the output will usually not be optimal in any given period because actual price generally will deviate from the expected price.

Consider what happens when the actual price is P_1 rather than $E(P)$. If the manager had known that the price was going to be P_1, he would have produced Q_1 units of output rather than Q_0. This inability to tell the future costs the firm in terms of reduced profits. In this particular case, the firm's profits were smaller by the area of shaded triangle *cde*. The revenue forgone was equal to rectangle Q_0deQ_1. The costs saved by not producing the extra output are equal to the area under the marginal cost curve between Q_0 and Q_1, which leaves triangle *cde* as forgone profit. This area can be expressed as

$$\frac{1}{2}(Q_1 - Q_0)[P_1 - E(P)]$$

The slope of the marginal cost curve can be represented as

$$m = \frac{P_1 - E(P)}{Q_1 - Q_0}$$

Algebraic rearrangement yields

$$Q_1 - Q_0 = \frac{P_1 - E(P)}{m}$$

---

[12]The following example is taken from Richard R. Nelson, "Uncertainty, Prediction, and Competitive Equilibrium," *Quarterly Journal of Economics*, vol. 75, February 1961, pp. 41–62.

[13]Since expected profit is given by

$$E(\Pi) = \overline{P}Q - C(Q)$$

the maximization of expected profit requires

$$\frac{\Delta E(\Pi)}{\Delta Q} = \overline{P} - \frac{\Delta C(Q)}{\Delta Q} = 0$$

In other words, equality of expected price and marginal cost is required.

which can be substituted into the expression for lost profit:

$$\Delta\Pi = \frac{[P_1 - E(P)]^2}{2m}$$

If we look at the expected lost profit, we have

$$E(\Delta\Pi) = \frac{E\{[P - E(P)]^2\}}{2m}$$

But $E\{[P - E(P)]^2\}$ equals the average squared deviation of the actual price from the mean price, which is the variance of the price. Accordingly, we have

$$E(\Delta\Pi) = \frac{\sigma_p^2}{2m}$$

where σ_p^2 is the variance of the price. This expected lost profit is the cost of uncertainty. Notice that this cost depends only upon the slope of the marginal cost curve and the variance of price. The manager will be willing to pay as much as this to remove all uncertainty.

Suppose that a forecaster develops a model for predicting future prices early enough to allow the manager to adjust his production plans. His model is not perfect and does not remove all of the uncertainty about future prices. Consequently, the manager must determine how much the forecaster's services are worth.

If the forecaster predicts the price to be $\hat{P}$, then

$$E[(P - \hat{P})^2] = \sigma_u^2$$

is the expected squared difference between actual price P and predicted price $\hat{P}$. In other words, σ_u^2 is the average squared error of the prediction. We can show that the expected lost profits from the remaining uncertainty

FIGURE 6.10 The costs of uncertainty and the value of forecasting.

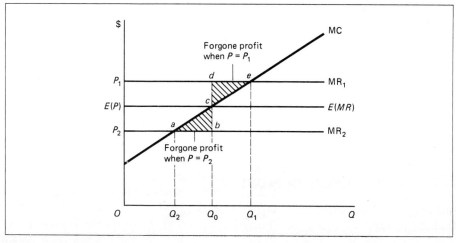

accompanying the forecaster's predictions are

$$E(\Delta\Pi') = \frac{\sigma_u^2}{2m}$$

Therefore, the *reduction* in lost profits that results from using the forecaster equals

$$E(\Delta\Pi) - E(\Delta\Pi') = \frac{\sigma_p^2}{2m} - \frac{\sigma_u^2}{2m} \tag{6.1}$$

In Chapter 3, the coefficient of determination (R^2) was defined to be

$$R^2 = 1 - \frac{\sigma_u^2}{\sigma_p^2}$$

in this case. With some algebraic manipulation, this becomes

$$\sigma_u^2 = \sigma_p^2(1 - R^2) \tag{6.2}$$

When equation (6.2) is substituted into equation (6.1) we get

$$E(\Delta\Pi) - E(\Delta\Pi') = \frac{\sigma_p^2}{2m} - \frac{\sigma_p^2(1 - R^2)}{2m} = \frac{R^2\sigma_p^2}{2m}$$

The manager should be willing to pay up to $R^2\sigma^2/2m$ for the forecaster's services

Question   An auto manufacturer calculates that the marginal cost of producing a car rises by \$1 with every 1,000 cars produced annually. The year-to-year variance in the price of automobiles (σ_p^2) equals 500^2. A forecaster is able to explain 80 percent of the annual variation in automobile demand (i.e., $R^2 = .80$). How much would the manufacturer be willing to pay for his services?

Answer   From the information given, $m = .001$. The value of the forecast thus equals

$$\frac{R^2\sigma^2}{2m} = \frac{.80 \cdot 500^2}{2 \cdot .001} = 100,000,000$$

Fortunately, because of competition among forecasters, automobile manufacturers do not have to pay this much for forecasters. While this technique may have limited applicability in determining whether *any* forecast is worthwhile, it can be quite useful in ascertaining whether a more sophisticated forecast justifies the additional expenditure associated with it.

6.8

MAXIMIZING EXPECTED UTILITY OF PROFIT

Let us consider how a risk-averse manager may behave when confronted by a random demand curve. For a competitive firm, random demand means that the manager cannot determine the price prior to her production decision. We shall assume that the product is highly perishable so that all of the output will be sold at the market-determined price. Under these circumstances, the manager will select the quantity of output that maximizes the expected utility of profit. The expected utility of profit equals

$$E[U(\tilde{\Pi})] = E\{U[\tilde{P}Q - C(Q)]\}$$

where E is the expectations operator. To achieve a maximum of expected utility, the manager must select the quantity of output where

$$\frac{\Delta E[U(\tilde{\Pi})]}{\Delta Q} = E\{U'(\tilde{\Pi})[\tilde{P} - C'(Q)]\} = 0$$

By the rules of expectations, we can write this condition as

$$E[U'(\tilde{\Pi})]E[\tilde{P} - C'(Q)] + \text{cov}[U'(\tilde{\Pi}), \tilde{P}] = 0 \qquad (6.3)$$

where cov $[U'(\tilde{\Pi}), \tilde{P}]$ is covariance between the marginal utility of profit and the price of the output;[14] the covariance between the marginal utility of profit and the price of the output equals the product of the correlation coefficient between the marginal utility of profit and the price, the standard deviation of the price, and the standard deviation of the marginal utility of profit. By algebraic manipulation, we can write equation (6.3) as

$$\bar{P} - C'(Q) = -\frac{\text{cov}[U'(\tilde{\Pi}), \tilde{P}]}{E[U'(\tilde{\Pi})]} \qquad (6.4)$$

Suppose that the manager was risk-neutral. The utility function would then be linear, as in panel (b) of Figure 6.2. For linear utility, the marginal utility of profit is constant. Since the covariance of a random variable ($\tilde{P}$) and a constant $[U'(\tilde{\Pi})]$ is zero, the risk-neutral manager would produce where

$$\bar{P} = C'(Q)$$

i.e., where the expected price is equal to marginal cost. This is the stochastic analogue of the usual model presented in Chapter 5.

The risk-averse case is more interesting. We can see that the utility function is concave in Figure 6.2. This means that the slope of the utility function decreases as profit increases. But profit will increase as the price increases. As a result, the marginal utility of profit and the output price move in opposite directions. Thus, the covariance between the marginal utility of profit and price {cov $[U'\tilde{\Pi}), \tilde{P}]$} will be negative. The expected marginal utility of profit $\{E[U'(\tilde{\Pi})]\}$ is always positive because the utility function increases monotonically. Thus, the right-hand side of equation (6.4) is positive. Now we can see the impact of uncertainty upon the risk-averse manager. She does not expand output to the point where marginal cost equals expected price. She stops short of that point because the covariance term in condition (6.4) acts like an additional cost.

These results are depicted in Figure 6.11. We have measured output on the horizontal axis and dollars on the vertical axis. A risk-neutral manager

---

[14]If X and Y are random variables, then the $E(XY) = E(X)E(Y) + \text{cov}(X, Y)$. In the present case, let $X = U'(\tilde{\Pi})$ and $Y = \tilde{P}$.

will select the output where expected price equals marginal cost, that is, Q_1 in the diagram. In contrast, a risk-averse manager will produce where expected price equals marginal cost *plus* the risk premium as measured by the covariance term. This output is Q_2 in Figure 6.11. At this output, the vertical distance between the marginal cost curve at Q_2 and the expected price $\bar{P}$ is equal to $-\text{cov}\,[U'\,(\tilde{\Pi}),\,\tilde{P}]/E[U'\,(\tilde{\Pi})]$.

Are these results consistent with our intuitive notions of risk aversion? The answer would appear to be yes. A risk-neutral manager will experience extra profits when price exceeds the average price and lower profits when price is less than the average. Owing to her linear utility function, equal deviations from the average profit are valued equally by the risk-neutral manager. In contrast, for the risk-averse manager, any decrease from the average profit has a greater effect on her utility than a comparable increase in profit. This stems from her concave utility function. The manager can reduce the chances of losses incurred from having to sell large quantities when the price happens to be low by systematically selecting a lower quantity of output. The risk-averse manager's caution is exhibited by a propensity to produce less than the risk-neutral firm.

Question   What happens when a risk-averse manager faces a known price, but her costs are random?

Answer   In this case, the expected utility of profit equals

$$E[U(\tilde{\Pi})] = E\{U[PQ - \tilde{C}(Q)]\}$$

Maximization of the expected utility of profit requires

$$\frac{\Delta E[U(\tilde{\Pi})]}{\Delta Q} = E\{U'\,(\Pi)[P - \tilde{C}'(Q)]\} = 0$$

FIGURE 6.11   Optimal output for a risk-averse and a risk-neutral manager.

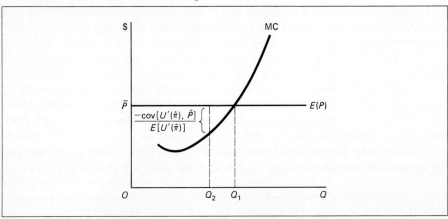

COPING WITH UNCERTAINTY

In this section, we have assumed that the firm can only cope with uncertainty by adjusting output levels. This, however, ignores many vehicles for dealing with uncertainty. The airline experience provides an example of a particularly aggressive way of handling uncertainty.

Commercial airlines are critically dependent upon reliable fuel supplies. In recent years, they have become dissatisfied with the current situation, where jet fuel is not always readily available. The consequence of their dissatisfaction is that they have begun to vertically integrate through contractual arrangements and actual ownership. In addition, the risk of being denied supplies has been reduced through supply-source diversification. TWA, for example, now buys jet fuel from 14 suppliers, where it used to buy from only 9.

Some airlines have become involved in the actual jet fuel distribution through owning and operating the support system (pipelines and storage tanks). Some airlines have even considered going into the refining business, but the costs of doing so have prevented this. American Airlines, however, has gone into the production of fuel. American hopes that it can produce enough fuel to reduce its dollar outlay for jet fuel.

Source: "The Airlines Move to Control Their Fuel Supplies," *Business Week,* Dec. 15, 1980, p. 103.

which can be written as

$$E[U'(\tilde{\Pi})]P - E[U'(\tilde{\Pi})]E[\tilde{C}'(Q)] - \text{cov}[U'(\tilde{\Pi}), \tilde{C}'(Q)] = 0$$

or

$$P - E[\tilde{MC}] = \frac{\text{cov}[U'(\tilde{\Pi}), \tilde{MC}]}{E[U'(\tilde{\Pi})]}$$

We know that $E[U'(\tilde{\Pi})]$ is positive because utility increases monotonically as profits rise. Furthermore, as marginal cost increases, profit falls, which increases the marginal utility of profit. Thus, $U'(\tilde{\Pi})$ and MC move in the same direction and the covariance is positive. Again, caution leads our risk-averse manager to restrict the firm's output to a point where price exceeds expected marginal cost.

6.9

SUMMARY

In this chapter, we have been concerned with risk and how it influences decisions. After defining risk and uncertainty, we examined the consequences for the manager's objectives. Uncertainty makes profit maximization an inappropriate goal of management since profit becomes a random variable. A search for an alternative objective function led us to examine the expected utility theory, which accommodates the random nature of profit and various attitudes toward risk. The impact of risk aversion, risk seeking, and risk indifference on decision making was analyzed. In particular, we compared some alternative investment options to gain an appreciation of how attitudes toward risk affected the choice of investments.

Since uncertainty causes some sacrifice of profit even for a risk-neutral firm, a reduction in uncertainty must be worth something. In fact, we developed the value of forecasting for a risk-neutral firm. Finally, we compared the output decision of a risk-neutral decision maker with that of a risk-averse manager. We found that risk aversion leads the manager to act cautiously by reducing the volume of output below the level that would maximize expected profit.

We shall return to these topics as we proceed through this book. Since uncertainty is pervasive in the business world, nearly every chapter will contain some topics that deal with risk.

IMPORTANT NEW TERMS

Risk

Risk aversion

Risk neutrality

Risk lover

Expected utility

Uncertainty

Efficiency frontier

Portfolio

PROBLEMS

6.1 In Figure 6.3, show why the actuarially fair gamble will be accepted by a risk lover.

6.2 Consider the example of investment options A and B analyzed in Figure 6.6. Prove that a risk lover will select option B rather than option A.

6.3 Examine Figure 6.7 where we found that project X was preferred to project Z because it provided higher expected utility. Will the project manager invest in either option if the other does not exist?

6.4 In the fire insurance example of Figure 6.4, suppose a new fire station is opened near the individual's home. As a result, the damage from a fire will be reduced by one-half from $W_1 - W_2$ to $(W_1 - W_2)/2$. What happens to the maximum fire insurance premium that can be charged?

6.5 In Figure 6.10, show that the forgone profit associated with producing Q_0 rather than Q_2 when actual price is P_2 is equal to triangle abc.

6.6 A popular hamburger chain outlet is located right across the street from Joe's Diner in Podunk, Florida. All the local residents eat at Joe's while the tourists eat at the chain outlet. Can this be explained by risk aversion?

6.7 There is a procyclical demand for many durable goods; that is, the demand for refrigerators and cars is greater in good times than in bad times. As a result, the demand for labor in these industries is greater in good times than in bad times and there is a tendency for earnings in these industries to be higher in good times than in bad times. Evaluate: if firms are risk-neutral and workers are risk-averse, there is an incentive for firms to provide earnings insurance (i.e., a more stable earnings stream) to workers.

6.8 Answer true, false, or uncertain: A firm with a relatively flat marginal cost curve has a greater benefit from a forecast about future prices than does a firm with a steep marginal cost curve.

6.9 Does the risk-loving manager produce more or less output than the risk-neutral manager? Why?

6.10 Consider a firm in a competitive industry with the following cost function:

$$\text{total cost} = .02 \, Q^2$$

where $Q =$ output

There is a 50 percent probability that the price will be $4 and a 50 percent probability that the price will be $8.

(a) Initially, the firm must set a production level prior to observing the price that it receives. Find (1) the output level that maximizes the firm's expected profits and (2) the expected profit associated with that output level.

(b) Suppose that the firm purchases an information service that enables it to know with certainty *prior to production* whether the price will be $4 or $8. (1) How much should the manager produce if he knows the price will be $4? (2) How much should the manager produce if he knows the price will be $8? (3) When the manager acquires the information service, he does not know what the price will be. He does know, however, that whatever the price turns out to be, the information service will apprise him of that price prior to production. Calculate the firm's expected profit when the information service is acquired.

(c) How much is a risk-neutral manager willing to pay for the information service described in (b)?

(d) Under what circumstances will the manager purchase the information service?

REFERENCES

Baumol, William: *Economic Theory and Operations Analysis*, Englewood Cliffs, N.J.: Prentice-Hall, Inc., 1977.

Green, H.A. John: *Consumer Theory*, New York: Academic Press, 1978.

Horowitz, Ira: *Decision Making and the Theory of the Firm*, New York: Holt, Rinehart and Winston, Inc., 1970.

Levy, Haim, and Marshall Sarnat: *Investment and Portfolio Analysis*, New York: John Wiley & Sons, Inc., 1972.

Nelson, Richard R.: "Uncertainty, Prediction and Competitive Equilibrium," *Quarterly Journal of Economics*, vol. 75, February 1961, pp. 41–62.

THREE

APPLICATIONS TO MANAGERIAL PROBLEMS

7 ORGAN-IZATIONAL DECISIONS

There are several managerial decisions that must be made before a potential firm begins its operation. These decisions are crucial to the firm's subsequent success. For example, someone must decide what, where, and how to produce the firm's output. In addition, someone must decide under what legal structure the firm will operate. These decisions are important because each can have a significant impact upon the firm's future profit or even survival. It is readily apparent that entry into the wrong industry, production in the wrong location, the wrong organizational form, or an inappropriate production process can result in a considerable loss of profit. What may not be so apparent is that such losses often can be prevented by the application of simple economic principles. In this chapter we shall examine several organizational problems that a manager may confront and apply some economic principles to them.

7.1

THE CHOICE OF PRODUCTS: ENTRY DECISIONS

Many businesses are not in existence for a long period of time; in fact, the average life expectancy of a business is 6 years. Most firms that go out of business do so because they have incurred economic losses. Some of these losses are needless and could have been avoided if there had been a careful analysis of whether the industries that these new firms entered could support additional firms. We will address this issue by analyzing first the case in which all firms in an industry have the same cost curves and subsequently the case in which cost curves vary from firm to firm.

IDENTICAL COST CURVES   Let us begin with the case where each potential firm in a particular industry has the cost curves shown in panel (a) of Figure 7.1. If each firm has access to the same inputs at the same prices, then the cost curves will be identical provided that the same production function is being used. We know from Chapter 5 that if there is a sufficient number of these potential firms, then the long-run industry supply curve would be horizontal at P_0, the price where the marginal cost curve and the average total cost curve intersect. The supply curve is horizontal because the entry and exit of firms over the long run will keep the price at P_0, where each firm is earning zero economic profit. When there is zero economic profit, total revenue is just large enough to cover implicit costs such as the value of the owner's time spent running the firm and the cost of capital equipment and buildings that are owned by the firm as well as explicit costs (e.g., salaries paid to truck drivers). Since each firm produces q_0 units in the long run, there will be

$$m_0 = \frac{Q_0}{q_0}$$

firms in the long run, where Q_0 is the quantity demanded at the price P_0.

If the number of firms currently in the industry (m_1) is less than the long-run number of firms, then each firm in the industry is making an economic profit. This situation is shown in Figure 7.2. With m_1 firms in the industry, the short-run industry supply curve is the summation of the m_1 marginal cost curves above the minimum point on the average variable cost curve. This supply curve intersects the demand curve at the price P_1. At that price, each firm's total revenue $P_1 q_1$ exceeds its total cost $c q_1$. Since the cost curve already includes the necessary payment for owned assets, the difference between total revenue and total cost represents an economic profit. It is these economic profits that attract entry into an industry.

Whether there are economic profits in the industry is a difficult empirical question. The existence of economic profits cannot be ascertained simply by observing them. The manager may infer economic profit by noting that the output per firm is greater than the long-run output per firm (q_0) or by noting that the current price exceeds the long-run price (P_0).

How can we reconcile the manager's pursuit of positive economic profit with the tendency of the market to push economic profits to zero for all firms? The managers of the first few firms that enter this industry are able to garner economic profit for some period of time. The entry of these firms, however, will shift the short-run supply curve to the right, causing the price to fall and each firm's profit to decline. As additional firms enter the in-

FIGURE 7.1   For a constant cost industry, long-run industry supply is horizontal [panel (b)] at a price equal to the minimum average cost of production [panel (a)].

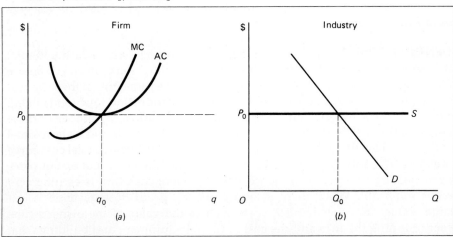

dustry, each firm's profit drops still further, and eventually (when the number of firms equals m_0) each firm makes zero profits.

There are, therefore, profits which a firm can make for a short period of time by entering an industry that does not have enough firms for there to be zero profits. A disequilibrium with respect to the number of firms in the industry arises because either the quantity demanded (Q) has changed or because the long-run output of each firm (q) has changed. To some extent, the changes in the quantity demanded and in firm output can be anticipated. The manager can use this knowledge to identify those industries with the greatest expected short-run profits. Moreover, good forecasting can be very important to the manager. This is because good forecasting helps the manager to be one of the first to discover short-run profit opportunities, and the first few entrants make the most profits.

Changes in the long-run output of each firm can be predicted with an understanding of the determinants of each firm's cost curves and of the nature of current technological change. A major factor behind many of the changes going on today in the optimal size of each firm is the computer. Computers have introduced additional scale economies into many firm operations. Because of this, the optimal size of each bank, for example, appears to be increasing. And an increase in the production of each bank, if not matched by a similar increase in the quantity demanded, must eventually result in a reduction in the number of banks. Such a reduction could be forecast with the appropriate information. This information obviously is not free. As we have noted, an understanding of cost curves and of the effects of technological

FIGURE 7.2   When there are too few firms in an industry, each firm earns positive economic profits [panel (a)] because the industry price P_1 exceeds the equilibrium price P_0 [panel (b)].

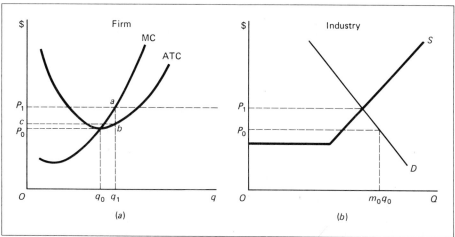

change on cost curves is required. Managers with an incomplete understanding of these factors will make mistakes. This is why managers use consultants who have specialized in these areas.

A temporary disequilibrium can also be caused by a change in the quantity demanded. We know from Chapter 3 that the quantity demanded of an industry's product depends on the price of that product, on real income, and on other prices. A change in any of these variables will result in a change in the quantity demanded and thereby in the number of firms. For instance, the number of firms in the fast-food business has increased as the demand for "fast food" has increased.

New firms, therefore, can best survive in industries where the quantity demanded is increasing or where optimal firm output is falling. A manager who is particularly astute in forecasting these trends can reap some short-run profits for his firm.

Question In the early 1970s, the Hyatt Regency in Atlanta was a very profitable hotel. The economic profits earned by the Hyatt Regency attracted entry, and five major hotels opened in the mid 1970s. None did well and two went bankrupt. What happened?

Answer The simultaneous entry of five new hotels caused occupancy rates at all major hotels to decline. This experience is not uncommon.

As a general proposition, some caution is necessary before leaping into an apparently profitable industry. This is because there are many other potential firms that could enter the industry. If enough of these potential entrants actually enter, all the firms in the industry would incur economic losses. For instance, suppose that there are 900 firms in an industry where the long-run equilibrium number of firms equal 1,000. The simultaneous entry of 500 firms into this industry would cause each firm in the industry to lose money. Consequently, information about the entry decisions of other potential firms can be very valuable; it may sometimes pay not to enter an industry that is attracting a lot of new firms.

DIFFERENT COST CURVES The assumption that each firm has the same cost curves is obviously an abstraction from reality. As we have noted, cost curves may vary from firm to firm because of differences across firms in managerial skills or in access to superior inputs. More efficient firms, by definition, are able to profitably produce at lower prices than are the less efficient firms. As the price rises, less efficient firms are drawn into the industry and the more efficient firms earn greater profits. In Figure 7.3, the price P_0 is too low for firm B to produce without losing money. Firm A, however, is making a profit at this price. Firm A would be willing to produce if the price were as low as P_1. For this reason, P_1 is called firm A's "entry price." It represents the price at which firm A enters the market.

In some ways, entry decisions are easier when there are differences across firms in cost curves. This is because it is easier to determine which firms will survive in any given industry: those firms with the lowest entry prices survive. A firm that is more efficient than the most vulnerable firm in the industry can make an economic profit by entering the industry. For example, the development of automation by Henry Ford made the Ford Motor Company more efficient than many other auto companies and was instrumental to the company's early success. An entrepreneur is therefore more likely to be successful if he establishes a company in an industry where he will be relatively efficient. In competitive industries, profits persist over the long run only for relatively efficient firms.

When there are differences in cost curves from firm to firm, some of the uncertainty about the entry responses of other potential firms is eliminated. When the product's price rises, only those firms with entry prices between the old price and the new price will enter the industry. Under these assumptions, there is no horde of identical potential firms to keep an eye on.

Potential firms, however, may have some uncertainty about how efficient they will be, and a significant fraction of business failures can be attributed to overoptimistic assessments of potential efficiency. To take one example, some people are not good at supervising others. If such a person opens a business, he may find this out through the failure of his firm.

Question Recently, a number of Asian agricultural economies were transformed from traditional economies where methods of farming were passed from generation to generation to dynamic economies characterized by the rapid development of new agricultural methods. What happened to the characteristics of farmers in this period?

Answer One of the benefits of education is that it helps us to recognize changes in our economy and to respond to them. More educated farmers are therefore more efficient in adopting new farming techniques than less educated farmers. The advent of rapid technological change in Asian ag-

FIGURE 7.3 When firms are heterogeneous they have different entry prices: A will enter at P_1, while B will not enter until the price is P_2.

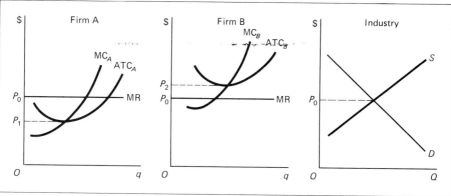

A PROBLEM IN
PRODUCT INNOVATION*

Due to the escalating prices of jet fuel and a change in the routing strategy of commercial airlines, there is an emerging demand for smaller, fuel-efficient commercial jets. Delta Air Lines was in the market for 60 such planes and wanted McDonnell Douglas's DC-11. The order, worth some $3 billion, would have been the largest commercial airplane sale in history. McDonnell Douglas turned down the order. Its DC-11 has not been built yet and may never be built as a result of McDonnell Douglas's risk aversion.

During the decade of the 1970s, McDonnell Douglas had not found commercial planes profitable. Consequently, the top management wanted to be careful about making DC-11 commitments. Since development and tooling for the DC-11 would cost $1 billion and the negative cash flow on early production would be another $1 billion in current dollars, McDonnell Douglas was trying to obtain a second airline's commitment before going forward with the DC-11. In addition to large guaranteed sales, McDonnell Douglas wanted the buyers to make substantial progress payments to help its cash flow during production. Moreover, it tried to spread its risk further by involving its future subcontractors. McDonnell Douglas wanted them to finance the development of their own components as well as make contributions to a general development fund. In return, each would receive a fixed percentage of the price of the plane.

While McDonnell Douglas was trying to piece this together, Boeing made the Delta sale by offering an exceptionally low price for an early commitment on its Boeing 757. Concern over being left out in the cold on the 757 may prompt United and American to make purchase commitments. If both United and American opt for the 757, there is a good chance that the DC-11 will never be built.

*Source: "The Big Deal McDonnell Douglas Turned Down," Business Week: Dec. 1, 1980, pp. 81–82.

riculture gave the more educated an advantage in farming which they did not experience under traditional agriculture.

7.2

INFLUENCE OF LICENSING FEES

In some industries, each firm must pay a lump-sum fee or tax for the privilege of conducting business. For example, many retail stores pay an annual operating license fee. This cost of doing business is rather interesting because it is a long-run fixed cost. Of course, it could be avoided by a firm's going out of business entirely and to that extent it is not really fixed. But in the short run or in the long run, it does not change with the size of the firm's output. To that extent, it acts like a long-run fixed cost. Let's see how the imposition of an annual operating license fee affects the manager's decisions.

We will consider a competitive industry in which some firms are more efficient than other firms. The demand curve and the long-run supply curve are represented in panel (c) of Figure 7.4 by D_0 and S_0, respectively. In long-run equilibrium, the industry produces Q_0 units of output at a price P_0. As can be seen in panels (a) and (b), the very efficient firm A produces q_0 at this output and the relatively inefficient firm B produces q_{10} at this price.

If a licensing fee equal to F per year is imposed, then the total cost of doing business in each year increases by F. Consequently, the average cost of producing q units per year rises by F/q. But since the fee does not vary with output, the marginal cost curve does not move. This means that MC in panels (*a*) and (*b*) goes through the minimum points on the pretax average cost curve AC_0 and on the posttax average cost curve AC_1.

As a result of the licensing fee, part of the original long-run supply curve of each firm is eliminated. For example, initially firm A's supply curve was that part of the marginal cost curve above the minimum point on AC_0. After the licensing fee was imposed, firm A's supply curve is that part of the marginal cost curve above the minimum point on AC_1. Thus, the bottom portion of each firm's supply curve is eliminated when a licensing fee is imposed. This is because a licensing fee makes production at low prices unprofitable.

At any given price, a licensing fee of $\$F$ per year reduces each firm's profits by $\$F$ per year. If a firm's pretax economic profits were less than $\$F$ per

FIGURE 7.4 A licensing tax raises average cost curves without affecting marginal cost curves. As a result, marginally profitable firms, like firm B, go out of business and more profitable firms, like firm A, expand production as the price rises.

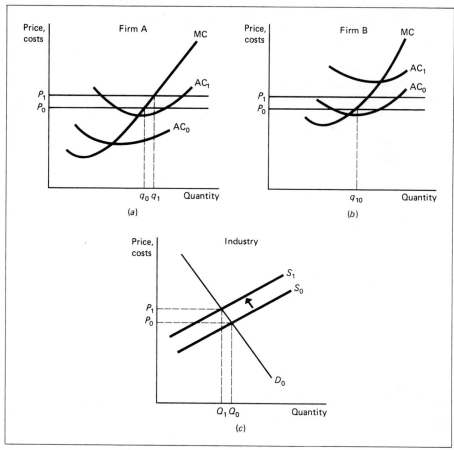

year, its manager would not find it profitable to continue production in the long run at that price. Thus, a licensing tax tends to reduce the number of firms producing at any given price, and as the bottom part of each firm's supply curve is eliminated, the industry supply curve shifts back.

In panel (c) of Figure 7.4, the industry supply curve shifts from S_0 to S_1, causing the price to rise from P_0 to P_1 and industry output to fall from Q_0 to Q_1. Firm B was making a very small profit prior to the imposition of the licensing fee. Under the licensing fee, this firm is unable to produce profitably at old price P_0 or at new price P_1. Firm A, on the other hand, was initially a very profitable firm. Under the licensing fee, firm A is able to continue to earn economic profits and in fact expands its production from q_0 to q_1 to take advantage of the higher price. We can therefore conclude that a licensing fee forces some marginally profitable firms out of business in the long run and elicits greater output from each of the more profitable firms that remain in the industry.

7.3

THE CHOICE OF PRODUCT QUALITY

Consider for a moment the purchase of an automobile from Fredd's Friendly Car Dealership. For $7,000, the customer may buy a car with a certain amount of fuel economy, comfort, and style and with a reputation for some level of durability. But the customer is also purchasing the proximity of the dealer to his residence or place of work, assistance in securing financing, a knowledgeable and honest sales and service staff, convenient hours for shopping and servicing, and so on. These are all components of product quality. When the manager alters any of these quality dimensions, she changes the product. Selecting quality in a sense is selecting the product to produce and sell. Thus, this analysis is very close to that contained in Section 7.1.

Consumers are willing to pay a higher price for a higher-quality good because a higher-quality good provides the consumer with more services. In the automobile example, consumers would be willing to pay more for cars that get 30 miles to the gallon than for cars that get 10 miles to the gallon, other things being equal. Consequently, each manager must choose between producing a low-quality good for a low price and producing a high-quality good for a high price.

It will be worthwhile to produce a higher-quality good if the increase in total revenue from producing the higher-quality good is at least as great as the increase in total cost associated with producing the higher-quality good. If it costs an auto manufacturer $100 per car to increase fuel efficiency from 15 miles per gallon to 20 miles per gallon and consumers are willing to pay $150 more for a car which gets 20 miles per gallon than for an otherwise identical car which gets 15 miles per gallon, then the manager can increase profits by improving the fuel efficiency of the automobiles her firm produces. But the manager will not choose to produce a car that gets 25 miles per gallon if it costs $130 per car to get the extra 5 miles per gallon while consumers are willing to pay only $105 more for cars with the additional fuel efficiency. We can see a principle that will become familiar: the profit-maximizing level of quality is the quality at which the increase in total revenue from adding 1 more unit of quality equals the increase in total cost associated with adding 1 more unit of quality.

This decision rule can be applied routinely to many quality decisions. It can be used effectively if managers recognize that the premium that consumers are willing to pay for higher quality varies over time and across customers. For example, the relative price of gasoline increased only 6 percent from 1969 to 1978. Consequently, consumers in 1978 were willing to pay very little more for fuel economy in 1978 than they were in 1969. Big cars were selling very well in 1978. In 1979, there was a dramatic increase in the relative price of gasoline, and the premium for fuel efficiency increased accordingly, resulting in plummeting big-car sales.

The premium for higher quality also varies across customers. To continue with our auto industry example, fuel has been relatively more expensive in Europe than in the United States for many years. For this reason, European auto manufacturers have found it more profitable to produce fuel-efficient cars than have American auto manufacturers. To take another example, working men and women and single persons are willing to pay more than others for items which reduce the time and effort in preparing meals, and much of the rapid growth in convenience foods in recent years can be attributed to the increase in the number of women working outside the home and in the number of single-person households. Another reason that the premium may vary is that some individuals may not be very efficient in securing financing for a major purchase. These individuals would be willing to pay a premium to get assistance in obtaining a loan.

Question Suppose the relationship between the price consumers are willing to pay and some index of product quality (v) is

$$P = 2v$$

The manager has discovered this relationship through many years of experience and experimentation. The cost of producing a unit of quality v is:

$$v + .1v^2$$

At what quality level is profit maximized?

Answer Profit equals total revenue (PQ) less total cost, or

$$\Pi = PQ - (v + 0.1\ v^2)Q$$

which can be written as

$$\Pi = 2vQ - (v + 0.1v^2)Q$$

by substituting for P.

Profit is maximized when the marginal impact on profit of a further increase in quality is zero:

$$\frac{\Delta\Pi}{\Delta v} = 2Q - Q - 0.2vQ = 0$$

This implies that

$$Q = .2vQ$$

or

$$v = 5$$

Profit is maximized by producing a commodity with 5 units of quality.

Consider the situation in Figure 7.5 where the original demand and supply of cotton shirts are denoted by D and S, respectively. The manager of a firm considers increasing the quality by processing the cotton to give it a "wrinkle-resistant" property. If he does so, the demand will shift to D' as consumers are willing to pay more for wrinkle-resistant cotton shirts. Of course, the costs of production will also rise. Thus, the supply function shifts to S'. The manager's optimal decision is to produce the lower-quality shirt. This conclusion follows from the fact that the demand price increases by the difference $P_1 - P_2$ while the cost increases by the difference $P_1 - P_3$. Since consumers value the wrinkle-resistant property by less than the cost of adding that property, the manager would lose profits by enhancing the shirt's quality.

FIGURE 7.5   If the cost of enhancing quality $(P_1 - P_3)$ exceeds the value placed on the higher quality by consumers $(P_1 - P_2)$, lower quality is optimal.

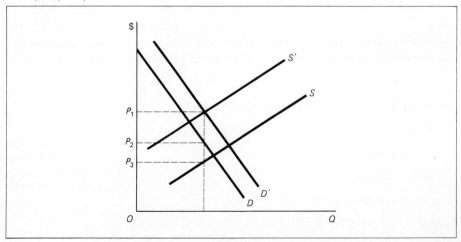

THE QUALITY OF AIR SERVICE*

Washington National Airport receives 68 percent of the passenger traffic destined for Washington, D. C., while Dulles Airport receives 14 percent and Friendship Airport (Baltimore) 18 percent. This is not surprising since National is just minutes from downtown, whereas Dulles is 26 miles away and Friendship 32 miles away. Due to congestion at National, it is very desirable to shift some of the traffic to Dulles. This, however, has encountered strong resistance from the carriers, and it is easy to see why.

Any product has several characteristics or dimensions. In the case of airline flights, there are the usual characteristics of convenience, comfort, safety, speed, and so on. One convenience feature is the proximity of the airport to the final destination. If an airline moved a flight to Dulles without any compensating change in its product, the quality would be deemed lower and the demand would fall.

Each airline is afraid to move unilaterally from National to Dulles because passengers will object to the inconvenience and switch to a competing airline that did not move. None of the airlines has mentioned offering a lower price to compensate for the added inconvenience. Instead, they have resisted pressures to move. One solution to the problem was offered by the Department of Transportation: move all high-density, long-haul flights to Dulles. In that way, no carrier would suffer a competitive disadvantage. In other words, each airline's product quality would fall by the same amount.

Question: Why might airlines still resist the above proposal?

Source: "Can Antitrust Immunity Lure Airlines to Dulles?" *Business Week,* Dec. 22, 1980, pp. 11–23.

7.4

THE SURVIVAL OF PRODUCTS[1]

In Chapter 3, we noted that consumers often have a demand for a collection of commodity characteristics rather than for the commodities themselves. Different types of food, for instance, provide calories, protein, and various vitamins in various proportions. Consumers purchase milk, butter, eggs, steak, and so on at least partly to obtain these calories, protein, and vitamins. In this section, we shall see that if the price of milk were sufficiently high, it would offer consumers an inefficient combination of protein and vitamin D. That is, consumers would be able to purchase this combination of protein and vitamin D at a lower price if they bought other foods. It is a grim fact of life in the market that goods that offer an inefficient combination of attributes are unlikely to survive for a long period of time.

The determinants of the survival of products are best understood if we examine a simple problem. Suppose that the consumer spends all her income—$100—on transportation services. There are two attributes associated with each mode of transportation: (1) distance traveled and (2) comfort. Let 4 miles of travel and 1 unit of comfort be associated with each unit of "walking." If a unit of walking costs $1 (in shoe leather), the consumer can purchase at most 100 units of walking with her $100 income. This allocation, represented as point A in Figure 7.6, would produce 100 units of comfort and 400 miles of travel.

---

[1] For an excellent treatment of this topic, see Kelvin Lancaster, *Consumer Demand: A New Approach,* New York: Columbia University Press, 1971.

The bicycle represents another mode of travel. Let us suppose that a unit of bicycling produces 4 units of comfort and 7 miles of travel and costs $2. Consequently, $100 would purchase 200 units of comfort and 350 miles of travel—position B in Figure 7.6. Positions on the line joining points A and B are possible if income is divided between walking and bicycling. In particular, if $50 is spent on bicycling and $50 is spent on walking, 375 miles are traveled and 150 units of comfort are obtained.

The streetcar or trolley represents still another means of travel. Let us assume that a unit trolley ride costs $2.50 and produces 10 units of comfort in the 2-mile ride. The consumer can buy up to 40 trolley rides. Point C in Figure 7.6 represents the purchase of 40 trolley rides. At this point, 400 units of comfort and 80 miles are obtained. As before, any point on the line between points B and C can be reached if the consumer divides her income appropriately between trolley rides and bicycle rides.

Similarly, any point on the line between points A and C could be obtained if income were allocated between trolley rides and walks. This, however, is an inferior allocation of resources because both more comfort and more distance can be obtained if income is allocated to some combination of trolley rides and bicycle rides *or* of bicycle rides and walks. Thus, in this simple model, consumers will *never* allocate their income between trolley rides and walks. They are better off if they choose other travel mode combinations, which are represented by line ABC. For example, by allocating income between trolley rides and walking, the consumer can spend all of her income and be at point D in Figure 7.6. But D is inferior to B because B

FIGURE 7.6 The efficient frontier with three goods—points below the frontier, such as D, are dominated by points on the frontier.

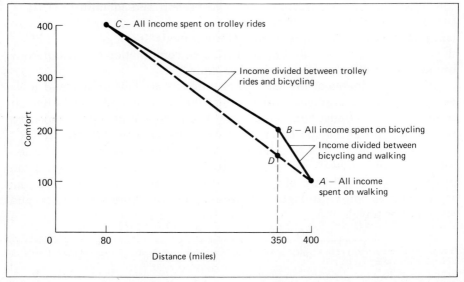

provides the same number of miles traveled but at greater comfort. All points below *ABC* are dominated by points on *ABC*.

Now let's consider what happens when a new mode of travel—the automobile—is invented. Under what circumstances will this new product survive? If it survives, will other products die?

We will assume that each unit automobile ride results in 1 unit of comfort and in 1 mile traveled. If a unit automobile trip costs $0.50, then the consumer is able to purchase 200 trips, which result in 200 units of comfort and 200 miles traveled. This position is labeled as point *D* in Figure 7.7. It is clear from the diagram that allocating money to automobile rides is inefficient because *D* lies below the frontier *ABC*. More comfort and distance can be obtained by allocating income between trolley rides and bicycling. Consequently, consumers will *never* allocate any money on automobile rides when the price is $0.50. At that price, the automobile is a new product that will not survive.

But this does not mean that the car is a product that is necessarily doomed to failure. If its price fell sufficiently, consumers would find that the automobile was an efficient mode of transportation. In particular, suppose that the price of a unit automobile ride fell to $0.357. The consumer then could purchase 280 car rides, producing 280 units of comfort and 280 miles of travel. In Figure 7.8, this allocation of income is given by point *D'*. Any point on *ABD'C* represents an efficient allocation of income, and consumers will choose some point on *ABD'C* as their most preferred point. That is, they will choose (1) to spend all their money on walking (point *A*), (2) to allocate their money between walking and bicycling (some point on *AB*), (3) to spend all their money on bicycling (point *B*), (4) to divide their income between

FIGURE 7.7 The introduction of the automobile—the automobile does not survive, because the price is too high.

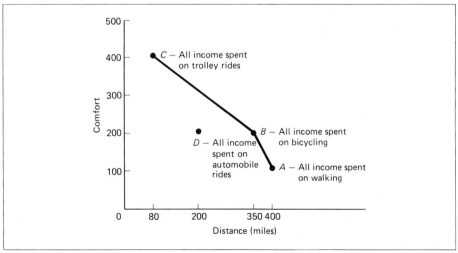

bicycle rides and car rides (some point on BD'), (5) to spend all their income on car rides (point D'), (6) to allocate their money between car rides and trolley rides (some point on $D'C$), or (7) to spend their money on trolley rides (point C). Allocating income between trolley rides and walks (AC), between trolley rides and bicycle rides (BC), or between walks and car rides (AD') is inefficient because these allocations lie below $ABD'C$. As a result, more comfort and distance can be obtained by picking a point on $ABD'C$ than by selecting inefficient allocations.

Sometimes a new product will force other products out of the market. It is easy to see why this happens. If a new product's price is sufficiently low, it is more efficient to use the new product in conjunction with several other existing products than to use some existing products in conjunction with the other existing products. Suppose that the price of a unit automobile ride falls to 0.30. Point D'' in Figure 7.9 depicts the combination of comfort and distance that is obtainable if all income is spent on car rides. Points on $AD''C$ represent an efficient allocation of income. Allocating *any* money to bicycling is then inefficient because more comfort and distance can be obtained by dividing income between car rides and walks. Thus, at this low price of automobile rides, there is no demand for bicycles. The attributes produced by bicycling are less expensively produced by using other modes of transportation. If, however, automobile trips were to become more expensive, bicycling would reemerge as a mode of transportation. And, in fact, the rising price of automobiles and of gasoline in recent years has been a major factor in the resurgence of bicycling in the United States.

We have seen that a new product offers consumers a slightly different combination of characteristics than do existing products. If a new product is

FIGURE 7.8 The introduction of the automobile—the automobile survives at a lower price.

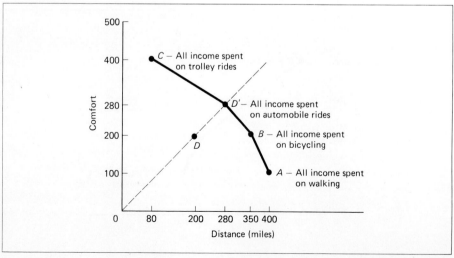

to survive, its price must be low enough to make that product an efficient choice. That is, products with relatively high prices will not be able to survive against other products offering a similar combination of the same characteristics. This principle of survivorship applies not only to new products but also to existing products. Accordingly, the introduction of a new product can make some existing products inefficient choices if the new product's price is sufficiently low. This was seen in our example where the introduction of the car led to the demise of the bicycle. To take other examples, slide rules went into oblivion when calculators became sufficiently cheap, and dried vegetables fell by the wayside with the development of frozen foods.

7.5

THE CHOICE OF PRODUCT MIX

The manager may wish to consider the production of more than one output. This decision is often affected by the relationships among products in the demand for products and in the supply of products. Let us first consider the effect on product mix of product relationships on the demand side.

Many products experience seasonal fluctuations in demand. For instance, the demand for soft drinks, ice cream, beach balls, and the like is greater in the summer than in other seasons. Consequently, in the off-months some relatively fixed inputs (e.g., equipment) are not fully utilized, and this is costly to the firm. One way in which the manager can reduce the cost of excess capacity in the off-season is to sell several products that have peak seasons at different times. This is one reason why swimming-pool supply

FIGURE 7.9   The introduction of the automobile—its price is so low that bicycling does not survive.

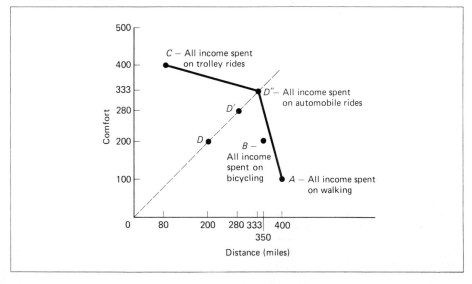

stores sometimes also sell snow-ski equipment and apparel. By doing so, the building and sales personnel are effectively utilized all year around. Similarly a department store manager is able to effectively deal with seasonality by reallocating floor space among departments; thus, toy departments expand at Christmastime and outdoor yard departments are larger in the summer.

Not all fluctuations in demand are seasonal, but a judiciously selected product mix can still be helpful to the firm. When demand rises and falls in some random fashion, the manager is unable to completely adjust the firm's resources to meet unanticipated demand changes. For this reason, some resources may be idle some of the time. Once again, excess capacity of some inputs is costly. The manager can reduce the costs of excess capacity by producing an array of products for which the peaks in demand occur at different times.

To see this, suppose that the demand for cola tends to rise when the demand for orange juice falls. Even if the manager cannot predict precisely when the demand for orange juice will be high, this negative correlation in demand can be beneficial. A firm that produces both orange juice and cola can save money by switching some of the inputs to cola production from orange juice production during periods of slack orange juice demand. It is clear that some inputs must be easily transferable from the production of one good to the production of the other good if cost savings from this product mix are to be realized.

This brings us to supply considerations. The production function may have a lot to do with the product mix selected by the manager. Some output mixes are simply more natural or cheaper than others. For instance, a manufacturer of leather wallets may find it profitable to use leftover scraps of leather to produce small leather items such as key holders. And a manager with a sufficient knowledge of chemistry to supervise one chemical process is also able to supervise other chemical processes. Furthermore, the by-product of one chemical process may be used as an input in other chemical processes. These are two reasons why chemical firms often produce more

CHANGING THE PRODUCT MIX IN A
FIGHT FOR SURVIVAL*

The market for heavy trucks has declined and is not expected to recover until 1985. Most firms in the industry feel that several of the seven existing producers will be forced to leave the industry. Since Freightliner is a small firm with only 7.8 percent of the market last year, one could be pessimistic about Freightliner's prospects. Freightliner's management, however, is confident that it will survive and expand its share to 10 percent by next year. In order to achieve this, Freightliner is planning to do two things to its product mix: (1) it will bring out heavier versions of its successful models for off-road uses—construction and logging—and (2) it will begin pushing a line of smaller trucks that Volvo produces for Freightliner.

Since all the truck producers will be competing for a smaller market, it is not certain that these efforts will work. The next few years will tell the tale.

*Source: "Freightliner: Girding for a Shake-Out by Broadening Its Truck Market," *Business Week*, Nov. 10, 1980, pp. 76, 78.

than one chemical output and do not combine the production of sulfuric acid with, say, the production of hamburgers.

These are some of the more important considerations that enter into the product-mix decision. Since a merger is one way of altering a company's product mix, these considerations also apply to merger decisions.

7.6

LOCATION DECISIONS

A manager, by properly choosing where to locate his plant, can have a considerable impact upon his firm's profits. He also must decide how many plants to operate. Should there be many small plants or a few large plants? The location of each of his plants is important because he may be able to reduce his transportation costs or take advantage of the geographic variations in wage rates, the price of land, and other input prices.

NO TRANSPORTATION COSTS To gain some perspective on the effect of transportation costs on the firm's decisions, let us first consider production in a multiplant setting with no transportation costs. Suppose that a particular plant has the cost curves shown in Figure 7.10. In a competitive industry, profit is maximized by producing q_0 units of output in this plant, for at this output, price equals marginal cost. This plant produces a profit of $(P_0 - AC_0)q_0$, which is given by the area of the shaded rectangle. Since this plant produces profits for the firm, the manager might be able to increase the firm's profit by adding another plant. Indeed, if there were no other considerations, profit would equal

$$n(P_0 - AC_0)q_0$$

where n = the number of plants

FIGURE 7.10 Profit maximization requires producing where price equals marginal cost. Profit equals the shaded area: $(P_0 - AC_0)\, q_0$.

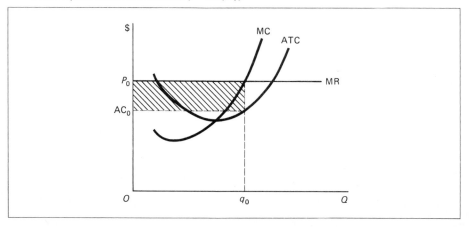

and profit would appear to be maximized by the operation of an infinite number of plants. The expansion of this particular firm, however, eventually would force the price down until the firm's profits equaled zero.

An increase in the number of plants may be accompanied, however, by an increase in the cost of producing in each plant. Reasons for this include managerial diseconomies. As the manager adds more and more plants, it becomes more difficult for him to supervise the firm adequately. The result of this is that per unit costs of production increase. Even so, it may still be desirable to add a plant. The criterion for adding one more plant can be illustrated by considering the decision to add a second plant. Suppose that each plant's marginal and average total cost curves rise from MC_0 and ATC_0 to MC_1 and ATC_1 when a second plant is added. As can be seen in Figure 7.11, the second plant itself has a profit which is given by the area of rectangle P_0abc, but when the second plant is added, the first plant experiences a reduction in profit which is given by the difference between the area of rectangle P_0def and the area of rectangle P_0abc. The second plant adds to the firm's total profit if the profit from the second plant is greater than the lost profit on the first plant. More generally, the nth plant adds to the firm's profit if the profit from the nth plant is greater than the lost profit on the first $(n-1)$ plants.

TRANSPORTATION COSTS: PRODUCTION COSTS INVARIANT Unfortunately, not much in the business world is free. Consequently, we must recognize that it takes resources to ship inputs (e.g., coal, wheat) to producers and to ship products to consumers. Let us assume for the moment that the producer pays the cost of shipping inputs to him and of shipping his product to

FIGURE 7.11   If the addition of plant 2 increases costs in plant 1, the manager must compare the additional profit contribution of plant 2 with the reduction in profit in plant 1.

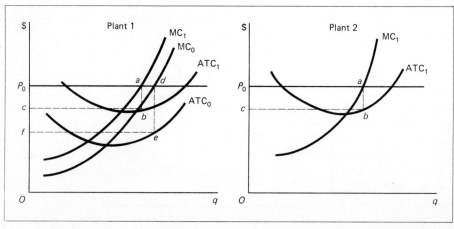

customers. For any given level of production and total revenue, profit maximization requires minimizing the total cost of transporting the inputs to the plants, producing the output, and transporting the output to customers. Let us assume for the moment that average production costs are not related to the number of plants or the output of each plant. Consequently, total costs are minimized by minimizing the sum of the cost of transporting inputs to plants and the cost of transporting outputs to customers.

For a number of services, like haircuts, the cost of transporting inputs (e.g., scissors) to the establishment is inconsequential. Consider an increase in the number of barbershops. As a result, there is a reduction in the number of customers served by each shop and the average customer travels a shorter distance to the barbershop. It is easy to see that total costs are minimized by locating a barbershop near each customer *if* input transportation costs are inconsequential and *if* average production costs are unrelated to the number of haircuts given in each barbershop. But we do not observe barbershops next to each house. As we shall see a little later, a likely explanation is that average production costs depend on how many haircuts are given.

For a great many products, however, input transportation costs are sizable. The manager is able to reduce the cost of transporting inputs to the plant by locating production closer to the source of the inputs (e.g., the coal mines, the wheat fields, the oyster beds, and so on). Generally, however, this causes production to be located farther from customers, which increases the cost of transporting the product to them. The manager will minimize costs by locating production so that the reduction in transportation costs that results from locating production closer to inputs is exactly offset by the associated increase in the cost of transporting the product to customers.

Question   If you were a cereal manufacturer, where would you locate your plant?

Answer   The principal ingredients in cereal are grain and sugar. Grains are grown in the Midwest, and sugar is a Southern product. A plant with a Midwest location would face low input transportation costs and would have very low distribution costs (i.e., the cost of distributing the product to consumers). In fact, many cereal companies have plants in the Midwest.

The location of plants thus depends on the benefits and costs of locating near inputs. These benefits and costs vary from product to product. In the early days of steel production, there were substantial benefits from locating steel plants next to coalfields because 4 tons of coal were used to produce each ton of steel. This is why Pittsburgh emerged as a center for steel production. In contrast to weight-losing processes like steel production, other processes involve a gaining of weight as inputs are combined. One such process is soft-drink production. Water, a major component in soft drinks, is readily available almost anywhere. Transportation costs are minimized if water is added in a location that is near the customers rather than near the source of other inputs such as sugar and flavorings. This is why soft-drink bottling plants are found in most large urban areas.

TRANSPORTATION COSTS: VARYING PRODUCTION COSTS Retail businesses exist to distribute products to consumers. For these and other firms, proximity to transported inputs is not a factor determining location. Under these conditions, we concluded that if average production costs were unrelated to the number of plants or the output of each plant, then costs would be minimized by locating a plant next to *each* customer.

But, in fact, production costs are related to the output of each plant and to the number of plants. For one thing, it may be very costly to supervise production in a large number of plants. Moreover, in large plants certain fixed inputs such as safes and office equipment are utilized more frequently and cost savings are realized that are associated with the specialization of inputs.

As a general proposition, a firm will reduce its costs by adding an additional plant if this results in transportation costs falling more than production costs rise. Only when the reduction in transportation costs associated with having smaller service areas equals the increase in production costs due to there being smaller plants will the firm have no incentive to increase the number of plants.

We should note that the firm has an incentive to minimize the sum of production and transportation costs even if the firm does not pay the transportation costs. This is because the customer is willing to pay a higher price to a firm that reduces the customer's transportation expenses. For example, the customer would be willing to pay up to $15 more for a product that reduces the customer's transportation expenses by $15.

Question Will hardware stores be larger in urban areas than in rural areas?

Answer Yes. It is easier to achieve production economies in urban areas. In an urban area, customers of a hardware store serving 30,000 people have no more than, say, a 6-mile round-trip drive to the store, while in a rural area, customers of a store serving the same number of people have as much as, say, a 30-mile round-trip drive to the hardware store. Because the increase in transportation costs associated with adding one more customer is greater in rural areas than in urban areas, stores will be smaller in rural areas than in urban areas.

We have seen that large stores are able to sell at lower prices than small stores because of production economies. The benefit to the customer of traveling to a large store to obtain a lower price depends on how much he is buying. The classic example of this is the purchase of groceries. Suppose that there are two types of trips involving the purchase of groceries: 2 units of groceries are bought on "spur of the moment" trips and 40 units of groceries are bought on "weekly" trips. There are also two types of grocery stores which are located at different distances from consumers. "Large" stores charge $1 per unit of groceries and "small" stores charge $1.25 per unit of groceries. The total cost to the consumer of making a "spur of the moment" trip to a "small" grocery store is

$$2(\$1.25) + T_S = \$2.50 + T_S$$

where T_S is the total transportation cost in getting to and from the small store. The total transportation cost T_S includes wear and tear on the car, the value of time, expenditures on gasoline, and so on. Similarly, the total cost of a "spur of the moment" trip to the large grocery store is

$$2(\$1.00) + T_L = \$2.00 + T_L$$

where T_L is the transportation cost in getting to and from the large store.

The consumer is indifferent between going to the large store and going to the small store when the total costs are equal:

$$\$2.00 + T_L = \$2.50 + T_S$$

or

$$T_L - T_S = \$0.50$$

In other words, if it costs $0.50 more to travel to and from the large store than to travel to and from the small store, a consumer will not care which store he visits. Any consumer who must spend more than an additional $0.50 to travel to and from the large store than to travel to and from the small store will go to the small store for his "spur of the moment" trips. Note that almost everyone will go to the large store for his "weekly" trip. This is because it must cost $10 more to go to and from the large store than to go to and from the small store for consumers to be indifferent between "weekly" trips to the two stores. In conclusion, those consumers who find small stores to be somewhat closer than large stores will frequent small, more expensive stores for their smaller purchases, and virtually all consumers will find it worthwhile to travel to the larger, less expensive stores for their larger purchases.

We can gain a better understanding of this process by taking a closer look at transportation costs. The difference in transportation costs between large and small stores can be written as

$$T_L - T_S = w(M_L - M_S) + p_t(d_L - d_S)$$

where w = value of consumer time
M_L = minutes spent traveling to and from large store
M_S = minutes spent traveling to and from small store
P_t = vehicular expense per mile traveled
d_L = distance to and from large store
d_S = distance to and from small store

We saw that a consumer will be indifferent between traveling to a large store for a "spur of the moment" trip and traveling to a small store for the same trip if it costs $0.50 more to travel to and from large stores. A consumer therefore will be willing to travel somewhat farther to the large store to take advantage of the lower prices that can be found there. How much farther he will be willing to travel will depend upon his value of time (w) and the price of vehicular transportation (p_t). Consumers with high values of time will not be willing to travel as far to go to a large store as will consumers with low values of time. And an increase in the price of gasoline or in the price of cars will send more consumers to convenience stores. Furthermore, in some areas (e.g., Manhattan) a great deal of traveling is done on foot. Because walking is so slow, consumers who live in these areas will not be willing to travel very far to go to a large store.

As we have seen, there is a tendency to bypass the expensive local stores and to shop at the less expensive regional store when transportation costs are a small part of the total cost of the good being bought. For some commodities (e.g., furniture, televisions, washers) there are no small purchases which would allow a small local store to coexist with a larger regional store. We can generalize these observations. When there are no sizable economies of scale in production and when transportation costs are an important part of the total cost, then small local stores (e.g., pizza parlors and bars) result. On the other hand, if there are significant economies of scale and transportation costs are a small part of total cost, then products will be sold only at regional stores (e.g., furniture stores, appliance stores). Both regional and local stores will generally get the most business if they locate in the center of the population that they are serving. The collection of regional stores in the center of a city or of a suburban area is often called a central business district, which exists to take advantage of the central location.

Regional stores in the central business district offer consumers a variety of goods, and consumers often look for more than one good when they go shopping. Since it can be very costly to travel from store to store, one of the major benefits of shopping centers is that they reduce the time spent going from store to store. Consumers therefore are willing to pay a premium for the convenience of shopping in a shopping center. This premium will increase as the cost of going from store to store rises. An increase in the value of time, in the price of gas, or in the price of cars will make transportation more expensive and thereby will increase the premium consumers are willing to pay to shop in a shopping center.

GEOGRAPHICAL VARIATION IN THE PRICES OF NONTRANSPORTED INPUTS   Some inputs are not transported. A plant in Akron employs workers who live in Akron or the area immediately around Akron. Very rarely is it profitable to pay a worker to commute to Akron from Chicago. To take another example, the land on which the plant is located is not transported.

For a variety of reasons, these nontransported inputs are often more expensive in some areas than in other areas. A manager therefore can reduce his costs by locating a plant in an area where these inputs are less costly. An understanding of the determinants of geographical variation in the prices of nontransported inputs is necessary, however, before plants can be located to take advantage of input price variation.

In Chapter 9, we shall develop the theory of compensating wage differentials. This theory states that workers are willing to work for lower wages if they are sufficiently compensated with some other reward. Accordingly, the theory predicts that wage rates will be lower in areas that are nicer or less expensive to live in. Furthermore, because competition for scarce land in urban areas forces urban land to be more expensive than the surrounding agricultural land, urban areas are more expensive to live in than are rural areas and wage rates are correspondingly higher in urban areas than in rural areas. There are also compensating wage differentials associated with the journey to work; firms that are located closer to their labor force are able to pay lower wages because their workers have a shorter distance to commute to work. Empirical evidence supporting this theory is cited in Chapter 9.

It is not just wages that are subject to geographic variation. There is a great deal of variation in land prices. As we have pointed out, the price of urban land will be greater than the price of nearby rural land. Land will also be more expensive in areas where agricultural land is more valuable. For example, it will cost more to rent an acre in the midst of a fertile wheat field than in Death Valley, California. Urban land prices also vary within a city. Most workers in large cities commute to the center of the city. These workers are willing to incur the additional expense of commuting an additional mile only if land prices fall sufficiently to make the workers indifferent between the two locations. Land prices therefore fall, other things being equal, as the distance to the center of the city rises. But other things are not always equal. Some locations experience more pollution than other locations, and the view from some sites is better than the view from other sites. Land prices adjust to reflect these differences. The resulting adjustments in land prices generally will not be sufficient to make all firms indifferent between locations. For example, land prices will be lower in relatively polluted areas, but the fall in land prices as pollution increases will not be great enough to induce outdoor restaurants and nurseries into polluted areas. Factories and other businesses that are relatively unaffected by pollution will outbid outdoor restaurants and nurseries for land with high levels of pollution.

Utility service is found at any location. Managers can purchase electricity and water and can arrange for the disposal of waste products. Electricity is less expensive in areas where it is produced by hydroelectric plants, and water tends to be more expensive in arid regions.

Businesses also are taxed by municipalities and by state governments, and the level of taxation differs considerably from area to area. A number of communities offer preferential tax status to any industry or to preferred industries in order to stimulate growth. Taxes sometimes fund services such as police protection or fire protection that are valuable to firms.

7.7

THE STRUCTURE OF OWNERSHIP

One of the more important decisions that must be made by a potential firm is how to allocate the ownership of the firm. Should the firm be set up so that the firm's residual gains go to a sole proprietor, to a group of partners, or to the stockholders in a corporation?

Owners have a unique role in firms, for only owners have the full incentive to maximize profit, which is the residual gain that accrues to owners. No one else has the proper incentive to make sure that supplies are being purchased at the lowest possible prices, that employees are not shirking, and that hired managers are not unnecessarily providing themselves with plush offices, "business" trips, and so on. This creates problems for the owners, because the information about these activities is not free. An owner cannot be certain how much business was conducted by a manager on a weekend with clients in the mountains unless the owner tags along, and this takes valuable time. Because of the owner's uncertainty about the manager's productivity, the manager who is not being watched on a weekend outing has an incentive to spend too much time skiing and hunting and too little time discussing business with clients. For similar reasons, managers have an incentive to give themselves nicer offices than is warranted and purchasing agents are tempted with "kickbacks" to purchase from more expensive suppliers.

This is not to imply that hired managers have no incentive to maximize profit. A manager who successfully directs one company will be sought by other firms, and proven managerial skills, if not rewarded by one firm, will be rewarded by other firms. The owners of the firms in which managers work, by offering profit sharing and bonus arrangements, can also give managers some incentive to act in the owners' interest. But these measures are not completely effective in motivating managers because of the information problems that were just discussed. Purchased inputs are therefore imperfect substitutes for the time spent by owners in managing their firms.

The optimal form of ownership will depend upon the size of the firm. To see this, let us see what happens as a firm grows. The owner of a very small firm spends very little time managing her firm. As her firm grows, she will employ more of each input, including the time she spends managing her firm. She will have to make more decisions and additional monitoring of inputs will be required. As her business grows her time eventually will become more valuable. This is because she will be infringing on the little time that remains for her family or friends or for sleep and recreation. Consequently, it becomes increasingly costly for the owner to allocate more of her time to managing her firm and she will search for ways of reducing this burden.

The time spent by owners in running a firm can be increased if the owner takes on a partner. The incentive to maximize profit is nevertheless smaller in a partnership than in a sole proprietorship. If a partner receives 50 percent of the firm's profit, then she gets only $500 when she increases her firm's profit by $1,000. A sole proprietor, on the other hand, receives the full increase in profit. The reduced incentive for profit maximization in a partnership is the result of each partner's receiving only a fraction of the increase in profit that results from one of her actions. The part of the increase in profit that goes to her partner(s) offers her no *direct* reward for her actions. If she cares about her partner(s), however, she does get some indirect benefit from increasing their welfare. Thus, a partner is more likely to spend time increasing her firm's profit when part of the increased profit goes to partners about whom she cares (friends or relatives) than when part of the increased profit goes to partners about whom she is indifferent.

Question Answer true, false, or uncertain: Family partnerships are more likely to succeed than partnerships among nonfamily members.

Answer True. Because family partners are more likely to care about one another than nonfamily partners, family partners will have a greater incentive to increase their firm's profits than will nonfamily partners. Family partnerships are therefore more efficient than nonfamily partnerships and accordingly are more likely to succeed than nonfamily partnerships.

There is no doubt that a smaller incentive exists to increase profit in a partnership than in a sole proprietorship. Nevertheless, as a business grows, the sole proprietor's time eventually becomes so valuable that ownership through a two-party partnership is less costly than ownership through a sole proprietorship. Further growth will lead to three- and four-party partnerships. We should note that with each addition of a partner, the incentive of each partner to increase his firm's profit falls.

At this point, it is appropriate to consider the laws which govern proprietorships, partnerships, and corporations. The owner of a sole proprietorship has unlimited liability for all debts incurred by her firm; all her property can be attached to meet these debts. Each partner in a partnership is liable without limit for all debts contracted by her partners. To be more specific, a partner who owns 10 percent of a firm has to pay 10 percent of the debts and may have to pay for the remaining debts if her partners are unable to pay. Her liability is limited only by her financial wealth. Entering a partnership is made even riskier by the fact that each partner has the power to commit the entire partnership without the approval of all the partners. Because of the liability for other partners' misdeeds and of the small incentive that each partner has to increase profit, large partnerships may find it difficult to attract partners and costly to raise funds. The corporate form offers a solution to this problem. An individual who owns 1 percent of the stock of a company receives 1 percent of the dividends disbursed by the company and may lose no more than what she paid for the stock. This limited liability is attractive to investors in large companies, and for this reason most large companies are corporations.

7.8

MAKE OR BUY DECISIONS

A firm must decide not only what outputs it will produce but also whether or not it will produce any of the inputs it uses. Should a food packing company produce or buy the cans that it uses? Should a factory have a shop that fashions equipment or should it purchase its equipment? These managerial decisions can have a significant impact upon profits.

Because of fixed costs, it often does not pay to produce a small quantity of any input. It is very costly to keep a carpenter on the payroll who makes only one worktable or bookshelf a year; it would be cheaper to order the table or bookshelf from a woodworking firm. To take another example, there may be considerable economies of scale in the production of cans. That is, a factory that produces 50,000 cans a day produces at a lower marginal cost than a factory that produces 1,000 cans per day. A cannery that uses only 1,000 cans per day therefore would have to sell many cans to other companies before it finds the production of cans to be economically sensible.

There are, however, some savings which result from producing an input rather than purchasing it. The most obvious savings are in transportation costs. A firm with its own carpentry shop does not have to pay carpenters to come to its plant every time something needs to be repaired. Communication about input specifications and needs may also be cheaper within a firm than across firms.

A firm will find it worthwhile to make its own inputs when the savings in transportation and communication costs outweigh any increased production costs associated with small scale. Because there are economies of scale in production, firms that use a large quantity of an input are more likely to find that the cost savings outweigh the increased production costs.

An example may help to sharpen the analysis of this problem. Suppose that a component for a radio can be purchased for $10 per unit. The manager of a small radio manufacturing company discovers that he can produce these components for $6. To do so, however, he must buy some equipment that costs $80,000. Should he continue purchasing the components or should he make them?

In order to answer this question for the manager, a firm like B & K Consultants needs to know three more things: (1) the firm's discount rate, (2) how long the necessary equipment will last, and (3) how many components are needed each year. Suppose that B & K finds out that the appropriate discount rate is 12 percent and that the equipment will last for 7 years. Whether the investment is worthwhile depends upon the anticipated quantity of components that will be used.

The value of the cost saving from producing the component is given in general form by

$$V = \sum_{t=1}^{n} \frac{(P-C)Q}{(1+r)^t}$$

A STRANGE MAKE OR BUY DECISION

The make or buy decision usually involves the determination of whether to vertically integrate backward to produce a needed input. General Host appears to have gone the other way. In 1971, General Host acquired Cudahy Foods, producer of fresh and processed meats. During the ensuing decade, Cudahy had fairly serious profit problems. In 1979, for example, Cudahy's sales represented 61 percent of General Host's total revenue, but the profit on those sales accounted for only 18 percent of total profits. Selling off the Cudahy subsidiary proved to be almost impossible because no one wants to acquire a meatpacker.

General Host seems to have hit on a plan to make the best of a bad situation. In 1980, it acquired Hickory Farms, the largest chain of specialty food stores in the country. Hickory Farms sells mostly salami, cured meats, and cheese through some 530 outlets. Currently, Hickory Farms buys its meat products from Armour & Co., but it could easily switch to Cudahy. Given Hickory Farms' sales of over $200 million worth of processed meat, this would be a huge boost for Cudahy. Before forcing such a switch, however, General Host had better examine why Cudahy was not Hickory Farms' supplier in the past. There is no sense in transferring any inefficiency from Cudahy to Hickory Farms.

Source: "General Host: Vertical Integration to Save a Subsidiary It Couldn't Sell," *Business Week*, Jan. 19, 1981, pp. 103–104.

where P is the purchase price, C is the production cost, Q is the annual quantity needed, and r is the discount rate. In this case,

$$V = \sum_{t=1}^{7} \frac{(\$10 - 6)Q}{1.12^t}$$

$$= 4Q \sum_{t=1}^{7} \frac{1}{1.12^t}$$

$$= 4Q(4.564)$$

$$= 18.256Q$$

The required investment is $80,000. Therefore, the manager must anticipate a need for at least 4,383 components per year for costs to be reduced by making components.[2] If the firm needs fewer than 4,383 units per year, the manager should buy them.

There are other considerations that affect the decision of whether to make or buy units. One of these is the need for secrecy. Through the use of pensions and the like, a firm has more control over the actions of its own employees than over the actions of the employees of the firm's suppliers. Because of this, a firm trying to protect its secrets may find it worthwhile to produce an input when other considerations would have led the firm to purchase the input. Furthermore, a firm may be more efficient in monitoring the quality of inputs it produces for its own use than other firms are in monitoring the quality of inputs produced for sale. Finally, patents and other legal barriers may prohibit a firm from producing certain inputs.

---

[2] Since $V = 18.256Q$, we solve the following equation to determine the break-even point:

$18.256Q = \$80,000$

7.9

SUMMARY

In this chapter, we have considered issues that determine the very nature of the firm. The first question we addressed was what to produce. We saw that the entrepreneur may be able to garner short-run profits by entering the right industry at the right time. We also saw that the very survival of a product in the marketplace depends on its price. The interrelationships among products were seen to determine a firm's optimal product mix.

Once it has been decided what to produce, several other questions immediately arise. We concluded that the location and number of plants should be chosen so as to minimize the sum of production costs and the costs of transporting inputs and outputs. Because of this, firms have an incentive to locate near the source of inputs, to locate near customers, and to take advantage of scale economies in production. The exact resolution of these conflicting forces depends upon the magnitudes of these transportation costs and of the scale economies in production. We also found that firms may be able to take advantage of geographic variation in wage rates, the price of land, and so on in selecting a site for production. Furthermore, the increasing value of supervisory time as the firm expands is the principal reason why inherently less efficient forms of ownership are eventually chosen as the firm expands. Finally, we saw that it often is worthwhile for a firm to "make" one of its own inputs if it uses enough of that input.

PROBLEMS

7.1 Answer true, false, or uncertain: Consumers who live closer to large grocery stores than to small grocery stores will never go to small grocery stores.

7.2 Answer true, false, or uncertain: Consumers in congested areas are willing to pay more (in higher prices) for the convenience of buying at shopping centers than are consumers in uncongested areas.

7.3 As the owner of a plant currently located in New York City, you are contemplating relocation. Where would you begin to search for a new plant site? Why?

7.4 Answer true, false, or uncertain: Firms entering expanding industries will never suffer losses.

7.5 PepsiCo, the manufacturer of Pepsi Cola, also owns Taco Bell and Pizza Hut, two restaurant chains. Why?

7.6 In Europe, gasoline is twice as expensive as in the United States. Other things being equal, will grocery stores be larger in Europe or in America?

7.7   Answer true, false, or undecided: Because corporations have limited liability, the corporate form of ownership is always less costly than other forms of ownership.

7.8   Will an increase in the cost of making a phone call make firms less likely to produce their own inputs?

7.9   On the basis of the usual considerations for optimization, when will an 11-member partnership elect to add a twelfth partner?

7.10 Answer true, false, or undecided: A lump-sum tax of $X per year which is assessed on firms leads to a reduction in *each* firm's output.

7.11 How can a company forecast whether or not a particular new product is likely to gain acceptance in the marketplace?

REFERENCES

Becker, Gary A.: *Economic Theory*, New York: Alfred A. Knopf, Inc., 1971.
Levy, Haim, and Marshall Sarnat: *Capital Investment and Financial Decisions.* Englewood Cliffs, New Jersey: Prentice-Hall, Inc., 1978.

DECISIONS ON FINANCE AND INSURANCE

Investment and financing decisions have an enormous impact upon a firm's future viability. Consequently, the manager must treat these decisions with the utmost care. In spite of having only imperfect information and operating with random economic variables, the manager will discover that several simple economic principles will serve him well in reaching optimal decisions. In this chapter, we shall not attempt to cover all aspects of finance and insurance. Rather, we shall focus our attention upon several financial decisions and explore the ways in which economics can be helpful. In addition, we shall analyze a fundamental insurance problem with simple economic tools.

8.1

OPTIMAL CAPITAL STRUCTURE

A firm's capital structure or financial structure refers to the mix of debt and equity that is used to finance the firm. When a firm uses some debt financing, it is said to have employed *financial leverage*, because the effect of the debt is to raise (or lever) the earnings per share. For any given total profit, if the rate of profit exceeds the interest rate on the debt, the earnings per share will be increased. As we have come to expect, however, not much of value is often free. In this case, the price paid for enhanced earnings per share is greater variability in earnings. As we saw in Chapter 6, additional variance indicates greater risk and will be avoided by risk averters. In other words, the use of debt can lever the earnings per share down as well as up.

An example will clarify this. Suppose that an unlevered firm faces a random operating profit of $10,000 or $5,000 with equal probabilities. If there are 1,000 shares of stock, the earnings per share will be $10 or $5 in each period. Now we can lever this firm by debt financing. Suppose the firm issues debt sufficient to reduce the number of shares to 500. Whatever the profit, it will be spread over only half as many shares. Suppose the fixed interest on the debt amounts to $3,500. This must be paid irrespective of the firm's realized profit in each period. As a result, in those periods where the firm earns $10,000 in profit, the earnings per share is

$$\frac{\text{Profit} - \text{interest}}{\text{Number of shares}} = \frac{\$10,000 - 3,500}{500} = \$13.00$$

which is an improvement over the unlevered figure of $10. But when profits are only $5,000, the earnings per share is levered down:

$$\frac{\$5,000 - 3,500}{500} = \$3.00$$

On average, the unlevered earnings per share is

$$\frac{\$10 + 5}{2} = \$7.50$$

whereas the levered earnings per share is a bit higher:

$$\frac{\$13 + 3}{2} = \$8.00$$

This is the good news. The bad news is that the variance in earnings per share for the unlevered firm is

$$\frac{1}{2}(\$10 - 7.50)^2 + \frac{1}{2}(\$5 - 7.50)^2 = \$6.25$$

while the variance for the levered firm is

$$\frac{1}{2}(\$13 - 8)^2 + \frac{1}{2}(\$3 - 8)^2 = \$25.00$$

Since both the expected earnings per share and the variance are higher for the levered firm, it is not clear that leverage is necessarily desirable. To determine this, we have to examine the effect of leverage on the firm's valuation.

The impact of leverage on the firm's value has been the subject of considerable intellectual attention. Fortunately, for our purposes a clear consensus has emerged regarding the effect of leverage.[1] We shall denote the value of the unlevered firm by V_u, which must equal the market value of the firm's stock S_u:

$$V_u = S_u$$

The value of the levered firm V_L is equal to the value of its stock S_L plus the value of its debt D_L:

$$V_L = S_L + D_L$$

For the purposes of determining the effects of leverage, we assume that the levered and unlevered firms are identical in all other respects. In particular, each firm enjoys an income stream before corporate taxes equal to X. The corporate tax rate is t. Finally, the borrowing and lending rate of interest for both is r.

If an investor purchases the fraction α of the levered firm's stock, he has invested αS_L in the firm. The firm's pretax income, after paying its debt, equals

---

[1] Franco Modigliani and Merton H. Miller, "Reply to Heins and Sprenkle," *American Economic Review*, vol. 59, September 1969, pp. 592–595, contains the most concise and easily understood proof. Our discussion follows theirs closely.

$$X - rD_L$$

After taxes,

$$(1 - t)(X - rD_L)$$

remains to be distributed to stockholders, and the investor's share of this equals

$$\alpha(1 - t)(X - rD_L)$$

This investor can obtain an identical return by purchasing stock in the unlevered firm and by personally borrowing money. In particular, he can buy the fraction α of the unlevered firm's shares. This investment of αS_U will generate a return of $\alpha X(1 - t)$. He can combine this with personal borrowing of $\alpha(1 - t)D_L$, which will generate a return of $-\alpha(1 - t)rD_L$. This total investment is

$$\alpha S_U - \alpha(1 - t)D_L = \alpha[S_U - (1 - t)D_L]$$

and the total return is

$$\alpha X(1 - t) - \alpha(1 - t)rD_L = \alpha(X - rD_L)(1 - t)$$

which is clearly equal to the return enjoyed by investing in the levered firm.

Ignoring risk for the moment, in equilibrium, when the returns on two investment opportunities are equal, the market valuation of the two opportunities must also be equal. Financial markets are very efficient. If the returns on two investments were equal, but their market valuations were not the same, arbitrage would occur. In other words, alert investors would sell the asset with the higher value or cost and buy the one with the lower value. This would continue until the market valuation of the two investment opportunities were equal. Thus,

$$\alpha S_L = \alpha[S_U - (1 - t)D_L]$$

or

$$S_L = S_U - (1 - t)D_L$$

The value of the levered firm is $S_L + D_L$ and the value of the unlevered firm is S_U; thus,

$$V_L = S_L + D_L = V_U + tD_L \tag{8.1}$$

Now we can see that the value of the levered firm is equal to the value of the unlevered firm plus a premium, which is equal to tD_L. Consequently, leverage increases the market value of a firm. The reason why leverage operates this way is that the levered firm can take advantage of the tax deduction that interest payments permit.

Question The manager of Fastbuck, Inc., is told to maximize the value of his firm. What debt-equity ratio will he select?

Answer   The careful reader will notice that equation (8.1) suggests a disconcerting answer. Any increase in debt increases the value of the levered firm relative to the unlevered firm. Thus, the manager should select a debt-equity ratio that approaches infinity. In other words, the optimal capital structure appears to involve nearly 100 percent debt financing. Since we fail to observe this in the world around us, one must wonder just what we have ignored. The answer is simple enough: the risk of bankruptcy.

IMPACT OF BANKRUPTCY RISK   In reality, firms are subject to the risk of bankruptcy. As the amount of debt that a firm issued rises, the risk of bankruptcy for the firm increases. Consequently, the interest rates that it must pay also rise to compensate the bondholders for the additional risk they face. As a result, the optimal capital structure will not involve 100 percent debt financing. We should expect something far short of that.[2] One way of incorporating the effects of bankruptcy risk is to add a term to the valuation relation in equation (8.1) that explicitly captures those effects. One can imagine that as the debt-equity ratio increases, the additional interest rate that the firm will have to pay on each dollar of debt because of the firm's default risk increases. Thus, the value of the levered firm becomes

$$V_L = V_U + tD_L - P(D_L)D_L \qquad (8.2)$$

where $P(D_L)$ is the penalty per unit of debt issued that a firm incurs as its total debt rises. We are assuming that $\Delta P/\Delta D_L$ is positive; i.e., the per unit penalty rises as the debt increases.

The firm receives some benefit from debt financing because there is a corporate tax. If there were no corporate tax (i.e., if $t = 0$), then the value of the firm would be maximized by having no debt. In the presence of a corporate tax, the benefit from additional debt rises as the corporate tax rate increases. In particular, the benefit from adding \$1 more of debt is equal to the tax rate t. Additional debt is, however, costly to the firm because (1) the risk penalty per unit of debt $[P(D_L)]$ rises and (2) the risk penalty per unit debt is applied to more debt.

Question   In a world where lenders are sensitive to bankruptcy risk and where corporations pay income taxes, what capital structure should the manager select to maximize the value of the firm?

Answer   The manager maximizes the firm's value by selecting the debt level at which the marginal benefit from \$1 more of debt t equals the marginal cost of \$1 more of additional debt $[P + (\Delta P/\Delta D_L)D_L]$. In other words, he will expand the firm's debt until

---

[2]Our discussion of bankruptcy risk and its impact upon the optimal capital structure follows that of Haim Levy and Marshall Sarnat, *Capital Investment and Financial Decisions*, London: Prentice-Hall International, Inc., 1978.

$$\frac{\Delta V_L}{\Delta D_L} = t - \left[P + \left(\frac{\Delta P}{\Delta D_L} \right) D_L \right] = 0$$

These relationships are shown in Figure 8.1. When bankruptcy risk is ignored [i.e., equation (8.1)], there is a positive linear relationship between the firm's debt and the firm's value; increasing the firm's debt *always* leads to an increase in the firm's value. In contrast, when bankruptcy risk is recognized, the firm's value increases, reaches a maximum, and then declines as the firm's debt rises. At low debt levels the benefits of leverage outweigh any penalties for bankruptcy risk, but at high debt levels the benefits of leverage are overcome by the cost of the punishment imposed on the firm by the financial community for incurring more and more bankruptcy risk.

Problem The manager of Mario's Pizza Company is interested in applying these principles to determine the optimal capital structure for his firm. The corporate tax rate is 30 percent. He estimates that the firm would be worth $45,000 if no debt were issued. Furthermore, he has found out that the present value of the interest payments on each dollar of debt rises by $0.01 for each $1,000 of debt that is issued; at zero debt there is no penalty.

Solution From the information given, the per unit penalty for debt equals

$$P = .00001 D_L$$

Accordingly, the value of the firm equals

$$V_L = 45,000 + .3D_L - (.00001 D_L) D_L$$

The firm's value is maximized where

FIGURE 8.1 Value of the levered firm with and without bankruptcy risk.

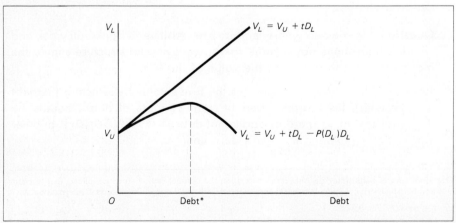

THE IMPACT OF A NONOPTIMAL CAPITAL STRUCTURE*

Tesoro Petroleum Corp. was founded by Robert V. West, Jr., when he bought a small group of oil-producing properties. An aggressive wheeler and dealer, West acquired many cheaply priced properties in the energy field. In doing so, Tesoro began to resemble a patchwork quilt: gasoline marketing, coal mining, petroleum refining, oil transportation and drilling, oil equipment rental and manufacturing, and petrochemical processing. As a result of these acquisitions, Tesoro had debt that reached 130 percent of its equity.

Tesoro's lenders placed restrictive covenants on its debt that limited the firm's flexibility. The covenants also cost Tesoro in terms of potential profitability. For example, during a period of soaring oil prices, Tesoro was compelled to sell off its North Sea oil interests. In addition, it had to dispose of many of its domestic oil and gas properties. Finally, it had to sell off the well-established Tesoro Pump and Valve Co.

Tesoro has now reduced its debt to just 20 percent of equity. Its new loan aggreements contain fewer restrictions on acquisitions and internal expansion. If the Tesoro management keeps its debt-equity ratio in proper balance, the firm should be able to proceed with a sound growth program.

*Source: "Tesoro Petroleum: The Irony of Becoming a Takeover Target," *Business Week*, Oct. 6, 1980, pp. 61–62.

$$\frac{\Delta V_L}{\Delta D_L} = .3 - .00002D_L = 0$$

$$D_L = 15,000$$

That is, the firm's value is maximized by incurring $15,000 worth of debt. With this amount of debt, the value of the firm equals

$45,000 + .3(15,000) - [.00001(15,000)] \ 15,000 =$
$45,000 + .3(15,000) - .15(15,000) =$
$47,250$

The benefit from incurring this debt is the tax write-off that is possible because of it [.3(15,000)]. But incurring this debt causes the firm to pay an interest rate that costs $0.15 more for each dollar borrowed than the zero debt interest rate. When this is applied to $15,000 of debt, the cost of debt financing equals .15($15,000), or $2,250. On balance, incurring $15,000 of debt increases the firm's value from $45,000 to $47,250.

8.2

CAPITAL BUDGETING

The term "capital budgeting" refers to the entire process of planning capital investments that generate returns in the future. Generally, the concern is with the expenditure or commitment of current dollars on projects whose benefits will accrue over more than 1 year.[3] The apparent reason for this arbitrary classification is that dollars spent or received within a calendar year are viewed as current and,

[3]For a thorough examination of capital budgeting, the interested reader may consult Levy and Sarnat, op. cit., pp. 1–114.

therefore, can be compared in nominal or undiscounted form.[4] In contrast, future years' receipts should be discounted for present-value calculations. The whole purpose of the exercise is to select those investment options that advance the goals of the firm and to reject those that do not. A successful manager will identify a set of capital investment decisions that will maximize the market value of the firm's outstanding stock.

NET-PRESENT-VALUE RULE   The net-present-value rule for evaluating investment options involves calculating the present value of each project's contribution to the firm's total profits. Assuming that the initial outlay in period 0 can be denoted by I_0 and that the net return in period t is R_t, then the net present value (NPV) of an investment is

$$NPV = \frac{R_1}{1 + r} + \frac{R_2}{(1 + r)^2} + \cdots + \frac{R_n}{(1 + r)^n} - I_0 \tag{8.3}$$

where r is the firm's appropriate discount rate and n is the number of years that the project generates returns. We must make it clear that R represents the total receipts minus the total operating costs in each year. The value of the net return need not be the same from year to year.

We should also pay attention to the economic interpretation of the firm's discount rate. It can be described as the minimum rate of return required of all new investments. Since the manager ties up money when she invests in a project, the discount rate should reflect the opportunity costs incurred by the firm. In other words, the discount rate must measure the value of the funds if those funds were invested in alternative pursuits.

The manager's decision rule is fairly obvious: if a project's NPV is positive, she should invest in that project; if the NPV is negative, she should reject that project. This follows from an examination of the NPV expression in (8.3). If the NPV is positive, that means that the present value of the project's profit stream exceeds the initial expenditure I_0. For example, suppose that a pinball machine will wear out at the end of 3 years. Earlier experience with such things leads the manager to anticipate annual net revenues as follows:

Year 1	$600
Year 2	800
Year 3	400

This particular pinball machine costs $1,400. Assuming that the discount rate is 10 percent, the net present value of this investment option is given by the following:

---

[4]This is strictly true only when the appropriate discount rate is low. If the rate of inflation is high, then the firm's manager will be concerned about the timing of payments and receipts during a year.

$$\text{NPV} = \frac{\$600}{1.10} + \frac{800}{(1.10)^2} + \frac{400}{(1.10)^3} - 1{,}400$$

$$= \$545.45 + 661.16 + 300.53 - 1{,}400$$

$$= \$107.14$$

Since the NPV of this option is positive, the present value of profits is increased by making an investment in the project. If the manager failed to make this investment, it would be analogous to producing a quantity of output short of the point where marginal cost and marginal revenue are equal.

Question   The manager of ABC, Inc., has been considering an investment of $100,000, which will finance her firm's entry into the combination lawn mower–snowplow manufacturing industry. Given the current production technology and input prices, the total cost (TC) function is

$$\text{TC} = \$10{,}000 - \$20Q + \$4Q^2$$

These production facilities will be highly specialized and have no scrap value at the end of 10 years. If the competitive price is $780 per lawn mower–snowplow and the firm's discount rate is 10 percent, should the manager invest in this project? Suppose the corporate tax rate were 50 percent and depreciation is not tax deductible, would your advice be the same? Would this project become viable if the discount rate fell to 8 percent?

Answer   To offer sound advice, we must calculate the net present value of this project. First, we have to find the stream of profits. Since the firm's optimal output occurs where profit is maximized, we must examine the profit function:

$$\Pi = PQ - TC$$

which is by substitution

$$\Pi = \$780Q - \$10{,}000 + \$20Q - \$4Q^2$$

For profit maximization, we must have

$$\frac{\Delta\Pi}{\Delta Q} = \$780 + 20 - 8Q = 0$$

which requires that the manager produce 100 units of output. If we substitute this into the profit function, we discover that yearly profits are

$$\Pi = \$780(100) - \$10{,}000 + \$20(100) - \$4(100)^2$$

$$= \$78{,}000 - \$10{,}000 + \$2{,}000 - \$40{,}000$$

$$= \$30{,}000$$

Now the net present value of this project is calculated as

$$NPV = \sum_{t=1}^{10} \frac{(\$30,000)_t}{(1 + 0.10)^t} - \$100,000$$

$$= \$184,337 - \$100,000$$

$$= \$84,337$$

which is clearly positive. Consequently, this is a worthwhile project.

If the corporate tax rate were 50 percent, the yearly aftertax profits would be $15,000. Substituting this into the net present-value calculation, we have

$$NPV = \sum_{t=1}^{10} \frac{(\$15,000)_t}{(1 + 0.10)^t} - \$100,000$$

$$= \$92,169 - \$100,000$$

$$= -\$7,831$$

which is clearly negative. Thus, the imposition of the tax alters the manager's decision.[5]

If the discount rate fell to 8 percent, the net-present-value calculation would be altered:

$$NPV = \sum_{t=1}^{10} \frac{(\$15,000)_t}{(1 + 0.08)^t} - \$100,000$$

$$= \$100,651 - \$100,000$$

$$= \$651$$

Now this project becomes viable once again. Consequently, the manager should invest in this project if the discount rate falls to 8 percent.

INTERNAL RATE OF RETURN RULE   An alternative approach is provided by the internal rate of return measure of an investment option's value. The *internal rate of return d* is that discount rate that would make the present value of the project's profit stream equal to the initial outlay:

$$\frac{R_1}{1 + d} + \frac{R_2}{(1 + d)^2} + \cdots + \frac{R_n}{(1 + d)^n} = I_0 \tag{8.4}$$

In other words, given the profit stream and the initial expenditure, the internal rate of return is the discount rate that would make the investment project's net present value zero.

The manager's decision rule is quite simple: if the internal rate of return d exceeds the opportunity cost of the firm's funds r, then the manager should invest in that project; if d is less than r, he should not invest in that project. For example, if the opportunity cost of the firm's funds is 12 percent and the

---

[5]Our assumption that depreciation is not tax deductible is clearly unsatisfactory. We shall examine the influence of taxation in Chapter 14.

internal rate of return on a particular investment option is 14 percent, the manager should invest in that project. Again, the economic reasoning behind this decision rule is straightforward. When the internal rate of return exceeds the opportunity cost of the firm's funds, the investment project generates enough revenue to cover these costs and provide some additional profit.

8.3	

CAPITAL BUDGETING AND UNCERTAINTY

In the preceding section, we assumed that the stream of future net returns was known with certainty. This, of course, will not often be the case. As we are all painfully aware, the future is filled with risks of many kinds. Input prices may shift around causing the cost function to be random. Alternatively, the demand function may move around in some random fashion that will cause the revenue function to be random. In either case, the future net receipts will not be known with certainty. As one might expect, this complicates matters to some extent. The same principles, however, can be applied.

First, let us suppose that the manager is *risk-neutral*. You will recall from Chapter 6 that a risk-neutral decision maker has a linear utility function. He focuses upon expected values and ignores the variance of a risky project. Thus, he will be concerned with the expected values of the various investment options and the net-present-value rule generalizes quite easily. For each period, the manager will evaluate the expected net return, which we shall denote by $\bar{R}_t$. The expected net present value $E(\text{NPV})$ of an investment can be written as

$$E(\text{NPV}) = \frac{\bar{R}_1}{1+r} + \frac{\bar{R}_2}{(1+r)^2} + \cdots + \frac{\bar{R}_m}{(1+r)^m} - I_0 \qquad (8.5)$$

where I_0 is the initial outlay and r is the riskless rate of interest.

For the risk-neutral manager, the decision rule under uncertainty differs only slightly from the decision rule where there is no uncertainty. If a project's expected net present value is positive, then the manager should select that project. Conversely, any project should be rejected if its expected net present value is negative. The reason behind this is apparent upon inspection of equation (8.5). When the manager invests in a project, the outlay of I_0 is made initially. If the $E(\text{NPV})$ is positive, then the present value of the expected returns exceeds the present value of the outlay. Forgoing this investment opportunity would reduce the firm's expected profits.

Somewhat more complicated is the case where the manager is *risk-averse*. In Chapter 6, we found that a risk-averse decision maker did not like risk and would pay something to reduce the risk he faced. When he is risk-averse, the manager will be concerned with the expected utility of the net returns during the future periods.[6] To understand this problem a bit more easily, we shall

---

[6]This discussion depends upon that contained in Charles Haley and Lawrence D. Schall, *The Theory of Financial Decisions*, New York: McGraw-Hill Book Company, 1979, pp. 189–193.

introduce the concept of the certainty equivalent for a random return. The return in, say, period 1 is random and provides an expected utility, which we denote as $E[U(\tilde{R}_1)]$. The certainty equivalent for this random return $\tilde{R}$ is the certain return CE_1 that provides the same utility. That is,

$$U(CE_1) = E[U(\tilde{R}_1)]$$

A brief example will help to clarify this important concept. Suppose the manager is confronted with the option of drilling for oil, which costs $1 million. If he drills and strikes oil, he receives $2 million, which is a $1 million profit. If the effort fails, he has lost the $1 million drilling cost. In Figure 8.2, we have drawn the manager's utility of wealth function. We see the firm starting from an initial wealth position at W_0. The probability of success is such that the expected wealth from drilling for oil $\overline{W}$ is greater than W_0. The expected utility of the uncertain option is given by the height of the chord connecting points A and B on the utility function directly above $\overline{W}$. We can see that the certain wealth level of CE_1 yields a level of utility equal to the expected utility of the uncertain option. This level of nonrandom wealth is the certainty equivalent of the uncertain investment opportunity.

When a manager attempts to evaluate an investment opportunity that involves a stream of future receipts that are random, he can employ the certainty-equivalent concept. For each future receipt, he calculates its certainty equivalent, for he is indifferent between this certain income and the uncertain receipt. These certainty equivalents must be discounted and summed to provide a value for the investment opportunity:

$$V = \frac{CE_1}{1+r} + \frac{CE_2}{(1+r)^2} + \cdots + \frac{CE_n}{(1+r)^n} \qquad (8.6)$$

FIGURE 8.2 Certainty equivalent of a risky option.

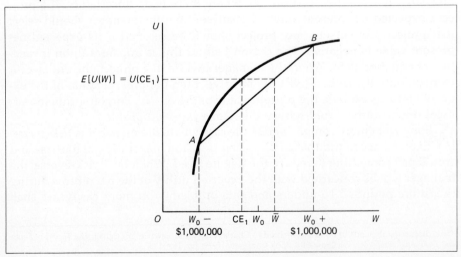

where r is the riskless rate of interest or the firm's opportunity cost for the funds to be invested. For the risk-averse manager, the decision rule is to invest in each opportunity where the present value of the certainty equivalent stream of net receipts V exceeds the initial outlay.

Question   Suppose that the manager can invest \$60,000 in a project that has an expected yearly profit of \$20,000 for 5 years. If the appropriate discount rate is 10 percent, will the manager pursue this option?

Answer   The risk-neutral manager will make this investment. Since the expected net present value is given by

$$E(NPV) = \sum_{t=1}^{n} \frac{\bar{R}_t}{(1+r)^t} - I_0 = \sum_{t=1}^{5} \frac{20,000_t}{1.10^t} - I_0$$

$$= \$75,816 - 60,000$$

$$= \$15,816$$

the expected net present value is positive. According to the decision rule above, the risk-neutral manager will proceed with this investment.

For the risk-averse manager, we have to examine the certainty equivalents of the expected annual profits. Suppose a particular manager would be indifferent between the risky option and a certain \$15,000 per year. For this manager, we must compare the present value of the certainty equivalents,

$$V = \sum_{t=1}^{n} \frac{CE_t}{(1+r)^t} = \sum_{t=1}^{5} \frac{\$15,000_t}{1.10^t}$$

$$= \$56,862$$

with the initial outlay of \$60,000. Since the initial outlay exceeds the value to the manager, he will reject this investment option.

8.4

INFLUENCE OF TAXATION

Taxation takes a variety of forms in the United States. A firm may be confronted with unit taxes or ad valorem taxes on output, sales taxes on purchases, and taxes on profits, to name just a few. We deal with most of these taxes elsewhere. In this section, we shall analyze the effect of an investment tax credit on the manager's investment decision.

If we let R_t represent the net receipts in period t and let r be the appropriate discount rate, the before-tax net present value is

$$NPV_{BT} = \frac{R_1}{1+r} + \frac{R_2}{(1+r)^2} + \cdots + \frac{R_{10}}{(1+r)^{10}} - I_0$$

where I_0 is the intial outlay. This is a special case of equation (8.3); here we have assumed an investment life of 10 years. Suppose that the firm faces a federal corporate income tax equal to 40 percent of profits. Now investment decisions must take account of the effects of taxation. For simplicity, we shall assume that the tax law permits straight-line depreciation of the investment over a 10-year period. This means that 10 percent of the investment may be deducted from the net return that the investment provides before calculating the tax. The firm, therefore, pays federal taxes equal to

$$.40 \ (R_t - .10I_0)$$

in the year t, and its aftertax net receipts in year t equal before-tax net receipts less taxes, or

$$R_t - .40(R_t - .10I_0) = .60R_t + .40(.10)I_0$$

If there were no depreciation allowance, the firm would be able to keep only 60 percent of its net receipts. The depreciation allowance enables the firm to retain an additional amount equal to the tax rate (.40) times the allowable depreciation ($.10I_0$), which is $.04I_0$ in this case.

The net present value of the investment on an aftertax basis is given by

$$\text{NPV}_{\text{AT}} = \frac{.60R_1}{1+r} + \frac{.60R_2}{(1+r)^2} + \cdots + \frac{.60R_{10}}{(1+r)^{10}} + \frac{.40(.10I_0)}{1+r} + \frac{.40(.10I_0)}{(1+r)^2}$$
$$+ \cdots + \frac{.40(.10I_0)}{(1+r)^{10}} - I_0 \tag{8.7}$$

It is clear that the tax on corporate profits affects the manager's decisions. The appropriate decision rule is to invest in projects where the net present value *after taxes* is positive. Since the influence of taxes is to reduce the flow of net receipts to the firm without affecting the cost of the initial outlay, we can see that taxation can make investment projects that were formerly desirable now undesirable.

On occasion, the government will attempt to stimulate investment by offering an investment tax credit of, say, 5 percent. This means that the firm that makes an investment of I_0 in a project is entitled to reduce its tax payment by 5 percent of I_0. The influence of this on the firm is obvious: it reduces the value of I_0 in the last term of the expression in (8.7):

$$\text{NPV}_{\text{AT}} = \sum_{t=1}^{10} \frac{0.60R_t}{(1+r)^t} + \sum_{t=1}^{10} \frac{.40(.10I_0)}{(1+r)^t} - 0.95I_0$$

It is clear that some projects that were almost profitable will become profitable after the tax credit legislation is passed.

8.5

PORTFOLIO DECISIONS WITH BORROWING AND LENDING

In Chapter 6, we examined a simple portfolio model that permitted neither borrowing nor lending. Incorporating borrowing and lending into this model yields some interesting results. Let's suppose that investors have the option of holding government securities that are free of risk. In other words, we assume that the government security provides a positive return with a zero variance. We consider the holding of risk-free government bonds to be lending. The return on the risk-free asset is called the "risk-free rate of interest," which we shall denote by r_0.

You will recall from Chapter 6 that the efficiency frontier consists of all risk-bearing portfolios that maximize the investor's return for any given standard deviation of return. In Figure 8.3, the efficiency frontier is labeled *EF*. Investors who are able to borrow and lend at risk-free interest rate r_0 can form a portfolio made up partially of risk-bearing assets from the efficiency frontier and made up partially of risk-free assets. Such a combination may provide the investor with better opportunities than are available solely from efficiency frontier *EF*. The most desirable set of combinations of risk-bearing assets and riskless assets or debts is obtained by rotating a line around risk-free interest rate r_0 on the vertical axis until the line is tangent to efficiency frontier *EF*. The reader should be able to verify that other lines passing through r_0 on the vertical axis and on some point on the efficiency frontier provide the investor with less desirable combinations of return and risk.

At the point of tangency, there is a portfolio of risky assets (*A*) with expected return r_A and standard deviation σ_A. In contrast, if the decision maker lends all his money, his portfolio will have a return of r_0 and a standard deviation of zero. Suppose, however, that he combines lending with some investment in portfolio *A*. For example, suppose he lends one-half of his money and invests the other half; let us call this portfolio *C*. Then his expected return on portfolio *C* will be

$$r_C = \frac{1}{2} r_0 + \frac{1}{2} r_A$$

FIGURE 8.3   The influence of borrowing and lending on the efficiency frontier.

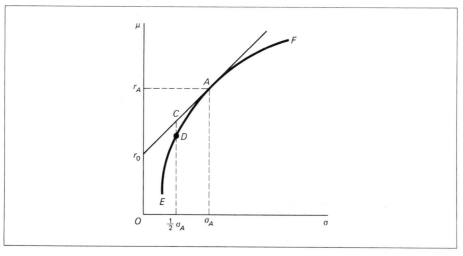

while the standard deviation of his return will be

$$\sigma_C = \frac{1}{2}\sigma_A$$

Thus, the risk and return are lower than the risk and return associated with portfolio A. Note, however, that portfolio C lies on the straight line connecting the risk-free return and portfolio A. Thus, by lending, the decision maker can reduce risk on more favorable terms than if he reduced his risk by moving along the efficiency frontier to portfolio D. Consequently, introducing the possibility of lending serves to enhance the investor's utility because more favorable risk-return options are made available.

Question Suppose the investor loaned one-quarter of his money and invested three-quarters in portfolio A, producing a porfolio that we shall call G. Where do we find G in Figure 8.3?

Answer The expected return on G is given by

$$r_G = \frac{1}{4}r_0 + \frac{3}{4}r_A$$

while the standard deviation of the return is

$$\sigma_G = \frac{3}{4}\sigma_A$$

Thus, G is also located on the straight line connecting r_0 and A. In this case, however, G lies three-quarters of the way toward A on the line rather than halfway toward A. As a general proposition, all portfolios that combine lending at the risk-free rate and investing in portfolio A will lie on the straight line to the left of A.

Suppose that the investor feels that portfolio A is so desirable that he would like to invest more than he currently owns in A. In other words, he wants to borrow in order to invest more in portfolio A. The effect of borrowing is to increase the expected return and the risk. Assuming that the investor can borrow an additional 25 percent at the risk-free rate, the expected return on portfolio H is

$$r_H = 1.25r_A - .25r_0$$

which is larger than r_A since r_A exceeds r_0. At the same time, the standard deviation of the return is also larger:

$$\sigma_H = 1.25\sigma_A$$

All portfolios that involve *borrowing* at the risk-free rate and investing in A will lie along the straight line to the right of A.

Under the assumptions that the investor can borrow and lend at the risk-free rate of interest, all optimal portfolios will involve A alone or some combination of A with borrowing or lending. Efficiency frontier EF is no longer the relevant budget line separating the attainable from the unattainable risk-return combinations. Instead, the tangent drawn from r_0 to EF becomes the relevant budget line.

The particular point along the tangent that will be selected depends upon the risk preferences of the individual. In Figure 8.4, we have two sets of indifference curves. In panel (*a*), the preferences of a very conservative investor are depicted. As a result, he holds risk-free assets (that is, he lends) as well as some risky assets. In panel (*b*), we find a more aggressive investor who borrows in order to maximize his utility. We should note that in both panels, the investment opportunities are the same. It is the difference in preferences that leads to different portfolios being selected. Each investor chooses to operate where the marginal cost of increasing risk relative to the marginal benefit of increasing the return (i.e., the slope of his indifference curve) is just equal to the reward offered to him in the market for bearing risk. The reward for bearing risk is given by the slope of the tangent from r_0 to A: $(r_A - r_0)/\sigma_A$; this shows the terms of trade that the market offers between risk and return. In other words, the manager will continue to take on additional risk until the marginal rate of substitution between risk and return in his preferences is equal to the trade-off that is compelled by the market.

8.6

MARKET INSURANCE, SELF-INSURANCE, AND SELF-PROTECTION

The real world is filled with many uncertainties. Events such as fires, burglaries, flooding, and the like can cost a firm a considerable amount of money. Confronted with these possi-

FIGURE 8.4   Utility maximizing portfolios with borrowing and lending.

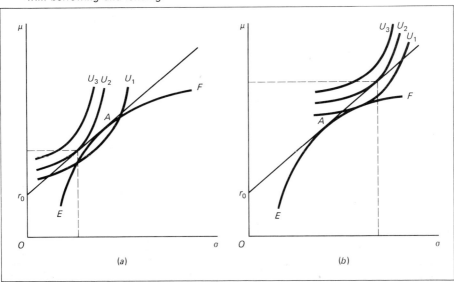

(a)

(b)

bilities, the manager of a firm must decide how to cope with such random occurrences. One possible reaction is to buy *market insurance*. In this case, the manager exchanges a certain, small loss in income for an uncertain and possibly large loss in income that an unfortunate event would entail. For example, when a manager buys fire insurance, the firm's annual profit is reduced by the insurance premium with certainty. But she avoids the possible large loss that would accompany a fire. A second option is *self-insurance*, which reduces the size of the loss that would result from a random event. Continuing with the fire example, the manager could invest in an automatic sprinkler system. Thus, the likelihood of a fire would be unaffected, but the extent of the loss in the event of a fire would be reduced. Finally, the manager could opt for *self-protection*, which reduces the probability of a casualty. With respect to a fire, the manager can reduce the likelihood of a fire's occurrence by substituting away from flammable building materials. Of course, these are not mutually exclusive options. In fact, these three options can be combined quite easily, and in this section, we will develop principles that aid the manager in deciding upon the appropriate mix of market insurance, self-insurance, and self-protection for her firm.[7] While it would be nice if there were no casualty losses, we shall see that reducing losses to zero generally will prove to be suboptimal.

Assume that the firm is faced with two possible states of the world. To provide this problem with concreteness, let these two states describe whether or not a flood occurs. Suppose that the manager does nothing initially to alter the probability of a flood or the magnitude of the loss that is imposed on the firm when there is a flood. Let us also assume that a flood (state 0) occurs with probability P. Consequently, there is a probability of $1 - P$ that no flood (state 1) will occur. There is a profit level associated with each of these states of the world: Π_{nf}^e is the profit when there is no flood and Π_f^e is the profit level when there is a flood. These profit levels constitute the firm's endowed position. Of course, $\Pi_{nf}^e - \Pi_f^e$ represents the firm's loss in the event of a flood.

MARKET INSURANCE   The firm is able to move away from its endowed position (Π_f^e, Π_{nf}^e) through the purchase and sale of flood insurance. Let the amount of actual insurance purchased equal the difference between the actual and endowed profits in the event of a flood:

$$I = \Pi_f - \Pi_f^e$$

Suppose that \$1 worth of flood insurance costs α in lost profits should there be no flood. The firm's expenditures on insurance in terms of "no-flood" profit can be written as

$$\Pi_{nf}^e - \Pi_{nf} = \alpha I = \alpha(\Pi_f - \Pi_f^e)$$

---

[7]This section was adapted from the perceptive analysis provided in Isaac Ehrlich and Gary S. Becker, "Market Insurance, Self-Insurance, and Self-Protection," *Journal of Political Economy*, vol. 80, August 1972, pp. 623–648.

This equation can be rewritten as

$$\Pi_{nf} = \Pi_{nf}^e - \alpha(\Pi_f - \Pi_f^e)$$

Thus, each dollar of insurance is bought by reducing the profit in the event of no flood by α dollars.

These relationships can be illustrated with the following example. A firm may be endowed with a profit of \$50,000 if no flood occurs and with a profit of \$10,000 if there is a flood. Suppose α is .3; then the manager can increase the firm's certain income in the event of a flood by \$1,000 for every \$300 reduction in certain income when no flood occurs. These relationships suggest the budget line depicted in Figure 8.5. We can see that the manager could choose to move from its endowed position E to the alternative position A, which involves a profit of \$44,000 if no flood occurs and \$30,000 if there is a flood. We emphasize the word "could" because this is what the insurance market will permit. To see this, note that \$20,000 of flood insurance must be bought to increase flood income from \$10,000 to \$30,000. Moreover, \$20,000 of flood insurance cost \$6,000 [= \$20,000(0.3)] in certain no-flood income. Thus, our budget line in Figure 8.5 serves the same function as budget lines generally: it separates attainable from unattainable combinations and shows the rate of exchange required by the market. To determine choices, one must consider the decision maker's preferences.

The manager has the preference function

$$U = U(\Pi_f, \Pi_{nf})$$

In other words, the manager's welfare is a function of flood profit and no-flood profit. Subject to the budget constraint, the manager maximizes her welfare by selecting Π_f and Π_{nf}. If the optimal level of Π_f exceeds the en-

FIGURE 8.5   Firm's budget line.

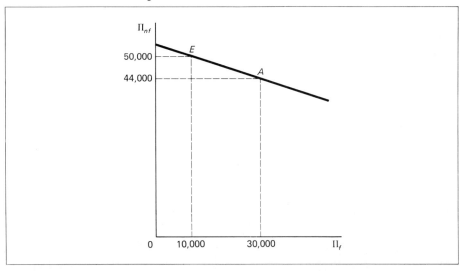

dowed level of Π_f, the manager will have to buy some insurance. As can be seen in Figure 8.6, insurance will be demanded if the slope of the indifference curve is steeper than the slope of the budget constraint at endowment E. Thus, we can see that if the amount of no-flood profit that the manager is willing to give up to increase the firm's flood profit by \$1 exceeds the amount of no-flood profit that the manager *must* sacrifice to buy \$1 worth of insurance, then the manager will buy some insurance. In Figure 8.6, we can see that a higher utility level is attained at Z than was provided by initial endowment E. In general, whether the manager elects to insure against flood loss depends upon her preferences, the firm's endowment, and the price of insurance.

Question   Will a firm have a larger incentive to insure rare losses or common losses?

Answer   First, we define a rare loss to be one with a relatively low probability of occurrence. Similarly, a common loss is one with a relatively high probability of occurring. Next, we should note that the odds of a loss are given by $P/(1 - P)$. Consequently, an actuarially fair exchange is defined to be an exchange of $P/(1 - P)$ units of no-loss income for an additional unit of loss income. The price of insurance can be written as

$$\alpha = (1 + \lambda)\,\frac{P}{1 - P}$$

where λ is known as the insurance loading factor. When λ is zero, the price of insurance equals the actuarially fair value. In this case, on the average, the insurance company's premium receipts will equal the casualty claims. This, however, leaves nothing to cover the resource costs of selling the insurance policies, processing the policies and the claims, in-

FIGURE 8.6   Utility maximization with insurance.

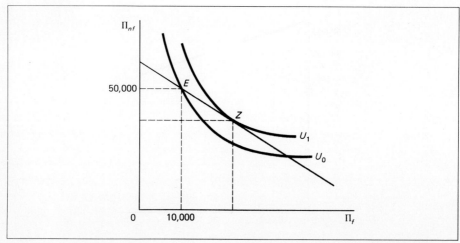

vesting money, and so on. Accordingly, to cover such costs, insurance companies must charge a price (α) such that the loading factor (λ) is greater than zero.

If the cost of processing and investigating claims increases as P increases, the loading factor λ will increase with increases in P. For example, suppose it costs $1 to process each claim. Then the expected claims processing costs for 1,000 policies, where the probability of a loss is .4, are $400. Similarly, if the probability of a loss is only .2, the expected claims processing costs are only $200. Accordingly, the loading factor must be higher when the probability of a loss is higher to cover the additional processing costs. Consequently, the price of insuring a rare loss (low P) would be closer to the actuarially fair price than would be the price of insuring common losses (high P). This gives the manager a greater incentive to insure rare losses.

SELF-INSURANCE As we indicated above, self-insurance reduces the size of a loss. For instance, the installation of an automatic sprinkler system reduces the loss from a fire in the event that a fire should occur. Assume that there is no market insurance available and that the firm's profit transformation possibilities are given by curve AB in Figure 8.7. Curve AB is likely to be concave because successive expenditures on self-insurance (e.g., buying an increasingly sophisticated sprinkler system) will probably bring about smaller and smaller increases in fire profit (that is, smaller and smaller reductions in losses). The manager will self-insure the firm if the slope of the preference function at endowment point E exceeds the slope of the profit transformation curve at E. This is true in Figure 8.7. As a result, the manager maximizes her welfare by choosing that point where the preference function is tangent to the profit transformation curve (D).

FIGURE 8.7   Utility maximization with self-insurance.

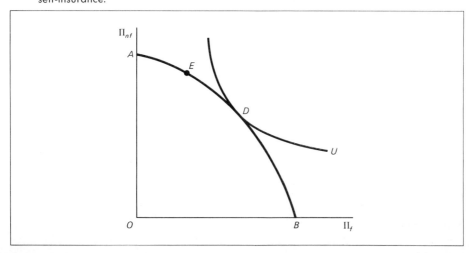

Now allow both market insurance and self-insurance to be available. At its endowed position (point E in Figure 8.8), the firm must choose between buying \$1 worth of insurance through the market and self-insuring to the same extent. The price of market insurance (α) is given by the slope of market insurance line CD through endowment point E. The price of self-insurance is similarly given by the slope of profit transformation curve AB at endowment point E. If the price of self-insurance is less than the price of market insurance, the manager will choose to increase her insurance coverage by \$1 by providing self-insurance. Self-insurance is chosen in this case because it is cheaper.

By providing \$1 worth of self-insurance, the firm moves along its profit transformation curve AB from endowment point E to the right to position H where fire income equals $\Pi_f^e + 1$ and where no-fire income equals Π_{nf}^*. At this point the firm is again faced with a decision about whether to increase its insurance coverage through self-insurance or through market insurance. Insurance may be increased through the purchase of market insurance by moving along a new market insurance line FG going through point H, which has co-

FIGURE 8.8   Utility maximization with market insurance and self-insurance.

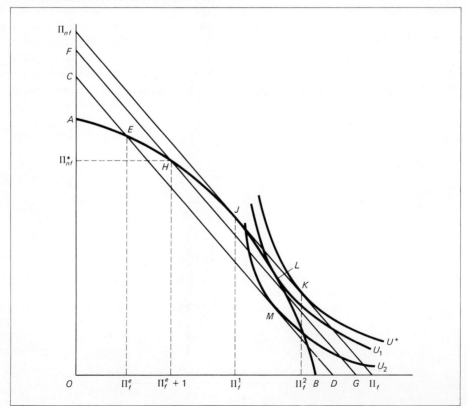

ordinates ($\Pi_f^c + 1$, Π_{nf}^*). For decision-making purposes, once $1 worth of self-insurance has been purchased, H is the new endowment point from which subsequent decisions will be made. Thus, at H, the manager must still decide upon market insurance versus self-insurance according to the usual decision criteria. The manager will increase the firm's insurance coverage through self-insurance if the price of self-insurance (measured by the slope of income transformation curve AB at H) is less than the price of market insurance (measured by the slope of market insurance line FG). At point H in Figure 8.8, the firm finds it cheaper to continue self-insuring. This state of affairs will continue until the manager reaches point J where the market insurance line is tangent to the profit transformation curve. At the point of tangency, the slopes are equal. Further increases in insurance coverage through self-insurance are more costly than increasing insurance coverage through market insurance. Thus, $\Pi_f^1 - \Pi_f^c$ insurance is bought through self-insurance. The market insurance line going through point J describes the combinations available to the manager. Her welfare is maximized if she chooses that point on this line where one of her indifference curves is tangent to the market insurance line. Thus, an additional $\Pi_f^2 - \Pi_f^1$ insurance is bought through market insurance. Utility level U^* is attained at this point. If only self-insurance were available, the firm would only attain the utility level U_1 at point L, and if only market insurance were available, the firm would only attain utility level U_2 at point M.

SELF-PROTECTION   Self-protection reduces the probability of undesirable events occurring. To take one example, the purchase of a good safe reduces the probability of a successful burglary. Self-protection does not, however, diminish the loss that accompanies a successful burglary, as market insurance or self-insurance would. This distinction between self-protection and insurance is illustrated more clearly in Figure 8.9.

FIGURE 8.9   Effect on the distribution of profit due to market insurance, self-insurance, and self-protection.

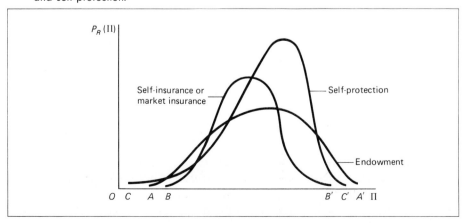

The probability of each profit possibility (Π) is graphed as a function of Π. The firm is endowed with profit distribution AA', and through self-insurance (e.g., a sprinkler) or market insurance, it is able to reduce the dispersion to BB'. The possibility of extremely low profits is eliminated, but at the cost of reducing the probability of extremely high profits.

Self-protection may shift the profit distribution to CC', which is clearly more skewed toward higher profits than either AA' or BB'. If chemicals are stored in separate rooms or buildings, the probability of a chemical reaction which results in a fire is reduced. Thus, self-protection reduces the probability of low incomes (associated with fires, for instance) and increases the probability of high incomes (e.g., associated with no fires).

Those who are more efficient providers of self-protection will face a lower cost of producing self-protection and therefore will demand more self-protection. For example, a manager with a background in chemistry probably will be more efficient in averting fires in a chemical plant than a manager with no training in chemistry; consequently, the former will choose more self-protection, and thus have a lower probability of fire, than the manager with no chemistry background. Thus, the observation that different people use different probabilities in their decision making does not necessarily reflect differences in the subjective evaluations of a single objective probability. Rather, it may reflect differences in the optimal probabilities due to differences in the marginal productivity of self-protection.

8.7

SUMMARY

In this chapter, we saw how simple principles of economics can be used in a variety of finance and insurance decisions. The capital structure of the firm was seen to depend upon the relative costs and benefits of using debt. An optimal capital structure was found where the marginal benefit of further debt was just equal to the marginal cost of adding more debt.

We also discussed capital budgeting decisions, and in a world with no uncertainty we concluded that any investment that increased the present value of the firm's profits should be undertaken. Decision criteria are more complicated in an uncertain world. We saw that a risk-neutral decision maker should approve any project that increases the firm's expected profits. A risk-averse manager can rely upon certainty-equivalent profits to help guide his decision.

The ability to combine lending and borrowing at some riskless interest rate with assets from a risk-bearing portfolio was found to expand the investor's opportunity set. We also learned that the manager should choose the point along this new opportunity set where his marginal benefit of achieving a higher return equals the marginal cost of bringing about the higher return.

Finally, we examined market insurance, self-insurance, and self-protection. Our familiar principle of optimization applied here as well: the manager should buy market insurance, produce self-insurance, or produce self-protection until the marginal benefit equals the marginal cost. Moreover, we once again discovered that the ability to combine options expands the firm's opportunities. In this case, the manager was better off combining market insurance and self-insurance than using either option by itself. Finally, we observed that a greater amount of self-protection should be chosen by those who are relatively efficient providers of self-protection.

IMPORTANT NEW TERMS

Certainty equivalent

Internal rate of return

Market insurance

Self-insurance

Self-protection

Risk-free asset

Leverage

Capital budgeting

PROBLEMS

8.1 Suppose we adopt the convention that all expenditures and receipts within a calendar year are counted as current dollars. Firm XYZ has an opportunity to invest $10,000 in a project on January 1. The firm will receive $875 at the end of each month for 1 year. Suppose the appropriate annual interest rate is 12 percent. Should the firm's manager take advantage of this opportunity?

8.2 Assume that the relevant discount rate is 10 percent. Calculate the net present value of the following investment project. For an initial expenditure of $5,000, the firm will obtain net receipts of $1,000 in year 1, $2,000 in year 2, and $3,000 in year 3. Should the manager accept this project? Suppose the discount rate were 8 percent. Is the project now more or less attractive?

8.3 Suppose there is a change in technology that caused all buildings to be less susceptible to fires. This would increase Π_f^e while Π_{nf}^e would remain unchanged, where Π_f^e and Π_{nf}^e represent endowed levels of fire and no-fire profit. What happens to the budget line in Figure 8.5? What is apt to be the effect on the quantity of insurance purchased?

8.4 Answer true, false, or undecided: An increase in the corporate income tax rate will cause the manager to decrease the debt-equity ratio.

8.5 Construct an efficiency frontier and find a utility-maximizing portfolio.

Now introduce the possibility of borrowing and lending at the same rate. Show that utility may increase but cannot decrease.

8.6 Suppose the borrowing rate for an investor exceeds the risk-free lending rate. Derive the budget line that separates attainable from unattainable risk-return combinations and indicate where the firm is borrowing or lending.

8.7 A manager calculates that through self-insurance, she can transform certain profit when there is no fire (Π_{nf}) into certain profit when there is a fire (Π_f) along the schedule

$$\Pi_{nf} = 20,000 - .001(\Pi_f)^2$$

The firm is endowed with a fire profit equal to $1,000 and a no-fire profit equal to $19,000. The price of market insurance (α) equals $8; this is equal to the loss of no-fire profit required to increase fire profit by $1 by buying insurance in the market. Find the optimal amount of self-insurance.

8.8 The time is 1920, and the Bluegrass Horseshoe Company has finished three-quarters of a new horseshoe plant. At this point, the introduction of the automobile causes the price of horseshoes to plummet and forecasts indicate that horseshoe prices will stay depressed for many years. Evaluate: It is pointless not to finish building the plant since it is three-quarters completed already.

8.9 Answer true, false, or undecided. A risk-averse firm will undertake the same investment projects that a risk-neutral firm undertakes.

REFERENCES

Ehrlich, Isaac, and Gary S. Becker: "Market Insurance, Self-Insurance and Self-Protection," *Journal of Political Economy*, vol 80, August 1972, pp. 623–648.

Haley, Charles, and Lawrence D. Schall: *The Theory of Financial Decisions*, New York: McGraw-Hill Book Company, 1979.

Levy, Haim, and Marshall Sarnat: *Capital Investment and Financial Decisions*, London: Prentice-Hall International, Inc., 1978.

9

LABOR MANAGEMENT DECISIONS

In Chapter 5, we examined the general problem of selecting the quantities of various inputs that were necessary for profit maximization. One of these inputs is labor. We shall focus on labor in this chapter for two reasons. First, labor is an important input; approximately three-quarters of the average U.S. firm's total cost is allocated to labor. Second, labor presents some interesting managerial problems that are not characteristic of other inputs. As we all know, in some respects dealing with humans is much more difficult than dealing with other inputs like machines, trucks, or cash registers. Humans strive to maximize their own welfare and managers must take this into account. For example, the cleanliness and noise level of the workplace has an impact upon humans that affects their willingness and ability to work. To a large degree, these factors have no effect on most other inputs. In addition, humans have personal problems that affect the quality of their work. They can be undependable—while a worker may come to the job with a hangover, his or her typewriter does not.

When it comes to employing the labor services of men and women, the news is not all bad. Workers can provide information about the production process. They can offer suggestions for improving the good or service being sold. But, perhaps most interesting, they can become more productive over time. With experience, workers can learn more efficient ways of producing a given product. Employees can also acquire additional skills and knowledge. Consequently, employers may find it desirable to alter production to take advantage of the learning that comes with additional experience or to invest in their employees by providing a training program. In all cases, sound managerial decisions depend upon balancing the incremental costs and benefits of the proposed actions. We now turn to some examples of labor management problems and a discussion of the economic principles for solving these problems.

9.1

OPTIMAL CUSTOMER QUEUING

As we have seen, the cost of obtaining a good or service includes not only the money price that is paid for it but also the value of the time that is spent obtaining the good or service. If the arrivals of the firm's customers are not perfectly predictable, the manager must deal with a randomness in the number of customers to be served at any point in time. This decision involves a trade-off between the time spent obtaining the good or service and its money price.

Consider the case of a supermarket. There may be some normal pattern in the arrival of customers. For example, there is usually some congestion during the lunch hour and immediately following the end of the normal workday. The manager can plan for these peak periods. To some extent, however, customers will arrive randomly and the manager must deal with this randomness in an optimal fashion. The manager of the supermarket could hire a sufficient number of cashiers such that no customer would ever have to wait in line. It is fairly obvious that this policy would result in most of the cashiers being idle a good deal of the time. The cost of providing this high standard of service, i.e., no waiting time, must be reflected in the price of the food sold by the supermarket. If the store manager reduces the number of cashiers, the time that each cashier stands idle would be reduced. This cost saving would decrease the money price of groceries to each customer but increase the waiting time for some of the customers. Consequently, the manager's problem is to find the correct combination of money price and waiting time.

The total cost of a trip to the grocery store is equal to the amount of money spent on the food purchased plus the value of the customer's time in getting to and from the store as well as the time spent in the store. In this problem, we shall ignore the commuting time; the problem of selecting the optimal location for the store is solved appropriately by employing the principles developed in Chapter 7. As a result, we will be concerned with the price of food and the value of the waiting time for the consumer. We can write the opportunity cost of a trip to the supermarket as

$$C = PQ + vT \tag{9.1}$$

where P and Q represent the price and quantity of food, v is the value of time to the customer, and T is the time spent in one trip to the supermarket. The price of the food depends upon the cost of the food to the store and the number of cashiers. The time spent in making one visit to the grocery store is also dependent upon the number of cashiers. In particular, a reduction in the number of cashiers leads to a decrease in the price of food, but it leads to an increase in the time spent shopping.

The manager's problem is to minimize the total cost of shopping for Q groceries by selecting the appropriate number of cashiers. If he fails to minimize these costs, another supermarket may offer his former customers a lower total cost and take them away. Curves depicting the monetary expenditures on food (PQ), the time cost of shopping (vT), and the total cost (C) are shown in Figure 9.1.

Consider what happens when the manager hires one more cashier. If each cashier costs $100 per week and the store has 1,000 customers, then hiring one more cashier adds $0.10 per week to the monetary cost of food. This is the slope of the PQ curve. The slope is constant because one more cashier adds $0.10 to each customer's weekly food bill whether there are 5 cashiers or 20 cashiers.

Similarly, the decrease in the time cost of shopping from hiring one more cashier is given by the slope of the vT curve. This curve gets flatter as the number of cashiers increases, because we expect a large reduction in waiting time from adding one more cashier when there are only a few cashiers and we expect a small reduction in waiting time from adding one more cashier when many cashiers are employed.

For the total cost to be minimized, the increase in the monetary cost of food from hiring one more cashier must equal the reduction in the time cost of shopping from hiring one more cashier. In Figure 9.1, the total cost is minimized by hiring N^* cashiers; at this point, the slope of the PQ curve equals the absolute value of the slope of the vT curve.

This result also can be obtained analytically. Suppose that the number of cashiers is represented by N. The increase in the price of a unit of food that results from adding one more cashier is represented by $\Delta P / \Delta N$, which is positive. Since Q units of food are purchased, adding a cashier raises the monetary cost of food by $(\Delta P / \Delta N)Q$. Similarly, the decrease in the time spent waiting in line that accompanies the use of one more cashier is given by $\Delta T / \Delta N$, which is negative. When this time savings is valued at the customer's value of time, we can see that using one more cashier reduces the time cost of shopping by $v(\Delta T / \Delta N)$. Accordingly, the total cost of shopping for a fixed quantity of groceries is minimized when the number of cashiers is adjusted to the point where

$$\frac{\Delta C}{\Delta N} = \frac{\Delta P}{\Delta N}Q + v\frac{\Delta T}{\Delta N} = 0 \tag{9.2}$$

The information required to make this decision is not difficult to obtain. As

FIGURE 9.1   In minimizing the costs of a fixed quantity of groceries, the manager must equate the marginal benefit of extra cashiers (slope of vT) to the marginal cost (slope of PQ).

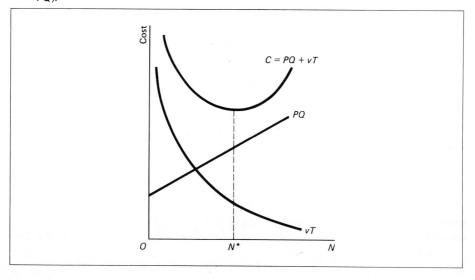

we have seen, the increase in the price of food associated with hiring one more cashier ($\Delta P/\Delta N$) can be calculated. Furthermore, the reduction in the average waiting time when an additional cashier is hired ($\Delta T/\Delta N$) can be observed.

FURTHER IMPLICATIONS   If one observes the length of the lines in various grocery stores, one is likely to find considerable variation in the amount of time that the average customer will have to stand in line. Generally, this suggests that the various store managers are catering to their respective clienteles. This can be seen by observing that the time cost of shopping depends upon the customer's valuation of his time. As we might expect, this valuation is personal and will vary across individuals. The manager must properly value his customer's time when choosing how many cashiers to employ.

> **Question**   Should we expect to find longer checkout lines in wealthy neighborhoods or in poor neighborhoods?

> **Answer**   Since an increase in the time spent in line that leads to a $1 decrease in the money cost of food is more likely to be worthwhile in stores whose clientele do not value their time highly, one should expect longer lines in poor neighborhoods.

The reason that reducing the customer's waiting time increases the money cost of groceries is that some of the cashiers will be idle part of the time. It follows that the higher the wage rate of the cashiers, the greater will be the money savings from having longer lines and thereby having the cashiers less idle. In terms of condition (9.2), the higher the cashier's wage rate, the higher $\Delta P/\Delta N$; this implies that the PQ curve in Figure 9.1 becomes steeper as the wage rate of cashiers increases. Consequently, for any given food purchase Q and value of time v, the optimal waiting time of the customer must increase as cashier wages increase. Thus, as a general proposition, the greater the value of the unoccupied resource, the more likely it is that customers will have to wait for service.

9.2

COMPENSATING WAGE DIFFERENTIALS

It was observed in Chapter 7 that nominal wages vary across geographic regions. As we have seen, that fact plays an important role in the location decision of the firm. We shall now examine the theory of compensating wage differentials, which is essential to an enlightened personnel policy. This starts from explicitly recognizing that workers are concerned not only with wages but also with job conditions, the location of the place of employment, fringe benefits, opportunity for advancement, and so on. A successful firm should be knowledgeable about the rate at which workers are willing to trade off wages for these other aspects of the job.

Let's consider two jobs with identical training and entrance require-ments. If both were equally enjoyable, then in equilibrium the wages must be equal. If the wages were not equal, then all workers would go to the job with the higher wage rate. When the wages in job 1 equal the wages in job 2, all workers will be indifferent between working in job 1 and working in job 2. The extreme form of this is where the jobs are identical in every respect ex-cept for the employer's identity. If one employer offers a lower wage rate, no one will want to work for that firm.

Now suppose that job 1 is more enjoyable than job 2. In selecting an oc-cupation, the worker will be influenced by the difference in wages between the two jobs and the value he or she places on the difference in the non-pecuniary aspects of the jobs. With "enjoyability" as an added dimension, the equilibrium condition is slightly more complicated. Since job 2 is less en-joyable, job 2 must pay higher wages. If this were not true, all workers would select job 1, which would have at least as high a wage rate plus greater non-pecuniary benefits. For example, sanitation workers command higher wages than workers in other jobs of comparable skill requirements in order to com-pensate them for the unpleasantness of having to deal with garbage. Similarly, police officers receive higher wages than security guards to com-pensate them for accepting greater physical risks.

But we can learn more from the theory of compensating wage differen-tials than that wages are higher in less pleasant jobs, other things being equal. Additional insight comes from the realization that people would increase the time they devoted to a relatively unpleasant job if the difference in wages exceeded the monetary value placed on the difference in non-pecuniary benefits. Consequently, in equilibrium, the difference in wages must equal the monetary value of the difference in nonmonetary benefits.

Question Why might university professors be paid more than sanitation workers when the nonpecuniary aspects of a university job are higher?

Answer University professors spend many more years in school acquir-ing knowledge than do sanitation workers. Some financial rewards (in earnings) are necessary to induce individuals to spend more time in school. The relationship between wages and market productivity is treated more fully in Section 9.3.

There are a number of useful applications of the theory of compensating wage differentials to business topics.

LOCATIONAL WAGE DIFFERENTIALS The theory of compensating wage dif-ferentials implies that nominal wages will adjust to keep the marginal worker of a given skill indifferent between locations. Wages necessarily will be greater in areas where the cost of living is high to fully compensate for the additional costs associated with living in these areas. Wages will be lower in areas which are nicer to live in; for example, many more workers would be willing to work for lower wages in Tahiti than in Anchorage, Alaska. Since workers are willing to work for less in nicer areas, the cost of locally produced goods such as restaurant meals, haircuts, and the like are lower in more pleasant areas. Accordingly, many components of the cost of living are lower in more desirable areas. In urban areas, however, competition for scarce land drives urban land prices above the prices of surrounding agricultural land. The cost of living (and consequently wages) will increase as land prices increase. Therefore, wages are predicted to be higher in urban areas and in less desirable areas.

Empirical evidence supporting this theory may be taken from a study of the determinants of primary and secondary teachers' salaries in 1970.[1] It was found that much of the variation in the nominal salaries of teachers of a given quality could be attributed to variation in urbanization and in the weather. School districts in completely urban areas were estimated to pay teachers between $400 and $1,300 more than schools in completely rural areas. The empirical evidence also supports the hypothesis that, other things being equal, wages adjust to *fully* compensate for geographical differences in the cost of living. The estimated relationship between salaries and January temperatures is graphed in Figure 9.2. The "optimal" climate in the sense of that climate where salaries are lowest, *ceteris paribus*, is estimated to be a belt which runs through Jacksonville, Atlanta, and New Orleans. School districts in areas with the winter climate of Detroit are estimated to pay teachers up to $1,800 more than school districts with the winter climate of Atlanta.

Furthermore, there is wage variation even within a city. Firms that are located closer to their labor force are able to pay lower wages because workers are willing to work for less when they have a shorter commute to work. One of the principal benefits of moving an office whose labor force is primarily white-collar out of the inner city and into the suburbs may be the reduction in wages that would accompany such a move.

JOB SAFETY AND THE EFFECT OF WORKMEN'S COMPENSATION   Let us examine the effects of job safety on a firm's personnel policies. Suppose the firms in industries A and B hire general maintenance workers of identical skills. Employment in industry A, however, is more dangerous than a similar job in industry B simply because accidents are more likely to occur in industry A. Initially, let us see what happens when injured workers are not directly compensated for time lost from the job or for any accident-related expenses. To focus on the safety aspect of the problem, assume that the work in industry A and the work in industry B are equally pleasant in all respects other than safety. It follows from the theory of compensating wage differentials that the wage rate must be higher in industry A than in industry B to compensate workers for the anticipated lost working time and for any losses associated with accidents. Moreover, if accidents entail subsequent medical payments, earnings (which equal the product of the wage rate and the time spent working) must be higher in industry A to cover these payments. It is

[1]Lawrence W. Kenny and David Denslow, Jr., "Compensating Differentials in Teachers' Salaries," *Journal of Urban Economics*, vol. 7, April 1980, pp. 198–207.

also reasonable to suppose that being sick or injured is less enjoyable than working. Provided that this is the case earnings in the relatively more hazardous industry will have to compensate for that discomfort also. Finally, if workers are risk-averse, some compensation will be required for the greater uncertainty about earnings in riskier jobs.

What happens if workmen's compensation is instituted? Suppose that the employer becomes fully responsible for any accident-related cost incurred by his employees: the employees will be compensated for all time lost from work because of an accident plus all of the resulting medical bills. If workers were risk-neutral and indifferent between being sick or injured and being on the job, the hourly wage rates would be equal in the two industries. But total earnings, if defined to include workmen's compensation, would still be higher in the relatively more hazardous industry A. As a first approximation, the total labor costs are the same for a firm in industry A whether there is a system of workmen's compensation or not.

Question Accident-prone workers are so called because they have more accidents than the average worker. Evaluate: Those who are accident-prone will leave industry 1, the riskier industry, if there is no system of workmen's compensation but may not if such a system is introduced.

Answer True. The first workers hired in industry 1 will be those who rarely have accidents, for the compensating wage differential necessary to induce these workers into industry 1 is less than the compensating wage differential required to induce more accident-prone workers into industry 1. Workers do not always know how prone they will be to industrial

FIGURE 9.2 The relationship between the salary that must be paid and the mean January temperature describes an aspect of compensating wage differentials.

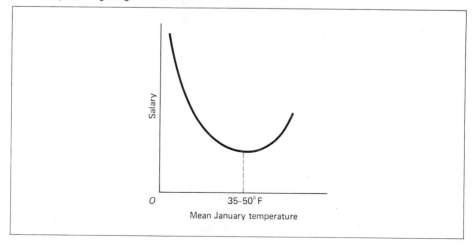

Salary

O

35–50° F

Mean January temperature

accidents; a worker who then discovers that he is accident-prone will leave industry 1 because the wage is not high enough to compensate for his frequent accidents. If a system of workmen's compensation is introduced, accident-prone workers have a much smaller incentive to leave industry 1.

It is of some interest to know whether workers are really willing to trade off job safety for wages. If they are, it is important for the firm to know something about the rate of exchange. Casual empiricism suggests that most people are willing to accept small risks in exchange for small rewards. For example, people will cross a busy street to buy ice cream. There is a positive probability of being killed for an ice cream cone, but rational consumers accept such small risks. Consequently, it is not outlandish to suppose that workers accept job-related safety risks in exchange for higher wages. In fact, Richard Thaler and Sherwin Rosen[2] have presented some empirical evidence that this is the case. They used the 1967 Survey of Economic Opportunity as a source of data for their study. Using this data, they estimated that annual earnings rose by some $176 to $260, other things being equal, as the occupation-specific probability of death increased by .001. Making some rather tenuous extrapolations, workers may be estimated to demand additional compensation of $1,760 to $2,600 per year to face an increased yearly probability of job-related death of 1 percent. Thus, the compensating wage differential associated with risk of life can be quite sizable.

Confronted with such information, the manager has the problem of selecting the cost-minimizing degree of risk that workers will be permitted to face. The total labor-related cost (C_L) to the firm can be written as the sum of expenditures on wages (wL) and expenditures on safety equipment

$$C_L = wL + P_s S$$

where S = safety equipment
P_s = price of safety equipment

One more unit of safety equipment costs the firm P_s in additional expenditures on safety equipment. But with additional safety equipment, the job becomes safer and workers are willing to work at lower wage rates. In particular, the reduction in the wage rate that results from 1 more unit of job safety equipment is given by $\Delta w/\Delta S$, where $\Delta w/\Delta S$ is negative. Since this reduction in the wage rate applies to L workers, the firm saves $(\Delta w/\Delta S)L$ in expenditures on wages when it purchases 1 more unit of job safety equipment. The manager wants to pick the quantity of safety equipment that will minimize her total labor-related cost. (How could this problem be depicted with a diagram similar to Figure 9.1?) The principle is both clear and familiar: expenditures on safety equipment should always be made if the resulting

---

[2]Richard Thaler and Sherwin Rosen, "The Value of Saving a Life: Evidence from the Labor Market," in Nestor E. Terleckyj (ed.), *Household Production and Consumption*, New York: National Bureau of Economic Research, 1975.

decrease in expenditures on wages exceeds the cost of the equipment because such an action will increase the firm's profits. The efforts at improved safety should be extended until the marginal cost of reducing risks (P_s) equals the marginal reduction in wages $[(\Delta w/\Delta S)L]$. Equivalently, total labor-related costs are minimized when

$$\frac{\Delta C_L}{\Delta S} = \frac{\Delta w}{\Delta S}L + P_s = 0$$

A capable manager will not provide her employees with too little safety. To see this, consider the following example. Suppose that a firm employs 50 workers in a certain occupation that involves a substantial risk, say, a 1 percent probability of being killed in a job-related accident. Using the Thaler-Rosen estimates, suppose that each employee must be paid an additional $2,400 per year for facing that risk. For 50 employees, the additional labor costs are $120,000 per year. The firm is contemplating the installation of safety equipment that will reduce the risk of death to .5 percent. If the equipment has an annual cost of less than $60,000, it will be installed because the savings in labor costs will exceed the cost of the equipment. Do you see why? In this instance, the workers place a value on the increased safety that exceeds the marginal cost of the increased safety. Since installation of the safety equipment will enhance the firm's profits, the manager's appropriate decision is to put in the equipment. Conversely, if the safety equipment costs more than $60,000, the workers would place a lower value on the increased safety than the cost of providing it. Consequently, the reduction in labor costs would be more than offset by the increased equipment costs. The manager would appropriately decide not to install the equipment. In both cases, the optimal action has been taken by the manager: safety equipment has been installed when the value placed upon it by the workers exceeds its marginal cost.

Question   Answer true or false: Since firms have incentives to supply their workers with the optimal level of job safety, it is not clear why there is a need for the Occupational Safety and Health Administration (OSHA), which imposes safety standards. Some supporters of OSHA claim that employers routinely mislead their employees regarding safety. Such a managerial decision may increase profits in the short run, but cannot succeed in the long run.

Answer   True. Initially, employers claiming to have more job safety than they do, in fact, often can hire workers at lower wages than they would otherwise have to pay. This increases profit in the short run. Eventually, however, information about the true job-related risk is acquired, and these firms then must pay the full compensating wage differential associated with true job-related risk. Moreover, a firm that has routinely misled its employees is unlikely to retain many of its employees after the firm's deceit is discovered. As we shall see in Section 9.6, quits are costly to the firm, and the loss of profit associated with a mass exodus of employees upon discovery of the firm's deceit may be greater than short-run increase in profit gained through deceit.

EMPLOYEE MALFEASANCE   When an employee of a firm acts in his own interest at the expense of the employer, we do not always have a case of malfeasance. For example, an employee could report a violation of safety regulations. But when the employee commits a wrongful act that he has no legal right to do, we have an instance of malfeasance. There are many ways in which an employee may further his own interests at the expense of the firm. A classic example is the purchasing agent who accepts a bribe for buying from a more expensive supplier. The cost to the firm of this instance of malfeasance is quite clear: it equals the overcharge on the order from the more expensive supplier.

Employee malfeasance increases the cost to the firm and thereby reduces the firm's profits. Thus, the managerial problem is to determine how best to deal with the possibility of malfeasance. The manager can deter the employee from engaging in acts of malfeasance by reducing the expected returns to malfeasance. For example, suppose that the employee's income is $10,000 if he does his job honestly. An unscrupulous supplier may offer him a bribe of $1,000 for purchasing overpriced inputs. Thus, his income will be $11,000 if he is not caught in this bit of malfeasance. Suppose that a sanction or penalty can be imposed upon the employee if he is discovered. In this situation, the expected income associated with accepting the bribe $[E(I)]$ will be given by

$$E(I) = p(\$10,000 + \$1,000) + (1 - p)(\$10,000 + \$1,000 - S) \qquad (9.3)$$

where p is the probability of not getting caught, $(1 - p)$ is the probability of being discovered, and S is the value of the penalty.

The manager can reduce the expected income from malfeasance in two ways: (1) she can increase the probability of detecting malfeasance and (2) she can increase the penalty to the employee should he be caught. There are several ways of increasing the probability of catching an employee engaged in malfeasance. First, the firm may purchase additional monitoring equipment. To reduce document theft, for example, electronic locks may be installed that lock when a specially treated item passes a sensing device. Second, additional labor may be employed to monitor the behavior and performance of the firm's employees. The added personnel will be allocated to the prevention, detection, and investigation of crimes against the firm. For example, guards may be hired to reduce employee theft, auditors may be hired to prevent or detect embezzlement, and foremen may be hired to ensure that workers do not become idle. Finally, employees may be "encouraged" to inform on the activities of their fellow workers. All of these efforts to decrease the probability of successful malfeasance require direct expenditures on inputs specifically designed to thwart someone bent on malfeasance.

Question   At what point will the firm stop hiring those inputs whose function is to deter malfeasance?

Answer   The firm will stop hiring those inputs when the cost of one more input equals the savings from reduced malfeasance that results from hiring one more input. In other words, such expenditures should stop when the marginal cost equals the marginal benefit.

The alternative means of deterring malfeasance is to increase the value of the sanction imposed upon the employee if he is caught. Since the firm cannot fine its employees, its options are somewhat limited. There are, however, two avenues open: (1) the firm may place money in a pension fund that is paid to the employee when he leaves the firm only if he has not been dismissed for malfeasance and (2) the firm may pay the employee more than his opportunity cost. For instance, a man may earn $18,000 per year as a policeman. Suppose his next best alternative occupation pays only $15,000. This provides an incentive of $3,000 per year to refuse the offer of a bribe. If one assumes that the cost to the employee of being fired is equal to the present value of the difference in earnings, we can readily calculate the value. Letting r represent the interest rate and V the value of the deterrent, we have

$$V = \$3{,}000 + \frac{\$3{,}000}{1+r} + \frac{\$3{,}000}{(1+r)^2} + \cdots + \frac{\$3{,}000}{(1+r)^{n-1}} \tag{9.4}$$

for an individual that has n more years to work before retirement. It is clear from this expression that the effectiveness of increasing an employee's wage above his alternative wages falls as the employee nears retirement. As the employee ages, the present value of the difference in earnings falls. In other words, it is less costly to accept a bribe when you lose only 5 years of excess wages than when you lose 10. The essence of this approach to dealing with malfeasance is that the manager makes the present job more attractive than alternative jobs.

Wage differentials can also be used to protect a firm's secrets. Since a company's secrets often can be quite valuable, this is an important consideration. The strategy of the Ford Motor Company provides an example. When the former president of Ford was released, he was given a trust fund that was worth over $1 million. But the proceeds went to him only in the event that he not work for another automobile company for at least 3 years. This sort of strategy is necessary because the employees of innovative firms can be bid away by firms that are not innovative. These employees will then be paid for the secrets that they bring with them. This raises the question of whether innovative firms are at a disadvantage. At first blush, one might suppose that they are because the innovative firm incurs the investment costs of being innovative and then may lose the benefits because key personnel take their secrets and expertise to other firms. But the analysis is not quite so clear because employees at innovative firms will be willing to supply their services for less in anticipation of the future benefits that are associated with being bid away by another firm. Suppose that a worker is considering two 1-year positions. Working at firm A pays $20,000 per year and offers no opportunities for stealing secrets. After 1 year at firm B, firm C would be willing to pay $4,000 for the knowledge about firm B's secrets which the worker has accumulated during that year. If the worker has no qualms about divulging a firm's secrets, then he will be willing to work for firm B for as little as $16,000 per year. This can be seen by noting that if firm B paid him $20,000, he could go to firm C after 1 year at firm B and make $24,000 for his year's work. Firm B could reduce the incidence of stealing its company secrets by offering part of the employee's compensation in a pension to be dispersed if no secrets were sold.

FRINGE BENEFITS Every employee considers the total value of the compensation package when he or she selects a job. The hourly wage rate may be the principal component, but the value of fringe benefits cannot be ignored. Health insurance and subsidized cafeterias are not gifts freely given to a firm's employees. They are part of the compensation package and should be viewed as such by managers. To the extent that fringe benefits can be substituted for wages, the manager may be able to increase the firm's profits. The first reason for this is that many fringe benefits are not subject to personal income tax.

Suppose the firm reduces an employee's gross wages by $1 to bring about an increase in fringe benefits. The sacrifice in income made by the employee to "purchase" the additional fringe benefits will be less than $1 because of personal income taxes. If the marginal tax rate is t cents per $1 then the employee's cost is $1.00 - t$ in aftertax terms. If the worker and the firm are equally efficient purchasers of the services provided by the fringe benefits, then the tax laws enable the firm to buy $1 worth of these services at a cost of only $1.00 - t$ to the employee. If the employee is willing to pay at least $1.00 - t$ for the services provided by a $1 wage reduction and the services cost no more than $1, then both parties can gain from the provision of fringe benefits. For example, suppose that $t = .30$ and that the firm reduces wages by $1 to spend $0.80 on fringe benefits. The manager thereby increases the firm's profits by $0.20. If the worker is willing to spend $0.75 for the resulting services, which have cost him $0.70, then he is also better off. Thus, the substitution of a fringe benefit for money wages can increase the firm's profits. It should be noted that the higher the employee's marginal tax rate, the greater the value of tax-free fringe benefits.

The second reason why fringe benefits may substitute for wages is that a firm may be a more efficient customer than the individual. Health insurance provides a good example. Owing to the fixed costs to the insurance company of writing a policy, the *individual* policy costs far more than the *per capita* cost of a group policy. Furthermore, the cost per employee falls as the number of employees in the group increases. Consequently, firms with larger numbers of employees pay less for a group health insurance policy than smaller firms. Again, the fact that the price of health insurance coverage is lower to the firm than to the individual allows the manager to reduce his total wage bill and thereby increase his firm's profits.

Question A union official discovered that "management" received free dental insurance as a fringe benefit while the unionized "labor" did not. He claimed that this was discriminatory. Was he correct?

Answer "Management" faces a higher marginal tax rate than does unionized "labor." Because of this, the cost to management in forgone wages of receiving any fringe benefit is less than the cost to labor in forgone wages of receiving that fringe benefit. Management therefore will find it beneficial to receive more wages in fringe benefits than will labor.

One of the characteristics of illness is that it is for the most part unforeseen. Even persons with high probabilities of getting cancer (e.g., heavy smokers) or of having heart attacks (e.g., overweight individuals) do not know when or if illness will occur. Unless individuals are protected, illness entails medical expenditures and a loss of income. Risk-averse individuals will reduce the uncertainty in their income and expenditures through the purchase of insurance. Medical insurance reduces the uncertainty in expenditures, and an allowance of sick days reduces the uncertainty in income. The demand for income insurance is therefore the motivating force behind the sick day allowance offered by many companies.

Sick day allowances, however, can be very costly, for when each employee is allowed to take D days off for being sick, the employee, by pretending to be sick, can increase his leisure without any loss of wages. This malingering reduces employee productivity and consequently reduces the wage rate that employers are willing to pay their employees; this is the cost to the employee of income insurance.

There are several ways of reducing the cost of income insurance. The employer could require a certification of sickness by the employee's doctor. This, however, increases the employee's medical expenditures for routine illnesses for which a doctor is often not consulted (e.g., for a cold or flu). Alternatively, the employer could pay the employee some fraction of his regular pay on sick days; this practice reduces malingering but also decreases the amount of income insurance which is, in fact, bought.

9.3

INVESTMENT IN SKILLS

In Chapter 5, we saw that a worker's wage rate is determined by the value to the firm of her productivity. Specifically, we found that a firm that is operating in competitive input and output markets would pay an employee the value of her marginal product:

$$w = \text{VMP}_L = P \cdot \text{MP}_L$$

which is determined by the price of the firm's output P and the worker's marginal product MP_L. Unlike most other inputs, workers can have an effect upon their marginal product. By investing in educational programs or even in on-the-job training, a worker can increase her productivity and consequently increase her wages.

Almost anyone can improve her productivity through the acquisition of additional skills or the improvement of existing skills. If the investment is to be worthwhile, however, the present value of the returns must exceed the costs. Consider an investment in a particular educational program that costs C dollars and yields benefits of B dollars next year and every year thereafter. The costs C must be inclusive: books, tuition, commuting costs, the value of earnings which are forgone for learning, and so on. The present value of the benefits of B per year equals

$$PV = \frac{B}{1 + r} + \frac{B}{(1 + r)^2} + \cdots + \frac{B}{(1 + r)^n} \qquad (9.5)$$

where we have represented the relevant interest rate by r and n is the number of working years that the employee still has left after the educational program. The investment will be worthwhile only if PV exceeds C. This is essentially the net-present-value rule that we examined in Chapter 8: when the NPV of an investment option is positive, the investment should be made. For example, if the interest rate were 10 percent, the present value of $100 per year for 30 years would be $942.70. Consequently, an educational investment that increased aftertax earnings by $100 per year when the interest rate equals 10 percent would be profitable only if its cost C is less than or equal to $942.70.

Question   Can an educational investment that is unprofitable when the interest rate is 10 percent become profitable if the rate falls to 8 percent?

Answer   Yes. As the interest rate falls, the present value of the returns on the investment rises. The rise in the present value of the returns may make a previously unprofitable investment now profitable. Thus, the net present value of an investment rises as the interest rate falls.

We have determined that some investments in increased productivity are economically sound; i.e., the returns properly discounted exceed the costs. The question then is, When should the firm pay the costs of education? The answer depends upon how specific the skills are to the firm in question. At one extreme, we may suppose that the increased skills can be used in many other firms. For example, a person may improve her typing skills through on-the-job training or she may become a better computer programmer. Since the skills are not firm-specific, i.e., only useful to the present employer, many firms will be willing to pay wages equal to the value of the worker's enhanced productivity. As a result, with an increase in productivity, the wages available at other firms will increase by the value of the increased productivity. If the manager agreed to pay for a computer programming course, he could not recoup the firm's investment. Essentially, the only way to recover the cost would be to pay the worker less than her full value to the firm after productivity was increased. But if the manager attempted to do this, the worker would simply move to a firm that paid her full worth. Consequently, the manager will not agree to pay for an investment in skills that can be used in many different firms. Workers will have to pay for on the job training in general skills through reduced current wages.

We may also consider the case where the skills in question are extremely specialized and cannot be used by any other firm. For example, a university employee whose job is to deliver mail to the various departments must learn their locations. This knowledge is not valuable to any other firm. If the employee pays for acquiring this knowledge, she would be investing in specific human capital. Because of her specialization, there is a gap between the value of her marginal product in this particular job and her alternative wages, which equal the value of her marginal productivity elsewhere. If she makes this investment in the belief that future wages at the university will reflect her increased productivity, she may be disappointed. The firm (in this case, the university) has no incentive to protect her investment by continuing to employ her. Similarly, if the firm were to pay for the investment, it could only benefit from the employee's increased productivity by not increasing her wages. The employee, however, has no incentive to protect the firm's investment by continuing to work for the firm. It is only when the costs and returns from investments in the firm-specific human capital are shared that *both* parties will suffer when the employee and the employer separate. Consequently, both the firm and the employee will pay for investments in firm-specific human capital.

Question   The U.S. Army provides some individuals with training as helicopter pilots. How does the Army protect its investment? Why don't firms do the same thing?

Answer   Soldiers are prohibited from leaving the Army before their period of enlistment is up. Those who do attempt to leave the Army before their period of enlistment is up are subject to long jail sentences. Firms have been unable to successfully enforce long-term labor contracts such as those found in the military. If *voluntary* long-term labor contracts were enforceable, additional investment in firm-specific human capital would take place.

9.4

EFFECTS OF FAIR EMPLOYMENT LAWS

Fair employment laws are designed to prevent job discrimination on the basis of race, sex, or any other seemingly irrelevant consideration. A law that requires "equal pay for equal work" has an ethical appeal that appears flawless. But such a law can pose problems for a firm's manager.

Consider two employees: one expects to work for 20 years and the other plans to work for 40 years. Each employee is contemplating an investment which costs C and which increases earnings by B next year and every year thereafter. The present value of the increased earnings will be greater for the individual planning to work for 40 years. As a result, he is more likely to find this investment profitable. Therefore, workers intending to work many years will tend to invest more in increasing their skills than workers who anticipate that they will spend only a few years on the job.

If productivity is not easily measured, a law or judicial ruling that requires equal pay for equal work may make differential investment more costly. Such a law or ruling may force employers to pay equal salaries to workers with the same experience on the job even if they have different productivities because of their having invested at different rates in on-the-job training.

The impact upon the employee that is planning to work more than the average number of years is clear: the incentive to invest more than others in increasing his skills is reduced. Since investment in on-the-job training is not rewarded as much when fair employment laws are (imperfectly) enforced, there will be less investment in on-the-job training.

The impact on the firm is equally clear: on the average the firm's work force will have lower productivity. Managers can react to this in a variety of ways. One of the easiest ways is to define narrow job classifications and reward productive employees through promotions. In the event of a complaint, however, the firm's manager will have to be able to prove that a man who was promoted in preference to a woman actually demonstrated superior productivity. Consequently, the manager will have an incentive to improve his measurement of employee productivity.

Question   Answer true or false: Minority quotas take the form of requiring, say, that 10 percent of a firm's employees must be members of a particular minority group. This will lead to a general increase in the demand for minority labor. If there was no discrimination initially, the firm would have to pay minority workers more than majority workers of equal quality.

Answer   True. With no discrimination initially, minority and majority workers of a given quality receive the same wage. The increased demand for minority workers drives the wage rate of minority workers of a given quality above the wage rate of identically skilled majority workers.

9.5

LEARNING BY DOING

In many manufacturing processes, one may observe that costs fall over time without any apparent changes in production technique. One of the most famous examples was reported by Lundberg.[3] Writing about the Horndal Iron Works, a Swedish firm, he noted that during a 15-year period the firm made no new investment and no change of any consequence in its production method. Nonetheless, output per worker showed an increase of some 2 percent per year. This phenomenon has been described by other economists for other industries. For example, costs have been observed to fall with increases in the total output produced

---

[3]E. Lundberg, *Produktivitet och Rantabilitet*, Stockholm: P. A. Norstedt and Sover, 1961.

in industries such as the aircraft,[4] home appliance, shipbuilding, and construction industries.

What appears to be happening is that workers are learning from their actual experience on the job. As a result, the output per worker increases over time. Where tasks are repeated, people become more efficient with more experience. They learn better ways of performing their assigned functions.

In some of the industries just mentioned, learning by doing is a very important phenomenon. In these industries, it has been observed that when total output doubles, the amount of labor needed to produce 1 unit of output is only 80 percent of what it formerly was. The quantity of other inputs is assumed to be constant. For instance, it may have taken 100 man-hours to assemble the fiftieth Piper Cub airplane ever produced and 80 man-hours to assemble the hundredth Piper Cub airplane ever produced.

In other industries, learning by doing is less important. In particular, there appears to be a lower rate of learning in highly automated processes. This is reasonable, for there is much less scope for innovation in a highly automated process.

As we discovered in Chapter 5, the manager of a competitive firm that experiences no learning by doing will find the firm's optimal output to be the quantity where marginal cost and marginal revenue (which is equal to price) are equal. In Figure 9.3, we see that the profit-maximizing quantity is Q_1

The manager's output decision is complicated by the phenomenon of

---

FIGURE 9.3 When the costs of future production fall because of present production, the manager will produce beyond the point where marginal cost equals marginal revenue.

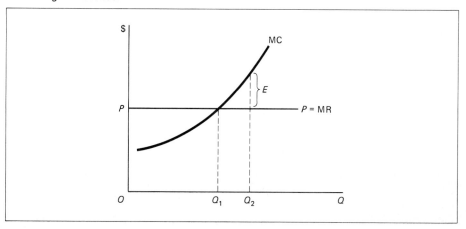

learning by doing. The marginal cost to the firm of producing 1 more unit today is still that firm's marginal cost (MC). The marginal benefit to the firm of increasing output by 1 unit, however, is equal to the price that it receives for that unit *plus* the present value of increased profits due to having 1 more unit of experience (and hence lower marginal cost) at each point in the future. The firm maximizes profits by equating the marginal benefit from increasing output to the marginal cost of increasing output. Thus, optimal output now requires

$$P + E = MC$$

where E represents the present value of experience. As can be seen in Figure 9.3, the firm that experiences learning by doing will produce beyond the point where price equals marginal cost; profit is maximized by producing Q_2. The firm will find that it has an incentive to produce more than the short-run profit-maximizing output because by increasing production today, it can increase future profits.

The firm's manager faces a very cumbersome maximization problem when the firm experiences learning by doing because the costs of production fall over time as a function of total previous production. Confronted with this intertemporal cost function, the manager must maximize the present value of profits. We can, however, simplify the manager's problem to gain some further appreciation of what the present value of increased profits from additional experience is. Suppose that the firm will experience learning by doing only in its first year of production. In Figure 9.4, we have the firm's cost

FIGURE 9.4 When learning by doing is important to a firm, the manager must take into account the effects of additional current production on the cost curves in the future: MC_1 and AC_1 as compared to MC_2 and AC_2.

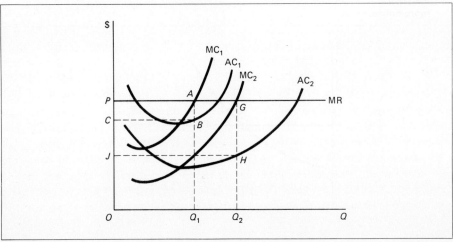

curves in the *second* year of production. These are assumed to remain in the same place for every year after the second. The average cost and marginal cost curves labeled AC_1 and MC_1, respectively, occur if the firm produces 100 units in the first year. The curves labeled AC_2 and MC_2 occur if the firm produces 101 units in the first year. Given the cost conditions AC_1 and MC_1, the manager will select output Q_1. The firm's maximum profits are given by

$$\Pi_1 = PQ_1 - AC_1 \cdot Q_1$$

which is area *PABC*. When the cost curves are AC_2 and MC_2, the manager maximizes the firm's profits by producing Q_2. Profit is given by

$$\Pi_2 = P \cdot Q_2 - AC_2 \cdot Q_2$$

which is area *PGHJ*. The annual increase in profits due to increasing the first year's production from 100 to 101 units equals

$$\Delta\Pi = \Pi_2 - \Pi_1 = PGHJ - PABC$$

These increased profits will be received indefinitely. In terms of present value, the added experience is worth

$$E = \frac{\Delta\Pi}{1 + r} + \frac{\Delta\Pi}{(1 + r)^2} + \cdots = \frac{\Delta\Pi}{r}$$

where r is the appropriate discount rate. If, for example, the interest (or discount) rate is 12 percent and the increase in annual profits $\Delta\Pi$ is $1,000, then the present value of the firm's increased experience would be $8,333. Consequently, the marginal cost of expanding production from 100 to 101 units in the first period could exceed the price by as much as $8,333 and the firm would still elect to produce the larger output.

9.6

HIRING AND LAYOFFS

The cost of using many inputs is negatively related to the duration of their use by the firm. This is equally true of labor inputs. Hiring costs are fixed costs associated with the employment of a particular worker. These costs include the expenses incurred in interviewing potential employees, relocating the worker who is hired, adding that employee to the payroll, and so on. The average cost per each day that the employee is with the firm decreases as the number of days that she is with the company increases. For example, suppose that it costs $100 to hire an employee. If this employee remains with the firm for only 10 days, then the hiring costs would amount to $10 per day. If the employee stayed with the firm 100 days, the hiring costs would amount to only $1 per day. Consequently, there are obvious cost savings that accrue to reduced personnel turnover. All else considered, the manager wants to minimize his hiring costs. This, of course, does not mean that he reduces his efforts to find suitable people for vacant positions. It means that he tries to keep the suitable people he has found.

Generally, it costs more to hire skilled workers than to hire unskilled workers. For one thing, it may be more difficult to ascertain the skills of skilled workers. That is, it may take more resources to ascertain whether a particular business executive is likely to be successful working for a new firm than to ascertain whether a manual laborer can dig a ditch or mow a lawn. Furthermore, skilled workers are more geographically dispersed than unskilled workers. In any given year, only a few good economic historians enter the market. The transportation costs associated with matching these job candidates with the small group of universities looking for economic historians are much greater than the transportation costs related to finding someone to mow the lawn. These observations are not limited to labor inputs. There is a similarly sizable transactions cost associated with the purchase of physical capital.

It seems natural to define a *variable* factor as a factor whose costs are independent of the duration of use and to define a *fixed* factor as a factor whose costs are inversely related to the duration of use. Thus, unskilled labor and raw materials are factors that are close to being variable factors and physical capital and skilled labor are factors that are close to being fixed factors.

These observations will influence how managers should respond to changing economic circumstances. For example, suppose output prices were to increase. As we know from Chapter 5, the manager would respond by increasing output. If the increase in price were expected to be of short duration, the manager would accomplish this by increasing his use of variable factors. Employees would work longer hours, and machines would work more intensively. If, however, the price increase were expected to be permanent, the cost of using fixed factors would fall, and the firm might optimally increase output by increasing fixed factors more and variable factors less. Additional workers would be hired and new machinery bought. Thus, in a temporary downturn, managers will tend to reduce output by reducing variable factors. The number of hours worked per employee falls much more in downturns than does the number of employees. Furthermore, most of the reduction in employment is in unskilled labor. This is partly due to the fact that skilled labor is more of a fixed factor than unskilled labor. Also, skilled labor may have more firm-specific human capital than unskilled labor. The firm would have less incentive to fire workers with firm-specific human capital because the firm loses part of the return on its investment in specific human capital when it fires workers with specific human capital.

Parenthetically, the empirical evidence suggests that at least 75 percent of workers laid off in manufacturing are subsequently rehired by their original employer; the generosity of unemployment insurance and the fact that unemployment insurance income is not taxed contributes to the high rate of "rehiring."[5]

---

[5]See Martin Feldstein, "Temporary Layoffs in the Theory of Unemployment," *Journal of Political Economy*, vol. 84, October 1976, pp. 937–957.

9.7

EFFECTS OF A MINIMUM WAGE

It is claimed that minimum-wage legislation increases the incomes of the poor. It is also claimed that the minimum wage prevents employers from exploiting the disadvantaged worker by paying him a wage that is below some socially acceptable standard. First, we shall examine the operation of a minimum wage to see its impact upon the labor market. Subsequently, we shall focus on its effects on the firm.

Consider a competive market for labor. In the absence of any constraints, the equilibrium wages will be determined by the intersection of supply and demand. In Figure 9.5, the demand for labor is given by DD. This represents the aggregation of all employer demands for this particular type of labor. As such, it shows the maximum quantities of labor that will be hired at various wage rates. The supply of labor is labeled SS and represents the aggregated preferences of workers with particular skills. It shows the maximum amount of labor that will be provided at various wage rates. At the point of intersection, the equilibrium wage and quantity of labor are found to be w_0 and L_0. The market is said to clear at this point both because anyone who is willing to work at a wage rate of w_0 can find a job and because any employer who is willing to pay at least w_0 can find an employee to fill a vacancy.

Suppose that a minimum-wage bill is enacted by the government. This law makes it illegal for an employer to pay a wage below the statutory minimum. Suppose the minimum wage is w_1. If the penalties for a violation of the minimum-wage law are sufficiently severe to deter all violations of the law, then the effect will be to change the supply curve. Originally, the supply was SS, but the law precludes wages below w_1. As a result, the supply curve becomes $w_1 aS$. In this case, the minimum wage was set below the market equilibrium. Being below the competitive wage rate, the statutory minimum is wholly ineffective. Thus, the quantity of labor supplied and demanded remains at L_0. For example, a minimum wage of \$1 when competitive wages equal \$2 will affect neither wages nor the quantity of labor employed.

For a statutory minimum wage to be effective, it must exceed the competitive wage. In Figure 9.5, if the minimum wage were w_2, it would have a market impact because w_2 exceeds w_0, the equilibrium wage. Now, the supply function becomes $w_2 bS$ because no wage can be paid below w_2. At the minimum wage, L_3 units of labor will be supplied, but only L_2 units of labor will be demanded. The market cannot clear because wages cannot fall below w_2. The effect of the minimum wage is clear: it creates an excess supply of $L_3 - L_2$ units of labor. Beginning from the initial equilibrium quantity of L_0, the minimum wages induced $L_3 - L_0$ more units of labor to offer their services at the same time that employers reduced the quantity demanded by $L_0 - L_2$ units.

Since there is excess supply, the available jobs must be rationed on a nonprice basis. Any employee with low productivity will be threatened with

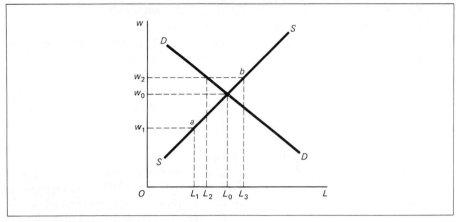

FIGURE 9.5   The impact of an effective minimum wage (w_2) is to cause excess supply of $L_3 - L_2$ and prevent the market from clearing. As a result, nonwage rationing of jobs can occur.

loss of employment. The employer is in a position of dispensing jobs with economic rent. A firm can give jobs to people that it favors particularly: friends, relatives of the owners, whites, males, and so on. The empirical evidence suggests that the minimum-wage law is a major cause of high unemployment rates for black males and teenagers.

It appears that any benefits that are alleged to accrue to unskilled labor from the imposition of a minimum wage are significantly reduced by the resulting loss of employment. As Figure 9.5 shows, *at least* $L_0 - L_2$ people who were previously employed will now be unemployed. To the extent that some of the new entrants to the labor market displace those originally employed, the number of unemployed people who previously had jobs will exceed $L_0 - L_2$. Of course, those who remain employed are better off at a wage of w_2 than they were at a rate equal to w_0.

Is anyone else better off as a result of the minimum-wage legislation? In fact, there are those who may benefit from a minimum wage. Since the minimum wage raises the price of unskilled labor, the ratio of the skilled wage rate to the unskilled wage rate will fall. This will lead a firm's manager to substitute toward skilled labor and away from unskilled labor as skilled labor becomes relatively cheaper. In essence, the minimum-wage law will cause the demand for skilled labor to increase. As the demand for skilled labor increases, the number of skilled workers employed will increase as will the wage rate of skilled workers. This is one explanation why the leaders of the AFL-CIO strongly support minimum-wage legislation.

Let's see how a national minimum wage affects an industry with geographically dispersed production facilities. We have already discovered that the wages paid to identical workers will vary from place to place to reflect compensating wage differentials. Suppose that the textile industry is composed of 300 firms located all over the country. These firms all employ the same production techniques and, therefore, demand the same kind of labor. Due to compensating wage differentials, however, the 300 firms pay different wage rates, which are summarized in the following distribution:

FIRM	WAGE
1	$4.00
⋮	⋮
2	3.95
⋮	⋮
150	2.85
299	2.05
300	2.00

On the basis of our earlier discussion, we expect to find the firms with northern and/or urban locations paying the higher wage rates. Those with a southern and/or rural setting will be paying the lower wages. The distribution of wages involves equilibrium differentials. Now suppose a minimum wage of $2.50 per hour is imposed. For the firms initially paying in excess of $2.50 per hour, the minimum wage is ineffective. Consequently, their cost functions are unchanged. The cost curves of firms that originally were paying less than $2.50 per hour for labor, however, are affected by the legislation. Labor becomes more expensive for these firms. This causes a shift in their marginal and average cost curves.

The effect of minimum-wage legislation on marginal and average costs is shown in Figure 9.6. In panel (a), we see that the cost curves of firm 2 are unaffected by the new law. Since firm 299 originally was paying only $2.05

FIGURE 9.6 Imposition of an effective minimum wage will help a firm (2) that pays a high wage and hurt a firm (299) that pays low wages.

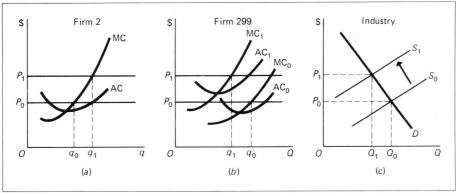

THE SEAMLESS HOSIERY INDUSTRY: AN
EARLY EXAMPLE OF THE IMPACT OF THE
MINIMUM WAGE*

In 1938, the first minimum wage was imposed at $.25 per hour. This had a substantial impact on the seamless hosiery industry, particularly those plants located in the South. Between 1938 and 1940, employment in northern plants increased by 4.9 percent, while employment in southern plants decreased by 5.5 percent. In contrast, total employment for all industries in the United States increased by 7.9 percent as the country pulled out of the Great Depression.

*Source: H. M. Douty, "Minimum Wage Regulation in the Seamless Hosiery Industry," Southern Economic Journal, vol. 8, October 1941, pp. 176–190.

per hour, however, its cost curves change from MC_0 and AC_0 to MC_1 and AC_1, as shown in panel (b). Industry supply, which was originally S_0, is an aggregation of the marginal cost curves of the 300 firms. When the marginal cost curves of the firms that originally paid less than the minimum wage of $2.50 shift to the left, the industry supply curve changes from S_0 to S_1. This causes the equilibrium industry price to rise from P_0 to P_1 and output to fall from Q_0 to Q_1 in panel (c) of Figure 9.6. We see that the increase in price to P_1 induces firm 2 to expand its production from q_0 to q_1. In general, the high-wage firm will increase production and experience an increase in profits. Firm 299 appears to reduce its output from q_0 to q_1. As a general proposition, since *industry* output falls and the high-wage firms increase their production, the low-wage firms must contract their production. Some may even go out of business. In general, the profits of the low-wage firms will decline. This analysis, therefore, suggests that northern and urban firms benefit from minimum-wage legislation at the expense of southern and rural firms. The empirical evidence supports many of the above propositions.[6]

9.8

SUMMARY

Compensating differentials played an important role in this chapter. We saw that customers are willing to pay higher prices to reduce the time spent waiting in line and that employees are willing to work for lower wage rates to obtain a more pleasant environment, additional safety, extra benefits, or training. A successful manager must have an intimate knowledge of these trade-offs.

A number of labor decisions involve incurring some cost in order to make future profits. We saw that when there is learning by doing, a manager should produce more than the usual profit-maximizing output to enhance future profits. We also discovered that because there are greater hiring costs associated with some types of labor than with others, the mix of labor that is hired or fired should depend on the duration of demand shifts.

Finally, we examined the minimum wage and discovered that its effects

[6]See Jacob J. Kaufman and Terry G. Foran, "The Minimum Wage and Poverty," in Readings in Labor Market Analysis, John F. Burton, Jr., et al. (eds.), New York: Holt, Rinehart and Winston, Inc., 1971, pp. 513–514.

are quite complicated. It creates a rationing problem for the manager, increases her demand for skilled labor, and hurts some firms more than others.

IMPORTANT NEW TERMS

Malfeasance

General human capital

Firm-specific human capital

Learning by doing

PROBLEMS

9.1   Answer true, false, or undecided: On the average, lines will be longer in a doctor's office than in a hardware store.

9.2   For whatever reason, some employees can be characterized as "company men"; i.e., they would not consider taking company secrets to another firm. These people are worse off if they work for an innovative firm. Why?

9.3   Can a profitable investment for a 25-year-old worker be unprofitable for a 35-year-old worker?

9.4   Answer true, false, or undecided: If Congress increases the FICA (Social Security) tax rate, all employers will be hurt by this.

9.5   Answer true, false, or undecided: If Congress increases the maximum FICA wages but not the tax rate, some employers will benefit from this.

9.6   Under what circumstances would a firm violate a minimum-wage law?

9.7   Answer true, false, or undecided: The lower the salaries of police officers, the more common will be the incidence of bribery of police officers.

9.8   Answer true, false, or undecided: An increase in the rate of learning by doing will encourage firms to increase production in the first few years of a production run.

9.9   Answer true, false, or undecided: A profit-maximizing firm will be less inclined to pay for women to acquire firm-specific skills than to pay for men to acquire firm-specific skills.

9.10 Answer true, false, or undecided: When the economy experiences a boom that is expected to be short-lived, the ratio of unskilled labor to skilled labor rises.

9.11 Answer true, false, or undecided: It is impossible to know how much workers value job conditions such as freedom from accidents, clean surroundings, and the like.

9.12 Answer true, false, or undecided: Raising the minimum wage leads to an increase in the crime rate.

9.13 Consider the provision of job safety. Assume that all information is free. In the widget industry, the annual cost of providing a worker with level S of job safety equals

$$C_{sw} = 2.5S^2$$

where $S =$ units of job safety

In the coal industry, the cost of providing a worker with level S of job safety equals

$$C_{sc} = 5S^2$$

Assume that both labor markets are competitive and that there are no differences in skills across industries. Furthermore, suppose that workers are willing to give up 1 unit of job safety only if their annual earnings rise by $50. (a) Find the levels of job safety provided in the widget and coal industries. (b) How do annual earnings in the coal industry compare with annual earnings in the widget industry? Be specific. (c) Suppose that OSHA requires at least 8 units of job safety in each workplace. What happens? Does this requirement enhance our well-being?

REFERENCES

Alchian, Armen: "Reliability of Progress Curves in Airframe Production," *Econometrica*, vol. 31, 1963, pp. 670–693.

Arrow, Kenneth: "The Economic Implication of Learning by Doing," *Review of Economics Studies*, vol. 29, 1962, pp. 155–173.

Becker, Gary S., and George J. Stigler: "Law Enforcement, Malfeasance, and Compensation of Enforcers," *Journal of Legal Studies*, vol. 3, January 1974, pp. 1–8.

Feldstein, Martin: "Temporary Layoffs in the Theory of Unemployment," *Journal of Political Economy*, vol. 84, October 1976, pp. 937–957.

Kaufman, Jacob J., and Terry G. Foram: "The Minimum Wage and Poverty," in John F. Burton, Jr., Lee K. Benham, William M. Vaughn, III, and Robert J. Flanagan (eds.), *Readings in Labor Market Economics*, New York: Holt, Rinehart and Winston, Inc., 1971.

Kenny, Lawrence W., and David Denslow, Jr.: "Compensating Differentials in Teachers Salaries," *Journal of Urban Economics*, vol. 7, April 1980, pp. 198–207.

Lundberg, E.: *Produktivitet och Rantabilitet,* Stockholm: P. A. Norstedt and Soner, 1961.

Oi, Walter: "Labor as a Quasi-Fixed Factor of Production," *Journal of Political Economy,* vol. 70, (December 1962), pp. 538–555.

Thaler, Richard, and Sherwin Rosen: "The Value of Saving a Life: Evidence from the Labor Market," in Nestor E. Terleckyj (ed.), *Household Production and Consumption,* New York: National Bureau of Economic Research, 1975.

10 LABOR MANAGE- MENT IN IMPERFECT MARKETS

In imperfect labor markets, one or more of the assumptions of perfect competition is violated: information about the productivity of labor or the location and offerings of workers and employers is costly; and/or a manager is unable to employ as many workers as he pleases at a fixed wage rate determined by the market.

There are a number of examples of imperfect labor markets. Unions raise the wage rate that a manager must pay his workers and may place limitations on his ability to hire and fire employees. An understanding of the causes and effects of unionization is helpful if a manager is to anticipate unionization and properly respond to it. To take another example, although there are many markets in which a manager can hire as many workers as he desires at a given wage rate, there are other markets in which additional labor can be obtained only if the wage rate is increased. How much labor should a firm employ if wage rates are positively related to the amount of labor employed? Furthermore, can a manager reduce the frequency with which workers quit by increasing wage rates, and if so, what is the optimal wage? These are some of the difficulties that a manager can face with imperfect labor markets.

10.1

TRADE UNIONS

Unions have had a pervasive effect on managerial decision making. Not only have they altered wage rates, but they also have made it necessary for some firms to ration labor, they have limited the ability of firms to promote qualified workers, and they have sometimes forced firms to employ more labor than they would have chosen. In this section we will consider a manager's optimal responses to these and other union-imposed constraints on a firm's behavior.

For the time being, let us assume that the *only* effect of unionization is to increase real wage rates, which are defined to include benefits. The empirical evidence on this topic suggests that unionization increases wages by 10 percent on average.[1] Later in this section we will investigate why the wage increase associated with unionization is greater in some industries than in others.

In the appendix to Chapter 5 we showed that the quantity of labor demanded by an industry falls when the wage rate rises. To be more specific, there are two effects of increased wages. Consider a competitive industry. An

---

[1]H. G. Lewis, *Unionism and Relative Wages in the United States*, Chicago: University of Chicago Press, 1963.

increase in the wage rate causes each firm's marginal cost curve to rise, and as a result, the industry supply curve also rises. The effects of this shift in the supply curve can be seen in Figure 10.1. Industry output falls from Q_0 to Q_1 and the price of the output rises from P_0 to P_1 when the supply curve shifts to the left from S_0 to S_1. Because less output is being produced, less labor is used; this is called the "output effect." The quantity of labor demanded by the industry also falls because labor has become more expensive relative to other inputs. Firms in the industry respond to this by substituting—if substitution is possible—away from labor and toward other inputs in the production of any given level of output. That is, less labor is used in the production of any output Q_0. The substitution away from labor as the wage rate rises is called the "substitution effect." Both substitution and output effects cause the quantity of labor demanded to fall as the wage rate rises.

In a competitive labor market, which by definition is not unionized, the price and quantity of labor are determined by the intersection of the supply curve of labor and the demand curve for labor. An industry demand curve for labor (D_0) is shown in Figure 10.2. The supply curve of labor to the industry is labeled S_0. The labor market equilibrium is given by the intersection of S_0 and D_0, where L_0 units of labor are employed at wage rate W_0. Suppose that this industry becomes unionized and as a result the industry wage rates rise to W_1. At the new wage, people are willing to supply L_1 units of labor but only L_2 units of labor are demanded. In fact, $L_1 - L_2$ more units of labor are supplied than are demanded. Initially, we shall assume that the industry is not forced to employ any more labor than it demands. Consequently, some rationing of labor supply is necessary to equilibrate labor supply and labor demand.

FIGURE 10.1   An increase in the wage rate shifts the industry supply curve up, causing a reduction in industry output and an increase in price.

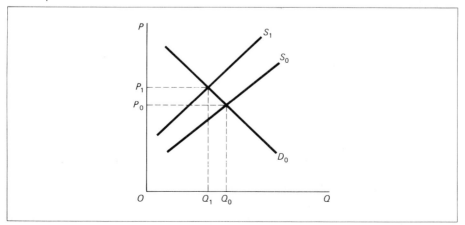

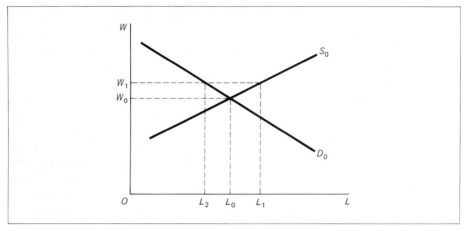

FIGURE 10.2   At the union wage rate W_1, there is an excess supply of labor equal to $L_1 - L_2$.

RATIONING THE SUPPLY OF LABOR   If there is some variation of skills within an occupation, it is possible to eliminate the excess supply of labor that results from unionization by raising the quality of labor. A concrete example will help to clarify the analysis.

Suppose that teachers in a school district form a union and that as a result their salaries increase from $10,000 to $11,000. When a worker is paid more than is absolutely necessary to keep him employed in a specific job, he is said to earn "economic rent." Teachers who were in the school district prior to unionization and who remain in the school district earn economic rents; in particular, these teachers earn $1,000 more annually than they could earn in comparable nonunionized school districts elsewhere.

The prospect of earning these economic rents will lead many similarly skilled teachers to apply for positions in this school district. The pile of applications on the school superintendent's desk can be shortened considerably if better qualified teachers are hired to fill vacancies.

Let's assume that a teacher's earnings in nonunionized school districts are proportional to his market skills. Consequently, in this district before unionization, teachers with, say, 1,000 units of human capital were earning $10,000 per year. That is, the school district paid $10 per unit of human capital. Since unionization causes salaries to rise to $11,000 per year, the school district will be able to hire teachers with as much as 1,100 units of human capital. The teachers with 1,100 units of human capital would earn no economic rent at this school district; they would be paid exactly what they could be earning in other similar districts. These more capable teachers often can be obtained by hiring teachers who attended better colleges or who were better students at their respective colleges.

Managers have an incentive to hire the most capable workers possible, given the wage rate set by the union, because this will maximize the firm's output for any total expenditure on labor. In other words, this strategy will result in output being produced at minimum cost. If the manager hires the most capable workers possible, workers will be indifferent between going to work for one of the unionized firms and working in a nonunionized firm. Workers accordingly will have no special incentive to apply for work in a unionized firm, and consequently hiring costs are lower than they would have been if rationing by worker quality had not been used. A manager who hires the most productive workers possible under the union wage rate thus not only increases her firm's output but also reduces hiring costs.

In firms where rationing by worker quality is used, employees who joined the firm prior to unionization earn economic rents and employees who joined the firm after the union was formed earn no economic rents. It is in the firm's interest for those earning economic rents to leave. Since these workers are earning more than they could elsewhere, only deaths, retirements, and resignations will reduce the fraction of employees who earn economic rents.

Rationing by worker quality is sometimes not feasible. In a number of occupations, there is very little variation in skills within the occupation. More importantly, rationing by worker quality may also be precluded by the union contract. If there is no rationing by worker quality, nearly every worker receives economic rents and either the firm or the union must ration the available places. A manager charged with this responsibility could allocate the available places on a first-come, first-served basis. Workers would respond to this system by forming long lines outside the employment office. The manager could receive some benefit from rationing, however, if she is able to bestow the economic rents associated with working in the unionized firm on those about whom she cares—family, friends, and so on. It is obvious that a job that gives its holder $1,000 to $2,000 more *per year* than he could earn elsewhere is a valuable gift. It is unlikely, however, that she gets much benefit from giving the fiftieth union job to a distant acquaintance.

The union appears to gain much more from bestowing the economic rents that go with union jobs. The union members together have many more sons and daughters to whom they would like to give union jobs than does the manager. If the union gains more from acquiring the right to bestow these economic rents than the manager does, we may reasonably expect that the union will end up giving out union jobs *if* union jobs are not allocated on a first-come, first-served basis.

The difficulty with this solution lies in obtaining the right to control who obtains employment. This control sometimes is exercised through licensure, which is generally administered by a licensure board. Thus, licensure boards are created which control the content of licensing examinations and the standards for passing. Consequently, these boards are able to affect who is licensed and how many licenses are awarded. Doctors, barbers, plumbers, electricians, hairdressers, and members of other occupations have persuaded various state and local governments that their occupations require regulation through licensure. Not surprisingly, the licensure boards are generally controlled by members of the occupation being regulated.

Employment may also be controlled through the use of closed shops. In a closed shop, only those *already in* the union can be hired by employers. The union, through its control of the size of the union, is able to determine the amount of economic rent each member receives and, through its control of the admission process, is able to determine who receives this economic rent. We are not surprised, therefore, to discover that a large fraction of the new members of some unions are children or friends of existing members.

THE FORMATION OF UNIONS   There are costs and benefits to forming a union, and a union presumably will be formed in a given industry only if the benefits outweigh the costs. A manager with some understanding of how the costs and benefits of union formation vary from industry to industry will be able to forecast more accurately the growth and the decline of unions in his industry. Predictions about the strength of unions can be used to help forecast product prices and industry output.

The principal benefit of unionization to employees is the increase in wage rates that results from unionization. In fact, a worker's earnings are maximized if the union drives the wage rate high enough so that only one worker is demanded. In Figure 10.3, the union maximizes the wage rate by moving to point A, where one worker is employed at a wage rate equal to W_1.

A union that chose to move immediately to this position would certainly please the worker who managed to stay employed and would just as certainly incur the wrath of its unemployed members. Thus, an immediate movement to an employment of one worker is unlikely.

The costs associated with displacing existing workers to get to point A do not prevent a union from relying on attrition to get there. The only benefit

FIGURE 10.3   The wage rate is maximized by moving up the demand curve until only one worker is demanded.

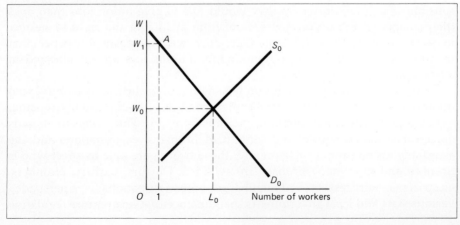

from hiring new workers to replace laborers who retire, die, or change jobs is the value that union members place on bestowing the economic rents that come with union jobs. For various reasons, however, many children choose a different line of work from that of their parents. Furthermore, replacing workers who die, retire, or change jobs is costly to the remaining union workers because it keeps their wage rates down. We may conclude that unions on net have some benefit from relying upon attrition to move toward the employment of one worker.

There are, however, costs to organizing a union and to maintaining wage rates above the competitive level. Let us first consider the organizational costs. Because there are fixed costs associated with organizing workers in each plant, the cost of organizing any given number of workers increases as the number of plants in which they are located rises.

> **Question** The percent of auto workers who belong to a union is much greater than the percent of retail clerks who belong to a union. Can you explain this difference in membership?

> **Answer** Part of the explanation relies on differences in organizational costs. Retail clerks are dispersed across many different stores, while auto workers are concentrated within a few plants. It is consequently much costlier to organize retail clerks into a union than to organize auto workers into a union. For this reason, the formation of a union of retail clerks is less likely to be beneficial than is the formation of a union of auto workers.

It is also costly to maintain wage rates above their competitive levels. Wages can be kept artificially high by restricting the supply of labor available to firms, but for this to be feasible the union must have the *power* to restrict supply. Closed shops and control over the licensure of workers are two techniques by which this power is obtained. Both these techniques, however, require some favorable action by public officials before they can be successfully implemented. That is, closed shops must be made legal or licensing ordinances must be passed. Somehow, the union must make it worthwhile for public officials to undertake these actions. This can be accomplished by furnishing votes for public officials who support unions. The electoral support that a union is able to offer politicians is proportional to union membership. Accordingly, a union that severely restricts employment reduces the support that it is able to offer politicians on election day and thereby endangers the legislation that makes it possible for the union to restrict employment.[2]

Unions are also able to maintain artificially high wage rates by striking or by threatening to strike. A strike is costly to both parties, for during a strike physical capital lies idle and workers are unable to utilize effectively their leisure because of uncertainty about the duration of the strike. These costs can be avoided by immediately agreeing to the terms that would be met at

---

[2]It should be noted that unions can also obtain favorable legislation by offering politicians campaign contributions.

the end of the strike, and in this sense both parties are worse off because of strikes. Economists have not been very successful in explaining why strikes ever occur.

Economic analysis has been more successful in explaining the duration of strikes. We would expect strikes to last longer when the costs imposed by strikes on either party are smaller. The lost production that results from strikes is not as costly when a sizable inventory is regularly maintained and can be used to meet demand during the strike. This is one reason why the strikes of auto workers and coal workers often last longer than other strikes. Coal mines maintain inventories of coal to deal with seasonal fluctuations in demand and auto manufacturers keep inventories of cars in response to the seasonal and cyclical demand for automobiles. To the union member, the biggest cost of being on strike is the lack of income. Unions, however, have developed strike funds to offer partial salaries to striking workers.

For a strike to be effective, striking union members must not be replaced by other workers. The new employees hired during a strike are sometimes called strikebreakers, and their employment reduces the cost imposed on the firm by the strike. In Figure 10.4, the demand for labor by a particular industry is labeled D_0 and the supply of labor to this industry is labeled S_0. At wage rate W_0, L_0 workers are employed while $L_1 - L_0$ workers are *willing* to work in this industry but are unable to find employment. The excess supply $L_1 - L_0$ represents a pool from which strikebreakers may be drawn if the union were to go on strike. The L_0 striking workers, therefore, must prevent the employment of a large number of strikebreakers from the excess supply of $L_1 - L_0$ and violence sometimes results. It becomes more difficult to prevent the employment of strikebreakers as the excess supply $L_1 - L_0$ rises relative to the number of striking union members L_0.

FIGURE 10.4   Striking is more difficult the more responsive the labor supply curve is to wage changes. At W_0, the excess supply associated with $S_1(L_2 - L_0)$ is greater than the excess supply associated with $S_0(L_1 - L_0)$.

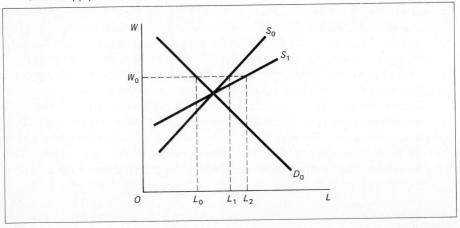

For any given price change, the more responsive labor supply is to increases in price, the greater the excess supply will be. In Figure 10.4, labor supply curve S_1 is more responsive to wage changes than labor supply curve S_0 is. Thus, the excess supply of labor is $L_2 - L_0$ as opposed to $L_1 - L_0$. A union faced with the labor supply curve S_1 is consequently less likely than a union faced with the labor supply curve S_0 to find that striking is a profitable way in which to raise wage rates.

The responsiveness of the labor supply curve to wage changes depends in part on the entry of workers into this labor market. If a small increase in the wage rate draws many workers into this labor market, then the market labor supply curve will be highly responsive to wage changes. On the other hand, the market labor supply curve will be relatively unresponsive to movements in the wage rate if a small increase in the wage rate draws very few workers into this market. This is apt to occur when a job appeals to a small segment of the population. For instance, a small increase in the wage rate of seamen will not cause many Americans to embrace the solitude and dangers of sea life. Thus, the supply curve of seamen is not very responsive to wage changes and seamen may find striking to be a profitable way in which to raise wage rates.

Furthermore, the excess supply will be greater the more responsive the demand for labor is to wage changes. In Figure 10.5, demand curve D_1 is more responsive to wage changes than demand curve D_0. At wage W_1, the excess supply associated with demand curve D_1 $(L_2 - L_1)$ is greater than the excess supply associated with demand curve D_0 $(L_2 - L_0)$. Accordingly, the potential benefits of a strike fall as the responsiveness of the demand for labor to the wage rate rises.

We have seen that an increase in the wage rate causes the quantity of

FIGURE 10.5   Striking is more difficult the more responsive the labor demand curve is to wage changes. At W_1, the excess supply associated with $D_1(L_2 - L_1)$ is greater than the excess supply associated with $D_0(L_2 - L_0)$.

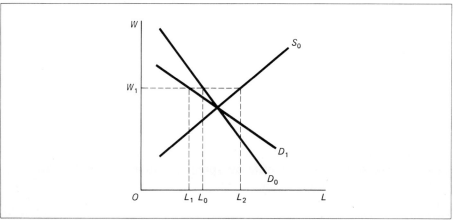

labor demanded to decrease for two reasons: (1) less output is produced when the product's price increases, and (2) there may be some substitution away from labor and toward other inputs when labor becomes relatively expensive. Accordingly, the responsiveness of labor demand to a wage increase depends on how much output falls when the output price rises and on how substitutable labor is for other inputs.

The magnitude of the fall in output depends upon the price elasticity of demand for the output. If the price elasticity is large (e.g., insurance), a wage increase results in a sizable decrease in output. Similarly, the fall in output accompanying a wage increase is small when the price elasticity is low (e.g., steel, shows, some government services). Thus, steelworkers, actors, and government workers have a greater gain from striking than do insurance workers.

The empirical evidence suggests that it is easier to substitute between unskilled labor and other inputs than it is to substitute between skilled labor and other inputs. To the extent that this is true, the demand for skilled labor is less responsive to wage changes than is the demand for unskilled labor. Skilled labor consequently has a greater benefit from striking than does unskilled labor.

In summary, unions are formed when the benefits outweigh the costs. An important deterrent to unionization is organizational costs, which are high when workers are scattered across many plants. Unions may keep wages above competitive levels by either controlling the supply of workers or threatening to strike. A union that determines wages through its control of supply cannot restrict the supply of labor too much or it will lose the political lease that enables it to control the supply of labor. Strikes are less costly to firms in industries where sizable inventories are normally maintained, and strikebreakers are more easily controlled in industries with relatively unresponsive demand and supply curves for labor.

This knowledge is useful to the manager in several ways. For example, she can use it to anticipate changes in the extent of unionization in her industry.

Question   Suppose that, as a result of increases in the relative price of gasoline, production takes place in a larger number of plants, each of which is smaller. How does this affect the cost of forming a union?

Answer   It is now costlier to form a union because there are more plants to organize and there is a fixed cost associated with organizing each plant.

The increase in wage rates that accompanies unionization raises the firm's costs and thus reduces its profits. Consequently, the manager may be able to increase the firm's profits by spending some money to reduce the probability that a union is formed in her firm. She may find it worthwhile to try to make it costlier to organize a union by influencing legislation on unions or by operating more than the cost-minimizing number of plants.

UNION RESTRICTIONS ON ALLOCATIVE DECISIONS Unions are able to affect not only the wage rate that a manager must pay her employees but also the conditions under which they work. Unions place restrictions on the decisions a manager is able to make. In this section, we will examine several of these restrictions and will consider the optimal response of managers to these restrictions.

When wage rates are raised above their competitive levels, managers attempt to substitute away from labor, which is now relatively expensive, and toward other inputs. As we have seen, this substitution makes striking more difficult. For this reason, unions sometimes try to limit the substitution that results from an increase in the wage rate. This is typically done in one of two ways.

Sometimes the wage contract entitles the union to some fraction of the product's price on each unit sold. Thus, the union receives the proceeds from what amounts to a tax on output instead of a wage increase. In this instance, the firm has no incentive to substitute away from labor because the wage rate has not risen.

Sometimes the manager is forced to use more labor in the production of each unit of output than she would choose to use. Unions claim that an increase in the labor-to-output ratio is sometimes necessary to eliminate "sweatshops" or to increase worker safety. Managers often label this practice "featherbedding." Examples include requirements for firemen on diesel locomotives and prohibitions against using spray guns in painting. "Featherbedding" rules cause a manager to employ more labor to produce each unit of output than she would choose to employ if she were minimizing costs. Thus, these rules cause marginal cost to rise, which, in turn, causes price to rise. Less output will be demanded at the higher price, and less labor will be required to produce the smaller output. Thus, the employment of labor will increase only if the additional labor used in the production of each output exceeds the fall in labor as output contracts.

Unions also restrict the manager's ability to fire and promote workers by insisting that these actions be based on worker seniority. To consider the evolution and effects of seniority, let's first examine promotion in a nonunionized firm. We have noted that entrepreneurial time is scarce. The owner(s) cannot make every decision in a large firm, and consequently some discretionary power is given to managers and foremen. Decisions on promotions are often allocated to foremen, who are supposed to promote the most industrious and capable employees. Once again, there is an opportunity for malfeasance, for the foreman can promote a friend or an employee who has done him a favor. Favoritism is, of course, more likely to occur in situations where favoritism is difficult to detect. Promotion based on seniority eliminates the favoritism that so many workers detest and may, through an improvement in employee morale, increase worker productivity. Nevertheless, seniority systems are costly because workers no longer have an incentive to show themselves to be more capable than their fellow workers and to learn additional skills. The worker who is first hired is always the first to be promoted. As before, a seniority system will be chosen if the benefits resulting from increased worker happiness outweigh the costs associated with reduced incentives to be productive and to learn. A firm that is "forced" by a union to adopt a seniority system probably incurs additional costs because the firm would have adopted a seniority system if the system had been expected to decrease costs.

10.2

INCENTIVE SYSTEMS

Suppose that a manager offered a job that paid $200 per week and required only that the employee show up at work. No productivity requirements would be imposed. Many individuals would respond to this "golden" opportunity by increasing their leisure on the job and correspondingly reducing their work effort. They would not exert themselves for their employer and might even sleep or read on the job. Worker productivity would be very low because workers are better off if they spend their time in more enjoyable activities than in increasing their employer's output. It is for this very reason that explicit or implicit incentive systems are found in almost every labor market.

Incentive systems operate through the observation and reward of productivity. An employee's productivity can be observed by either her manager or the firm's customers. In some situations, the total cost of providing a product is minimized when the customer tips the employee after good service has been rendered. This is because tipping frees the manager from having to monitor the employee and allows customers, who may be in a better position to observe the quality of service provided by employees, to reward good service.

Tipping accordingly gives employees an incentive to provide customers with prompt, courteous, and individualized service. This incentive is greater the more responsive tips are to good service. Thus, tipping is apt to be an inefficient mechanism for controlling the quality of service if almost every customer leaves a 15 percent tip. Conversely, tipping is a more reliable control when there is repeat business. A waitress, for example, then has an opportunity to build up a clientele by providing good service.

Most incentive systems, however, rely on managers to monitor and reward an employee's output. Before we turn to a discussion of explicit incentive systems, we should note that there are also many implicit incentive schemes. In firms that rely on implicit incentives, there are no contracts which explicitly tie salaries to output. Instead, there is an understanding that resourceful and energetic workers will eventually be rewarded with a raise, a promotion, or some other thing of value.

Bonuses, piece rates, and commissions have been used in various explicit incentive systems. Each of these devices encourages employees to put forward a greater effort. The increased intensity of work is beneficial to the firm in two circumstances: (1) the capital that workers use is otherwise underutilized (e.g., the value of the marginal product of the company car or personal computer terminal that the employee uses exceeds the marginal cost of additional usage), and (2) the increased intensity of work increases the return on the firm's investment in hiring and training the employee. The benefits that come from increased utilization of capital or from acquiring a greater return on company investments in employees must be weighed against the costs of running an incentive system. Part of these costs are administrative. It is costlier to count output and to reward an employee according to her output than to give her the same check week after week. The remainder of the costs of running an incentive system are related to the income risk that results from these schemes. An insurance agent, for example, does not know exactly how many policies he will sell in any given month. Consequently, there is an element of randomness in his output. In Chapter 6, we showed that risk-averse individuals must be compensated to take on additional risk. In this case, risk-averse employees must be compensated with an increase in income if they are to be induced to give up a salaried income for the risky income that comes with an incentive system. In conclusion, incentive systems should be implemented only if the benefits described above outweigh these costs.

Question   Clothing salespeople are paid W_1 dollars per year plus a commission equal to α dollars per garment sold times the number of garments sold annually. Annual earnings in the best alternative occupation are W_0 dollars. (1) How are W_1 and α determined? (2) Under what circumstances will α be "high"? "low"?

Answer   (1) If the two jobs are equally enjoyable and have the same locational characteristics, then the earnings must be equal in the two jobs. That is,

$$W_0 = W_1 + \alpha G \tag{10.1}$$

where G = number of garments sold annually. If selling clothes is more enjoyable than working in the alternative profession, then

$$W_0 > W_1 + \alpha G$$

There are obviously many combinations of W_1 and α at which a worker is indifferent between selling clothes and working in the next best alternative occupation. To simplify the exposition, let's assume that both jobs are equally enjoyable and have the same locational characteristics. Then equation (10.1) holds. Rearranging (10.1), we get

$$W_1 = W_0 - \alpha G$$

which is represented by line AB in Figure 10.6. To see this, we first recognize that if the commission rate α is zero, then the salespeople receive no

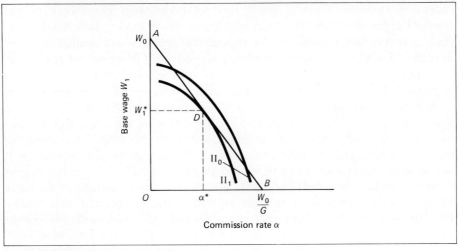

FIGURE 10.6   Profit is maximized by
operating where the isoprofit line is tangent
to the set of feasible combinations (line *AB*).

income from commissions and require a base income W_1 equal to their alternative income W_0. This solution is point A in Figure 10.6. At the other extreme, commission income αG must equal their alternative income W_0 if there is no base income (i.e., $W_1 = 0$). This outcome is given by point B in Figure 10.6.

The manager's task is to pick a base wage–commission rate combination on line AB, which depicts the feasible combinations of base wages and commission rates available to the manager. The manager will choose that combination that maximizes profits. In Figure 10.6, curve Π_0 gives the set of combinations of base wages and commission rates that yield profit level Π_0. The curve is negatively sloped because the commission rate must fall when the base wage rises if profits are to remain constant. Similarly, curve Π_1 depicts the combinations yielding profit level Π_1. Because Π_1 involves smaller base wage rates and commission rates than Π_0, Π_1 represents a higher profit level than Π_0. In fact, Π_1 is the highest profit that the manager can attain. Accordingly, profit is maximized by paying base wage rate W_1^* and the commission rate α^*.

(2) The more profitable it is for the firm to use an incentive system, the more the firm will rely upon that payment mechanism. In terms of Figure 10.6, incentive systems are more profitable when the isoprofit curves are flatter. If isoprofit curve Π_1 became flatter at point D, the new tangency would be to the right of point D on AB. Thus, when incentive systems become more profitable, a higher commission rate is chosen. But what makes incentive systems more profitable? Incentive systems are more profitable when it is less costly to count output and to adjust paychecks. Incentive systems are also more beneficial to the firm when it is particularly costly to have unproductive employees—that is, when hiring and

training costs are high or when the cost of maintaining an inventory of clothes is substantial.

The other determinant of the optimal commission rate is the cost to the firm of increasing the commission, which is given by the slope of line *AB* in Figure 10.6. It is costlier to increase the commission on each garment by $1 when salespeople sell 1,000 garments per year than when salespeople sell only 500 garments per year. As a result, the commission will be lower in stores where it is "easy" to sell clothes. Other aspects of the incentive system decision are difficult to incorporate into a diagram. If employees are risk-averse, then incentive systems are less costly when sales are not very random because employees are not assuming much risk. Accordingly, α will be higher when sales are steady.

10.3

MONOPSONY

We have defined a competitive factor market as a market in which individual firms are unable to affect the price they pay for the factor. One such market is depicted in Figure 10.7, where the curve that shows the supply of unskilled labor to the individual firm is graphed. Any single firm will pay $2 per hour for unskilled labor, whether the firm employs 1 worker or 50,000 workers. The marginal cost of hiring the unskilled worker for 1 more hour is equal to the wage rate of $2.

In factor markets that are not competitive, a firm is able to affect the price it pays for a factor by altering the quantity of the factor that the firm uses. Firms in these markets are called "monopsonists," and the U.S. government as an employer of astronauts is one example of a monopsonist. The government can find seven qualified astronauts who are willing to undertake risky space trips at relatively low wage rates; these men probably enjoy the adventure of space travel. The government, however, must turn to more circumspect and cautious men if it is to hire 100 qualified astronauts. These more

FIGURE 10.7 Supply curve to an individual firm in a competitive labor market.

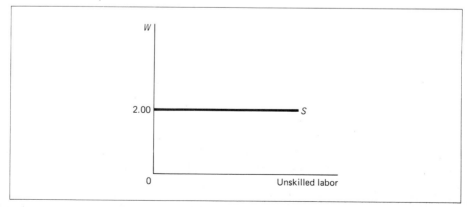

cautious men require higher wage rates to induce them to undergo the risks of space travel. For this reason, the supply curve of qualified astronauts to the U.S. government is positively sloped.

The supply curve facing a representative monopsonist is labeled S_L in Figure 10.8. The firm can purchase 10 units of labor at a wage rate of $8. To purchase 11 units of labor, however, it must pay *each* employee a wage rate of $9.[3] The cost to the firm of increasing its use of labor from 10 units to 11 units is equal to the difference in the expenditures on labor at these two quantities, or

$$\$9 \cdot 11 - \$8 \cdot 10 = \$19$$

This $19 cost may be decomposed into two elements: (1) the $9 actually paid for the eleventh unit, and (2) the increase in price ($9 − $8) on the first 10 units ($10).

DEFINITION ◗   The *marginal factor cost* (MFC) is the increase in the total expenditures on a factor accompanying a 1-unit increase in the employment of that factor.

The marginal factor cost of the eleventh unit of labor is thus $19. The

---

[3]It is assumed that the first employees hired at the lower wage rate can always quit and be rehired at the higher wage rate.

FIGURE 10.8   Supply curve to an individual firm in a monopsonistic labor market. Profit is maximized by equating the value of the marginal product (MR · MP_L) to the marginal factor cost (MFC_L).

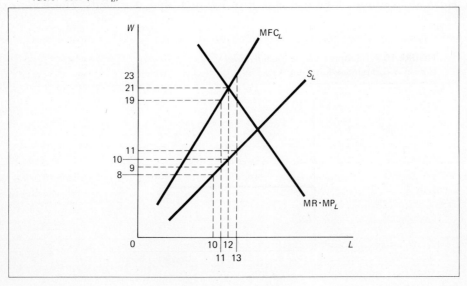

marginal factor cost curve is labeled MFC_L in Figure 10.8; the numbers behind the calculation of the marginal factor cost of labor are given in Table 10.1. It is interesting to note that the marginal factor cost curve lies above the supply curve. That is, the *marginal* factor cost of labor is greater than the wage rate, which is the *average* cost of labor. This is because hiring 1 more unit of labor costs the firm not only the wage rate that must be paid this last laborer but also the increase in the wage rate of all other laborers.

On the other hand, in a competitive labor market, the marginal factor cost equals the wage rate. This is because hiring 1 more unit of labor in a competitive labor market does not affect the wage rate that must be paid other workers.

We saw in Chapter 5 that a firm maximizes its profit by operating where the increase in total revenue from using 1 more unit of a factor equals the increase in the total cost from using 1 more unit of a factor. The increase in total revenue from using 1 more unit of a factor is equal to the marginal revenue of selling additional output times the additional output produced by hiring that 1 more unit. The increase in total cost from hiring an additional unit of an input is the marginal factor cost. The profit-maximizing quantity of labor, therefore, occurs where

$$MR \cdot MP_L = MFC_L$$

The monopsonist depicted in Figure 10.8 maximizes his profit by employing 12 units of labor, for it is at this quantity that the marginal factor cost of labor equals the product of the marginal revenue and the marginal product of labor. At this quantity, employees are paid $10 per hour and the marginal factor cost of labor equals $21.

The astronaut labor market described earlier in this section is a good example of a monopsonistic market. Some care is necessary, however, in ascribing monopsony power in other circumstances. For instance, the fact that the ABC Tool Company is the only employer of engineers in Sharpsburg, Maryland, does not imply that the ABC Tool Company is a monopsonist. When it is hiring engineers, it must compete with thousands of companies across the country, and if it does not offer a nationally competitive wage rate, it will be unable to attract any new engineers. A firm that does not offer a nationally competitive wage rate not only will be unable to attract

TABLE 10.1

WAGE RATE	LABOR	W·L	MARGINAL FACTOR COST OF LABOR
8	10	80	
9	11	99	19
10	12	120	21
11	13	143	23

new workers but also will lose workers who migrate to take more attractive jobs. These losses, coupled with retirements and deaths, make it very difficult for a firm to keep wages below the nationally competitive level for an extended period of time.

Consequently, a local monopsony is unlikely to coexist with a national labor market for a long period of time, although coexistence for a short period of time is possible. There is no strong evidence which supports the existence of monopsony outside of professional sports. This is a reasonable result, for virtually all of the skills found in labor markets are not sold in labor markets in which there are only a few firms that demand a particular skill. Thousands of firms employ welders, architects, janitors, teachers, and so on. Monopsony, therefore, appears to be a relatively rare phenomenon.

Question   In some sports, once a player has been drafted, no other team can bid for him. He has the option of playing for that team or not playing at all. (1) Does this practice of "ownership" of players confer monopsony power on the owners of teams? (2) Will the elimination of this practice (a) raise athletes' salaries and (b) increase the cost of tickets to sports events?

Answer   (1) Each player will choose to leave professional sports when the earnings in professional sports fall below his earnings in other professions, other things being equal. As an owner reduces the wage rate he pays his players, some players will find it worthwhile to leave professional sports. The owner, therefore, faces a positively sloped supply curve of labor and consequently is a monopsonist.

(2) When this practice is removed, owners are forced to compete for players' services. This competition drives up wage rates and makes the supply curve facing each owner flatter because players have options other than leaving the sport. That is, each owner must pay every player his competitively determined wage or the player will go to another team; owners no longer have the ability to push wages down that they once enjoyed. It is unclear what happens to the marginal factor cost of players. The marginal factor cost equals the wage rate *plus* the increase in the wages paid other workers when one more player is hired. The increase in the wage rate raises the marginal factor cost, but the flattening of the supply curve facing each owner reduces the marginal factor cost. It is entirely possible for the marginal factor cost of labor to fall when this practice is removed, and a fall in the marginal factor cost of labor would result in a fall in the marginal cost of sports, causing ticket prices to fall.

10.4

JOB SEARCH

In our discussion of labor markets, we have assumed that every laborer is aware of her employment opportunities at every conceivable job. Obviously, this is an unrealistic assumption. Time and money are required to acquire information about the wage rates that are offered by different firms. Because this information is costly, laborers will not find it worthwhile to become completely informed about job possibilities.

Suppose that the distribution of wage rates that would be offered to a particular worker is shown in Figure 10.9.[4] Firm A would offer her $6 per hour if she applied for work. Firm B, on the other hand, would offer her only $4 per hour if she applied for work. The worker does not know which firm will offer her the highest wage rate, for if she did, she would immediately apply for work at that firm and firms offering lower wage rates would be unable to attract workers. Only by going from firm to firm is the worker able to obtain information on which firms are offering various wage rates.

If this worker applies for a job at firm B, she will be offered $4 per hour. She can accept this job or search for a more lucrative job. The benefits of rejecting firm B's job offer to search for a better job are equal to the present value of the expected increase in wage rates that results from getting one more job offer. As can be seen in Figure 10.9, a worker who receives a $4-per-hour job offer has a much greater benefit from searching for a better job than a worker who receives a $6-per-hour job offer.

The cost of searching for one more job includes forgone earnings and out-of-pocket expenditures. A person who allocates time to job search could have allocated that time to earning money. Job search consequently "costs" the individual the money that could have been earned had there been no job search. Thus, job search is more expensive for an individual with a high wage rate than for an individual with a low wage rate. Searching for a job may also entail the purchase of newspapers, the use of employment agencies, the purchase of clothes, and/or the use of a car.

The optimal amount of job search depends on the benefits and costs of

---

[4]Assume there are no differences across firms in the cost of living or in job or locational amenities. Alternatively, the nominal wage rate can be adjusted to reflect differences in these factors.

FIGURE 10.9 The distribution of wage offerings.

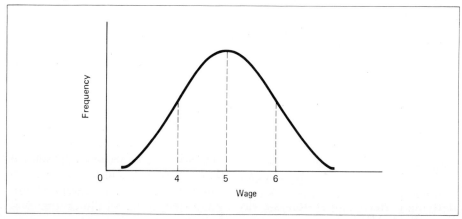

search. If the benefits of undertaking one more search outweigh the costs, additional search is beneficial. A worker should stop searching for additional job offers when the marginal benefit from one more search equals the marginal cost of one more search. Because search is costly, workers will not find it worthwhile to search until they find the highest wage rate. It is the optimality of incomplete search which allows some dispersion of wage rates to persist.

Question Suppose that search were subsidized with unemployment benefits. What would happen to the duration of search?

Answer The creation of unemployment benefits makes it less costly to turn down job offers and hence leads to more job search. There is considerable empirical evidence supporting the proposition that the duration of unemployment increases when unemployment benefits become more attractive.

The problem facing the manager is how to best respond to a labor market characterized by job search. As we have noted, workers who are offered a high wage rate have a smaller benefit from additional search than workers who are offered a low wage rate. A manager, therefore, is able to increase the frequency with which job applicants accept job offers by raising the offered wage rate. Managers who find it particularly costly to have job vacancies or who face a high cost of interviewing each applicant will find it worthwhile to offer high wage rates. Job vacancies will be costly when it is difficult to substitute between capital and labor. For example, a particular machine may be unusable unless there is an operator to run it. Interviewing costs may be related to skill levels; it may be costlier to ascertain whether a skilled worker is qualified to be a chef than to ascertain whether an unskilled worker is qualified to be a busboy.

A manager who pays his employees high wage rates can also reduce the frequency with which his employees quit his firm. Because offering high wage rates reduces vacancy and interviewing costs, high wage rates will be beneficial to firms for which these costs are large. High wage rates, in reducing quit rates, also reduce costs associated with firm-specific training. To take one example, firm-specific training is particularly important in government agencies, where each employee must be taught the regulations that she is to enforce. It is for this reason that (1) government agencies pay their employees higher wage rates and (2) government employees have lower quit rates than are observed in private industry.

10.5

SUMMARY

In this chapter, we turned our attention to labor management problems that arise in imperfect markets. A factor market is said to be imperfect when any of the assumptions underlying perfect competition is seriously violated. Much of the chapter was devoted to the effects of unions upon the labor markets and the resulting impact upon managerial decisions.

When a union suddenly raises the wage that a manager must pay, the manager will try to respond by substituting away from labor in favor of other inputs and by hiring more productive workers. The union contract, however, may forbid these substitutions.

We analyzed the formation of unions. An appreciation of the conditions conducive to unionization will enable a manager to prepare for and even forestall unionization. We saw that the development of unions depends on the concentration of workers and on the ability of the union to exert political influence and to strike.

Since a worker should be paid according to the value of his marginal product, we investigated the managerial problem of monitoring a worker's marginal product. From this perspective, several incentive schemes were analyzed: customer tipping, straight salaries, commissions. Each has its good and bad points from a managerial point of view.

Monopsony exists when a firm is large enough relative to an input market to affect the market price of the input by his hiring decisions. A firm with monopsony power does not maximize profits by equating the value of the marginal product to the input price. Instead, the manager should hire the input until the value of the marginal product equals the marginal factor cost. This will be at a smaller quantity. Very few firms, however, appear to exercise monopsony power.

Finally, we analyzed managerial problems associated with the lack of full information in the labor market. Because workers are searching for the best jobs, managers can increase the number of employees hired and decrease the number of employees who quit by raising the wage rate. The benefits of doing this depend on the costs of vacancies and quits.

IMPORTANT NEW TERMS

Economic rent

Monopsony

Marginal factor cost

PROBLEMS

10.1 Answer true, false, or undecided: Unions would prefer that a firm faced with eliminating the excess supply of labor that results from unionization *not* ration by worker quality.

10.2 Are unions more likely to be found in industries with rapid job turnover than in industries with slow job turnover?

10.3 Answer true, false, or undecided: Strikes are more likely to occur in industries where there is seasonal unemployment than in other industries.

10.4 A monopsonist in the labor market is paying his workers $10 per hour. The marginal product of labor equals 5 and the monopsonist increases his total revenue by $2 with each unit sold. Is the monopsonist maximizing his profit?

10.5 Which of the following is most likely to be a monopsonist? (a) the Speedo Plumbing Company, (b) the all-volunteer U.S. Navy, (c) Citibank.

10.6 Is the dispersion of wage rates likely to be greater in a college town, where many people stay with an employer for a relatively short period of time, or in other small towns, where workers spend a relatively long period of time in any one job?

10.7 Name some other methods in addition to raising wage rates which can be used to increase the rate with which a manager is able to fill vacancies.

10.8 How can a manager determine which commission structure maximizes her profits?

10.9 Answer true, false, or undecided: A decrease in the cost of job search (e.g., gasoline becomes cheaper) has no impact on the dispersion of wage rates which is found in the market for a particular kind of labor.

REFERENCES

Alchian, Armen, and William R. Allen: *Exchange and Production: Competition, Coordination and Control*, Belmont, California: Wadsworth Publishing Company, Inc., 1977.

Ben-Zion, Uri, and Edi Karni: "'Tip' Payments and the Quality of Service," in Orley C. Ashenfelter and Wallace E. Oates (eds.), *Essays in Labor Market Analysis in Memory of Yochanan Peter Comay*, New York: John Wiley and Sons, 1977.

Lippman, Steven A., and John J. McCall: "The Economics of Job Search: A Survey," *Economic Inquiry*, vol. 14, June 1976, pp. 155–89.

Rees, Albert: *The Economics of Trade Unions*, Chicago: University of Chicago Press, 1962.

11

PRODUCTION DECISIONS

Our discussion of the firm in Chapter 5 made the production decision appear fairly simple. Although the manager may have to experiment a bit, she will adjust output until marginal cost equals marginal revenue. At that point, profit will be maximized. A real manager, however, must deal with a variety of complications. For example, technological change, which we may term "progress," changes the cost of production. As we shall see, it is possible for a manager, through investment, to alter the technology that she uses. Should she then invest her firm's resources in the quest for such progress? If so, how much should she invest? To take another example, there may be some randomness in demand. This randomness affects the manager's desired inventory levels and the type of contracts that she will be interested in making. Finally, it takes only a moment's reflection to recognize that many government actions affect the manager's output decisions. The purpose of this chapter is to examine how a manager makes the optimal production decision in the face of these sorts of complications.

11.1

SPOT MARKETS AND LONG-TERM CONTRACTS

In Chapter 6, we saw that uncertainty about prices caused risk-averse managers to reduce their production, thereby reducing their expected profits. Risk-averse managers produce less than the expected profit-maximizing output because they value the $1 increase in profit associated with a higher actual price less than the $1 decrease in profit associated with a lower actual price.

In Chapter 8, we found that risk averters could make themselves better off by purchasing insurance. A long-term contract reduces a manager's uncertainty about the price he will receive just as an insurance policy reduces uncertainty about income. A long-term contract does this by specifying the price that the firm will receive for its product over a number of years. The firm thereby avoids the fluctuations in price that are associated with selling from year to year at the price prevailing at the time that the product is brought to the market. This latter current price is called the "spot price." Because a risk-averse manager would prefer to reduce his uncertainty and a long-term contract reduces his uncertainty about prices, he would be willing to pay a premium to sell through long-term contracts. That is, he would be willing to accept a lower long-term contract price than the price he could expect to receive from selling his product on the spot market each year. How much less would depend upon his specific risk preferences. This means that long-term contract prices would be less than average current or spot market prices. The manager's willingness to "pay" for risk reduction is one of the reasons why long-term contracts exist.

We should note that the presence of risk does not lead risk-neutral managers to favor long-term contracts. This is because risk-neutral managers maximize expected profits and enjoy no gain from the reduction in price uncertainty that long-term contracts bring.

Accordingly, because of their attitudes toward risk, *risk-averse* managers are willing to accept a lower price for long-term contracts than they receive in the spot market even if their cost of supplying goods under long-term contracts is the same as their cost of supplying goods to the short-term market. *Risk-neutral* managers, in contrast, are unwilling to accept a lower price under long-term contract when their costs of supplying long-term and short-term markets are the same.

The cost of supplying a unit of output under long-term contract, however, may be less than the cost of supplying a unit of output to the spot market.[1] As we shall see, this will result in differences between long-term contract prices and average spot prices that are unrelated to attitudes toward risk. There are several reasons why production under a long-term contract may be cheaper than production for the spot market. Long-term contracts eliminate the transactions costs associated with finding buyers each year in the spot market. Furthermore, by reducing the variability in the price that the firm receives for its product, long-term contracts reduce the variability in the firm's total revenue over time. As we saw in Chapter 8, a reduction in the variability of total revenue lowers a firm's risk of bankruptcy and thus enables the manager to borrow money at lower interest rates. A fall in the variability of total revenue also reduces the need for the manager to borrow and save to meet his payroll. Long-term contracts are also beneficial to the firm because they provide information about the future level of demand. Plants can then be designed specifically to meet this level of demand. Production under these conditions is cheaper than it would be if plants were designed to be flexible enough to handle many different production levels.

Question   Do firms in markets characterized by great volatility in prices or firms in markets with relatively stable prices receive greater benefit from long-term contracts?

Answer   Long-term contracts bring about a greater reduction in price variance in volatile markets than in stable markets and hence are more beneficial in volatile markets than in stable markets.

If markets are competitive and if managers are risk-neutral, then the difference between the average spot price and the long-term contract price must equal the difference in the cost of producing for the two markets. That is,

$$E(P_s) - P_{LT} = MC_s - MC_{LT} \qquad (11.1)$$

[1]This argument is developed in Dennis W. Carlton, "Contracts, Price Rigidity, and Market Equilibrium," *Journal of Political Economy*, vol. 87, October 1979, pp. 1,034–1,062.

where $E(P_s)$ equals the average or expected price in the current or spot market, P_{LT} equals the long-term contract price, MC_s equals the marginal cost of producing for the spot market, and MC_{LT} equals the marginal cost of producing under a long-term contract. If the price difference is not as great as the difference in the cost of producing for the two markets, the manager loses money if he sells on the spot market. For example, suppose that the average spot market price is $3 more than the long-term contract price while it costs $5 more to supply a good to the spot market than under long-term contract. Then selling a good on the spot market rather than under long-term contract is unwise because it costs the firm $2 in lost profit. Conversely, the manager has no incentive to sell under long-term contract if the price difference more than compensates for the additional cost of producing for the spot market. Only when equation (11.1) holds will the manager be indifferent between selling 1 more unit on the spot market and selling 1 more unit under long-term contract.

Of course, the difference in marginal costs $MC_s - MC_{LT}$ may differ from firm to firm in a given industry. If this is the case, managers that find it much more expensive to produce for the spot market will specialize in long-term contract production. Similarly, managers for whom spot market production is only slightly more expensive than production under long-term contracts will specialize in spot market production.

Question Are firms with a significant risk of bankruptcy more likely to use long-term contracts than other firms?

Answer Yes. A firm with a large bankruptcy risk experiences a greater reduction in interest payments than do other firms when it reduces its variability in total revenue by using long-term contracts.

Finally, we may ask why buyers use the more expensive spot market at all. A long-term contract commits a buyer to purchase so many units at an agreed-upon price for n years. Agreeing to purchase too many units can be very costly at some point in the future. Consequently, the buyer may be willing to pay a slightly higher price in the spot market to avoid these costs.

11.2

OPTIMAL INVENTORIES

The production or delivery of most products could be arranged so that a unit is produced or delivered as it is sold. But it is very costly to set up production so that a pie emerges from the oven the moment a customer desires one or to arrange deliveries so that a truck from the factory arrives with a typewriter whenever a customer wants to purchase a typewriter from Sears. Fortunately, many products can be stored from one period to the next. This enables managers to reduce their production or delivery costs by keeping an inventory of the goods they produce or sell. But there are carrying costs associated with holding an inventory. This means that there is an optimal inventory level that minimizes costs. We shall examine the inventory problem in a situation where there is perfect certainty and subsequently where demand is random, thereby creating some uncertainty.

DETERMINISTIC CASE   The principles that we want to develop can be observed in a simple model of inventory analysis. Suppose that a retailer anticipates selling Q_0 units of output during the next year at a market-determined price of P_0. We shall assume that this demand is known with certainty and is spread evenly over the year. Our retail manager has several options. For example, he could order Q_0 at the beginning of the year and let his inventory be depleted gradually over time. This strategy would maximize the size (and expense) of the warehouse necessary for storage. It would also maximize the forgone earnings on the capital tied up in the inventory. To conserve on these costs, the manager could order $Q_0/52$ each week. By increasing the frequency of deliveries, he reduces the average inventory level. As a consequence, the costs associated with holding an inventory are reduced, but this cost saving is not free. There are fixed costs associated with each order: our manager would have to pay 52 bills instead of 1, he would have to submit 52 orders instead of 1, he would have to pay for 52 deliveries instead of 1, and so on. The manager must optimize by choosing the order size at which the marginal cost of an additional order equals the reduction in inventory costs that result from placing one more order.

Let Q_D represent the quantity delivered to the firm with each order. The average inventory held by the firm will be equal to $Q_D/2$ because the demand is spread evenly. For example, suppose a store sells 10 boxes of El Fumo cigars per day. If the store manager receives an order of 70 boxes every week, his average inventory will be $70/2 = 35$. On Monday, he starts off the day with an inventory of 70 boxes. In the course of the day, 10 boxes are sold, leaving an inventory of 60 boxes at the end of the day. Thus, the average inventory on Monday is 65 boxes. Similarly, the average inventory on Tuesday is 55 boxes, and so on. For the week, the average inventory is $(65 + 55 + 45 + 35 + 25 + 15 + 5)/7 = 35$.

We shall let C_I equal the interest and other carrying costs associated with holding each unit in inventory. Included in C_I are warehousing costs and the cost of shelf space while the item is on display waiting to be purchased. The total annual inventory costs are equal to the product of the cost per unit held in inventory (C_I) and the average number of units held in inventory ($Q_D/2$), or $C_I Q_D/2$.

If Q_D is delivered in each order, then the number of orders is equal to the total quantity purchased during the year (Q_0) divided by Q_D, or Q_0/Q_D. There are both fixed and variable costs associated with each order

$$C_F + C_V Q_D$$

where C_F is the fixed costs (submitting the order, processing the bill, delivering the order from the plant to the store, etc.) and C_V is the variable costs. Obviously, a large fraction of the cost of any order goes toward paying for the production of the good; that is, variable costs are a large part of the order cost. The total annual order costs equal the number of orders (Q_0/Q_D) times the cost of each order $(C_F + C_V Q_D)$.

$$\frac{Q_0}{Q_D}(C_F + C_V Q_D) = C_F \frac{Q_0}{Q_D} + C_V Q_0$$

Total cost (C) is, of course, equal to the sum of the inventory costs and the order costs:

$$C = C_I \frac{Q_D}{2} + C_F \frac{Q_0}{Q_D} + C_V Q_0 \qquad (11.2)$$

Our retail manager minimizes total annual cost by selecting the quantity ordered each time (Q_D) so that small changes in the order quantity do not change total cost.[2]

$$\frac{\Delta C}{\Delta Q_D} = \frac{C_I}{2} - \frac{C_F Q_0}{Q_D^2} = 0 \qquad (11.3)$$

We can interpret (11.3) in a sensible way. The manager should expand the size of his order until the marginal cost of expanding the average inventory by ordering 1 more unit each time $(C_I/2)$ is just equal to the cost saving associated with reducing the number of orders during the year that results from ordering 1 more unit with each order $(C_F Q_0/Q_D^2)$.

The solution to the optimality condition (11.3) provides an interesting result:

$$Q_D = \sqrt{\frac{2 C_F Q_0}{C_I}}$$

This is the famous "square root rule" of inventory analysis. To see how this works, consider the optimal inventory decision facing the Businessman's Office Supply store. It sells 1,000 secretarial desks a year. The annual cost of holding one of these desks in inventory is $20. The fixed cost of each order is $4, and the cost of ordering one more desk in each order is $150. From the information given, $Q_0 = 1,000$, $C_I = 20$, $C_F = 4$, and $C_V = 150$. Accordingly, the cost-minimizing quantity to be ordered is

$$Q_D = \sqrt{\frac{2(4)(1,000)}{20}} = \sqrt{400} = 20$$

Readers should plug this order quantity and other order quantities into (11.2) to verify that costs are indeed minimized when the manager of the Businessman's Office Supply store orders 20 desks with each order. The *average* inventory held by the office supply store will be 10 ($= {}^{20}/_2$) desks. Furthermore, to order 1,000 desks over the year, 50 orders will have to be placed.

There are a number of things to note about the square root rule. The cost-minimizing order quantity does not depend in any way on the variable cost of order C_V, for this cost is incurred no matter when the item is ordered. In

---

[2]This optimality condition can be derived analytically by taking the first derivative of (11.2) with respect to the order quantity.

our example, the fact that desks cost $150 did not directly affect the inventory decision.

We can also see that the optimal inventory level decreases as the cost of holding a unit in inventory C_I rises. The manager responds to the increased cost of inventories by holding less in inventory and ordering more frequently. Bulky or expensive items cost more to hold in inventory than small or cheap items. Inventories are also more expensive when the warehouse or store space devoted to holding inventories is costlier.

There are a number of factors that affect the fixed cost of each order C_F. As the computer has become cheaper, C_F has fallen. To take another example, an increase in the price of gasoline makes it more expensive to send a truck over to the Businessman's Office Supply store with a shipment of desks and consequently C_F rises. A rise in the fixed cost of each order leads the manager to reduce the number of orders and in so doing to increase the average inventory level.

Question   Suppose that the community in which the Businessman's Office Supply store operates goes through an economic slump, and as a result, the manager anticipates selling only 250 desks over the next year. What is the new cost-minimizing order quantity?

Answer

$$Q_D = \sqrt{\frac{2(4)\,250}{20}} = \sqrt{100} = 10$$

This means that 25 orders will have to be placed over the next year. Since orders and inventory levels are each expensive, the manager minimizes costs by reducing both the number of orders and the average inventory level when sales fall off. In particular, a drop of sales to one-fourth of former levels has caused the optimal order quantity, and thus the optimal inventory, to fall to only one-half of its former value. In contrast to this square root rule, a decision rule that dictates inventories be a constant percentage of sales volume would result in inventories that are too large for popular items (large Q_0) and in inventories that are too small for unpopular items (small Q_0).

Exercise   Show that a quadrupling of the fixed cost of ordering causes cost-minimizing inventories to double. In addition, show that a quadrupling of the cost of holding a unit in inventory cuts optimal inventories in half.

STOCHASTIC CASE   The easiest stochastic or random model of inventories will not appear to be very simple, but in actuality the principles behind the analysis are familiar and intuitively obvious.

First, we have to specify the problem facing the manager.[3] Suppose the

---

[3] This problem, along with many others, is examined in admirable fashion by Ira Horowitz, *Decision Making and the Theory of the Firm*, New York: Holt, Rinehart and Winston, Inc., 1970.

firm is a bakery that supplies bread. The manager observes a price of P_0 and must select a quantity of bread to produce. We introduce demand uncertainty by assuming that the manager does not know the precise quantity that will be sold at a price of P_0. He does, however, have a probabilistic notion of how much he can sell. For ease of exposition, we shall assume that the average variable costs are constant and represented by C_V. If our bakery manager cannot sell all of his output on the day it was produced, he must reduce the price below C_V to P_S and sell it in a secondary market. In other examples, one may deduct from the secondary price the costs of storage, some adjustment for spoilage, and the like.

The costs associated with overproduction would lead a manager to decrease production. But if the demand for bread is high at the price of P_0 and the bakery runs out of bread, the profit that could have been made selling additional loaves of bread is lost. In particular, given the fixed costs, the bakery loses $P_0 - C_V$ on each lost sale. Consequently, the prospect of lost sales encourages a manager to bake more bread. The optimal output decision will balance these two sources of lost profit.[4]

For any output decision that the manager makes, there is an expected loss. One component of this expected loss is the expected lost profits associated with the probability that the manager will not produce enough output to meet demand. The other component is the expected loss associated with the probability that the manager produces too much output and has to sell at a loss in the secondary market. A risk-neutral manager will want to minimize the total expected loss through an optimal choice of output.

The benefit from baking one more loaf of bread stems from having that additional loaf to sell if it is needed. On any day that the loaf is needed, it is sold at a profit of $P_0 - C_V$. The probability that the loaf will be needed equals the probability that the actual quantity demanded (Q) is at least as great as the quantity produced (Q^*). This probability is denoted as $\Pr(Q \geq Q^*)$. Thus, the expected profit increases by $(P_0 - C_V)[\Pr(Q \geq Q^*)]$ when one more loaf is baked to meet large demands. Equivalently, the change in the expected loss is $-(P_0 - C_V)[\Pr(Q \geq Q^*)]$, which is negative.

The cost of baking one more loaf of bread results from having one too many loaves on days when demand is low. On one of these days, the extra loaf of bread is sold at a loss of $C_V - P_s$ on the secondary market. There is a probability, which is denoted as $\Pr(Q < Q^*)$, that the additional loaf will not be demanded on the primary market. Accordingly, the expected loss increases by $(C_V - P_s)[\Pr(Q < Q^*)]$ because there is a possibility that the additional loaf will not be sold on the primary market.

The expected loss (L) is minimized when the benefit of baking one more loaf equals the cost of baking one more loaf, or

$$\frac{\Delta L}{\Delta Q^*} = -(P_0 - C_V)[\Pr(Q \geq Q^*)] + (C_V - P_s)[\Pr(Q < Q^*)] = 0 \qquad (11.4)$$

[4]The mathematical analysis of this problem is a little messy. Nonetheless, it is presented in Section 11A.1 of the mathematical appendix to this chapter.

By the usual rules of probability, $\Pr(Q \geq Q^*) + \Pr(Q < Q^*) = 1$. We can substitute this into (11.4) to get

$$-(P_0 - C_V)[1 - \Pr(Q < Q^*)] + (C_V - P_s)[\Pr(Q < Q^*)] = 0$$

Solving this equation for $\Pr(Q < Q^*)$ provides an interesting decision rule:

$$\Pr(Q < Q^*) = \frac{P_0 - C_V}{P_0 - P_s} \tag{11.5}$$

The optimal quantity of output occurs where the probability that demand will be less than that output equals the profit per unit sold $(P_0 - C_V)$ divided by the difference between the price in the primary market and the price in the secondary market $(P_0 - P_s)$.

The optimal level of output depends on the benefits and costs of expanding production. With an increase in the profit per unit sold in the primary market $(P_0 - C_V)$, the benefits of producing larger quantities rise. Similarly, the costs of expanding output diminish as the magnitude of the loss in revenue from selling in the secondary market $(P_0 - P_s)$ falls. Either of these changes should cause the manager to expand production. In equation (11.5), we can see that an increase in $P_0 - C_V$ or a decrease in $P_0 - P_s$ results in an increase in the optimal probability that demand will be less than output. This means that the optimal level of production increases; at higher levels of production, there is a greater probability that the quantity demanded will be less than the quantity produced.

Often uncertainty about demand is coupled with a seasonal demand. For example, clothing store managers do not know how many bathing suits they will sell in a particular year. But they know for sure that almost no bathing suits are sold in October. At the end of the selling season, the manager is faced with a decision. She could hold her leftover bathing suits until next year's selling season, when they can be sold for P_0 dollars each, or she could sell them at a reduced price. It is costly to hold an inventory of bathing suits. For example, suppose that it costs C_I to hold each bathing suit in inventory until it is sold next year. The net yield to the retailer is therefore $P_0 - C_I$. Consequently, the manager would be willing to sell a bathing suit at the end

---

INTEREST RATES AND INVENTORIES*

An example of the effects of inventory cost changes on the optimal inventory levels can be seen in the automobile industry. Automobile dealers pay for their inventories of new cars with business loans that are indexed to the prime rate. As the prime rate has risen considerably over the past 2 years, the dealers' inventories have been decreased correspondingly. Here we can use condition (11.3) to see the impact of higher interest rates and the consequent decrease in inventory levels.

When interest rates rise, inventory costs C_I rise. This causes an imbalance in condition (11.3). In order to return to an optimal position, the automobile dealer should reduce the size of his inventory. This process will continue until the marginal benefit of reducing the inventory level is just equal to the marginal cost of increasing the number of orders during the year.

---

*Source: "Autos: Distress That Won't Go Away," *Business Week*, Jan. 12, 1981, pp. 52–53.

of the selling season for as little as $P_0 - C_I$ to avoid having to hold the item in inventory. One of the functions of special sales is to reduce inventory levels on seasonal items.

11.3

OPTIMAL BIDDING BEHAVIOR

In most theoretical treatments of the demand for the products of the firm, the firm receives business more or less automatically. But there are a large number of products that are sold on a competitive bid basis. For example, cast-iron water pipe, steel reinforcing bars, asphalt, concrete, fleet cars, milk, bread, and many other products are often sold to government agencies or contractors on the basis of competitive bids. Generally, there is an absence of negotiation. The buyer announces that he wants to buy a specific quantity of a carefully specified product according to a set delivery schedule. Each firm must evaluate its own situation and that of its competitors and quote a price. A firm can fail to win a contract award for trivial amounts of money. In contrast, a winning bidder may "leave a lot of money on the table," i.e., may be the low bidder by a wide margin and therefore earn lower profits than was necessary. Consequently, bidding for contracts is an important responsibility that requires the processing of a lot of information. In this section, we shall examine a simple model that illustrates some of the complexities.

Since there are several (or perhaps many) firms bidding on a contract, the manager cannot know for sure whether she will win the contract award. Based upon market intelligence, the past performance of her competitors, and her own firm's situation, she must select a single price to offer. The manager cannot know what her competitors will bid and, therefore, the outcome is uncertain. In many bidding contexts, however, the manager is able to increase the probability of being awarded the contract by lowering the bid that she submits on the proposed project. There is, of course, a cost to lowering the firm's bid on the project: if it wins, the resultant profits will be lower because the quantity sold is fixed. Consequently, the manager cannot just submit an extraordinarily low price. Suppose that the manager is risk-neutral. You will recall from Chapter 6 that a risk-neutral manager wants to maximize expected profit. Thus the optimal bid is one that maximizes expected profit.

Let the probability that the firm will receive the contract that it bid on be p. If the manager wins the contract, the firm's profits will be equal to the difference between contract bid C_B and the total cost of performing contracted work TC. The probability of losing the contract is equal to $1 - p$. If the manager does not win the award, profits will be zero. The firm's expected profits can be written as

$$E(\Pi) = p(C_B - TC) + (1 - p)\,0$$

$$= p(C_B - TC)$$

Since the contract will be awarded to the firm submitting the lowest bid, a decrease in the contract bid will increase the probability that the firm's bid will be the lowest bid. This, of course, would increase the probability that the firm receives the contract. Accordingly, we may specify that the probability of receiving the contract is a function of the contract bid;

$$p = f(C_B)$$

where $\dfrac{\Delta p}{\Delta C_B} = \dfrac{\Delta f(C_B)}{\Delta C_B} < 0$

In other words, as bid C_B goes down, the probability of winning rises.

The manager will select the contract bid that maximizes the firm's expected profits. This occurs when the marginal impact on expected profits of a further change in the contract bid is zero:

$$\frac{\Delta E\,[\Pi]}{\Delta C_B} = p + (C_B - TC)\frac{\Delta p}{\Delta C_B} = 0$$

The manager has found the right bid when the expected marginal benefit of increasing the contract bid is just equal to the marginal cost. More specifically, the expected marginal benefit from increasing the contract bid by \$1 is probability p that the firm wins the contract and thus is able to receive the additional \$1 in profits that results from a contract with a \$1 higher contract bid. This must be equal to the marginal cost of increasing the contract bid by \$1, which is the loss in expected profit associated with the resulting fall in the probability of receiving the contract. This is $(C_B - TC)\,\Delta p/\Delta C_B$ in the optimality condition.

These results may be a little more tangible if the probability of winning the contract is assumed to be a linear function of the contract bid:

$$p = a - bC_B \qquad 0 \le a \le 1 \qquad 0 \le C_B \le \frac{a}{b}$$

Expected profit is then written as

$$E(\Pi) = (a - bC_B)(C_B - TC)$$

$$= aC_B - bC_B^2 - aTC + bC_BTC$$

The optimality condition for maximizing expected profit with respect to the contract bid is

$$\frac{\Delta E(\Pi)}{\Delta C_B} = a - 2bC_B + bTC = 0$$

This can be solved for the otpimal contract bid:

$$C_B = \frac{a + bTC}{2b} \tag{11.6}$$

Question   Let the trade-off between the contract bid and the probability of receiving the contract be

$$p = 1 - .0001111C_B$$

Furthermore, let the total project cost be $7,000. What is the optimal bid? What is the firm's expected profit?

Answer   By direct substitution into equation (11.6) the optimal contract bid is given by

$$C_B = \frac{1 + .0001111(\$7,000)}{2(.0001111)}$$

$$= 8,000$$

The expected profit depends upon the probability of winning

$$p = 1 - .0001111C_B$$

$$= 1 - .0001111(\$8,000)$$

$$= .1112$$

and the profit margin if the manager wins the contract

$$C_B - TC = \$8,000 - 7,000$$

$$= \$1,000$$

Specifically,

$$E[\Pi] = p(C_B - TC)$$

$$= .1112(\$1,000)$$

$$= \$111.20$$

Equation (11.6) tells us that the total cost and the parameters of the contract bid–probability relationship determine the optimal bid. We now examine how these variables affect the optimal bid. First, consider an increase in the total cost of the project. If the parameters of the trade-off between the probability of receiving the contract and the contract bid remain unchanged, then this particular firm's costs rise relative to other firms. A $100 increase in TC will lead to an increase in the optimal contract bid of less than $100 because every $1 increase in the contract bid reduces the probability that the contract will be awarded. In particular, if TC rises to $7,100 while a and b remain at 1 and .0001111, respectively, then the optimal contract bid rises from $8,000 to

$$C_B = \frac{1 + .0001111(\$7,100)}{2(.0001111)} = \$8,050$$

Thus, the contract bid is increased by one-half of the cost increase. This result is fairly general as can be seen by examining equation (11.6) and the effect of a change in total cost:

$$\frac{\Delta C_B}{\Delta TC} = \frac{1}{2}$$

Suppose that the trade-off between the bid and the probability of receiving the bid becomes steeper. Specifically, let b rise from .0001111 to .00012 while $a = 1$ and $TC = 7,000$. In Figure 11.1 the line shifts from AB to AC. Now, it is more costly to increase the contract bid because a $1 increase in the bid leads to a greater fall in the probability of receiving the contract than when b was equal to .0001111. The optimal contract bid accordingly falls from $8,000 to

$$C_B = \frac{1 + .00012(\$7,000)}{2(.00012)} = \$7,667$$

Qualitatively, this result can be confirmed by examining equation (11.6) and the effect of changes in b:

$$\frac{\Delta C_B}{\Delta b} = -\frac{a}{2b^2}$$

which is clearly negative, indicating that an increase in b decreases the optimal contract bid.

11.4

JOINT PRODUCTS

Many production processes yield more than one product. In some cases, the "other" products are undesirable wastes that have no economic value. In fact, the firm may have to pay someone to remove these wastes and dispose of them. In other cases, however, the other products have considerable economic value. For example, when a petroleum firm refines crude oil to make gasoline, there are several by-products: jet fuel, kerosene, number 1 heating oil, diesel fuel, number 2 heating oil, numbers 4, 5, and 6 fuel oils, and asphalt. These prod-

FIGURE 11.1 The tradeoff between the contract bid and the probability of winning.

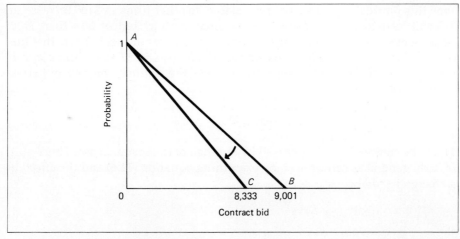

ucts all have substantial market values. Interestingly, the ratios of these various products to one another can be adjusted within certain limits, and the manager therefore is able to increase or decrease profit by altering these output ratios. There are other products, however, that are produced in fixed proportions; in this situation, the manager's ability to alter profits is more limited. We shall examine these two cases in this section.

FIXED PROPORTIONS   The fixed proportions case is the easiest case for the manager. First, however, let's investigate the market properties of joint products. Consider, for example, the fact that one steer produces one hide and two sides of beef. In Figure 11.2, we display the demand curves for pairs of sides of beef and for hides. These are labeled D_B and D_H, respectively. The price that buyers are willing to pay for a steer is equal to the sum of what people are willing to pay for the component parts. Thus, the demand curve for steers D_S is equal to the *vertical* addition of the demand curve for hides and of the demand curve for pairs of sides of beef. If the cattle market is competitive, market equilibrium will occur where the total demand curve intersects the supply curve for steers. In Figure 11.2, this occurs at an output of Q_0 steers. The price of a steer ($75) is equal to the price of its hide ($25) plus twice the price of a side of beef ($50).

> **Question**   Suppose that an epidemic of hog cholera kills a substantial number of hogs. This causes the price of pork to rise dramatically and causes the price of shoes to fall. Why is the price of shoes affected?
>
> **Answer**   Pork is a substitute for beef. When the price of pork rises, the

FIGURE 11.2   The demand for steers D_S is the *vertical* sum of the demand for beef D_B and the demand for hides D_H.

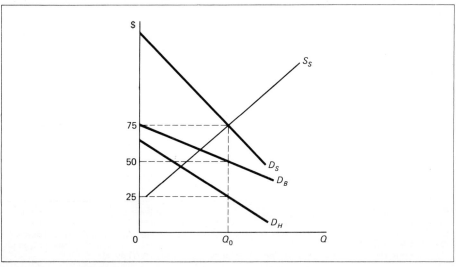

demand function for beef shifts from D_B to D'_B in Figure 11.3. Of course, The vertical sum of D'_B and D_H now shifts to D'_S. The new equilibrium price of steers is P'_S, which is composed of $2P'_B$ and P'_H. Notice that because the demand for hides did not change, the higher equilibrium quantity of steers causes the price of hides to fall, for a fall in the price of hides is necessary if the quantity of hides consumed is to increase. Since shoes are made of leather and its price has fallen, the costs of producing shoes will decline. This results in a price decrease for shoes. Consequently, managers who must purchase leather can benefit from keeping an eye on beef demand.

On the other hand, the producer of steers simply responds to the price of steers because of the fixed proportions in which beef and hides are produced through the production of steers. The price of steers is equal to the price of hides plus two times the price of a side of beef:

$$P_S = P_H + 2P_B$$

If steer production is competitive, the manager will act as a price taker and produce the number of steers where the marginal cost of production equals the price. This is the usual result for profit maximization.

VARIABLE PROPORTIONS   The case of variable proportions is more interesting and somewhat more complicated. We shall make use of the production possibilities curve, which is defined as the locus of output combinations that fixed quantities of inputs can generate.[5] For simplicity, we shall assume that we can get two products (gasoline and fuel oil) from a single variable input (crude oil) plus a fixed input (the refinery). Having already fixed the refinery capacity by some prior decision, we can plot the gasoline–fuel oil trade-off for a given quantity of crude oil.

In Figure 11.4, we see that the production possibilities curve is a concave function, which is labeled PPC: $CO° = g(G, FO)$. This curve shows the quantity of gasoline G that must be sacrificed to obtain an extra gallon of fuel oil (FO) from a given quantity of crude oil ($CO°$). For example, to expand fuel oil output from FO_1 to $FO_1 + 1$, the refinery manager must reduce his gasoline production from G_1 gallons to G_2 gallons. In contrast, at higher levels of fuel oil output, producing 1 more gallon of fuel oil requires a larger reduction in gasoline output. In particular, gasoline production drops from G_3 to G_4 when fuel oil production rises from FO_3 to $FO_3 + 1$.

The slope of the production possibilities curve indicates the rate at which the manager must reduce the output of gasoline in order to expand the output of fuel oil for a fixed quantity of crude oil. In other words, the slope measures the rate at which the existing technology will permit the manager

---

[5]P. Wonnacott and R. Wonnacott (*Economics*, New York: McGraw-Hill Book Company, 1979, p. 731) define the production possibilities curve as follows: "A curve showing the alternative combinations of outputs that can be produced if all productive resources are used. The boundary of attainable combinations of outputs." The following exposition is adopted from the treatment in James M. Henderson and Richard E. Quandt, *Microeconomic Theory*, 2d ed., New York: McGraw-Hill Book Company, 1971, pp. 89–98.

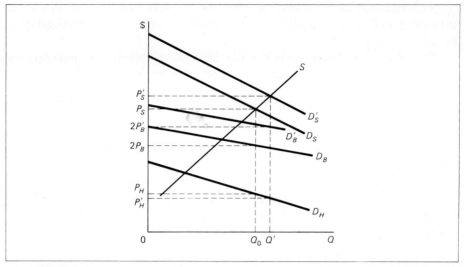

FIGURE 11.3   An increase in the demand for beef causes the price of hides to fall.

to transform one product into the other. Minus this slope is usually called the "marginal rate of transformation":

$$\text{MRT}_{G, \text{FO}} = -\frac{\Delta G}{\Delta \text{FO}}$$

FIGURE 11.4   The production possibilities curve shows technologically feasible combinations of outputs from fixed quantities of inputs.

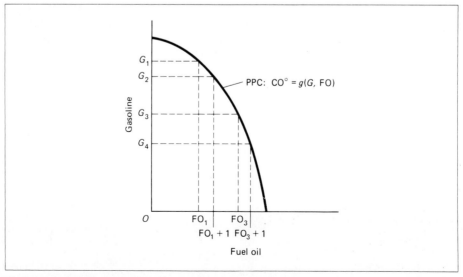

The marginal rate of transformation can be expressed in terms that are a bit more familiar. Suppose that gasoline production changed by ΔG gallons.

Question What change in the use of crude oil would be necessary to bring about a change in gasoline production of ΔG gallons?

Answer By definition, the marginal product of crude oil in the production of gasoline is the increase in gasoline that results from using 1 more gallon of crude oil

$$\text{MP}_{\text{CO}}^{G} = \frac{\Delta G}{\Delta \text{CO}}$$

The reciprocal of the marginal product of crude oil in the production of gasoline is the amount of crude oil that is required to produce 1 more gallon of gasoline.

$$\frac{1}{\text{MP}_{\text{CO}}^{G}} = \frac{\Delta \text{CO}}{\Delta G}$$

Thus a change of $(\Delta \text{CO}/\Delta G)\Delta G$ gallons of crude oil is necessary to alter gasoline production by ΔG gallons.

Similarly, $(\Delta \text{CO}/\Delta \text{FO})\Delta \text{FO}$ more gallons of crude oil are required to increase fuel oil production by ΔFO gallons. If we want to vary gasoline and fuel oil production so that crude oil usage remains constant, then

$$\Delta \text{CO} = \frac{\Delta \text{CO}}{\Delta G} \Delta G + \frac{\Delta \text{CO}}{\Delta \text{FO}} \Delta \text{FO} = 0$$

Thus, we have

$$\text{MRT}_{G,\text{FO}} = -\frac{\Delta G}{\Delta \text{FO}} = \frac{\Delta \text{CO}/\Delta \text{FO}}{\Delta \text{CO}/\Delta G} = \frac{\text{MP}_{\text{CO}}^{G}}{\text{MP}_{\text{CO}}^{\text{FO}}}$$

where $\text{MP}_{\text{CO}}^{\text{FO}}$ is the marginal product of crude oil in the production of fuel oil.

The manager wants to choose the combination of gasoline and fuel oil that maximizes profit. The profit function can be written as

$$\Pi = P_G G + P_{\text{FO}} \text{FO} - p\text{CO}$$

where P_G is the market price of gasoline, P_{FO} is the market price of fuel oil, and p is the price of crude oil. Profit is maximized by selecting the production levels of gasoline and fuel oil at which a marginal change in gasoline production or a marginal change in fuel oil production leaves profit unchanged:

$$\frac{\Delta \Pi}{\Delta G} = P_G - p \frac{\Delta \text{CO}}{\Delta G} = 0$$

(11.7)

$$\frac{\Delta \Pi}{\Delta \text{FO}} = P_{\text{FO}} - p \frac{\Delta \text{CO}}{\Delta \text{FO}} = 0$$

Solving these conditions for p and substituting the marginal products, we find at the optimum that

$$p = P_G \text{MP}_{\text{CO}}^G = P_{\text{FO}} \text{MP}_{\text{CO}}^{\text{FO}} \qquad (11.8)$$

In other words, the manager will have maximized the firm's profits when the price of the variable input is equal to the value of its marginal product in each of the two uses.

The profit-maximizing solution can also be seen graphically. The manager wants to find the output combination on the production possibilities curve that maximizes profit. Any point on the production possibilities curve represents a level of gasoline and a level of fuel oil that together use some constant quantity of crude oil. This means that total cost does not vary along the production possibilities curve. Thus, to maximize profit, the manager must find the point on the production possibilities curve at which total revenue is the greatest.

Total revenue equals

$$TR = P_G G + P_{\text{FO}} \text{FO} \qquad (11.9)$$

For some level of total revenue TR_0, equation (11.9) can be written in slope-intercept form as

$$G = \frac{TR_0}{P_G} - \frac{P_{\text{FO}}}{P_G} \text{FO}$$

This straight line represents the combinations of gasoline and fuel oil that yield the level of total revenue TR_0. This is called an "isorevenue line."

The manager's task is to find the highest isorevenue line passing through the production possibilities curve. This isorevenue line is the one that is tangent to the production possibilities curve. At the tangency, the slope of the isorevenue curve equals the slope of the production possibilities curve. This means that

$$\frac{P_{\text{FO}}}{P_G} = \frac{\text{MP}_{\text{CO}}^G}{\text{MP}_{\text{CO}}^{\text{FO}}} \qquad (11.10)$$

Equation (11.10) is merely a rearrangement of the last equality in equation (11.8). The tangency solution is shown in Figure 11.5, where G_1 gallons of gasoline and FO_1 gallons of fuel oil are produced, yielding total revenue TR_1.

11.5

TECHNOLOGICAL CHANGE

Technology or the "state of the arts" is embedded in the production functions that relate the quantities of inputs to the quantities of outputs. When society experiences technological change or progress, the quantity of output that a given set of inputs can generate increases. Since a firm obtains more output from the same quantity of inputs, the costs of production fall.

Normally, technological change operates through the marginal products of the various inputs. In Chapter 5, we found that a firm operating in competitive output and input markets maximizes profit by equating the price of input (p_i) to the value of the marginal product of input i. That is,

$$p_i = P \cdot MP_i$$

where P is the price of the product and MP_i is the marginal product of input i. A competitive firm equates price to marginal cost. Accordingly,

$$MC = \frac{p_1}{MP_1} = \frac{p_2}{MP_2} = \cdots = \frac{p_n}{MP_n}$$

Thus we can see immediately that an increase in the marginal products will cause marginal cost to fall.

INDUCED TECHNOLOGICAL CHANGE In the course of history there have been a few instances where technological change has occurred more or less accidentally with no apparent economic motivation. But there is considerable evidence that supports the hypothesis that the rate of innovation is affected by economic incentives. As a result, we should consider the level of technology as a managerial decision variable that is subject to economic interpretation. For example, Food and Drug Administration regulations have made it costlier for U.S. pharmaceutical firms to introduce new drugs. As a result, U.S. drug firms are now much less important in the discovery of new drugs than they were at one time.

The firm's manager can invest resources in increasing the marginal product of each of the inputs that are employed. She can develop machines that

FIGURE 11.5 Profit maximization requires producing those quantities where the marginal rate of transformation equals the ratio of output prices.

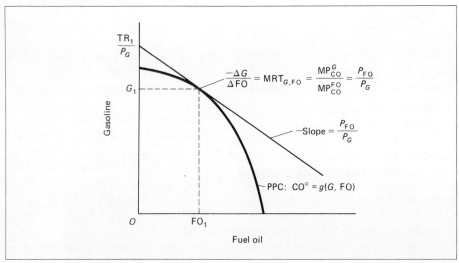

more efficiently handle her production needs, and she can discover production processes in which labor is more productive.

Because the firm must spend resources to bring about an increase in marginal productivity, such induced technological change is not a free good. As a result, the manager will want to find the level of expenditures on increasing input productivity that maximizes the firm's profit. This implies that each firm will have a profit-maximizing level of technology.

Question   Does the manager of a small firm have more incentive to invest in research and development than the manager of a large firm?

Answer   No. Suppose that a proposed innovation could increase the marginal product of labor by 2 units. A firm that produces more output than another firm will use a greater quantity of labor simply because it produces more output. As a result, the 2-unit increase in marginal productivity will accrue over a greater quantity of labor in a large firm than in a small firm. Thus, a given expenditure on technological progress is more likely to be profitable in a large firm than in a small firm. This can be seen easily when the firm has a constant returns to scale production function.

A firm is said to have constant returns to scale if a 5 percent increase in each input causes output to increase by 5 percent. It can be shown (see Section 11A.3 of the mathematical appendix to this chapter) that if a firm's production function.

$$Q = f(L,K)$$

exhibits constant returns to scale, then

$$Q = \mathrm{MP}_L L + \mathrm{MP}_K K \tag{11.11}$$

where Q denotes output, L and K are the quantities of labor and capital, and MP_L and MP_K represent the marginal products of labor and capital.

Suppose that a firm is contemplating research and development expenditures which are expected to increase capital's marginal product by 2 units. Equation (11.11) tells us that the increase in output, and consequently the increase in total revenue, which results from this improved technology increases proportionately as capital increases. A firm with 200 units of capital has twice the increase in total revenue of a firm with 100 units of capital.

Therefore, the empirical finding that large firms invest more in R&D than small firms need not rest on arguments that large firms face lower interest rates when they borrow money or have monopoly power. It follows from the fact that such expenditures are not continuous and large firms obtain more benefits than small firms from any given expenditure.

The analysis could be modified to allow an increase in expenditures on R&D by the manager of a firm to increase the technology of all other firms in the industry. For instance, a new process may be copied by other firms. Under this assumption, an innovating firm would not be able to capture all of the benefits of its innovation and accordingly would have a reduced incentive to innovate. This provides some justification for the granting of exclusive ownership rights (i.e., a patent) to innovations.

PATENTS   At this time in the United States, a patent grants exclusive rights lasting for 17 years to the owner of the patent. This gives the patent holder an opportunity to appropriate the benefits resulting from his invention. Consider an individual who has patented a cost-reducing invention that may be used in a competitive industry. For simplicity, assume that this industry has a perfectly elastic preinvention supply curve at price C, as shown in Figure 11.6. Thus $C = P = MC = AC$. Let the use of the patent reduce the average cost (exclusive of royalty payments for use of the patent) from C to $\bar{C}$.

As long as the new competitive price P is less than the old competitive price C, firms in the competitive industry would be willing to pay a positive price for the right to use the patent, for then if they did not adopt the patent, they would be driven out of business by those firms that did adopt the patent. Each firm willingly would pay the difference between its new total revenues PQ and its new total costs $\bar{C}Q$ for the right to use the patent. The competitive industry would be willing to pay $PQ - \bar{C}Q$ for the use of the patent. The patent holder, therefore, wishes to choose a royalty that will maximize her patent revenue $PQ - \bar{C}Q$.

Notice that $PQ - \bar{C}Q$ represents industry profit when there are no patent royalties. Thus, the patent holder wants to induce the competitive industry to produce where this industry profit is greatest. But industry profit is maximized when the industry produces the monopoly output and charges the monopoly price. For this strategy to benefit the patent holder, she must extract this industry profit by charging the appropriate royalty rate.

FIGURE 11.6   A patent holder's optimal royalty will lead the competitive industry to produce the profit-maximizing quantity. The royalty will be $P_1 - \bar{C}$.

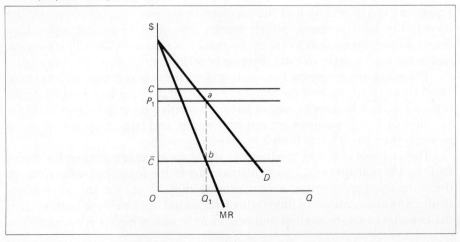

Let's now be more specific. In Figure 11.6, the patent holder wants the industry price and output to be P_1 and Q_1, which were determined by equating industry marginal revenue MR and industry marginal cost $\bar{C}$. If the patent holder sets a per unit royalty at $P_1 - \bar{C}$, the competitive industry will have a marginal cost equal to P_1 and will produce the optimal output from the patent holder's perspective. The total royalties will be given by the area of $P_1 ab\bar{C}$, which is $(P_1 - \bar{C})Q_1$. The manager of an inventive firm has an incentive to undertake the research leading to the invention if the cost of the invention is less than the present value of the patent royalties.

Question   Suppose the manager of XYZ Corporation is offered a chance to buy the patent described above. The patent holder wants XYZ Corporation to pay the present value of the royalties that the patent generates:

$$PV = \sum_{t=1}^{17} \frac{(P_1 - \bar{C})Q_1}{(1 + r)^t}$$

Is this an appropriate price?

Answer   If the manager could be certain that no competitive inventions were possible, this would not be an unreasonable price. But there is a serious problem. Suppose that another inventor devises an imperfect alternative to the invention in question. As a specific example, suppose ABC, Inc., is prepared to offer an invention that reduces the production cost from C to C' where the difference $C - C'$ is only one-half the cost saving $C - \bar{C}$. This option makes it impossible for XYZ Corporation to charge a royalty of $P_1 - \bar{C}$. The maximum per unit royalty is now $C' - \bar{C}$, which is obviously less than $P_1 - \bar{C}$. Thus, even if a competitive invention is inferior, the possibility of its existence reduces the market value of the original invention. Of course, if a superior invention were to emerge, the original cost-reducing invention would be worthless. Given such risks, the manager would be unwise to purchase the patent at the patent holder's asking price.

11.6

SHUT-DOWN DECISIONS

On the basis of the quest for maximum profits, we know that the manager searches for the output where marginal cost and marginal revenue are equal. Although profits are maximized here, they need not be positive. Indeed, one of the key questions facing a manager whose firm has negative profits is whether or not to shut down.

In this instance, the manager's responsibility is to minimize the firm's losses. Even if the existing firm does not produce, there are certain fixed costs TFC which must be paid. This means that the firm loses its TFC if it shuts down. If the firm stays open, its profit equals

$$\Pi = TR - TVC - TFC$$

where TR equals total revenue and TVC equals total variable cost. Only if total revenue TR exceeds total variable cost TVC does remaining open produce a smaller loss than shutting down. Equivalently, the manager should keep the plant open if price $(= TR/Q)$ exceeds average variable cost $(= TVC/Q)$.

As time passes, fewer and fewer costs remain unavoidable. Workers may be fired, machines and buildings may be sold, and leases may not be renewed. In the long-run, all costs are avoidable. In fact, this is the somewhat circular definition of the long run. Consequently, the manager will choose to produce in the long run if and only if total revenue is at least as great as total costs.

Question   Why would the manager want to produce in the long run if total revenue is just equal to total cost?

Answer   The appropriate definition of total cost includes a competitive rate of return on investment. In other words, all inputs are paid enough to keep them employed in that particular endeavor.

The naive shut-down rule is that output should be zero if price is less than average variable cost at the point where marginal cost equals marginal revenue. This ignores a few complications. For example, suppose that the manager has signed supply contracts for a certain quantity of output. The contract price may be less than the average variable costs of production, but shutting down does not make the firm's contractual obligations disappear.[6] Consequently, when the manager elects to produce zero output, the loss is not confined to the usual fixed costs. Rather, the loss is larger than the fixed costs to the extent that the firm's breach of contract imposes additional costs. Partial or full payment of the contracted costs is frequently required when a contract is broken. These payments must be added to the usual fixed costs to determine the losses associated with shutting down.

Question   The Hog Town Electronics Company has a contract to supply 1,000 adapter switches at $10 per unit. Owing to unforeseen circumstances, costs have risen to the point where average variable cost is $12. Although the current market price is $15, the contract price is below average variable cost. Should the manager close the plant?

Answer   If the manager honors the firm's contract, the firm will lose $(\$12 - 10)(1,000) = \$2,000$ in addition to its fixed costs. Normally, one recommends shutting down. But the customer would have to pay $15 for the adapter switches and would have a valid claim against Hog Town Electronics for the $5-per-unit difference. Thus, shutting down would lead to losses of $5,000 plus the fixed costs. Production is obviously cheaper than breaching the contract.

[6]An interesting article on this topic is provided by John H. Barton, "The Economic Basis of Damages for Breach of Contract," *Journal of Legal Studies*, vol. 1, June 1972, pp. 277–304.

The shut-down decision is further complicated by demand instability. When demand is unstable, we should not expect the manager to shut down the firm every time that price falls below average variable cost. In the first place, even if the instances when price is below average variable costs were perfectly predictable, there can be considerable transactions costs in shutting down. For example, one cannot turn a steel plant on and off with the flick of a switch. There are large costs of attaining the necessary heat for the basic steel process. Similarly, a firm that operates an assembly line operation cannot lay off and recall its labor force without substantial personnel costs. As a result, if the manager feels that the situation is only temporary, he may not shut down when price dips below average variable cost.

Finally, the manager may not know precisely when the price will be too low. Demand may be random, which means that the price shifts up and down in a probabilistic fashion. Accordingly, the manager will be unable to predict on which days the price will fall below average variable cost. This, of course, precludes shutting down intermittently. Consider the situation depicted in Figure 11.7. We are looking at a competitive firm that produces a perishable product. It will be able to sell its output at a price equal to P_1 or P_2 depending upon the random process that determines the actual price. Half of the time, the price will be P_1, and it will be P_2 the other half of the time. The expected price is $E(P)$ in Figure 11.7. Faced with this situation, the manager cannot maximize profits because profits are random. One solution would be to maximize expected profits, which would require producing Q_3 units of output in each period. Note that the expected price equals marginal cost at Q_3. When the price is P_1, the firm earns positive profits. In contrast, if the manager could have known beforehand when the price would be P_2, he would not have produced anything on those days because the firm loses money on those sales. But he cannot know just when the price will equal P_2,

FIGURE 11.7 Maximizing expected profit requires producing where $E(P) = MC$. Some output will be sold at P_2, which is below AVC.

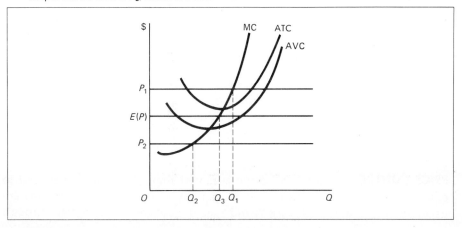

WHEN OPTIMAL OUTPUT IS ZERO

The decision to produce no outputs, i.e., to shut down, is not an easy one to reach. For one thing, to make such a decision often requires admitting a mistake. After all, someone had to decide to enter the industry. Nonetheless, when it becomes clear that continued operation makes no sense, the sensible thing to do is minimize future losses by exiting from the industry. Recently, such a decision was made by the Sun Company.

For 64 years, Sun Ship, Inc., produced ships in its Chester, Pa., shipyard. Sun Ship was the largest employer in Chester, accounting for some 4,200 jobs. In addition, each of the jobs led to four service-industry jobs. Combined with the fact that 40 percent of Sun's employees were minorities, tremendous pressure was put on Sun to remain open. But the prospect of continuing losses made remaining open a serious mistake. During the 1976–1979 period, Sun Ship lost some $62 million. In 1977, Sun's management made a decision to pump funds into the shipyard in an effort to increase profitability. When this did not seem to help, Sun decided to stop the construction of new ships.

Source: "Why Sun Will Stop Building New Ships," *Business Week*, Jan. 26, 1981, p. 32.

---

and this precludes intermittent shutdowns. Owing to the product's perishability, he cannot use inventories to help deal with the uncertainty that he faces.

Question   Suppose that firm XYZ owns the building in which it operates. It is a specially designed building that cannot be leased or sold to anyone else. Yearly payments of $12,000 must be made on the mortgage for 10 more years. How does this asset affect the manager's shut-down decision?

Answer   During the 10-year period, the annual payments should be treated like any fixed cost. These mortgage payments cannot be avoided by shutting down. Since the building has unique characteristics, the manager cannot get anyone else to assume these fixed costs. After the building is paid for, the cost is sunk and should have no effect upon the managerial decision regarding production levels.

11.7

OPTIMAL RESPONSE TO GOVERNMENT PROGRAMS

Many government programs interfere to some extent with the market mechanism. Other programs alter the institutional framework in which markets operate. We shall examine two cases in this section: price controls and environmental restrictions. In each instance, we are not concerned with making any normative judgment regarding the wisdom of such programs. Rather, we are interested in how the manager of a firm might optimally respond to the business opportunities posed by the government's activities.

PRICE CONTROLS   So far, we have assumed that prices alone are used to equilibrate markets. The truth is that many other rationing mechanisms are used, too. For example, during World War II, gasoline was rationed through the use of gasoline coupons. Some form of nonprice rationing is necessary whenever prices are not permitted to equate supply and demand. The nature of the problem is plain enough to see in Figure 11.8. Given the supply and demand, the equilibrium price and output are P_1 and Q_1, respectively. If price is stuck at P_2, for some reason, the market does not clear. At price P_2, firms are collectively willing to provide only Q_3 units of output. In contrast, consumers collectively want Q_2 units of output. Consequently, some rationing device must be used to allocate the available quantity of output. The alternatives vary from the simple to the complex.

There is a more fundamental question: Why is there nonprice rationing? Many prices are set for a specific period without full knowledge of the quantities demanded and supplied. Nonprice rationing is frequently used to deal with unforeseen increases in demand. For instance, airlines, motels, and symphonies set their prices without knowing exactly how many people will wish to use their services on a given day. If an unusually large number of people wish to fly between Buffalo and Chicago on a particular day, only those who were first in line will be able to do so. Another source of nonprice rationing is the government, which frequently charges less than the market price. For instance, public housing is often subsidized by the government and thereby sold at a price below its market value.

A principal source of nonprice rationing is government regulation of market prices. Government-imposed minimum or maximum prices can be considered as discontinuous excise taxes. In the case of a price ceiling, the firm incurs no penalty for selling at or below ceiling price P_C in Figure 11.9. A price ceiling therefore does not alter the firm's supply curve at or below P_C; the "tax" rate in this region equals zero.

A firm choosing to violate a price ceiling does so at some potential cost. Suppose that each time a firm sells at a price greater than the ceiling price, its

FIGURE 11.8   Price controls at P_2 will not allow this market to clear, as Q_3 will be supplied and Q_2 will be demanded.

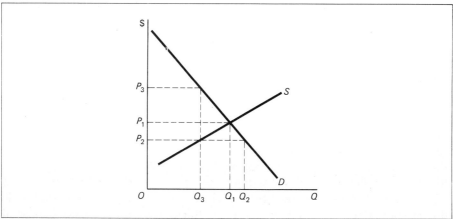

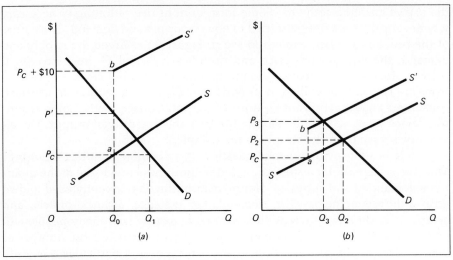

FIGURE 11.9   The effect of price controls (a)
when there are severe penalties for violations
and (b) when penalties are not severe.

probability of being caught is .001. If caught, the firm is fined $10,000 per
unit sold in violation of the law. The expected fine associated with selling 1
unit in violation of the price ceiling therefore is given by

$$E(\text{fine}) = (\$10{,}000 \cdot .001) + (0 \cdot 0.999) = \$10$$

That is, there is a .001 probability that the firm will be caught and accordingly
be fined $10,000 and a .999 probability that the firm will not be caught and
therefore suffer no losses. For any price greater than the ceiling price, producers will require the old marginal cost *plus* the compensation required for
violating the price ceiling. In our example, a risk-neutral industry would
require $P_C + \$10$ to be induced to produce an infinitesimal amount past Q_0 in
panel (a) of Figure 11.9. Since the industry supplies Q_0 at ceiling price P_C, the
new supply curve [$SabS'$ in panel (a) of Figure 11.9] is discontinuous at P_C.

The supply and demand curves do not intersect. At Q_0, producers have
no incentive to produce more than Q_0, for the price that consumers are
willing to pay (P') is less than the price that producers would demand
($P_C + \$10$) to produce more than Q_0. Consumers would end up paying P_C for
Q_0 goods, and nonprice rationing would be necessary to ration the excess demand ($Q_1 - Q_0$).

Suppose, however, that the expected punishment for violating the
price ceiling is quite small. This may be because the fines are low or because
the government employs only a small number of agents to ascertain whether
the law has been violated. If the expected punishment is small enough, then
the supply and demand curves will intersect and the price ceiling will lead to
an *increase* in market prices and a reduction in output. This situation is
depicted in panel (b) of Figure 11.9. Here, the imposition of a price ceiling at

P_C causes the supply curve to contract from SS to $SabS'$. Output falls from Q_2 to Q_3 and price rises from P_2 to P_3. Firms have found it worthwhile to violate the law.

Thus, price ceilings do not necessarily lead to nonprice rationing. Nonprice rationing will be observed only if the expected punishment is sufficiently great. The government, of course, can increase the expected punishment by (1) increasing fines or prison terms associated with violating price ceilings or (2) increasing the resources devoted to detecting violations of price ceilings, and thereby increasing the probability of detection.

An owner of a firm who finds it worthwhile to engage in nonprice rationing has several options to choose from. The firm gains very little from using long lines (e.g., lines for World Series tickets) to discourage demand and hence ration the excess demand. Other methods of rationing directly increase the owner's utility or profits. For instance, a bank faced with a mortgage rate ceiling reduces its expected losses from default and hence increases its profits by granting loans only to those with a great deal of collateral. In 1978, New York banks responded to an interest rate ceiling on mortgages at $8^1/_2$ percent when nationally mortgages were going for $9^1/_2$ to 10 percent by requiring 50 percent down. An owner of a rent-controlled apartment may increase her utility by giving that apartment to a friend, a relative, a person of similar ethnic background, a college classmate, or a good-looking man. Each rationing technique benefits certain groups at the expense of other groups. It is often quite difficult to determine on an a priori basis who benefits and who suffers from rationing.

ENVIRONMENTAL CONTROLS   In response to mounting evidence that air pollution is detrimental to personal health, society decided to do something about the problem. At the federal level, this response took the form of the Clean Air Act. This act gave the administrator of the Environmental Protection Agency the authority to prescribe standards for various pollutants. In other words, he could set a maximum quantity of certain air pollutants that could be emitted into the air. The determination of the optimal quantity of air pollution is an incredibly complex problem. Nevertheless, the government established certain pollution standards, and we can analyze the consequences of these standards for business.

One way of encouraging firms to reduce pollution is to tax the emissions.[7] The manager of a firm subject to the pollution tax will maximize profits by adjusting the firm's output to account for the tax. An example will clarify this prescription.

Suppose that there is a pollution tax on smoke. For the firm that we shall consider, smoke is directly related to the quantity of fuel that is used in the production process. Thus, the tax on smoke can be expressed as a tax on the fuel consumed in the production process. If the firm's production function is

$$Q = f(L,\ K,\ F)$$

---

[7]This problem was analyzed by William Baumol and Wallace Oates, "The Use of Standards and Prices for Protection of the Environment," *Swedish Journal of Economics*, vol. 73, March 1971, pp. 42–54.

where Q is output, L is labor, K is capital, and F is fuel, the profit function *without the tax* is

$$\Pi = PQ - wL - sK - pF$$

where w, s, and p are the prices of the labor, capital, and fuel inputs, respectively.

Profit maximization requires employing all inputs until the value of the marginal product of each input is equal to its price:

$$P \cdot \text{MP}_L = w$$

$$P \cdot \text{MP}_K = s$$

$$P \cdot \text{MP}_F = p$$

If the use of fuel is taxed, the profit function becomes

$$\Pi = PQ - wL - sK - (p + t)F$$

where t is the tax per unit of fuel. Profit maximization now requires adding inputs until

$$P \cdot \text{MP}_L = w$$

$$P \cdot \text{MP}_K = s$$

$$P \cdot \text{MP}_F = p + t$$

In other words, the manager hires labor and capital until their values of marginal product equal their prices. For fuel, however, she equates its value of marginal product to its price plus the tax. This, of course, will reduce the use of fuel and lead the manager to substitute away from the use of fuel in favor of labor and capital.

The government policy *in practice* often takes the form of standards that are applied to each firm. In such cases, the manager will maximize the firm's profits subject to the usual constraints plus the governmentally imposed constraint that the level of emissions E be less than or equal to the standard E^*:

$$E \leq E^*$$

If the standard is ineffective, the constraint is said to be not binding. This means that the profit-maximizing level of emissions is less than E^*. In this case, the manager's decision is unaffected.

If the standard is effective, however, the constraint is said to be binding. Consequently, the constraint would force firms to use a hitherto unprofitable combination of inputs. This, of course, leads to an increase in marginal costs. The manager would respond by substituting toward inputs that were less pollution-intensive. For example, firms would substitute away from the use of high-sulfur fuel toward the use of low-sulfur fuel. They may even replace capital equipment, thereby altering the production function employed. Finally, the manager may add capital equipment, e.g., scrubbers in smoke-stacks to arrest the emissions.

The principle for deciding whether such expenditures make any sense economically is a familiar one. If such an expenditure increases the firm's revenues by more than it increases its costs, then the expenditure should be made. If not, the manager will elect to forgo the expenditure. This works for pollution control equipment as well as other investment options.

11.8

SUMMARY

In this chapter, we examined a number of rather specific production decisions—decisions regarding the length of sales contracts, size of inventories, bid prices, expenditures on innovation, patent royalties, shutting down, and compliance with price controls and with standards. The decision rules that we developed are merely variations on what are by now familiar themes.

A number of these decisions involve continuous variables. We saw that inventories should be expanded, bid prices lowered, and patent royalties increased until the relevant marginal benefit equals the relevant marginal cost. In each instance, it was necessary first to set up the problem. After some thought, we discovered what the marginal benefits and costs are, and the solution followed.

Many of the other decisions involve comparing the firm's profits in one situation with the firm's profits in another situation. Thus, a manager should enter into long-term contracts if they generate more profits than operating on the spot market, and should shut down if less money is lost under this solution than would be lost by staying open. Similarly, innovation is worthwhile if a firm has a relative advantage in utilizing or developing a new technology. Finally, investment in pollution-control equipment is warranted only if profits rise.

PROBLEMS

11.1 Suppose the trade-off function between the contract bid and the probability of winning a contract is given by

$$p = 1 - .0001111C_B$$

and let the total project cost be $7,000. Calculate the probability of winning and the expected profit for bids of $7,000, $7,500, $7,900, $8,000, $8,100, and $8,500.

11.2 Consider the value of the cost-saving invention described in the text. What would happen to the value if the patent laws were amended so that no patent would be issued if a new invention failed to reduce costs by more than an existing invention? What would happen to the incentive to invent?

11.3 Some plants are designed specifically to produce a particular output level. These plants produce this output level at lower cost than other plants can but are relatively inefficient in producing other output levels. Other, flexible plants can produce a wide range of outputs without much change in marginal cost. Suppose that the flexible plants became cheaper relative to the inflexible plants. What would happen to the incidence of long-term contracts?

11.4 Examine the square root rule of optimal inventories. Differentiate the rule with respect to C_I and C_F to determine the impact on the optimal inventory of changes in these costs.

11.5 Answer true, false, or uncertain: The Sleazo Office Supply Store sells twice as many Cheap typewriters as Ritz typewriters. This store should therefore stock twice as many Cheap typewriters as Ritz typewriters.

11.6 The rate of interest that banks are allowed to pay on savings accounts cannot exceed a particular interest rate. (a) Under what circumstances will banks give their customers gifts (e.g., calculators, china, barbecues) when they add money to their savings accounts? (b) What happens to the value of the gifts that are given to bank customers when the rate of return on alternative assets (bonds, homes, etc.) rises?

11.7 Answer true, false, or undecided: Price controls always lead to some form of nonprice rationing.

11.8 Consider a bakery that sells fresh bread in its own store and sells leftover bread to a thrift store. Suppose that the community becomes wealthier and will purchase the day-old bread at the thrift store only if its price falls. How does this affect the bakery's production decision?

11.9 As the price of energy rises, what will happen to research on energy-saving devices? Why?

11.10 The current spot market price for a truckload of lumber is $31. The price that lumber producers are receiving for a truckload of lumber under long-term contract is $42. Evaluate: Lumber producers must not be maximizing profits, since long-term production for the spot market is costlier than production under long-term contract.

REFERENCES

Baumol, William: *Economic Theory and Operations Analysis*, Englewood Cliffs, N.J.: Prentice-Hall, Inc., 1977.

Becker, Gary: *Economic Theory*, New York: Alfred A. Knopf, Inc., 1971.

Ferguson, C. E.: *Neoclassical Theory of Production and Distribution*, London: Cambridge University Press, 1969.

Henderson, James M., and Richard Quandt: *Microeconomic Theory*, New York: McGraw-Hill Book Company, 1971.

Horowitz, Ira: *Decision Making and the Theory of the Firm,* New York: Holt, Rinehart and Winston, Inc., 1970.

MATHEMATICAL APPENDIX

11A.1

STOCHASTIC INVENTORY MODEL

We can use the same notation as in Section 11.2:

P_0 = price in primary market
C_V = average variable costs
P_S = price in secondary market
$f(Q)$ = probability of quantity Q

The expected loss associated with an output decision of Q^* can be written as

$$L = (P_0 - C_V) \int_{Q^*}^{\infty} (Q - Q^*) f(Q) \, dQ + (C_V - P_S) \int_0^{Q^*} (Q^* - Q) f(Q) \, dQ$$

$$(A11.1)$$

where the first term on the right-hand side is the expected opportunity loss due to insufficient quantity and the second term is the expected loss on sales in the secondary market due to insufficient demand. A risk-neutral manager will want to minimize this expected loss through his choice of Q^*.

To find the optimal value of Q, we set the first derivative of (A11.1) equal to zero:

$$\frac{dL}{dQ^*} = -(P_0 - C_V)\Pr(Q > Q^*) + (C_V - P_S)\Pr(Q < Q^*) = 0 \qquad (A11.2)$$

where $\Pr(Q > Q^*)$ is the probability that more than Q^* will be demanded and, similarly, $\Pr(Q < Q^*)$ is the probability that less than Q^* will be demanded. Thus, we can see that output should be expanded until the marginal reduction in the expected loss due to insufficient quantity is equal to the marginal increase in the expected loss due to insufficient demand. By the usual definitions of probability, $\Pr(Q > Q^*) + \Pr(Q < Q^*) = 1$. Thus, we can write first-order condition (A11.2) as

$$-(P_0 - C_V) + (P_0 - C_V) \Pr(Q < Q^*) + (C_V - P_S) \Pr(Q < Q^*) = 0$$

or

$$\Pr(Q < Q^*) = \frac{P_0 - C_V}{(P_0 - C_V) + (C_V - P_S)} = \frac{P_0 - C_V}{P_0 - P_S}$$

Thus, the optimal quantity of output occurs where the probability that demand will be less than that output equals the profit per unit sold $(P_0 - C_V)$ divided by the difference between the price in the primary market and the price in the secondary market.

11A.2

JOINT PRODUCTS—
VARIABLE PROPORTIONS

The firm's production possibilities curve can be written as $L^0 = g(X,Y)$ where L^0 denotes a specific value of the variable input and X and Y are the two products. The marginal rate of transformation is minus the slope of the production possibilities curve:

$$-\frac{dY}{dX} = \text{MRT}_{XY}$$

We can take the total differential of the production possibilities curve:

$$dL^0 = \frac{\partial g}{\partial X} dX + \frac{\partial g}{\partial Y} dY$$

which equals zero for movements along the production possibilities curve. Thus, we have

$$\text{MRT}_{XY} = -\frac{dY}{dX} = \frac{\partial g/\partial X}{\partial g/\partial Y}$$

But $\partial g/\partial X = \partial L/\partial X$ and $\partial L/\partial X$ is the reciprocal of the marginal product of labor in producing X. Similarly, $\partial L/\partial Y$ is the reciprocal of the marginal product of labor in producing Y. Consequently, we can write

$$\text{MRT}_{XY} = \frac{\partial Y/\partial L}{\partial X/\partial L} = \frac{\text{MP}_L^Y}{\text{MP}_L^X}$$

The firm's profit function can be written as

$$\Pi = P_X X + P_Y Y - wL$$

It is convenient to substitute the production possibilities function for L and write the profit function as

$$\Pi = P_X X + P_Y Y - wg(X,, Y)$$

The manager's problem is to select the appropriate quantities of X and Y to produce in order to maximize profits. The first-order conditions for maximum profit require the first partial derivatives to be zero:

$$\frac{\partial \Pi}{\partial X} = P_X - w\frac{\partial g}{\partial X} = 0$$

$$\frac{\partial \Pi}{\partial Y} = P_Y - w\frac{\partial g}{\partial Y} = 0$$

Solving these conditions for w and substituting the marginal products, we find at the optimum that

$$w = P_X \frac{\partial X}{\partial L} = P_Y \frac{\partial Y}{\partial L}$$

In other words, the value of the marginal product of labor in each of its uses must equal its price.

11A.3

Suppose $Q = f(L,K)$ is a constant returns to scale production function. The total differential of Q is

EULER'S THEOREM

$$dQ = \frac{\partial f(L,K)}{\partial L}\, dL + \frac{\partial f(L,K)}{\partial K}\, dK$$

We can multiply the left-hand side by Q/Q and the first and second terms on the right-hand side by L/L and K/K, respectively. Then, we would have

$$Q\,\frac{dQ}{Q} = MP_L \cdot L\,\frac{dL}{L} + MP_K \cdot K\,\frac{dK}{K}$$

By the definition of a constant returns to scale production function, if each input is increased by the same proportion, i.e., if

$$\frac{dL}{L} = \frac{dK}{K}$$

then the output will increase by the same percentage:

$$\frac{dQ}{Q} = \frac{dL}{L} = \frac{dK}{K}$$

Thus, we can cancel these terms, which leaves

$$Q = MP_L \cdot L + MP_K \cdot K$$

12 PRICING DECISIONS IN IMPERFECT MARKETS

The pricing of a firm's output is one of the most important of all managerial decisions. The impact of price on profit is clear and direct. For firms in competitive industries, managers find it most sensible to set price at the level dictated by the market. Higher prices would not attract any customers, and lower prices would result in lower profit. Thus, there is not much pricing discretion for managers of competitive firms. For all other firms, however, there is some degree of pricing discretion. Finding the appropriate price is an important task. In this chapter, we shall consider a variety of pricing decisions when the firm is not in a perfectly competitive industry. These decisions include the pricing of new products, setting discriminatory prices, and peak-load pricing. In addition, we shall examine the pricing for a cartel. Finally, we shall investigate the effect of taxation on pricing decisions.

12.1

PRICING NEW PRODUCTS

When a firm introduces a new product, the manager is faced with a problem: determining the price that will maximize the firm's profits. We can suppose that he knows the production costs of his firm. If he also knew the demand function for his product, the pricing decision would be a familiar one. As we can see in Figure 12.1, the manager would equate marginal cost MC and marginal revenue MR to produce profit-maximizing quantity Q_1. The profit-maximizing price would be P_1 in that case. This, of course, is no different from the analysis in Chapter 5. There are, however, several complications that arise for brand new products. For one thing, the manager may not know just where the demand curve is. His natural response will be to turn to the marketing people for their demand forecasts. Their forecasting or prediction can be quite accurate. In that event, the manager can act as we have described above. But there are many situations where new products are sufficiently novel that the marketing forecasts will be rather imprecise. In these cases, the manager can use the forecasted demand curve to pick an initial price and quantity. On the basis of his intuition that the forecast will prove to be inaccurate, the manager will be prepared to experiment with price in an effort to find the optimal price. In other words, the manager uses the best information that he can get to select a starting point. Subsequently, he gropes around in an effort to improve the profits of the firm. After this process ends with the manager satisfied that he has found the optimal price, the firm will be in a position such as the one depicted in Figure 12.1, where Q_1 is produced at price P_1.

For some purposes, commodities can usefully be characterized as *inspection* goods or *experience* goods.

DEFINITION ▶   An *inspection* good
is one whose relevant characteristics
can be determined by a potential
buyer's inspection.

Thus, a potential buyer of an inspection good will know whatever would be pertinent to her decision prior to actually purchasing the commodity. For example, if a woman is considering the purchase of a new dress, that commodity is an inspection good. Prior to purchase, she can determine the color, style, fit, quality of the material and sewing, and so on.

DEFINITION ▶   An *experience*
good is one that has one or more
important characteristics that can
only be determined by consuming the
commodity.

Thus, shoppers for experience goods must take a bit of a gamble when they buy an unfamiliar brand. For example, if a shopper considers buying a package of frozen beans, the shopper can ascertain significant characteristics like appearance, smell, and taste only after the beans have been bought, cooked, and eaten.

In some cases, the initial pricing strategy will be affected by whether the

FIGURE 12.1   Profit-maximizing price and
quantity are determined by equality of
marginal cost and marginal revenue.

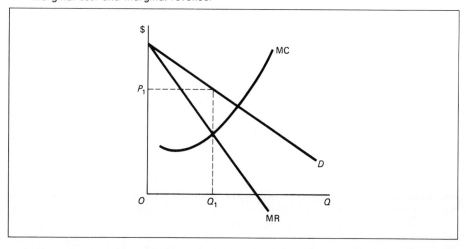

commodity in question is an inspection good or an experience good. When a new inspection good is introduced, the major promotional problem is making consumers aware of its existence. Once they are acquainted with the commodity, each consumer can make a rational (utility-maximizing) choice. The manager, therefore, can set a profit-maximizing price at once. For an experience good, however, simply making the consumer aware of its availability is not enough. Somehow, consumers must be induced to sample the product. One way of doing this is through promotional pricing. Low, introductory offers are common pricing strategies for gaining some market penetration. The purpose of the low price is to reduce the amount that the consumer risks by trying a new product. These price reductions should be viewed as promotional costs or investments just like advertising. Subsequently, after a position is established in the market, the manager can cut back on this form of promotion and set the usual profit-maximizing prices.

The manager's pricing strategy is affected not only by whether the good is an inspection or experience good but also by the duration of the firm's monopoly position. Some new products provide an initial monopoly position that is quickly eroded by other firms. For example, the Mr. Coffee brewer and the Water Pik Shower Massage both experienced some monopoly power for 1 or 2 years before other manufacturers began producing essentially identical products. Even though the manager may expect his monopoly position to be of short duration, the correct pricing decision can yield monopoly profits. Suppose that the new product is one that can be imitated quite easily, but only after a time lapse. That is, other firms will require some time to recognize the fact that this is a product worth imitating and some additional time to implement the imitation. This could

---

A PROBLEM IN PRICING
NEW AUTOMOBILES*

For several years, small, fuel-efficient imports have been replacing domestically produced gas guzzlers in the U.S. automobile market. Detroit has responded by introducing in the 1981 model year some fuel-efficient models of its own. These cars are fundamentally different from the small U.S. cars of earlier years. The earlier small models were cut-rate cars in appearance and performance. This is not the case with the 1981 models, which are smaller and fuel-efficient but are fully equipped and comfortable. Consequently, the U.S. producers are introducing something of a new product and should price it accordingly. Many observers feel, however, that the U.S. producers have exceeded the optimal entry price.

The U.S. producers are facing serious problems: low profits, an even lower cash flow, rising labor costs, and rising production costs due to environmental and safety legislation. In response to this situation, they have elected to follow a high-price strategy. One problem with such a strategy is that it raises the price of trying one of the new cars. Since cars are experience goods, this strategy will work against rapid market penetration.

The longer that the U.S. producers permit incursions by imports, the more difficult it will become to reverse the trend. Recapturing market share will become more difficult the longer the U.S. buyer's experience with satisfactory imports. Consequently, the high-price strategy could be a disaster for the U.S. automobile industry.

---

*Source: "Detroit's High-Price Strategy Could Backfire," Business Week, Nov. 24, 1980, pp. 109, 111.

provide, say, a 3-year period during which the original innovator has a monopoly. After that, the market may be quite competitive. The innovator will
maximize the present value of his profit stream by charging the monopoly
profit-maximizing price for 3 years and the competitive price thereafter.

There are other instances where a new product's price falls over time. For
example, one observes this price pattern in the distribution of many movies.
The so-called first-run movie theaters charge higher prices than the second-
run theaters. In cases like this, however, the monopoly position is not deteri-
orating. Rather, the distributor is engaging in price discrimination, which
we shall examine next.

12.2

PRICE DISCRIMINATION

Monopolists sometimes find it profitable to charge different prices to
different customers for essentially
the same commodity. Consider a
monopoly with different demand
curves in two markets. The manager must determine the prices to be charged
in these two markets. Suppose he has only one production facility. Associated with this production facility is a marginal cost curve that is a function of total output. In Figure 12.2, we have the demand and corresponding
marginal revenue curve for market 1 in panel (a) and the same curves for
market 2 in panel (b). In panel (c), we have the horizontally combined
marginal revenue curve along with the firm's marginal cost curve.

After the usual groping around, the manager will discover that the firm's
profits are maximized when he produces where the summed marginal revenue ΣMR equals the firm's marginal cost MC. To maximize profits, this output should be allocated between the two markets in such way that the
marginal revenues are equal. Thus, the profit-maximizing condition is that

FIGURE 12.2 Monopolistic price
discrimination yields maximum profits when
$MR_1 = MR_2 = MC$.

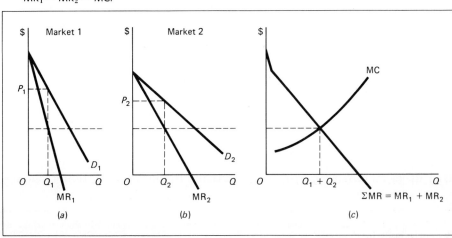

$$MC = MR_1 = MR_2$$

If the marginal revenues were not equal, then a reallocation of the total quantity produced would increase profits. For example, suppose that MR_1 exceeded MR_2. Taking 1 unit of output away from market 2 would reduce total revenue by MR_2. Sending this unit to market 1 would increase total revenue by MR_1. Since MR_1 exceeds MR_2, the gain exceeds the loss, and profits are increased. Profits are increased still further by continuing to reallocate until the marginal revenues are equal. During this whole process, total output remains constant and, consequently, so does total cost.

Profit maximization thus requires that marginal revenues be equal (i.e., $MR_1 = MR_2$). Furthermore, for the usual reasons, marginal revenue must equal marginal cost. That is, the increase in total revenue from selling 1 more unit in either market must equal the increase in total cost that results from producing that additional unit.

In Figure 12.2, profits are maximized by allocating Q_1 to market 1 and Q_2 to market 2. The prices are P_1 and P_2, respectively. As we can see, P_1 is higher than P_2 while the marginal cost of production is the same for both markets. This is a case of price discrimination. When a firm sells a homogeneous output simultaneously to two different markets such that the price–marginal cost ratios are not equal, the firm is said to be engaging in price discrimination.[1]

When we examine Figure 12.2, we notice that the market with the steeper demand curve has the higher price. Intuition suggests that this may be more than coincidence. Although it is not always the case, this time our intuition is pointing us in the right direction. We have seen that MR_1 will equal MR_2 when profits are maximized. But we saw in Chapter 3 that

$$MR = P\left(1 - \frac{1}{\epsilon}\right)$$

where ϵ is the elasticity of demand. Consequently, if the marginal revenues are equal, we know that

$$P_1\left(1 - \frac{1}{\epsilon_1}\right) = P_2\left(1 - \frac{1}{\epsilon_2}\right)$$

Suppose that at any price, the elasticity of demand in market 2 exceeds that in market 1: $\epsilon_2 > \epsilon_1$. Then $1/\epsilon_2$ is less than $1/\epsilon_1$ and $(1 - 1/\epsilon_1) < (1 - 1/\epsilon_2)$. Thus, P_2 will be less than P_1. This is a very plausible result. A higher price is charged in the market that is less responsive to price increases while a lower price is charged in the market that is more responsive to price changes.

There are numerous examples of price discrimination. Movie theaters, amusement parks, and airlines charge lower prices for children than for adults. Utility companies charge consumers more for electricity than industrial users are charged. For many journals, library subscription rates are

---

[1] A generalized price discrimination model for more than two markets is presented in the mathematical appendix to this chapter.

higher than individual subscription rates. Each of these price differences presumably reflects differences in demand elasticities. Are the implied differences in demand elasticities reasonable?

Question   The manager of ABC, Inc., a monopoly producer, has been advised that the demand curve in market 1 is

$$P_1 = 40 - 2Q_1$$

while the demand curve in market 2 is

$$P_2 = 92 - 4Q_2$$

He knows that his firm's total cost curve is

$$TC = 22 + 4Q$$

What prices should be charged in each market?

Answer   B & K Consultants have advised the manager to produce where marginal revenue in each market is equal to the marginal cost of producing the total output in order to maximize profits. Total revenue in market 1 is

$$P_1Q_1 = 40Q - 2Q_1^2$$

and total revenue in market 2 is

$$P_2Q_2 = 92Q - 4Q_2^2$$

Consequently, the marginal revenues for markets 1 and 2, respectively, are

$$MR_1 = 40 - 4Q_1 \quad \text{and} \quad MR_2 = 92 - 8Q_2$$

Since marginal cost is 4 in this example, the optimal quantities are determined by solving the following equations:

$$40 - 4Q_1 = 4 \quad \text{and} \quad 92 - 8Q_2 = 4$$

which require $Q_1 = 9$ and $Q_2 = 11$. As a result of substituting these optimal quantities in the demand functions, the profit-maximizing prices are

$$P_1 = 22 \quad \text{and} \quad P_2 = 48$$

The manager will find his total profit by the usual calculation:

$$\Pi = P_1Q_1 + P_2Q_2 - C(Q)$$

$$= 22(9) + 48(11) - [22 + 4(20)]$$

$$= 624$$

Question   The boss's son, Failing Phil, tells the manager that price discrimination does not produce greater profits than the standard monopoly solution. In support of this, he points out that B & K Consultants have not even advised a change in total output. How should B & K respond?

Answer   B & K should simply point out that to charge a single price the manager would have to determine the total demand curve by solving the separate curves for quantity, adding them together, and then solving for price:

$$Q_1 = 20 - \frac{1}{2}P_1$$

$$Q_2 = 23 - \frac{1}{4}P_2$$

At any price P, the total quantity demanded by both markets equals

$$Q = Q_1 + Q_2$$

$$= \left(20 - \frac{1}{2}P\right) + \left(23 - \frac{1}{4}P\right)$$

$$= 43 - \frac{3}{4}P$$

Solving for P in terms of Q,

$$P = 57\frac{1}{3} - \frac{4}{3}Q$$

As a result, marginal revenue would be

$$MR = 57\frac{1}{3} - \frac{8}{3}Q$$

which should be equated to marginal cost:

$$57\frac{1}{3} - \frac{8}{3}Q = 4$$

Solving for Q reveals that the optimal quantity is 20, which was the same total output as in the price discrimination case. Substituting the optimal output into the demand curve, we see that the profit-maximizing price is $30^2/_3$, which falls between the optimal prices for markets 1 and 2. Finally, substituting the optimal price and quantity into the profit function,

$$\Pi = PQ - C(Q)$$

$$= 30\frac{2}{3}(20) - [22 + 4(20)]$$

$$= 511\frac{1}{3}$$

which is less than when the manager set discriminatory prices. B & K then point out that nepotism is not always consistent with profit maximization.

Price discrimination appears to increase the profits of firms with monopoly power, yet many managers do not engage in price discrimination. It seems reasonable to infer, therefore, that price discrimination is often not profitable or possible even when it is legal. Arbitrage is the practice of buying in the low-price market and reselling in the high-price market. This practice may thwart the manager's efforts at price discrimination. Consider a firm that sells its output in several geographic locations. A manager's ability to charge different prices in different locations is determined by the cost of transportation between locations. If a good sells in different markets at a price differential that exceeds the cost of transportation between the two markets, arbitrageurs would find it profitable to buy in the cheap market and resell the good in the expensive market, which would drive the price down in the expensive market. For instance, suppose oranges were sold to retailers in Miami for $0.50 per orange and to retailers in Atlanta for $1 per orange. If it cost $0.05 per orange to transport oranges between Atlanta and Miami, then merchants could buy oranges in Miami and sell them to retailers in Atlanta for any price between $0.55 and $1. Competition among these resellers, unless their actions were constrained by the orange monopoly, would eventually drive the price of oranges in Atlanta down to $0.55 (assuming the Miami price remained at $0.50).

Similar incentives exist to arbitrage away price differences between groups. Children would try to resell their cheaper movie tickets to adults, and if grocery stores attempted to charge higher prices to the elderly for prunes, the elderly would attempt to get their children, grandchildren, or younger friends to purchase prunes for them.

Price discriminating firms should try to stamp out such arbitrage by forbidding the product's resale. Airlines and theaters can easily monitor who ultimately uses plane and movie tickets; an adult is simply not allowed to enter a theater with a child's ticket. In other markets, it may be more difficult to reduce the incidence of resale. For example, Heinz sells ketchup to the retail grocery market as well as to the restaurant market. The restaurant market has a higher price elasticity of demand for ketchup and appears to be charged a lower price. The bottles of ketchup which are sold to restaurants are labeled "not for resale"; this facilitates policing against arbitrage between the two markets. If a Heinz representative were to see a restaurant bottle (labeled "not for resale") in a grocery store, he could punish the grocery store for its activities by withholding Heinz products. We should note that this form of punishment is not costless for Heinz. A grocery store, at one extreme, is virtually powerless in preventing arbitrage among customers. For instance, it is unable to stop younger customers from reselling prunes to their retired relatives and acquaintances.

Of course, the firm is better off if it does not have to pay for policing against resale. One way to accomplish this is to persuade the government to make resale of the firm's product illegal. Through "sharing" some of the additional profits that result from price discrimination with legislators or through lobbying, a firm may be able to "enlighten" politicians on the evils of resale. As an example, milk producers at the turn of the century were able to get laws passed that banned the resale of milk.

In general, efforts to prevent arbitrage are costly. Resources must be expended to separate markets that are not naturally distinct. If the cost of preventing arbitrage exceed the increased profits due to price discrimination, the manager will decide not to engage in price discrimination.

In summary, a manager will find that price discrimination will lead to enhanced profits whenever

1   His customers can be separated in to two or more groups that have different demand elasticities

2   It is worthwhile to prevent arbitrage

12.3

PEAK-LOAD PRICING

In the price discrimination case the firm faces two different demand functions simultaneously. A different situation exists whenever the firm faces sequential demand for an output produced with a fixed amount of capital. There are many examples of products that exhibit such sequential demands: personal income tax advice, airport landing privileges, tourist hotels, long-distance telephone service, computer time, and urban transportation services, to name just a few. In each case, there is a period of peak demand that requires a large productive capacity but there is also a period with substantially less demand. Sometimes these periods occur in the same day. For example, the demand for bus service is quite heavy during the morning and evening rush hours but is fairly light at other times of the day. The so-called peak and off-peak periods also can be a seasonal phenomenon. As an example, there is a relatively heavy demand for tourist hotels on Cape Cod during the summer months and an almost nonexistent demand during the rest of the year.

Question   Confronted with sequential demands, the manager of Computer Time Sharing is confused about how much computer capacity her firm should have. She is also concerned about the optimal quantities of service to supply in each period and the prices to charge her customers in each period. She called on B & K Consultants for their advice on how to make these decisions so that the firm's profits would be maximized.

Answer   On the basis of our earlier analyses, we should expect that the optimum will be characterized by the equality of marginal revenues and marginal costs. In fact, we shall see that this is the case. B & K prepared the following general analysis.

In Figure 12.3, the peak demand is labeled D_1 while the off-peak demand is labeled D_2. The corresponding marginal revenue functions are denoted MR_1 and MR_2, respectively. The horizontal line at height b represents the marginal operating cost, which is assumed to be constant in this case. This represents the cost of producing another unit of output, given some level of productive capacity. For Computer Time Sharing, the cost of the electricity, paper, and labor involved in turning out a "standard" computer job would be included in b. We have used β to represent the cost of a unit of capacity that is just large enough to produce 1 unit of output per period. In the case of Computer Time Sharing, β equals the cost of the additional computing capacity that would allow one more "standard" computer job to be turned out each period. This constant cost is added to the marginal operating cost and is plotted as $b + \beta$ in Figure 12.3.

Capacity is chosen to accommodate peak demand, and consequently the peak customers must support the costs of capacity. Thus, the marginal cost of providing 1 more unit of output to peak customers is the sum of the marginal operating cost (b) and of the marginal capacity cost (β). To maximize profits, the marginal cost of providing a unit of output to peak customers ($b + \beta$) is equated to the marginal revenue associated with selling a unit of output to peak customers (MR_1). In Figure 12.3, this occurs at output Q_1. Consequently, peak customers pay P_1 for each of the Q_1 units of output that they purchase. Finally, we note that by our definition of β, the optimal peak output Q_1 determines the optimal level of productive capacity.

Since the peak customers have financed the productive capacity, the manager can ignore the capacity costs when determining price and

FIGURE 12.3 In a peak-load situation, profit maximization requires $MR_1 = b + \beta$ and $MR_2 = b$, where capacity is determined by the output level Q_1.

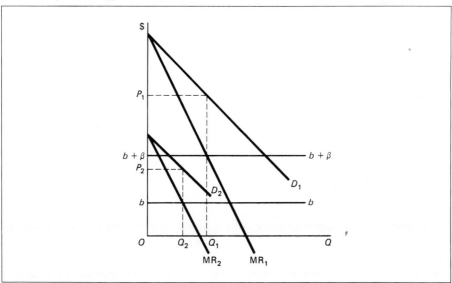

output for the off-peak customers. Profit maximization requires that the manager reduce the off-peak price and expand output as long as marginal revenue exceeds the marginal operating costs. Accordingly, the manager will supply Q_2 to off-peak customers and charge them P_2 per unit. This follows from the equality of off-peak marginal revenue MR_2 and marginal operating cost b. The firm's total profits are given by the sum of the peak and off-peak profits:

$$\Pi = (P_1 - b - \beta)Q_1 + (P_2 - b)Q_2$$

Any other price and output would yield a lower total profit.[2]

Question   Answer true, false, or undecided: Since the peak demand accounts for the capacity, the peak price will always exceed the off-peak price.

Answer   False. While the assertion has some intuitive appeal, we see upon closer examination that it is not always true. For example, consider the demand functions in Figure 12.4. In spite of the fact that the peak demand is D_1, peak price P_1 is less than off-peak price P_2. This results from the fact that the off-peak demand is relatively less elastic than the peak demand.

12.4

THE MULTIPLANT FIRM

Suppose that ABC, Inc., sells its output in a single market but has two production facilities. Each production center has a manager that supervises the production process. These people, however, are not in a position to decide upon the optimal quantity to produce. A higher-level manager must decide upon the firm's total output and the allocation of production responsibility between the two plants.

Question   How does this manager decide on the optimal price and output?

Answer   She does this in the usual way. To determine the profit-maximizing output of the firm, the manager must equate the firm's marginal cost and marginal revenue. By doing this, she will find the profit-maximizing output level. The firm's marginal cost is equal to the sum of the separate plants' marginal cost curves. In Figure 12.5, we depict the marginal cost curve of plant 1 [mc_1 in panel (a)] and the marginal cost curve of plant 2 [mc_2 in panel (b)]. In panel (c), we have added these curves horizontally to provide the firm's marginal cost curve (MC). Equating MC and MR indicates that the optimal price and quantity are P_0 and Q_0, respectively.

---

[2]The peak-load pricing model is developed mathematically in the mathematical appendix to this chapter.

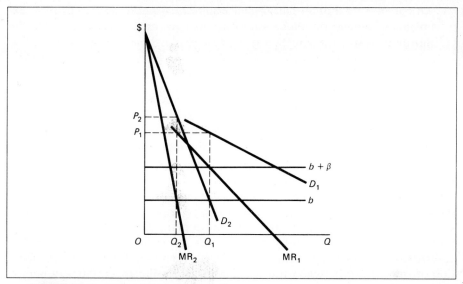

FIGURE 12.4   Optimal peak price may be less than the off-peak price profit maximization when off-peak demand is relatively less elastic.

Question   How will the production of Q_0 be divided between the two plants?

Answer   The manager of plant 1 will be assigned the responsibility for producing Q_1 units of output. Similarly, the plant 2 manager will be required to produce Q_2 units of output. Owing to the construction of MC,

FIGURE 12.5   For the multiplant firm, profit maximization requires producing where MC = MR and allocating production such that $mc_1 = mc_2$.

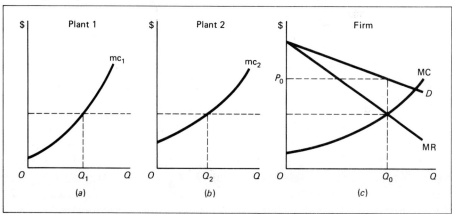

we can be sure that Q_1 plus Q_2 will equal Q_0. We can see that profit-max-imization involves an allocation of production responsibility such that the marginal costs of production are equal across both plants:

$$MR = mc_1 = mc_2$$

To appreciate why this is necessary, let's see what the consequences are of not having this condition satisfied. Suppose that the profit-maximizing quantity Q_0 is produced, but the production responsibility is misallocated. For example, let's suppose that mc_1 equals 5 while mc_2 is only 3. Profit, of course, is total revenue minus total cost. Total revenue is fixed once the total output is determined. Thus, profit maximization requires cost minimization. When mc_1 is not equal to mc_2, however, costs are not minimized. In this example, the cost reduction that results from reducing production in plant 1 by 1 unit is 5. To hold final output constant, output in plant 2 must be increased by 1 unit. This will increase cost by only 3. Since the cost saving (5) exceeds the cost increase (3), costs are reduced and profits increased by 2 by this realloca-tion of production between the two plants. A similar incentive will persist until the marginal costs are equal.[3]

Question Suppose that XYZ Company is the monopoly supplier of hyperflex. The marketing department has determined that the demand for hyperflex is

$$P = 300 - 2Q$$

XYZ Company has two production centers. The manager of plant 1 has found that his plant can produce according to the linear total cost curve

$$TC_1 = 4Q_1$$

Plant 2, in contrast, has a total cost curve of

$$TC_2 = .05(Q_2)^2$$

Find the profit-maximizing output for the firm and the production respon-sibility for each plant. Also, find the firm's total profit.

Answer To obtain the profit-maximizing output, we must sum the marginal cost curves of the two plants to find the firm's marginal cost curve. Plant 1's marginal cost curve is horizontal at a height of 4. Plant 2's marginal cost curve is found by differentiating TC_2 with respect to Q_2:

$$MC_2 = .10Q_2$$

It is clear that it is cheaper to produce the first unit of output in plant 2 for $0.05 than to produce 1 unit in plant 1 for $4. For the second unit of out-put, incremental cost is $0.15, which is lower than production in plant 1.

---

[3]A mathematical derivation of these results is presented in Section 3 of the mathematical appendix to this chapter.

This relationship continues until the firm produces 40 units of output in plant 2, at which point production is shifted to plant 1. Arithmetic confirms that producing more than 40 units in plant 2 is costlier than producing 40 units in plant 2 and producing the remainder in plant 1. The summed marginal cost curve is given in Figure 12.6.

The manager will want to produce that output where marginal revenue is equal to the summed marginal cost. Since demand is

$$P = 300 - 2Q$$

total revenue will be

$$TR = PQ = 300Q - 2Q^2$$

and marginal revenue will be

$$MR = \frac{\Delta PQ}{\Delta Q} = 300 - 4Q$$

Equating marginal revenue and marginal cost yields the optimal output:

$$300 - 4Q = 4$$

$$4Q = 296$$

$$Q = 74$$

Substituting the optimal quantity into the demand function yields the optimal price

$$P = 300 - 2Q$$

$$= 300 - 2(74)$$

$$= 152$$

Thus the manager will sell 74 units at a price of $152 each.

FIGURE 12.6   Sum of $MC_1 = 4$ and $MC_2 = 0.10Q_2$.

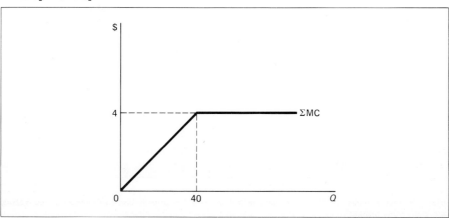

Since total output exceeds 40 units, production in plant 2 equals 40 units. Production in plant 1 equals the difference between total sales and production in plant 2: $74 - 40 = 34$. Substituting the price and quantity data into the profit function yields the firm's profit:

$$\Pi = TR - TC_1 - TC_2$$

$$= \$152(74) - \$4(34) - \$.05(40)^2$$

$$= \$11,248 - \$136 - \$80$$

$$= \$11,032$$

12.5

CARTELS

Sometimes a group of firms that have been competing among themselves want to limit this competition in a joint effort to earn greater profits. Such a group is called a "cartel." In the United States, cartel activity is generally illegal because it restrains trade.[4] Nonetheless, it is important for managers of U.S. firms to understand cartel theory for several reasons. First, it is useful for a manager to recognize when either his customers or his suppliers have stopped competing and started colluding. Second, participation in some international cartels may be mandatory for foreign subsidiaries of U.S. firms. For example, in the 1970s there was a uranium cartel operating outside the U.S. The Canadian government required U.S. subsidiaries located in Canada to participate in this cartel. Finally, it will be a lot easier to predict the behavior of cartels like OPEC if a manager knows how a cartel operates.

We shall assume that the cartel's goal is to organize production in such a way that the industry profits are maximized. This goal can be accomplished if the firms collectively act like a multiplant monopolist. Let us see what this prescription involves for a large number of firms. We begin by assuming that industry demand is linear and remains stable throughout the analysis. Variations in the industry's use of its inputs are assumed to have no impact on input prices. Finally, we assume at this point that each firm (1) has access to the same technology, (2) faces the same input prices, and (3) has the same managerial skills. Each firm, therefore, has the same cost curves. We have shown the cost functions of a typical firm in panel (a) of Figure 12.7.

Competitive Solution Let's now derive the long-run supply curve of this industry. Each firm would be willing to enter the industry when the price equaled P_2. At that price, each firm in the industry would produce q_2 units of output and its total revenue $(P_2 q_2)$ would equal total cost $(ATC \cdot q_2)$. Each firm in the industry would have zero economic profits from producing

---

[4]The Sherman Act's first section prohibits "every contract, combination, . . . or conspiracy in restraint of trade among the several states. . . ." The courts have held that this covers price fixing, market sharing, bid rigging, and many other things.

and would be indifferent between entering the industry and not entering the industry.

Any firm in the industry would be willing to produce additional units if the price rose above P_2. But then there would be positive profits in the industry and enough firms would enter to drive the price back to P_2. The long-run supply curve of the industry is therefore perfectly elastic at P_2. Variations in industry output come entirely from variations in the number of firms producing in the industry. In panel (b) of Figure 12.7, the long-run supply curve and the demand curve intersect at price P_2 and output Q_2. If we assume that there are 100 firms in the industry, then $Q_2 = 100 \, q_2$.

Question   Suppose that the 100 separate firms continue to be owned independently. These firms, however, are attempting to improve their profits by obeying the dictates of the cartel planning group with regard to price and output. What will be prescribed?

Answer   The cartel planning group must select the profit-maximizing price and output. This requires a knowledge of the cartel's marginal cost and marginal revenue curves. First, let's consider the determination of the cartel's marginal cost curve.

Since the cartel has 100 plants, the planning group must allocate output among these 100 plants. Suppose it selects an output level that exceeds Q_1, which is equal to $100 q_1$ (see Figure 12.7). Then the output will be evenly divided among the 100 plants in order to minimize costs. To see this, suppose output were not evenly divided. The marginal cost in one plant then would exceed the marginal cost in another plant; say, $MC_1 > MC_2$. Move 1 unit of output from plant 1 to plant 2, and the cost *reduction* in plant 1 (MC_1) would exceed the cost *increase* in plant 2

FIGURE 12.7   Long-run supply is horizontal in a constant cost industry with identical firms.

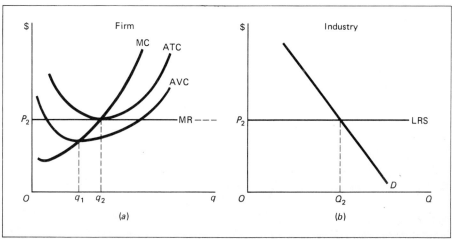

(MC_2). Thus, costs are not minimized unless marginal costs are equal across plants.

Suppose the cartel were to select an output smaller than Q_1. It is not profitable to operate any plant at an output level below q_1, for revenues do not cover variable costs. Consequently, any output Q less than Q_1 will be allocated equally among Q/q_1 plants, each of which will produce q_1. There will be $100 - Q/q_1$ plants idle in this case. Any other solution would have higher variable costs.

Since total fixed costs are constant and total revenue is fixed once the output is selected, maximizing profits requires minimizing total variable costs. For the cartel, the average variable cost (AVC) function is a horizontal line at a height equal to the minimum point on the average variable cost curve in panel (a) of Figure 12.7 until Q_1 is reached. At that point, AVC is positively sloped. The monopolist's short-run marginal cost coincides with AVC until Q_1, and then it is positively sloped and is above AVC. These relationships are depicted in Figure 12.8, which reproduces panel (b) of Figure 12.7 and adds the short-run functions. The short-run average total cost curve is U-shaped with a minimum at Q_2 because Q_2 can be produced most efficiently (at an average total cost of P_2) when there are 100 plants in the industry and other output levels can be produced most efficiently (again at an ATC equal to P_2) when the number of plants is *not* equal to 100. Constraining the number of plants in the industry to be 100, forces costs at output levels not equal to Q_2 to be higher than they would otherwise be.

In the short run, the cartel maximizes profits by equating marginal

FIGURE 12.8 Short-run profit maximizing price and output decision for the cartel: equate MR with industry MC.

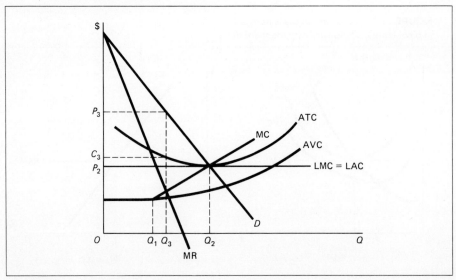

cost and marginal revenue. In this case, a total output of Q_3 will be produced and sold at the short-run profit-maximizing price of P_3. The monopoly profits are given by the rectangle of area $(P_3 - C_3)Q_3$. These profits may then be shared equally by all firms in the industry.

In the long run, we should expect that these economic profits will attract entry and perhaps a return to the original competitive price and output. Nonetheless, the short-run economic profits may persist for some time. Consequently, collusive activity, organized through the formation of a cartel, appears to enhance profits. But collusion does not seem to be prevalent in many industries. Why not? For the answer to this question, we need a positive theory of collusion.

A POSITIVE THEORY OF COLLUSION   As with any other economic decisions, there are benefits and costs to forming a cartel.[5] The benefits are related to the elasticity of the industry demand function and to the elasticity of the industry marginal cost curve. Now, let us examine the following question.

Question   Are the benefits to collusive activity greater when demand is less elastic or more elastic?

Answer   Recall that the cartel increased its profits by restricting output. Our intuition should suggest that for any price increase, the resulting profits will be larger where demand is less elastic because the consequent reduction in quantity demanded will be smaller than it would be if demand were more elastic. In this instance, our intuition provides the correct answer. Consider Figure 12.9 where we have labeled the competitive supply LRS and have demand curves D and D' intersecting supply at the same point. For either demand curve, the competitive price and output will be P_1 and Q_1, respectively. Since D and D' are linear, the associated marginal revenue curves (MR and MR') intersect the industry marginal cost at the same point. (You should be able to prove this.) Thus, the industry profit-maximizing output is Q_2 for either demand curve. But the optimal prices are P_2 for demand curve D and P_3 for demand curve D'. Thus, profits are $(P_2 - P_1)Q_2$ for D and $(P_3 - P_1)Q_2$ for D'. It is obvious that $(P_2 - P_1)Q_2$ exceeds $(P_3 - P_1)Q_2$ since P_2 exceeds P_3.

We can show that the steeper demand function D is less elastic than the flatter demand function D'. Recall that the elasticity of demand is given by

$$\epsilon = -\frac{\Delta Q}{\Delta P}\frac{P}{Q}$$

[5]This section owes much to Gary Becker, "Crime and Punishment: An Economic Approach," *Journal of Political Economy,* vol. 76, April 1968, and to George Stigler, "A Theory of Oligopoly," *Journal of Political Economy,* vol. 72, February 1964.

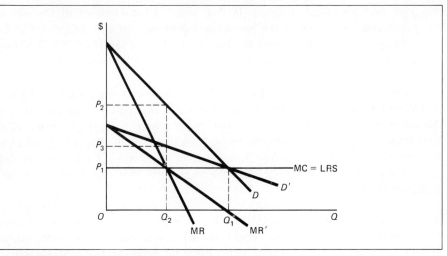

FIGURE 12.9   Cartel profits are greater
when demand is less elastic at the competitve
price.

In evaluating the elasticity of demand at the point of intersection, the
appropriate price and quantity are P_1 and Q_1. Since $-\Delta Q/\Delta P$ is minus
the reciprocal of the slope of the demand function, we have

$$\frac{-\Delta Q}{\Delta P} = \frac{Q_1 - Q_2}{P_2 - P_1}$$

for demand function D and

$$\frac{-\Delta Q}{\Delta P} = \frac{Q_1 - Q_2}{P_3 - P_1}$$

for demand function D'. We can substitute these expressions into the
definition of price elasticity to discover that

$$\frac{Q_1 - Q_2}{P_3 - P_1} \frac{P_1}{Q_1} > \frac{Q_1 - Q_2}{P_2 - P_1} \frac{P_1}{Q_1}$$

In other words, the price elasticity of demand for D' exceeds that for D
at the point of intersection. Therefore, industries with less elastic demand
curves will have greater gains from collusion than industries with more
elastic demand curves.

Similarly, the gains from collusion are related to the elasticity of the industry marginal cost curve. As with different demand elasticities, we may
wonder precisely how the elasticity of marginal cost affects the gains from
participation in a cartel. This raises the following question.

Question   Are the benefits to collusive activity greater when industry
marginal cost is less elastic or more elastic?

Answer   In Figure 12.10, we have demand and marginal revenue labeled D and MR. There are two marginal cost curves intersecting demand at output level Q_1. The MC curve is more elastic than the MC' curve. (You should be able to prove this.) Consider what happens when the cartel reduces output by 1 unit from Q_1 to Q_1 minus 1. Total revenue is reduced by the height of the marginal revenue curve, and total cost is reduced by the height of the marginal cost curve. The net increase in profit is given by the difference between the marginal cost and marginal revenue curves. For the industry with marginal cost MC, a cartel will reduce output from Q_1 to Q_2 since marginal revenue equals marginal cost at Q_2. Adding up all the marginal cost—marginal revenue differences we find that the total benefit associated with reducing output from Q_1 to Q_2 equals triangular area ABC. In contrast, suppose that MC' is the industry marginal cost curve. In that case, the profit-maximizing output is Q_3. The benefit of the cartel, as measured by the summed differences between the marginal cost and marginal revenue curves, is triangular area ABE. A comparison of areas ABC and ABE demonstrates categorically that the more elastic the industry marginal cost, the greater the benefit to collusive activity.

The costs of forming and maintaining a cartel are formidable. Most of us are familiar with the costs associated with collective decision making in casual settings such as clubs, fraternities, and sororities. These costs are no less important when independent firms are negotiating over prices and outputs. An even more important problem arises, however, because each firm has an incentive to cheat on the cartel agreement. Recall that the cartel would like to

Figure 12.10   Cartel profits are higher when industry marginal cost is more elastic at the competitive output.

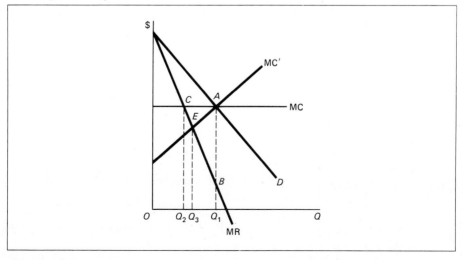

operate where industry marginal cost equals industry marginal revenue. This may be accomplished by allocating output such that each firm produces where its marginal cost equals the optimal industry marginal cost. To take one example, firm 1 in Figure 12.11 is supposed to produce q_1 units of output. The difficulty with this solution is that firm 1 could increase its profits by expanding its production past the cartel's allocation to where marginal cost equals price. This is because firm 1 believes that it can get cartel price P_m for each unit that it produces. Accordingly, it could increase its profits by the shaded area in panel (a) of Figure 12.11, which equals the summed differences between P_m and firm 1's marginal cost, if it increased output from q_1 to q_0. But if each firm were to produce more than its cartel allocation, the resulting excess supply at P_m would force the price down and thus cause total industry profits to fall. Obviously, if the cartel is to be successful, the cartel must *discover* at least some of the firms who violate the cartel's allocation plan and must also punish known violators. Both discovery and punishment are costly.

Without going into much detail, the cost of determining which firms are violating the cartel's agreement will be related to the number of firms, the number of customers, the behavior of buyers, and the attitude of government. Each firm's output could be monitored by placing spies outside each firm's gates and counting the number of trucks leaving the firm's plant. In an industry with many firms, this would be very costly. Alternatively, a spy could be placed outside the office or residence of each buyer to monitor whose trucks are supplying each buyer. This form of information gathering becomes very costly as the number of buyers rises and as the fraction of buyers who are new in the market increases. It is also less costly to check up on the behavior of cartel members when buyers report correctly and fully the

FIGURE 12.11 Each cartel member has an incentive to cheat on the cartel agreement.

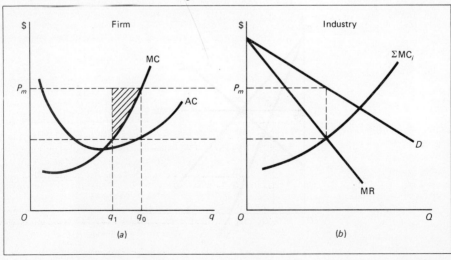

prices offered to them as in competitive sealed-bid situations. Finally, a hostile government may force the cartel to use less efficient, and thus more costly, methods of monitoring.

If a cartel is to be successful, not only cheaters must be discovered but also known cheaters must be punished. And any form of punishment is either costly or ineffective. For example, the cartel could impose fines on the cheaters, but this may be ineffective if there is no legal way in which to compel payment. The expulsion of a cheater from a cartel often does not accomplish anything. Retaliatory price cuts can be used to reduce a cheater's profits, but these price cuts also reduce the cartel's profits. Other, illegal methods are sometimes used to punish cheaters. For instance, a cartel may decide to burn down a cheater's warehouse. The members of a cartel who resort to these illegal means may be fined or go to jail if they are caught.

The managers in an industry must weigh the costs and benefits of collusion and decide (1) whether or not to collude, and (2) if colluding, how "much" to collude. If the costs are large relative to the gains, collusion does not pay, and a competitive solution will emerge. If the costs are small relative to the gains, collusion is profitable, and a position near the monopoly position will be adopted. Solutions that fall between the monopoly solution and the competitive solution are also possible. In particular, it is possible that both costs and gains are sizable when collusion is profitable and that in the optimal solution a sizable number of violations occur.

THE PRECARIOUS INTERNATIONAL COFFEE CARTEL*

Nearly every cartel is concerned about raising the price of its product and thereby increasing the industry profits above the competitive level. In order to be successful, however, the cartel members must reduce their output. This, as we have seen, causes instability, because each member has an incentive to cheat on his fellow cartel members. These pressures can be seen in the efforts to elevate the world price of coffee.

Following a severe frost in Brazil, coffee production fell and the price of coffee rose to $3.40 per pound—a 400 percent increase—in early 1977. The coffee-producing nations experienced a most welcome and substantial increase in their export earnings. Since that time, production has expanded and the world price has fallen.

In an attempt to counter this recent trend, the major Latin American coffee producers pooled some of their financial resources for buying and selling contracts in the futures markets. Although these efforts to manipulate the price of coffee largely failed—coffee prices fell to $1.25 per pound for December 1980 delivery—the United States pressured them to stop these disruptive activities. In return, the International Coffee Organization, which has 62 members, agreed to stabilize prices by establishing an export quota system.

Most observers are skeptical about the likely success of this effort. In the first place, actual coffee production has been substantial. With no serious frost damage, the Brazilian output, for example, could be as much as 50 percent higher than last year's. In addition, some of the producing nations are unhappy with the size of their quotas. Finally, many of the producers need additional revenue to pay for their oil imports. At the low coffee prices agreed upon, they cannot afford to reduce the volume of exports. If the quota system fails, what will happen to the price of coffee?

---

*Source: "The Coffee Producers' Precarious Quota Plan," *Business Week*, Oct. 20, 1980, p. 47.

12.6

DOMINANT-FIRM MODEL

Cartels often are formed in industries where there are few firms, all similar in size. As we have seen, these firms maximize cartel profits net of detection and punishment costs. There is a somewhat different problem confronting the manager of what is known as a "dominant firm." In this situation, the dominant firm is surrounded by a competitive fringe, that is, by a large number of small firms. If these firms are too numerous or too unreliable to organize, the manager of the large firm must decide how to set his firm's price, taking into account the behavior of these fringe firms.

One strategy is to adopt a live-and-let-live philosophy. Specifically, the manager of the dominant firm accepts the presence of the fringe firms, assumes that they will react to his price by producing where their marginal cost equals price, and sets his price to maximize his firm's profit, taking into account the fringe firms' behavior.[6]

In essence, the dominant firm shares the industry demand with the competitive fringe. The effect of this strategy can be seen in Figure 12.12, where D is the industry demand and S is the supply of the competitive fringe. If the dominant firm's manager is going to permit the competitive fringe to sell all it wants at the price he sets, then the dominant firm will be able to sell the difference between industry demand and the competitive fringe supply. For example, at a price of P_1, the competitive fringe will supply a sufficient quantity to clear the market. The dominant firm will not have any residual demand to fill. At a price equal to P_2 or below, the competitive fringe will not supply anything. Thus, at this price the dominant firm will have the entire

---

[6]A mathematical version of this model is presented in the mathematical appendix to this chapter.

FIGURE 12.12 Demand facing dominant
firm is market demand minus fringe supply.

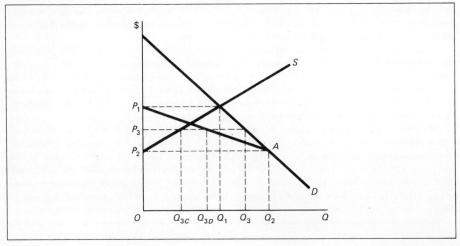

market. For prices between P_1 and P_2, the competitive fringe and the dominant firm share the market. At a price of P_3, for instance, the consumers will demand Q_3, which is supplied collectively by the fringe firms and the dominant firm. The fringe firms supply Q_{3C} and the dominant firm supplies $Q_3 - Q_{3C} = Q_{3D}$. Performing this calculation for all possible prices between P_1 and P_2 yields the dominant firm's residual demand function P_1AD. The manager of the dominant firm will select a price to maximize his firm's profits.

We can examine the profit-maximizing price and output in Figure 12.13. Industry demand D, competitive fringe supply S, and residual demand P_1AD are depicted as well as the marginal revenue for residual demand curve mr. The manager will maximize profits by equating the marginal revenue associated with the residual demand curve to the dominant firm's marginal cost MC. Thus, the dominant firm will set price P_4 and supply Q_{4D}. Consumers will demand Q_4 at P_4; therefore, the competitive fringe will supply Q_{4C} at price P_4 and the market will clear.

12.7

INFLUENCE OF TAXATION

Certain forms of taxation will have an influence on pricing decisions. Other forms of taxation will have no effect on the profit-maximizing price selected by the manager. We shall consider two types of taxes that may influence the pricing decisions of a firm's manager: (1) a tax on the firm's profits and (2) a unit tax on output.

Question   A state government decided to put a tax on corporate profits. The manager of Apex, Inc., hired B & K Consultants for advice on the appropriate price and output response. What did B & K advise?

FIGURE 12.13   Dominant firm selects industry price by equating mr and MC.

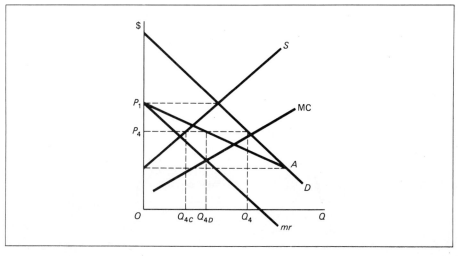

Answer   B & K told the manager that his pretax price and output should remain optimal after the tax was imposed. They told him that this was because the tax would not affect the revenue function or the cost function. As a result, whatever price and output maximized pretax profit would also maximize posttax profit. To illustrate, suppose that the tax rate on the firm was 40 percent. Then $0.40 of every $1 of profit would go to the government. If the manager had determined the profit-maximizing price was $10 per unit and that the corresponding optimal output was 250 units, then the total revenue would be $2,500. If the average cost is $7 per unit when total output is 250 units, the firm's pretax profit is

$$\Pi = P \cdot Q - AC \cdot Q$$

$$= \$10(250) - \$7(250)$$

$$= \$750$$

A 40 percent tax on profits means that Apex will retain $450 in profit and send $300 to the government.

What happens if the manager attempts to adjust price and quantity in response to this tax? The answer is that posttax profits must fall. Since the price of $10 and the output of 250 units were found to be profit-maximizing, any change will reduce profit. If pretax profit is reduced, 60 percent of the now lower profit must also be lower than the $450 that the firm would have retained if it produced 250 units. This also can be seen in Figure 12.14. This result is demonstrated more formally in the appendix.

Question   The state of Florida wanted to raise additional revenue by taxing phosphate, an important ingredient in fertilizers. Suppose a unit

FIGURE 12.14   A tax on profit does not alter the optimal output.

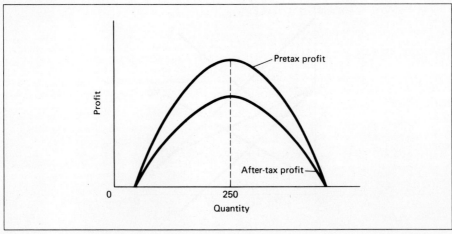

tax of $10 per ton was imposed. How would this tax affect the manager's price and output decision?

Answer   The key to answering this question is to analyze the impact of the tax on the firm's revenue function. Unit taxes are fairly common. For example, taxes on cigarettes, gasoline, and liquor are often unit taxes. Such taxes do not vary with the price of the product. These taxes create a difference between the demand price paid by the customer and the price received by the firm. This obviously has an effect on the firm's revenue function and may affect the manager's determination of the optimal price and output. We can analyze these changes for a monopolist in Figure 12.15.

Before the tax is imposed, the optimal price and output are determined by the intersection of marginal cost MC and marginal revenue MR. Given demand function D and marginal cost MC, we can see that the optimal price and quantity are P_1 and Q_1, respectively. Since there is no tax, P_1 is the price that customers pay and the price that the firm receives for its phosphate.

When a unit tax is imposed, the firm's perceived demand function shifts from D to D'. The vertical difference between D and D' is the per unit tax levied by the government. A manager will attempt to operate where the firm's profits are maximized, taking into account the influence of the tax. This will involve a reduction in phosphate output from Q_1 to Q_2. The price paid by the consumer will be P_2, while the price received by the firm will be P_2'. The difference between P_2 and P_2' is the tax that goes to the government.

FIGURE 12.15   The effect of a unit tax is to reduce the quantity and increase the price to the consumer.

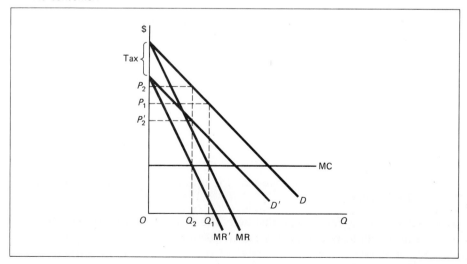

12.8

SUMMARY

In this chapter we have been concerned with the pricing decisions of a manager whose firm has some market power. The standard case was developed in an earlier chapter. Here, we have focused upon some more complicated cases. For example, we examined the optimal price and output decisions for new products, for cartels, and for dominant firms. In addition, we examined the profit-maximizing decisions of a manager practicing price discrimination and peak-load pricing. Finally, we investigated the multiplant firm and the influence of various forms of taxation.

In all these situations, we found that we could rely upon fundamental principles of optimization. Equating marginal revenue to marginal cost provided the answer to most of the questions posed. The trick was to find the appropriate marginal revenue and marginal cost functions. Once that was accomplished, the rest of the problem was familiar.

IMPORTANT NEW TERMS

Inspection good

Experience good

Price discrimination

Arbitrage

Cartel

PROBLEMS

12.1 Answer true, false, or undecided: Collusion is more likely to occur in industries where there are a large number of firms than in industries where there are a small number of firms.

12.2 A monopolist is able to separate two markets. In one market, the demand can be expressed as $Q_1 = 10 - P_1$. In the second market, the demand is $Q_2 = 20 - 2P_2$. The monopolist's marginal cost equals \$4. Evaluate: Therefore, the monpolist maximizes profit where $Q_1 = 6$ and where $Q_2 = 12$. (If the statement is false, give the correct answer.)

12.3 Answer true, false, or undecided: Oil prices can be expected to skyrocket in the future because of the monopoly power enjoyed by the OPEC cartel.

12.4 Answer true, false, or undecided: The imposition of a price ceiling on a monopolist will lead to a fall in output.

12.5   Answer true, false, or undecided: Skimming (the practice of charging a high price in the first month, a lower price in the second month, etc.) will be unprofitable in a community of identical individuals.

12.6   Why is it optimal for some resort motels to be fully occupied in the off-season while resort motels in other areas either close down or have high vacancy rates in the off-season?

12.7   Suppose that the price elasticity of demand for electricity by consumers is 2 and that the price elasticity of demand for electricity by manufacturers is 3. Also suppose further that the electric company is a profit-maximizing monopoly that is able to separate the two markets. How does the price charged consumers for electricity relate to the price charged manufacturers? Be specific.

12.8   Answer true, false, or undecided: Collusion will be more prevalent in industries with more elastic demand curves than in industries with less elastic demand curves.

12.9   Answer true, false, or undecided: Any monopolist who does not engage in price discrimination must be stupid.

12.10 In the multiplant firm problem, why is it not optimal for each plant manager to select her own output?

12.11 Classify the following as inspection or experience goods, and explain your choice. (*a*) B & K light beer, (*b*) fashion jeans, (*c*) electric typewriter (be careful).

REFERENCE

Ferguson, C. E., and John Gould: *Microeconomic Theory*, Homewood, Illinois: Richard D. Irwin, Inc., 1975.

MATHEMATICAL APPENDIX

12A.1

GENERALIZED PRICE DISCRIMINATION MODEL

For a firm that operates in n markets but produces from a single production facility, the objective function is

$$\Pi = \sum_{i=1}^{n} P_i Q_i - C(Q) \qquad (A12.1)$$

where $Q = \sum_{i=1}^{n} Q_i$. The first-order conditions for a profit maximum are

$$\frac{\partial \Pi}{\partial Q_i} = P_i + Q_i \frac{\partial P}{\partial Q_i} - C'(Q) \frac{\partial Q}{\partial Q_i} = 0 \tag{A12.2}$$

$i = 1, \ldots, n$. Since $\partial Q / \partial Q_i = 1$, we can write the first-order conditions as

$$MR_i = MC \qquad i = 1, \ldots, n \tag{A12.3}$$

This corresponds to our earlier result:

$$MR_1 = MR_2 = \cdots = MR_n = MC \tag{A12.4}$$

12A.2

PEAK-LOAD PRICING

For a firm facing sequential demands where only one demand presses on capacity, the objective function is

$$\Pi = P_1 Q_1 + P_2 Q_2 - b(Q_1 + Q_2) - \beta Q_1 \tag{A12.5}$$

where period 1 customers are assumed to impose the peak demand on capacity. The first-order conditions for maximum profit require that the partial derivatives of (A12.5) vanish:

$$\frac{\partial \Pi}{\partial Q_1} = P_1 + Q_1 \left(\frac{\partial P_1}{\partial Q_1} \right) - b - \beta = 0$$

$$\frac{\partial \Pi}{\partial Q_2} = P_2 - Q_2 \left(\frac{\partial P_2}{\partial Q_2} \right) - b = 0 \tag{A12.6}$$

The optimal prices can be determined from (A6) as

$$P_1 = \frac{b + \beta}{1 - 1/\epsilon_1}$$

$$P_2 = \frac{b}{1 - 1/\epsilon_2} \tag{A12.7}$$

where ϵ_1 and ϵ_2 are the price elasticities of demand for the peak and off-peak consumers, respectively.

In the so-called shifting peak case, the demands of customers in both periods press upon capacity. Consequently, the objective function becomes

$$\Pi = P_1 Q_1 + P_2 Q_2 - b(Q_1 + Q_2) - \beta Q^* \tag{A12.8}$$

where $Q^* = Q_1 = Q_2$, because both groups of customers contribute to the need for productive capacity. The first-order condition for a profit maximum is provided by differentiating (A12.8) with respect to Q^*. Since $\partial Q_1 / \partial Q^* = \partial Q_2 / \partial Q^* = 1$, we may write this as

$$\frac{\partial \Pi}{\partial Q^*} = \left[P_1 + Q_1 \left(\frac{\partial P_1}{\partial Q_1} \right) \right] + \left[P_2 + Q_2 \left(\frac{\partial P_2}{\partial Q_2} \right) \right] - 2b - \beta = 0 \tag{A12.9}$$

In other words, the sum of the marginal revenues must equal the sum of the marginal costs.

12A.3

THE MULTIPLANT FIRM

A firm may sell its output in a single market but produce it in several plants or production centers. The manager's problem is to select the total output that will maximize profits and optimally allocate the production responsibility among the plants. For a firm with n plants, the objective function is

$$\Pi = P \cdot Q - \sum_{i=1}^{n} C_i(Q_i) \qquad \text{(A12.10)}$$

where $Q = \sum_{i=1}^{n} Q_i$, and Q_i is the output produced in plant i.

The first-order conditions for maximum profit require that the partial derivatives of (A12.10) vanish:

$$\frac{\partial \Pi}{\partial Q_i} = \left(P + Q\frac{\partial P}{\partial Q} \right) \frac{\partial Q}{\partial Q_i} - C_i'(Q_i) = 0 \qquad \text{(A12.11)}$$

$i = 1, 2, \ldots, n$. Due to the constraint that $Q = \sum_{i=1}^{n} Q_i$, $\partial Q/\partial Q_i$ must equal 1. Thus the first-order conditions (A12.11) can be written as

$$\text{MR} = \text{MC}_1 = \cdots = \text{MC}_n \qquad \text{(A12.12)}$$

which is analogous to the condition in the text.

12A.4

THE DOMINANT-FIRM MODEL

The market demand for a homogeneous product supplied by a dominant firm is

$$Q_M = Q_M(P) \qquad \text{(A12.13)}$$

where Q_M is the quantity and P is the price. The supply of the competitive fringe is an increasing function of price:

$$Q_C = Q_C(P) \qquad \text{(A12.14)}$$

If the market is to clear, the residual demand facing the dominant firm must be equal to the difference between the market demand and the competitive supply:

$$Q_D = Q_M(P) - Q_C(P) \qquad \text{(A12.15)}$$

Under the live-and-let-live philosophy of the dominant-firm model, the dominant firm's profit function is

$$\Pi = P(Q_D) - C(Q_D) \qquad \text{(A12.16)}$$

where $C(Q_D)$ is the dominant firm's total cost function. Profit maximization requires that

$$\frac{d\Pi}{dQ_D} = P + Q_D \frac{dP}{dQ_D} - C'(Q_D) = 0 \tag{A12.17}$$

12A.5

IMPACT OF A PROFITS TAX

In the text, we claimed that a tax on economic profits would not affect the price and output decisions of the firm. This conclusion can be shown quite easily in mathematical form.

Prior to the introduction of the tax, the firm's objective function was

$$\Pi = PQ - C(Q) \tag{A12.18}$$

The maximization of profit requires the price and output implicit in the solution to the first-order condition

$$\frac{d\Pi}{dQ} = P + Q\frac{dP}{dQ} - C'(Q) = 0 \tag{A12.19}$$

After the tax is imposed, the objective is to maximize after-tax profits:

$$(1 - t)\Pi = (1 - t)[PQ - C(Q)] \tag{A12.20}$$

where t is the tax rate. The first-order condition for this objective function is

$$\frac{d(1 - t)\Pi}{dQ} = (1 - t)\left[P + Q\frac{dP}{dQ} - C'(Q)\right] = 0 \tag{A12.21}$$

Since $(1 - t)$ is assumed to be a positive constant in the unit interval, we must still have $P + QdP/dQ - C'(Q)$ equal to zero. This reduces to the requirement in (A12.19).

13

MARKETING
DECISIONS

Many marketing decisions can be analyzed fruitfully within the framework of maximizing behavior which is provided by economics. Profits often can be increased not only by altering factors in the production of output but also by altering the level and location of advertising and the number and location of the sales force. The models that determine the profit-maximizing level of advertising also have implications for the prevalence of false advertising. Furthermore, in Chapter 7 we showed how the organization of firms was related to scale economies of different operations. In this chapter, we show in particular how private brands and franchises result from differences in the scale economies of production, distribution, and advertising. Our purpose is not to teach the principles of marketing. Rather it is to show how principles of economics can be used in making some marketing decisions.

13.1

OPTIMAL ADVERTISING[1]

Advertising has many functions. One of its principal functions is to provide information to the public about a product's price and attributes; a store's location, hours, and selection of products; and so on. Advertising may also alter a consumer's preferences. In this section, we will see how the optimal level of advertising is determined in the context of the various functions that advertising performs.

THE IDENTIFICATION OF SELLERS: BASICS One of the roles of advertising is making consumers aware of the existence of sellers. There are two reasons why this is necessary. First, the identity of buyers and sellers changes over time. Of particular interest to any one seller is the changing identity of buyers. New buyers continuously enter a market: buyers emigrate from other sales markets, and another set of individuals becomes of age financially and begins to purchase goods. Both sets of new buyers require information about the identity of sellers, and advertising performs this function. Second, buyers sometimes forget some of what they learned. For this reason, sellers need to refresh the knowledge of infrequent buyers.

One of the determinants of the fraction of potential buyers who are aware of a particular seller is the amount of advertising that takes place each period. Admittedly, there are many possible ways in which to advertise a firm's exis-

[1]Much of the material in this section is drawn from George Stigler, "The Economics of Information," *Journal of Political Economy*, vol. 69, June 1961, pp. 213–225.

tence, and some are more effective than others. The decision about where to advertise will be addressed in Section 13.3. For the time being, it is most instructive to consider advertising in homogeneous units (e.g., number of minutes of prime time television commercials per week or the number of quarter-page ads in the local newspaper). Suppose that during each period a firm purchases a units of advertising and that as a result of this advertising some fraction c of potential customers is informed about the existence of this seller. Consequently, c is a function of a:

$$c = g(a)$$

Increasing the level of advertising (a) will increase the fraction of potential customers who are informed each period (c). We will also assume that there is a total of N potential customers, who are initially uninformed. Thus, at the end of the first period, cN customers are informed about this seller's existence.

Another determinant of the fraction of potential buyers who are aware of a seller is the amount of information that is lost each period. Let us also suppose that at the beginning of each period, fraction b of the informed customers either lose their knowledge or leave the market. We should expect that b will be high in communities characterized by a high rate of turnover of permanent residents (e.g., university towns, Hollywood), a large fraction of tourists (e.g., Hawaii, Cape Cod), or a sizable mortality rate (e.g., elderly communities). Of the cN customers who were informed in the first period, $(1 - b) \, cN$ remain informed at the beginning of the second period.

In the second period, information about the seller is once again brought to the public. For those $(1 - b)cN$ customers who remain informed at the beginning of the second period, advertising is unnecessary. Advertising brings them no new information. But advertising may inform those who were not reached by the first period's advertising $[(1 - c)N]$ and those who were informed but subsequently lost their information (bcN). Advertising will reach a fraction (c) of these uninformed people. Therefore, by the end of the second period

$$\lambda N = (1 - b)cN + c[bcN + (1 - c)N] \tag{13.1}$$

of all potential customers are aware of the seller, where λ represents the fraction of potential buyers who are aware of a particular seller. Equation (13.1) may be simplified to

$$\lambda N = cN[1 + (1 - b)(1 - c)]$$

Following this process over many periods is a very tedious task, and we will spare the reader from having to go through these details. It can be shown that at the end of k periods,

$$\lambda N = cN[1 + (1 - b)(1 - c) + (1 - b)^2(1 - c)^2 + \cdots + (1 - b)^{k-1}(1 - c)^{k-1}]$$

buyers are informed. This is a series with the property that as k approaches infinity,

$$\lambda N = \frac{cN}{1 - (1 - c)(1 - b)} \tag{13.2}$$

That is, the number of informed buyers equals cN in the first period and increases in each successive period, approaching $cN/[1 - (1 - c)(1 - b)]$. The path of the number of informed buyers over time is depicted in Figure 13.1.

An examination of equation (13.2) shows how the number of informed buyers depends on c and b. Just as we would expect, an increase in the retention rate on advertising knowledge $(1 - b)$ results in an increase in the number of informed buyers. We can see that as $(1 - b)$ rises, the denominator in (13.2) falls, which increases the fraction of total customers who are informed. In other words, λN rises as b falls. Similarly, more consumers know about a seller's existence when advertising reaches more people in each period. Equivalently, an increase in c leads to a rise in N. That is why advertisers are interested in influencing the retention rate $(1 - b)$ and the contact rate (c).

THE IDENTIFICATION OF SELLERS: MONOPOLY A monopolist sets his price (P) and the level of advertising (a) so as to maximize profit. Since profit equals total revenue less total production costs (TC_p) and expenditures on advertising, we may express the firm's profit as

$$\Pi = PQ - \text{TC}_p - P_a a \tag{13.3}$$

where Q denotes the total quantity sold and P_a represents the price of a unit of advertising (e.g., the price of a minute of prime time television time). We assume that every potential customer who is aware of this monopolist's existence buys from him. Thus, the total quantity sold is equal to the product of the number of customers who buy from the monopolist (λN) and the quantity purchased by each customer (q).

FIGURE 13.1   The path of the number of informed buyers over time.

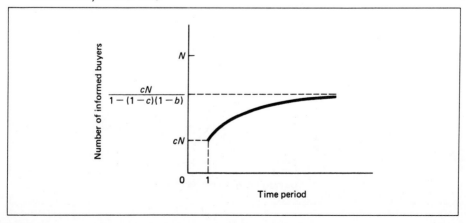

$$Q = \lambda N q \tag{13.4}$$

By substituting equation (13.4) into equation (13.3),

$$\Pi = P\lambda N q - TC_p - P_a a \tag{13.5}$$

we can express the firm's profit as a function of the number of informed buyers (λN), the quantity purchased by each customer (q), the product price (P), the costs of production (TC_p), and the expenditure on advertising ($P_a a$).

Each customer decreases the quantity that she purchases (q) when the product's price rises. This negative relationship between the price and the quantity purchased by each customer is depicted in Figure 13.2. The manager must choose the point on this demand curve that maximizes his profit.

Let's see what happens when the manager decreases the price sufficiently to get each customer to purchase 1 more unit. This causes the quantity sold to increase by λN, which is the number of informed customers. As a first approximation, total production costs increase by the product of the marginal cost of production (MC_p) and λN when output increases λN units. That is, total production costs rise by $MC_p\lambda N$. Total revenue also changes when each customer is induced, through a fall in price, to purchase 1 more unit. The total revenue from each customer equals Pq. Let us define the change in the total revenue per customer from increasing q by 1 unit to be MR. The total revenue received by the firm therefore increases by $MR\lambda N$ when each customer is led to buy 1 more unit. The manager maximizes the firm's profit by equating the increase in his total revenue from selling one more item to each customer ($MR\lambda N$) to the increase in his total cost from selling one more item to each customer ($MC_p\lambda N$).

$$MR\lambda N = MC_p\lambda N$$

FIGURE 13.2   The customer's demand for the product.

Price (P)

O

Quantity purchased per customer (q)

D

or

$$MR = MC_p \tag{13.6}$$

This last condition is the usual profit-maximizing condition for the monopolist.[2]

The manager also can increase his profit by adjusting the level of advertising. Additional advertising raises the fraction of potential customers who are aware of the monopolist's product (λ). By definition, increasing the level of advertising (a) by 1 unit raises the fraction of potential customers who buy from this monopolist (λ) by ($\Delta\lambda/\Delta a$). Consequently, the number of actual customers rises by $N(\Delta\lambda/\Delta a)$. Since each customer purchases q units, production and sales increase by $Nq(\Delta\lambda/\Delta a)$ units. But the firm has to spend P_a for the 1 unit of advertising that increases output by $Nq(\Delta\lambda/\Delta a)$ units. If we divide the price of advertising (P_a) by the increase in sales that an additional unit of advertising causes $[Nq(\Delta\lambda/\Delta a)]$, we have the amount that the firm must spend to increase sales by 1 unit: $P_a/[Nq(\Delta\lambda/\Delta a)]$. The benefit to the monopolist from creating one more sale at price P through advertising equals the difference between the price that is received for that sale (P) and the marginal cost of producing that last unit (MC_p). Accordingly, the manager maximizes profit by equating the marginal cost of selling 1 more unit through advertising $P_a/[Nq(\Delta\lambda/\Delta a)]$ to the marginal benefit of selling 1 more unit through advertising ($P - MC_p$).[3] In other words, the manager should increase his expenditures on advertising until

$$P - MC_p = \frac{P_a}{Nq(\Delta\lambda/\Delta a)} \tag{13.7}$$

Equations (13.6) and (13.7) are necessary conditions for profit maximization. We shall see how to use (13.7) below.

It is not as difficult a task as it might seem to select the price and level of advertising that maximizes profit. Setting marginal revenue equal to the marginal cost of production is a familiar problem. The really new task here is to find the level of advertising that satisfies condition (13.7). Using the techniques described in Chapter 3, the manager can estimate a demand function relating quantity demanded to price, the level of advertising, and other pertinent variables. This demand function will provide him with an estimate of the effect of advertising on demand.[4] This estimate and the price of advertising together imply how much it costs to sell 1 more unit through advertising. The optimal level of advertising is then readily obtained.

It is helpful to graphically illustrate the first-order condition for profit

---

[2]The profit-maximizing condition expressed in equation (13.6) is derived more formally in Section 13A.1 in the mathematical appendix to this chapter.

[3]This is shown more formally in Section 13A.2 of the mathematical appendix to this chapter.

[4]We should note that in the absence of better information, using a guess about the effect of advertising on demand is better than ignoring the optimal advertising decision altogether. Though a trial and error process, the manager can search around for the optimum described by conditions (13.6) and (13.7).

maximization that is expressed by equation (13.7). As advertising increases, production rises, and the marginal cost of production increases if there are decreasing returns to scale. Accordingly, $P - MC_p$ falls as advertising increases. This is shown in Figure 13.3 for the hypothetical values shown in Table 13.1. In this model, the number of potential customers (N) and the quantity purchased by each customer (q) do not change as a company varies the level of its advertising. Furthermore, the price of advertising (P_a) does not vary with the amount of advertising undertaken by a firm if the advertising market is competitive and there are no fixed costs in advertising. It is, however, plausible to expect the effectiveness of advertising ($\Delta\lambda/\Delta a$) to decline as the level of advertising rises. If this is true, the marginal cost of selling 1 more unit through advertising $\{P_a/[Nq\,(\Delta\lambda/\Delta a)]\}$ increases as the level of advertising rises, as can be seen in Figure 13.3 and in the data in Table 13.1. Profit is maximized by using 12,000 units of advertising in Figure 13.3, for at this level of advertising, the marginal benefit of increasing output through advertising equals the marginal cost of increasing output through advertising. This can be seen in Table 13.1 where $P - MC_p = P_a/[Nq(\Delta\lambda/\Delta a)] = 9$.

Of course, a change in the benefit or cost of advertising will alter the optimal level of advertising. A firm with a higher marginal profit per unit of output (i.e., a higher value of $P - MC_p$) has a greater benefit from advertising

TABLE 13.1
THE OPTIMAL LEVEL OF ADVERTISING

a	$P - MC_p$	$P_a/Nq\ \dfrac{\Delta\lambda}{\Delta a}$
0	15	3
2,000	14	4
4,000	13	5
6,000	12	6
8,000	11	7
10,000	10	8
12,000	9	9
14,000	8	10
16,000	7	11
18,000	6	12
20,000	5	13
22,000	4	14
24,000	3	15
26,000	2	16
28,000	1	17
30,000	0	18

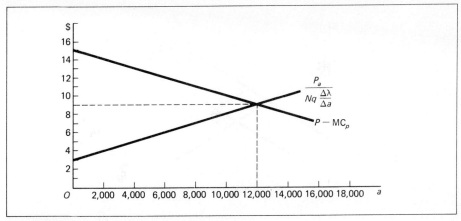

FIGURE 13.3 The optimal level of advertising.

and will choose a higher level of advertising. In Figure 13.4, a shift in the marginal benefit schedule from $(P - MC_p)_0$ to $(P - MC_p)_1$ causes the optimal level of advertising to rise from a_0 to a_1. In this model, a competitive firm, which operates at $P = MC_p$, has no incentive to advertise.

Similarly, the optimal level of advertising rises when the marginal cost schedule falls from $\{P_a/[Nq(\Delta\lambda/\Delta a)]\}_0$ to $\{P_a/Nq(\Delta\lambda/\Delta a)]\}_1$ in Figure 13.5. There are several possible reasons why the marginal cost of advertising schedule may shift to the right: (1) the cost of each unit of advertising (P_a) falls; (2) the potential market reached by advertising is larger—that is, N rises; (3) each customer who is made aware of the monopolist's existence

FIGURE 13.4 The effect of an increase in the benefits of advertising on the optimal level of advertising.

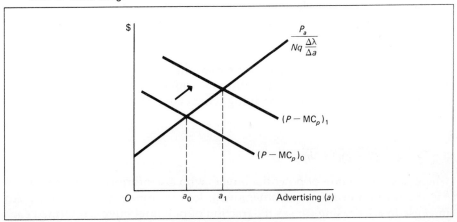

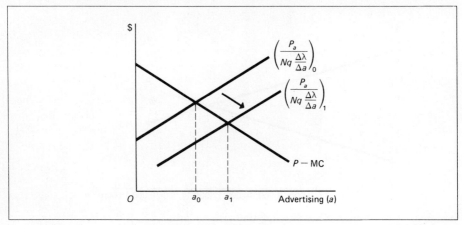

FIGURE 13.5 The effect of a fall in the cost of advertising on the optimal level of advertising.

through advertising purchases more units—i.e., q rises; (4) advertising is more effective—i.e., $\Delta\lambda/\Delta a$ increases.

Question Answer true, false, or undecided: A brewer who produces a beer (Gusto) that appeals to heavy beer drinkers should advertise more than a brewer who produces a beer (Classo) that is popular with occasional beer drinkers.

Answer In general, true. Suppose that advertising in each instance has the same effect on the fraction of potential consumers who buy a particular brand of beer (i.e., $\Delta\lambda/\Delta a$ is the same for both beers). That is, 1 unit of advertising causes n_0 more people to buy Gusto beer or causes n_0 more people to buy Classo beer. But each Gusto buyer purchases more beer than each Classo buyer. This means that q is higher for Gusto beer than for Classo beer. Consequently, $\{P_a/[Nq(\Delta\lambda/\Delta a)]\}$ is lower for Gusto than for Classo. As a result, Gusto finds it cheaper to sell one more bottle of beer through advertising than does Classo, and Gusto will maximize profit by advertising more than Classo.

Most of the variables that shift the marginal cost of advertising schedule are fairly straightforward. Some additional understanding is gained, however, by spending some time examining what causes $\Delta\lambda/\Delta a$ to increase. Recall that

$$\lambda = \frac{c}{1 - (1 - c)(1 - b)}$$

where c is the fraction of potential buyers who are informed each period and b is the fraction of informed buyers who lose information each period. An increase in advertising causes the fraction of potential buyers informed each period (c) to rise and thus leads to an increase in λ. If additional advertising reaches more people each period (i.e., there is a greater rise in c from 1 unit of advertising), $\Delta\lambda/\Delta a$ rises.[5] Consequently, it is now cheaper to sell an additional unit through advertising, and profit will be maximized by using more advertising.

Generally, an increase in the "death" rate of informed customers (b) will cause more advertising to be optimal. The logic here is that advertising about a local monopoly is more beneficial in a community where there is some geographic mobility (e.g., a university town), and hence a relatively great need for information, than in a community where there is very little geographic mobility and a large number of residents already know (from previous advertising) about the particular monopoly. On the other hand, if there is too much mobility, people may not stay around long enough for advertising to be effective, and an increase in the "death" rate of informed customers may lead to a fall in the optimal level of advertising.[6]

THE IDENTIFICATION OF SELLERS: MANY SELLERS A slightly more complicated but more interesting situation arises when many sellers are selling the same item. Changes in demand and supply conditions continually alter the equilibrium price. Since consumer search is costly, at any point in time there will be a distribution of prices offered by different sellers. Consumers go from store to store searching for the lowest price. One of the primary functions of advertising is to induce consumers to go to a particular seller in their search for lower prices.

Accordingly, let us assume that a manager is able to increase the number of potential customers who canvass his store (T_i) by increasing the level of advertising (a). Each consumer goes to several stores before deciding where to buy, and a particular manager can increase the fraction of canvassers who buy from her (M) by lowering her price. The total revenue received by this firm equals

PT_iMq

where T_i represents the number of potential customers who canvass a store, M is the fraction of those canvassing the store who buy from the store, and q denotes the quantity bought by each buyer. The manager wants to maximize her firm's profits, which equal

$$\Pi = PT_iMq - TC_p - P_a a \qquad (13.8)$$

and this can be accomplished by setting the appropriate price and level of advertising.

As we have seen, advertising has its benefits and costs. The optimal level of advertising occurs where the marginal benefit of selling 1 more unit through advertising equals the marginal cost of selling 1 more unit through

[5]This is derived in Section 13A.3 of the mathematical appendix to this chapter.
[6]See Section 13A.4 in the mathematical appendix to this chapter.

advertising. As before, the marginal benefit of selling 1 more unit through advertising equals the difference between price and the marginal cost of obtaining 1 more unit for resale. Let's now examine the marginal cost of selling 1 more unit through advertising. By definition, the number of consumers who canvass a store rises by $\Delta T_i/\Delta a$ when the level of advertising increases by 1 unit. Because only a fraction M of canvassers buy from a store and each buyer purchases q units, a unit increase in advertising brings about an increase in sales of $Mq\ (\Delta T_i/\Delta a)$. But it costs P_a to bring this about. Accordingly, the cost of selling 1 more unit through advertising equals $P_a/[Mq(\Delta T_i/\Delta a)]$. Profit is maximized when

$$P - MC_p = \frac{P_a}{Mq(\Delta T_i/\Delta a)} \tag{13.9}$$

Question   A store sells tires for $50 apiece. The tires cost the store $35 apiece in purchasing, inventory, and installation costs. The manager estimates that 1 minute of television advertising, which costs $100, brings 10 potential customers into the store. One-third of these buy tires and each buyer purchases 4 tires. Should the manager increase or decrease his advertising?

Answer   He should increase his advertising. In the context of this question, $P = 50$, $MC_p = 35$, $P_a = 100$, $M = {}^1/_3$, $q = 4$, and $\Delta T_i/\Delta a = 10$. The firm receives a $15 profit on each tire that is sold through advertising:

$$P - MC_p = \$50 - 35 = \$15$$

and it costs only $7.50 to sell a tire through advertising

$$\frac{P_a}{Mq(\Delta T_i/\Delta a)} = \frac{100}{1/3 \cdot 4 \cdot 10} = \$7.50$$

To maximize profit, the manager must not only pick the correct level of advertising but she must also choose the correct price. Her pricing decision is more complicated when there are other firms selling the same product than when her firm is the only firm selling a particular product. We have seen that the manager of a monopoly maximizes the firm's profit by equating the increase in the total revenue from selling 1 more unit to each customer to the marginal cost of production. We will now derive a similar condition for a seller competing with other sellers in a market characterized by imperfect information.

At any given level of advertising, a store is able to sell more of its product when it lowers its price. This is true for two reasons. As the price falls, each buyer purchases more; this is seen in panel (*a*) of Figure 13.6. A price decrease also causes a greater fraction of canvassers to purchase from this particular store. This relationship is shown in panel (*b*) of Figure 13.6. Both these effects are taken into account in the negative slope of the demand curve *D* facing the firm in panel (*c*) of Figure 13.6. Associated with this demand curve is a marginal revenue curve labeled MR. The marginal revenue curve

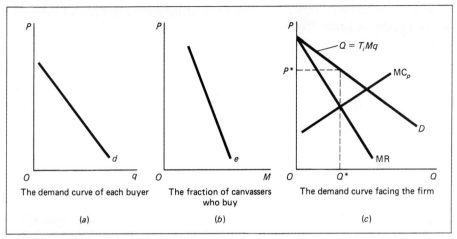

(a) The demand curve of each buyer

(b) The fraction of canvassers who buy

(c) The demand curve facing the firm

FIGURE 13.6 The profit-maximizing price in a world of sellers.

(MR) gives the change in the firm's total revenue associated with a 1-unit increase in the firm's sales. As we have noted, this increase in the firm's sales comes from the increased consumption of each buyer *and* from an increase in the fraction of canvassers who end up buying from this store. Profit is maximized when MR equals the marginal cost of production.[7] Profit is maximized by setting the price at P^*. At this price, Q^* units will be sold.

The determination of the profit-maximizing price is not as forbidding a task as it might seem to be. As we have seen, profit is maximized by setting the marginal cost of production equal to marginal revenue. Knowledge about the marginal revenue line can be obtained by varying the seller's price and observing the effect on total revenue. Through a trial-and-error process, the manager can get a good feeling for marginal revenue. This information then can be combined with knowledge about the marginal cost of production to find the profit-maximizing price.

Each seller is able to charge a price that exceeds the marginal cost of production. This is because information is costly. If information were free, *all* consumers would buy from the seller offering the lowest price. A seller that sold goods at a price slightly above the prevailing price would be unable to attract any buyers, while a seller who set a price slightly below the prevailing price would capture the entire market. Consequently, under free information, both the curve labeled *e* in panel (*b*) of Figure 13.6 and the demand curve facing the firm in panel (*c*) of 13.6 would be horizontal at the same price, and profit would be maximized by selling at a price equal to marginal cost.

We have seen that sellers are able to sell at prices that exceed marginal

---

[7] This is shown using calculus in Section 13A.5 of the mathematical appendix to this chapter.

cost because some buyers do not find it worthwhile to search out the seller with the lowest price. In fact, the less responsive the fraction of canvassers who purchase from a given seller is to price changes, the higher will be the profit-maximizing price. (The reader should review the factors that determine this responsiveness.)

CHANGING CONSUMER TASTES   Many economists argue that producers are able to alter consumer preferences by advertising appropriately. That is, as a result of advertising, consumers value a particular product more highly and consequently are willing to pay a higher price for it. Under this scenario, the advertiser is something of a pied piper who leads impressionable consumers to purchase whatever goods the advertiser chooses for them.[8]

Once again, the manager must compare the benefits and costs of advertising in order to maximize profits. Suppose that 1 unit of advertising shifts the demand curve out from D_0 to D_1 in Figure 13.7. Furthermore, suppose that the manager maximizes the firm's profit along demand curve D_0 by producing Q_0 units. One more unit of advertising enables the firm to charge P_1 rather than P_0 for each of these Q_0 units of output. Consequently, advertising increases the firm's total revenue by $(P_1 - P_0)Q_0$ when Q_0 units of output are sold. Consequently $(P_1 - P_0)Q_0$ is a measure of the benefit to the firm of using 1 more unit of advertising.[9] Since a unit of advertising costs P_a, the manager should expand his advertising campaign if $(P_1 - P_0)Q_0$ exceeds P_a

---

[8]We should note that the informational approach to advertising provides another explanation of the positive relationship between advertising and price. Under this approach, advertising provides information about a product's characteristics, and as a result of this additional information, consumers are willing to pay a higher price for the product.

[9]This can be shown using calculus in Section 13A.6 of the mathematical appendix to this chapter.

FIGURE 13.7   The benefit of advertising.

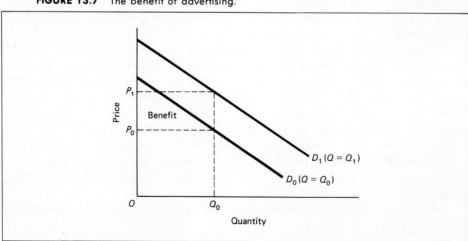

and should reduce the level of advertising if $(P_1 - P_0)Q_0$ is less than P_a. Profit will be maximized when $(P_1 - P_0)Q_0$ equals P_a.

Along any demand curve (e.g., D_1 in Figure 13.7), profit will be maximized by setting price so that marginal revenue equals marginal cost. This should be a familiar conclusion by this time.

13.2

FALSE ADVERTISING

False advertising is the provision of incorrect information. Typically a product's qualities are exaggerated in order to increase sales. When can this strategy be successful?

In Chapter 12, we divided goods into inspection goods and experience goods. By definition, the characteristics of inspection goods can be ascertained prior to purchase. Advertising can inform buyers that a particular store carries a certain inspection good at a specific price. Advertising, however, cannot successfully misinform buyers about the characteristics of the inspection good because these characteristics can be observed prior to purchase. As an example, if a store manager falsely advertises that she has red pens for sale when the store only carries blue pens, the buyer cannot be deceived. Upon arrival, the buyer will know that the claim was false and will not buy a blue pen if he needs a red one. It is silly to lie about inspection goods because it cannot deceive and it is bound to anger potential customers.

There is, however, some potential to mislead buyers about the characteristics of *experience* goods because a consumer has to use an experience good before he can ascertain its characteristics. But the potential for misleading buyers is also limited. This is because of repeat sales. Once a consumer has experienced a particular good, he knows its characteristics and will purchase it again only if he values it sufficiently. A producer cannot continue to mislead frequent purchasers of an experience good.

Accordingly, the potential for false advertising is greatest for seldom-purchased experience goods. Some manufacturers and sellers of these goods can be expected to engage in false advertising. Of course, false advertising will be less prevalent the more severe the legal penalties for false advertising and the less expensive the acquisition of information (e.g., the purchase of *Consumer Reports*).

Some sellers of seldom-purchased experience goods have a greater opportunity for making money from false advertising than do others. Consumers who are led through false advertising to purchase a lower-quality good than they would have otherwise purchased become dissatisfied with their purchase. As a result of this dissatisfaction, they and some of their friends choose not to purchase from this store in the future. Consequently, the more buyers there are who are new to a particular community, the more buyers there are who can be "suckered" once. As a result, false advertising is more prevalent in communities with transient populations (e.g., university towns) and in communities with a large number of visitors (e.g., resort towns, tourist areas).

13.3

ADVERTISING MEDIA

Various media can be used to advertise a firm's product. The manager must allocate her advertising budget among the media so as to maximize her firm's profit. For the manager who is armed with information about the effectiveness of the various media, this is not a difficult task.

The economic principle is familiar: $1 of advertising expenditure should go to that medium of advertising that produces the greatest increase in company profits. Money should be reallocated from media in which $1 produces a small increase in company profits to media in which $1 produces a larger increase in company profits. This reallocation should continue until a $1 in advertising expenditure produces the same increase in company profits in all media.

Question   A manager calculated that a one-page ad in the *New York Times* results in 300 additional sales and that a 1-minute ad on WABC radio produces 150 additional sales. The ad in the *Times* costs $100, while the ad on WABC costs $50. Has she maximized company profits?

Answer   To the extent that $1 produces the same increase in company profits in both media, she has. The ad in the *Times* costs $100 and produces 300 sales. Thus, $1 produces 3 sales. Similarly, a $50 ad on WABC produces 150 sales. Again, $1 results in 3 sales. This is the familiar equimarginal principle:

$$\frac{MS_T}{P_T} = \frac{MS_R}{P_R}$$

where MS_T is marginal sales in the *Times*, MS_R is marginal sales on the radio, and P_T and P_R are the respective prices for space in the *Times* and on WABC.

13.4

PRIVATE BRANDS AND FRANCHISES[10]

Firms are organized around the production, advertising, and distribution of products. Differences across products in the scale economies associated with these functions will result in differences in the organization of firms. We shall examine a couple of these differences.

We will define private brands to exist whenever physically identical products are sold under the producer's own brand name and under the brand name(s) of one or more distributors. For example, Del Monte may sell green beans under its own label and produce identical green beans for A&P stores under the Ann Page label. Obviously, every brand of green beans is not

---

[10]The analysis in this section draws on Roger D. Blair and Yoram Peles, "Private Brands and Antitrust Policy," *UCLA Law Review*, vol. 24, October 1977, pp. 46–69.

equally tasty. There are, however, instances in which a producer sells the same good under different labels, and this is what we mean by private brands.

Private brands sometimes emerge when the economies of scale in production exceed the economies of scale in distribution. In Figure 13.8, the average cost of distribution is represented by curve AC_d and the average cost of production is represented by curve AC_p. The cost of production is minimized at output level Q while the cost of distribution is minimized at output level q. This figure is drawn so that $Q = 2q$. Consequently, the cost of distributing Q units of output is minimized when there are two distribution facilities, each distributing q units. This is easily seen by examining Figure 13.8. Two distribution facilities can each distribute q units at an average cost of C_0. In contrast, the average cost of having one distribution facility handling Q units of output equals C_1, which is considerably higher than C_0.

One way in which several firms can successfully distribute a product that is produced by one firm is for each firm to sell the product under its own brand. The reputation of each distributor then provides the customer with information about the quality of the product. Private brands are commonly used to distribute tires, major appliances, and a wide array of food products, among other things. Presumably, this reflects the fact that the minimum-cost output in distribution is less than the minimum-cost output in production. These are products that experience considerable scale economies in production.

Franchising may occur when the opposite is the case. Specifically, franchises arise when the minimum-cost output in advertising exceeds the minimum-cost output in production. In this instance, costs are lower when one firm specializes in advertising a particular product (and perhaps in monitoring output quality) than when several firms advertise the product. Costs are also lower when several firms are producing the product than when

FIGURE 13.8 Economies of scale in distribution and in production.

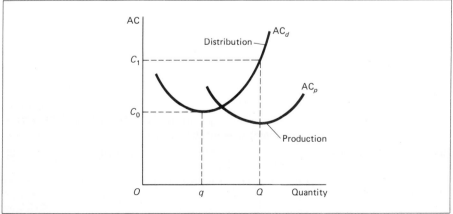

one firm produces the product. As a result, the organizational structure that minimizes cost is one where one firm advertises a commodity that is produced by several firms; this essentially is the franchise system.

The profitability of a franchise will depend on the scale economies in advertising and in production. Products where the minimum-cost levels of production are low (e.g., locally produced products) are likely candidates for franchises. Consequently, it makes sound economic sense for some fried chicken outlets to be franchised operations. Similarly, products that can realize considerable scale economies in advertising may be products which are most efficiently organized in a franchise. Advertising removes some of the uncertainty about a product, and much of the advertising done by restaurant, hotel, and hardware franchises is designed to establish the quality of the product being advertised. Consumers know what they are buying when they walk into a McDonald's restaurant or a Holiday Inn anywhere in the country. Similarly, products that appeal to a very specialized market are unable to take advantage of significant scale economies in advertising. This is one reason why franchises exist for restaurants specializing in steaks, seafood, hamburgers, or chicken and do not exist for restaurants specializing in German, Chinese, or French cuisine.

Question   What has been the impact of television on the prevalence of franchises?

Answer   When television was introduced, the scale economies that were associated with advertising a number of products for which visual information is important increased. Consequently, some franchises became more profitable, and franchises became more prevalent in our society.

13.5

ALLOCATION OF SALES REPRESENTATIVES

A manager must allocate her salesmen to maximize company profits. She must decide how many sales representatives to put in each territory and which ones to assign to which territory. We will consider each of these decisions in turn.

THE OPTIMAL NUMBER OF SALES REPRESENTATIVES   The decision on how many sales representatives to place in each territory is very similar to the optimal advertising decision, because sales representatives generate sales in much the same way that advertising does. The benefit to the firm of selling 1 more unit through a sales representative's effort equals the difference between the price and the marginal cost of producing the good and shipping it to the buyer. The cost to the firm of selling 1 more unit through a sales representative's effort equals the sales representative's wage rate multiplied by the time required to sell 1 unit.[11] The manager maximizes profits by allocating

---

[11]To simplify the exposition, commissions are ignored in the discussion in this section. It is a straightforward matter to incorporate commissions.

her sales representatives such that the benefit of selling 1 more unit through a sales representative equals the cost of selling 1 more unit through a sales representative. Thus, the difference between price and the marginal costs of producing and shipping the good must equal the sales representative's wage rate times the time required to sell 1 unit.

The manager accordingly will take into account territorial differences in the selling price, the marginal cost of production and shipping, the wage rate, and the productivity of sales representatives when she decides on the size of the sales force in each territory. Other things being equal, she will allocate more sales representatives to territories with a high "profit" per unit (i.e., a large difference between price and the marginal cost of production and shipping) than to territories with a low "profit" per unit. Because of compensating wage differentials, wage rates are higher in territories that sales representatives find less desirable to work in. The higher cost of selling in these territories will lead the manager to place fewer sales representatives in these territories than in other territories. Similarly, more sales representatives will be allocated to territories where it is easy to sell the product than to territories where it is difficult to sell the product.

A numerical example may help to clarify these matters. Suppose that there are two sales territories: territory 1 and territory 2. In each territory, the relationship between the number of sales representatives (S) and the number of units sold (Q) is

$$Q = 2,500S - 150S^2 \qquad (13.10)$$

In territory 1, output sells for \$100 per unit and costs \$80 per unit to produce and ship. Output in territory 2 sells for \$105 per unit. This territory is farther away from the plant, and the per unit cost of production and shipping equals \$95. Sales representatives in territory 1 are paid \$8,000 per year, and sales representatives in territory 2, a most unpleasant place, are paid \$13,000 per year. Consequently, the firm's profit equals

$$100Q_1 + 105Q_2 - 80Q_1 - 95Q_2 - 8,000S_1 - 13,000S_2$$

where Q_1 is the output sold in territory 1, Q_2 is the output sold in territory 2, S_1 is the number of sales representatives in territory 1, and S_2 is the number of sales representatives in territory 2. Collecting terms, we can simplify the expression for profit:

$$\Pi = 20Q_1 + 10Q_2 - 8,000S_1 - 13,000S_2 \qquad (13.11)$$

Substituting (13.10) into (13.11),

$$\Pi = 20(2,500S_1 - 150S_1^2) + 10(2,500S_2 - 150S_2^2) - 8,000S_1 - 13,000S_2 \qquad (13.12)$$

Profit is maximized by selecting the appropriate number of sales representatives for each territory. This can be determined by adjusting the number of sales representatives in each territory until the change in profit from any further change in the number of sales representatives is zero. In other words, by setting $\Delta \Pi / \Delta S_1$ and $\Delta \Pi / \Delta S_2$ equal to zero, we will be able to find the optimal number of sales representatives for each location:

$$\frac{\Delta \Pi}{\Delta S_1} = 20(2,500) - 20(300)S_1 - 8,000 = 0$$

$$42,000 = 6,000 S_1$$

$$7 = S_1$$

$$\frac{\Delta \Pi}{\Delta S_2} = 10(2,500) - 10(300)S_2 - 13,000 = 0$$

$$12,000 = 3,000 S_2$$

$$4 = S_2$$

Accordingly, the manager should put seven sales representatives in territory 1 and four sales representatives in territory 2. The reader can verify that operating in each territory adds to the company's profit by substituting $S_1 = 7$ and $S_2 = 4$ into the profit function (13.12). To be sure that these assignments maximize profits, try substituting other values for S_1 and S_2 in (13.12).

THE OPTIMAL ASSIGNMENT OF SPECIFIC SALES REPRESENTATIVES   So far the problem of assigning sales representatives to territories has been considered under the assumption that all sales representatives are equally productive. It is more realistic to assume that sales representatives differ in their productivity and, moreover, that some will perform better than others in specific territories. Some sales representatives will be more effective in one part of the country because of their background and temperament, while others will be more effective in other parts of the country. Similarly, some types of accounts will be more effectively handled by some sales representatives, and other types of accounts will be more effectively handled by others.

The manager's problem is to allocate her sales force so that the firm's profit is maximized. The firm's profit from assigning salesman A to territory 1 equals

$$\Pi_{A1} = (P_1 - MC_1)Q_{A1} - W_{A1}$$

where P_1 denotes the price that can be obtained in territory 1, MC_1 is the marginal cost of producing a good and transporting it to territory 1, Q_{A1} represents the number of units sold by salesman A in territory 1, and W_{A1} is the salary paid to salesman A in territory 1. Thus, the territorial profit is equal to the "profit" per unit ($P_1 - MC_1$) times the number of units sold, less the salary. The manager must assign sales representatives to territories so that the sum of these territorial profits over all territories is maximized. This is a particular kind of linear programming problem, which is not surprisingly called the "assignment" problem. A standard algorithm exists to solve it.[12]

---

[12]See C. W. Churchman, R. L. Ackoff, and E. L. Arnoff, *Introduction to Operations Research*, New York: John Wiley and Sons, Inc., 1957, chap. 12, "The Assignment Problem."

A simple example will help to clarify some of these points. Consider the problem of assigning four salesmen to four territories. The teritorial profits associated with each salesman are given in Table 13.2. Salesman A brings $9,000 in profit to the company if he is assigned to territory 1, $5,700 if he is assigned to territory 2, and so on. Clearly, if there were no other sales representatives, the manager would maximize profit by assigning salesman A to territory 1. This is called the territory in which salesman A has an absolute advantage. Similarly, salesman B has an absolute advantage in territory 2, salesman C has an absolute advantage in territory 2, and salesman D has an absolute advantage in territory 4.

But it is not possible to assign all the salesmen to territories in which they have absolute advantages, for this would result in territory 3 being uncovered. How can we best assign a salesman to territory 3? Moving salesman D from the territory in which he has an absolute advantage (territory 4) to teritory 3 results in a $2,400 (= 7,500 − 5,100) loss of profit. Moving salesman B or salesman C from territory 2, in which they have an absolute advantage, to territory 3 results in a $2,000 or $3,500 loss in profit, respectively. On the other hand, moving salesman A from the territory in which he has an absolute advantage (territory 1) to territory 3 results in only an $800 loss in profit. Salesman A has a *comparative* advantage in territory 3. Similarly, very little profit is lost when salesman C is moved from territory 2 to territory 1.

This reasoning suggests why the assignment A3, B2, C1, D4 produces the greatest total profit ($32,500) among all 4! = 24 possible assignments of four men to four territories. While there is a tendency to place productive sales representatives in lucrative territories, the optimal assignment does not rigidly adhere to this strategy. The maximization of the *sum* of territorial profits allocates some salesmen to territories where they have a comparative advantage but not an absolute advantage.

We may also note that just as there is a tendency to send productive salesmen to lucrative territories, there is a tendency to send sales representatives to territories in which they enjoy working. The manager can pay lower salaries under this allocation and accordingly will reap higher profits.

TABLE 13.2
ESTIMATES OF THE PROFITS ASSOCIATED WITH VARIOUS ASSIGNMENTS OF SALESMEN TO TERRITORIES

SALESMAN	TERRITORY			
	1	2	3	4
A	9,000	5,700	8,200	4,500
B	9,200	9,500	7,500	7,000
C	7,300	7,500	4,000	5,100
D	6,000	3,000	5,100	7,500

13.6

SUMMARY

In this chapter, we have not attempted to cover all the topics found in marketing courses. Rather, we have sought to bring an economist's perspective to some marketing decisions, which were not analyzed in the previous chapters.

We saw that advertising provides information about prices, the characteristics of products, the existence of products and sellers, and so on. To maximize profit, the manager must simultaneously set the appropriate advertising and price levels. These occur where the increased profit from selling 1 more unit through advertising equals the additional advertising expenditures necessary to sell 1 more unit through advertising and where marginal revenue equals marginal cost. We also analyzed false advertising and concluded that since false advertising provides incorrect information, false advertising can succeed only when consumers can be fooled—that is, in the case of infrequently purchased experience goods. Our discussion of advertising ended with an analysis of how to allocate advertising funds among various advertising media.

We also saw that the organization of the firm was at least partially the result of scale economies in the production and distribution of the product. Private brands are likely to be optimal when the minimum-cost output in production exceeds the minimum-cost output in distribution. Franchises result from the minimum-cost output in advertising exceeding the minimum-cost output in production.

Finally, we considered the optimal allocation of sales representatives. A manager can increase profit by allocating more sales representatives to profitable areas and by allocating *particular* sales representatives to areas in which they have a comparative advantage.

IMPORTANT NEW TERMS

Informed buyers

Canvass

False advertising

Private brand

Franchise

Comparative advantage

PROBLEMS

13.1   Consider the advertising decision faced by one store (of several) selling a particular item. Suppose that gasoline becomes more expensive and as a result people who come into this store are more likely to buy from this store than was previously the case. Do the new search conditions warrant a change in the firm's advertising policy? Does the answer depend on whether the store is a high-priced or low-priced seller?

13.2   Consider the same changes outlined in Problem 13.1. Do the new search conditions warrant a change in the firm's pricing policy?

13.3   Answer true, false, or undecided: A firm can *never* make money by engaging in false advertising.

13.4   Examine the impact of an increase in the minimum-cost output in production on the prevalance of private brands and of franchises.

13.5   Suppose that a young salesman turns out to be unexpectedly productive in dealing with a particular type of clientele? Should he be reassigned? If so, where?

13.6   The optimal condition for quantity per customer is given in the mathematical appendix to this chapter in (A13.2). This is satisfied where λN equals zero. Will this maximize profit? What is wrong?

13.7   Florida orange growers advertise the benefits of orange juice and through advertising increase the price that people are willing to pay. The growers estimate the following demand function for orange juice:

$$P = c - .000032X + .0001521I + .038P_t + .75TV$$

where X = number of cans of frozen orange juice sold per year
$\quad\quad P$ = price of orange juice
$\quad\quad I$ = real income of consumers
$\quad\quad P_t$ = price of can of tomato juice
$\quad\quad TV$ = minutes of TV advertising
$\quad\quad c$ = constant term

They wish to maximize profits, which equal

$$P(X, TV)X - TC_p(X) - P_{TV}TV$$

The price of orange juice is currently \$0.50, and 1 million cans are sold per year. The price of 1 minute of television is \$200,000. Should the growers increase or decrease their TV advertising budget?

13.8   Joe's Bar and Grill sells the best hamburgers in the vacation resort town of Pleasant Beach. All of the locals eat at Joe's while all of the tourists eat at Burger King and McDonald's. Explain this.

13.9   Suppose that there are sizable costs associated with creating an advertising campaign for any particular advertising medium. How do these "fixed" costs affect the choice of advertising media?

13.10   If a manager allocates *one* salesperson to a particular territory, the firm receives the following profit:

	PROFIT FROM TERRITORY 1	PROFIT FROM TERRITORY 2
Salesman A	4,000	8,000
Saleswoman B	7,000	9,000

If salesman A *and* saleswoman B are both allocated to territory 1, the company's total profits from territory 1 equal $9,500. If salesman A and saleswoman B are both allocated to territory 2, the company's total profits from territory 2 equal $14,000. Find the optimal allocation of these sales personnel.

REFERENCES

Blair, Roger D., and Yoram Peles: "Private Brands and Antitrust Policy," *UCLA Law Review*, vol. 24, October 1977, 46–69.

Kotler, Philip: *Marketing Decision Making: A Model Building Approach*, New York: Holt, Rinehart and Winston, Inc., 1971.

Stigler, George: "The Economics of Information," *Journal of Political Economy*, vol. 69, June 1961, 213–225.

MATHEMATICAL APPENDIX

13A.1

ADVERTISING BY A MONOPOLY— OPTIMUM OUTPUT

The firm's profit can be written as in equation (13.5) in the text:

$$\Pi = P\lambda Nq - TC_p - P_a a \quad (A13.1)$$

The optimal (i.e., profit-maximizing) quantity per customer is found where the first partial derivative of the profit function vanishes. First, note that

$$\frac{\partial \Pi}{\partial q} = \lambda N \left(P\frac{dq}{dq} + q\frac{dP}{dq} \right) - \frac{dTC_p}{dq}\lambda N$$

$$= \lambda N \left[\left(P + q\frac{dP}{dq} \right) - MC_p \right]$$

$$= \lambda N(MR - MC_p)$$

Profit is maximized by adjusting output to the point where

$$\lambda N(MR - MC_p) = 0 \quad (A13.2)$$

which requires that marginal revenue equal marginal cost.

13A.2

ADVERTISING BY A MONOPOLY—OPTIMUM LEVEL OF ADVERTISING

We begin with the profit function shown in (A13.1) above. The profit-maximizing quantity of advertising is found where the first partial derivative of (A13.1) with respect to a vanishes. Differentiation yields

$$\frac{\partial \Pi}{\partial a} = PNq \frac{d\lambda}{da} - MC_p Nq \frac{d\lambda}{da} - P_a$$

Profit is maximized by changing the quantity of advertising until

$$PNq \frac{d\lambda}{da} - MC_p Nq \frac{d\lambda}{da} - P_a = 0$$

Algebraic manipulation provides a more precise expression for that found in condition (13.7) in the text:

$$P - MC_p = \frac{P_a}{Nq \dfrac{d\lambda}{da}} \tag{A13.3}$$

13A.3

EFFECT OF ADVERTISING ON THE FRACTION OF BUYERS WHO ARE INFORMED

Recall that the fraction of buyers that remains informed is given by

$$\lambda = \frac{c}{1 - (1-c)(1-b)}$$

Using the chain rule, we can determine the qualitative impact upon λ of more effective advertising:

$$\frac{d\lambda}{da} = \frac{d\lambda}{dc} \frac{dc}{da}$$

$$= \frac{1 - (1-c)(1-b) - c(1-b)}{[1 - (1-c)(1-b)]^2} \frac{dc}{da}$$

$$= \frac{b}{[1 - (1-c)(1-b)]^2} \frac{dc}{da}$$

which is positive because b and dc/da are both positive. Consequently, additional advertising causes λ to rise. If dc/da increases, then $d\lambda/da$ will also increase.

13A.4

EFFECT OF THE LOSS OF INFORMATION ON THE EFFECTIVENESS OF ADVERTISING

From Section 13A.3, we know that the effectiveness of advertising $(d\lambda/da)$ rises if

$$\frac{d\lambda}{dc} = \frac{b}{[1 - (1-c)(1-b)]^2}$$

increases. Consequently, the question is whether an increase in b causes $d\lambda/dc$ to rise. If so, advertising is more beneficial.

If

$$\frac{d}{db}\left\{\frac{b}{[1-(1-c)(1-b)]^2}\right\} > 0$$

advertising will become more beneficial as b rises. Now,

$$\frac{d}{db}\left\{\frac{b}{[1-(1-c)(1-b)]^2}\right\}$$

$$= \frac{[1-(1-c)(1-b)]^2 - 2b[1-(1-c)(1-b)](1-c)}{[1-(1-c)(1-b)]^4}$$

$$= \frac{1-(1-c)-b(1-c)}{[1-(1-c)(1-b)]^3}$$

$$= \frac{1-(1-c)(1+b)}{[1-(1-c)(1-b)]^3}$$

and this is greater than zero if

$$1 > (1-c)(1+b)$$

If $c > .5$, this condition always holds. If $c < .5$, b must not be too large relative to c.

13A.5

ADVERTISING BY A "COMPETITIVE" FIRM—OPTIMUM PRICE

We begin with the expression for profit that appears in equation (13.8) in the text:

$$\Pi = PT_iMq - TC_p - P_aa \quad (A13.4)$$

Optimization requires operating where the first partial derivative of (A13.4) equals zero. Differentiating (A13.4) with respect to price and setting the derivative equal to zero yields

$$\frac{\partial \Pi}{\partial P} = T_i\left[M\frac{d(Pq)}{dP} + Pq\frac{d(M)}{dP}\right] - MC_pT_i\left[M\frac{d(q)}{dP} + q\frac{d(M)}{dP}\right] = 0$$

This can be manipulated to show that

$$MC_p = \frac{M[d(Pq)/dP] + Pq[d(M)/dP]}{M(dq/dP) + q(dM/dP)}$$

$$= P\left(1 - \frac{1}{\epsilon_{q,p} + \epsilon_{M,P}}\right)$$

where $\epsilon_{q,p} = -\left[\frac{d(q)}{dP}\right]\frac{P}{q}$ = elasticity of q with respect to P

$\epsilon_{M,P} = -\left[\frac{d(M)}{dP}\right]\frac{P}{M}$ = elasticity of M with respect to P

$\epsilon_{q,P} > 0$ and $\epsilon_{M,P} > 0$

13A.6

ADVERTISING WHEN "TASTES" CAN BE CHANGED—OPTIMUM LEVEL OF ADVERTISING

Starting with a familiar expression for profit,

$$\Pi = PQ - TC_p - P_a a \qquad (A13.5)$$

where $P = P(Q,a)$, we may examine one of the necessary conditions for a maximum. The first partial derivative of (A13.5) with respect to a is

$$\frac{\partial \Pi}{\partial a} = \frac{\partial P}{\partial a} Q - P_a = 0$$

In the text, $(P_1 - P_0)$ corresponds to $\partial P/\partial a$, which measures the change in price generated by a unit of advertising.

14 ACCOUNT-ING AND MANAGE-RIAL DECISIONS

For all managerial decision making, the manager's job is easier when he has the appropriate information. By this we mean that the information is neither too detailed nor too aggregate. Moreover, the data provided must accurately measure the economic variable(s) of interest.

Accountants traditionally have organized and kept records to serve a variety of purposes. Data obviously must be kept and organized so that taxes may be paid. Accountants furthermore produce information (e.g., financial reports) for use by investors, creditors, and others. But accountants can also provide the manager with information about the cost of operation, the value of assets, the value of inputs that are produced within the firm, and so on. In fact, the accounting department should be regarded as the principal source of financial information within the business.

Businesses traditionally have turned to their accounting departments for financial data on their activities and an analysis of those data. Increasingly, managers expect their accountants to provide information that (1) helps to identify the existence of problems, (2) provides a description of alternative courses of action, and (3) helps to evaluate these alternatives. In most of the previous chapters, we have simply assumed that the relevant information was available. We did not worry about the source of the information. If, however, the manager wants to assure himself that the appropriate information is available, he must coordinate with his accountant. The manager may not know precisely what information can be provided. Moreover, he may not even know just what information is necessary. Candid discussions with the accounting staff may resolve these difficulties.

14.1

BREAK-EVEN ANALYSIS

Suppose ABC, Inc., is considering a new product line: medium-priced men's wallets. In order to be fairly competitive in this market, the marketing staff has advised selling each wallet for $10. The fixed cost for the necessary plant and equipment is $100,000 per year. Direct (variable) materials and labor costs will amount to $6 per wallet according to the purchasing and production departments.

Question Should ABC, Inc., add medium-priced men's wallets to its product line?

Answer The answer to this question depends, of course, upon whether ABC, Inc., can sell a large enough volume of wallets to justify the investment in plant and equipment. Break-even analysis can be helpful to the manager who must face this decision. Consequently, he may ask the accounting department to perform this analysis.

Break-even analysis informs the manager of the quantity at which he will begin to make a positive profit. Profit equals total revenue less total cost, or

$$\Pi = TR - TC$$

In this case,

$$\Pi = 10Q - (100{,}000 + 6Q) \tag{14.1}$$

Accountants usually assume that total revenue and total cost are each linear functions of output. They are graphed in panel (a) of Figure 14.1. Equation (14.1) can be simplified to

$$\Pi = 4Q - 100{,}000 \tag{14.2}$$

To find the point at which profit equals zero, set $\Pi = 0$ in equation (14.2) and solve for output.

$$0 = 4Q - 100{,}000$$

$$Q = 25{,}000$$

The firm experiences a loss if output falls below 25,000 and experiences a profit if output exceeds 25,000. This is seen in panel (a) of Figure 14.1. Consequently, the manager must turn to his marketing department to assess the chances of selling more than 25,000 wallets at the price of $10.

FIGURE 14.1 The determination of the break-even quantity for a competitive firm with a linear total cost curve.

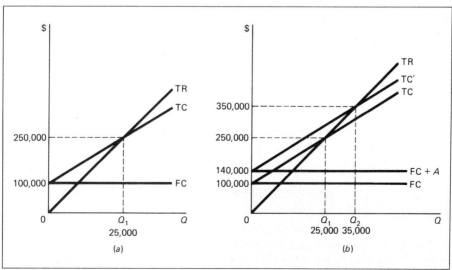

Since definitive answers are unlikely to guarantee that result, the manager must trust his intuition and judgment. But he had been aided in this by the break-even chart.

Question   Suppose the sales promotion expert promises that a market penetration of 30,000 at a price of $10 is virtually certain if ABC, Inc., spends $40,000 on advertising. Should the manager authorize that expenditure and add the wallets to his product line?

Answer   No. The accounting department will quickly point out that the *old* break-even chart did show that sales of 30,000 wallets would yield a profit. But a new break-even chart is now necessary. In panel (b) of Figure 14.1, the $40,000 advertising expenditure (A) has been added to the $100,000 in fixed costs. As a result, the new total cost (TC') starts at $140,000 and our new break-even quantity will be 35,000 wallets. Consequently, the promised quantity of 30,000 wallets would be insufficient to warrant the investment in advertising and productive capacity.

The break-even chart in panel (a) of Figure 14.1 suggests that sales in excess of 25,000 will generate total revenues that are greater than total costs (assuming no advertising). We can see that the difference between total revenue and total cost, which is profit, gets larger as sales expand. This implies, in the absence of other considerations, that profit is maximized by producing an infinite quantity. Since this conclusion is ridiculous, most break-even analysts assume that this process is only viable until full capacity is reached, say, a maximum quantity equal to Q_M. Thus, according to break-even analysis, the firm's profits will be maximized when the firm is operating at full capacity.

APPLICATIONS OF BREAK-EVEN ANALYSIS   In the example we have been considering, break-even analysis was used to assist in determining whether a new product should be introduced. Additionally, we analyzed whether an advertising expenditure was sensible. There are, however, many other kinds of questions that can benefit from break-even analysis. For example, suppose the manager is trying to decide whether the quality of an existing product should be changed. A quality change will result in different costs and may alter the price that the firm can charge for the product. The accounting department can perform a break-even analysis under the altered cost and demand conditions. This will assist the manager in reaching his decision. Almost every decision that will change costs and/or revenues can be analyzed through the careful use of break-even analysis.

SOME QUALIFICATIONS AND REFINEMENTS   In the above example, the total revenue and total cost functions were assumed to be linear. These assumptions may be challenged. For most decisions that involve small changes, linear approximations to nonlinear functions will perform satisfactorily. Some decisions, however, involve substantial changes that require more precision than linear approximations can provide. In these instances, one may wish to refine the break-even chart to include nonlinear functions. For example, in Figure 14.2, the total cost curve (TC) is consistent with the U-shaped average cost curves that we are used to seeing. Figure 14.2 shows two break-even points. Quantities Q_2 and Q_3 generate revenues that are equal to the costs of production. All quantities between Q_2 and Q_3 yield positive profits. One of these intermediate points—specifically, Q_1—yields maximum profits.[1] The vertical distance between TR and TC is greatest at this point. We have retained a linear total revenue curve on the assumption that the firm can sell all it wants at the market-determined price. In other words, we have assumed that the firm is doing business in a competitive industry.

If the firm has some market power, the demand curve will be negatively sloped. In other words, the manager must lower the product price in order to sell larger quantities. This may make the total revenue curve nonlinear. A nonlinear total revenue curve is shown in Figure 14.3. Again, there are two break-even points: Q_1 and Q_2. At an output of Q_3, the manager will maximize the firm's profits.

In all of the break-even analyses, the accounting department reports and charts the cost data that the manager requests. There are some types of cost information that accountants do not normally provide. Consequently, a manager must give explicit instructions in order to obtain this information. In the next section, we shall see that without proper instructions it is possible for

---

[1]At Q_1, the slope of the TC curve is equal to the slope of the TR curve. As we know, this means that marginal revenue equals marginal cost, which is a familiar optimization rule.

FIGURE 14.2   The determination of the break-even quantity for a competitive firm with a nonlinear total cost curve.

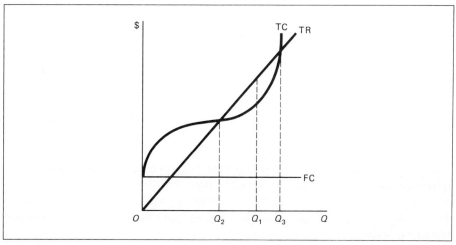

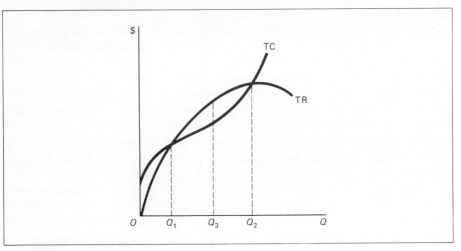

FIGURE 14.3   The determination of the
break-even quantity for a monopolist with a
nonlinear total cost curve.

the manager to use inappropriate cost data and thus to make the wrong
decision.

14.2

**DEFINING COSTS
APPROPRIATELY**

It is the manager's responsibility to
see that she is provided with the cost
data that suit her needs. In particular, she must assure herself that costs
are being allocated appropriately and
that all relevant costs are being considered. The preceding analyses in this
book have been based upon the implicit assumption that the accounting
department has, in fact, provided the right cost data. At this point, however,
we should note that the accountants are quite good at providing certain
kinds of cost information, but require some direction and assistance in other
areas. Appropriate managerial decisions depend upon correctly measured
costs.

For an economist, the relevant concept of cost is captured by market alternatives. Many inputs are purchased in the marketplace and used immediately in the firm's production or distribution process. Since these inputs
were offered for sale on the open market, the alternative cost or opportunity
cost of any specific employment is obviously equal to the market price of the
input. For example, suppose the manager of Super Sub buys ham for the submarine sandwiches that are its specialty. Anyone could have purchased that
ham. Consequently, the opportunity cost of Super Sub's using that ham is
given by the price that was paid for the ham. For these types of inputs, i.e.,
those that are purchased in the open market, the accountants can provide accurate and appropriate cost data for managerial decisions. These costs are
called *explicit* costs.

There are other costs that a business may incur that do not involve explicit payments. These are called *implicit* costs and involve a firm's use of its own assets. As an example, suppose Super Sub operates out of a small building that it owns and provides a delivery service with an automobile that it owns. The manager could increase her revenue by renting out the building and car. By choosing not to rent out these assets, the manager forgoes this rental income. Consequently, the opportunity cost of Super Sub's employing these assets is given by the prices that the assets could command in the market, i.e., the market alternative. If the manager does not include the lease value of Super Sub's building and the rental value of its car in her total cost, she will understate the cost of the submarine sandwiches that she is selling. The implicit costs of a business can be considerable. In addition to the rental value of tangible assets, implicit costs include the implicit interest that the owner's capital investment could earn and the alternative income that the owner could earn by working for someone else.

The accountant tends to regard costs as an outward flow of assets. His focus is sharpest when dealing with historical explicit costs incurred by a business. He will need some help in providing full cost information because of the presence of implicit costs. But without considering implicit costs, a manager cannot make accurate managerial decisions. Thus, some effort must be made to measure the implicit costs being incurred by the firm. We can see the importance of this in a break-even example.

Example   Sam's Service Station sells gasoline for $1.25 per gallon. Sam himself manages the service station. He pays $500 per month rent for the physical facility and $1,000 per month in salaries to his employees who pump gas. Sam must pay $1.00 per gallon for the gasoline. He wants to know how many gallons of gasoline he must sell per month to break even. One answer is 6,000 gallons, which can be calculated as follows:

Total revenue is $1.25G where G is the number of gallons sold and total costs are $1,500 for rent and salaries plus $1G. Then total revenue equals total cost at 6,000 gallons:

$$\$1.25G = \$1,500 + \$1.00G$$

$$(\$1.25 - 1.00)G = \$1,500$$

$$G = 6,000$$

But this answer is wrong because Sam's salary has been forgotten. Certainly, Sam would consider this to be a serious omission. The correct answer depends upon Sam's opportunities. Suppose that he could earn $800 per month managing someone else's service station. Then the correct calculation would be :

$$\$1.25G = \$1,500 + 800 + 1.00G$$

$$(\$1.25 - 1.00)G = \$2,300$$

$$G = 9,200$$

This is a substantial difference!

The accuracy of managerial decisions depends not only on the measurement of all relevant costs but also on the appropriate allocation of costs.

In many instances, the allocation of costs is a relatively straightforward matter. For example, the manager of Super Sub purchases 100 pounds of ham and 50 pounds of beef each week. In order to price her subs properly, she needs to know that it costs, say, $0.10 more to make a sub with roast beef in it than to make a sub with ham in it. This information can be obtained from her records of ham purchases and beef purchases if she knows how much ham or beef is used to make each sub.

There are a number of other situations in which additional information is necessary before costs can be correctly allocated.

Question   Suppose that the Amalgamated Phosphate Company needs to borrow $1 to pay for the equipment required to mine *each* ton of phosphate per year. That is, if a company mines 50,000 tons of phosphate per year, it must borrow $50,000 for the equipment. The phosphate is sold either under a long-term contract, where the firm's revenue per ton is certain, or in the spot market, where the firm's revenue per ton in any given year depends on supply and demand conditions in that year. The interest rate that banks charge the Amalgamated Phosphate Company is given by

$$r = .10 + (.02)\alpha$$

where α = fraction of total tons which are sold on the spot market. (a) Find the total annual interest payment (do not worry about the complications associated with paying off the principal) if the company sells 500,000 tons per year under long-term contract and 1.5 million tons per year on the spot market. (b) The accounting department is charged with allocating interest costs to long-term sales and to spot market sales in such a way as to guide decision making. How would you do this?

Answer   (a) Since the firm sells 1.5 million out of 2 million total tons on the spot market, α equals .75. Accordingly,

$$r = .10 + (.02)(.75)$$

$$= .115$$

That is, the firm pays an interest rate of 11.5 percent. The annual interest payment (in perpetuity) equals

$$.115(2,000,000) = \$230,000$$

(b) If the firm sold only under a long-term contract, the interest payments on the equipment necessary for the 500,000 tons produced under the long-term contract would equal $50,000 [= \$500,000(.10)]$. It seems reasonable to allocate the remaining $180,000 in interest payments to the 1.5 million tons sold on the spot market, and this in fact is the correct allocation. At the base interest rate (10 percent), the equipment necessary to produce this rock generates $150,000 in interest payments each year. Furthermore, Amalgamated Phosphate pays a 1.5 percent higher interest rate on the *entire* $2 million loan *because* three-quarters of its production goes to the spot market; this amounts to $30,000 [= $2,000,000(.015)] each year. Thus $180,000 in annual interest payments are attributable to the 1.5 million tons of phosphate rock mined for the spot market each year. Allocating three-quarters of the total interest payments to production for the spot market would be incorrect.

In this problem, we have been able to allocate interest payments between production under long-term contract and production for the spot market because we know how the interest rate is related to the share of production going to the spot market. Similar information may be called for in other problems involving the allocation of costs.

14.3

HISTORICAL COSTS VERSUS REPLACEMENT COSTS

In the previous section, we were concerned with the possibility of overlooking certain relevant costs. Specifically, we found that the implicit costs of using owned assets should not be ignored. When these costs are forgotten, the cost accounting is incorrect and appropriate managerial decisions are more difficult to make. A similar problem arises when asset values are changing over time. We may gain a better appreciation for this difficulty from the following problem.

Question In December, the purchasing agent for MGH Publishers bought a year's supply of paper for $12 million. Each month, the firm produces 800,000 books. If they are all the same size and therefore require the same amount of paper, a cost accountant may suggest a paper cost of $1.25 per book:

$1,000,000 \div 800,000 = $1.25

Is this correct?

Answer The arithmetic is correct but the economics may not be. In fact, the suggestion is correct only in the event that the price of paper remains constant during the entire year. In contrast, suppose that the price of paper rises by 1 percent per month. This means that the paper used in January had a historical cost of $1 million but a replacement cost of $1.01 million:

$1,000,000(1.01) = $1,010,000

On the basis of replacement costs, the books produced have a paper cost of

$1,010,000 \div 800,000 = $1.2625

which is not such a big difference. But by October, the replacement cost of the paper is

$1,000,000(1.10) = $1,100,000

and the per book paper cost is

$$\frac{\$1,100,000}{800,000} = \$1.375$$

which is a 10 percent increase over the per book paper cost calculated on the basis of historical costs.

The conflict between using historical costs or replacement costs arises because of the time lag between the purchase of an input and its use. If the input price changes during this time lag, a choice must be made between historical and replacement costs. Resolution of the conflict should depend upon the principle that opportunity costs are relevant. In an intertemporal context, the opportunity cost of using an input out of inventory is that input's replacement cost. Thus, the cost accountant should use replacement costs. More importantly, the manager should use replacement costs in production and pricing decisions. If he fails to follow this advice, incorrect decisions are bound to follow.

INVENTORY VALUATION: LIFO VERSUS FIFO   The dispute between historical costs and replacement costs surfaces in the distinction between LIFO and FIFO methods of drawing down inventory. It is normally a good practice to rotate inventories of inputs. Thus, those supplies that have been in inventory the longest will be used before the more recently acquired inputs. In other words, on the basis of *physical* inventory control, most firms will use a FIFO (first in first out) procedure. But the *accounting* procedure may deviate from this practice. A firm that follows the LIFO (last in first out) costing procedure uses the price most recently paid for an input as the current cost. In contrast, a firm that uses the FIFO costing method uses the price paid on the oldest units in its inventory as the current cost.

We can see that the LIFO concept approximates replacement costs. In our earlier example, MGH Publishers bought its paper requirements at yearly intervals. As we saw, price changes caused the original purchase price to deviate substantially from replacement costs. In other cases, however, inputs are purchased at frequent intervals—monthly, weekly, or even daily. When inputs are purchased frequently, using the LIFO method will result in input valuations that are close to replacement costs. In contrast, the FIFO method is the historical cost method of inventory valuation. In a period of rising input prices, FIFO provides deceptively high profit figures that are unrealistic. A dramatic example may make this clear and highlight the sort of managerial error that can accompany an incorrect cost accounting.

Suppose that the Fine Jewelry Company purchased gold at $200 per ounce. Partly on the basis of this input price, it sold a small gold pendant, using 1 ounce of gold, for $400. These pendants generated profits of $100 each. Subsequently, the market price of gold rose to $600 per ounce. Since Fine Jewelry used the FIFO accounting method, it thought that its pendants still contained $200 worth of gold. As a result, it continued to sell the gold pendants for $400 until its inventory of $200-per-ounce gold was depleted. Not surprisingly, sales of these pendants were brisk. Did the manager of Fine Jewelry make a mistake in producing or pricing these pendants? It is not hard to find a more profitable alternative than the one he adopted. The manager could have sold the inventory of gold for $600 per ounce. This would have provided a profit of $400 per ounce. Instead, he produced pendants that generated only $100 in profit per ounce used. Consequently, he was replaced by a manager who endorsed the LIFO method of inventory, which more closely measures the opportunity costs of using inputs.

It must be understood that the relevant replacement cost is the one that exhausts all efficiencies. It is not sensible to compare efficient prices of inputs with inefficient prices. Consider this final problem.

Question Suppose that the Super Staple Company gets an exceptional buy on the wire it uses for making staples. As a result, its inventory of wire is sufficient for an entire year's worth of output. On the basis of the bargain price paid for the wire and storage costs, each box of staples requires $0.25 worth of wire for production. If Super Staple had purchased its requirements on a monthly basis, the wire costs per box of staples would be $0.30. How should Super Staple's accountants value the wire actually used?

A PROBLEM IN VALUING
INTERNATIONAL ASSETS*

International business provides an interesting problem in the valuation of assets owing to changing exchange rates. The Financial Accounting Standards Board (FASB) has been grappling with this problem for some time without an obvious solution. Currently, the foreign currency translation rule, FASB-8, is extraordinarily unpopular with business executives. Let's see why.

Prior to consolidation with the U.S. parent, each foreign subsidiary's financial report is expressed in its so-called functional currency. This is normally the currency in which most of the subsidiary's business is conducted. Subsequently, the subsidiary's current monetary assets (cash and accounts receivable), its current liabilities, and its long-term debt are converted into dollars at *current* exchange rates. In contrast, the fixed assets (plant, equipment, and inventory) are converted into dollars at the exchange rates that were in effect at the time that the assets were acquired. Any gains or losses that result from the conversion must be included in the U.S. parent's income statement. Since these gains and losses may be reversed later due to changes in exchange rates, the FASB-8 rule distorts the parent's income. In addition, the financial statements lack economic reality because some of the subsidiary's costs are not being properly valued. This occurs for two reasons: (1) Historical costs rather than replacement costs are being used. (2) The historical costs are being converted into dollars at irrelevant exchange rates.

Problem: Design and defend an appropriate revision of the FASB-8 rule.

Source: "Why FASB-8 Reform Isn't Easy," *Business Week,* Dec. 22, 1980, pp. 70–71.

Answer The appropriate cost to impute for the wire is $0.25. This is not a case where opportunity costs diverge from explicit costs. The manager of Super Staple determined that the optimal order size was equal to a full year's supply. The fact that less efficient order sizes would raise the per box cost of wire does not mean that a different valuation should be used. There is no indication that the market value of the wire has changed. In fact, the $0.25 cost is based upon purchasing efficiencies and, consequently, should be regarded as an efficient price. A less efficient purchasing pattern generates a higher cost of $0.30. But this should be viewed as an inefficient price and should not be used.

14.4

VALUATION OF INTANGIBLE ASSETS

The accounting department also can provide the manager with information related to the firm's intangible capital (e.g., goodwill, advertising capital, and firm-specific human capital). As we shall see, this information can be important in obtaining loans, obtaining a fair price when a firm is sold, or allocating inputs.

ADVERTISING CAPITAL Advertising often affects sales with a lag. This may be because it takes time for consumers to assimilate the information that advertising provides or to adjust their spending patterns. Whatever the reason, advertising in current and past periods produces additional sales in future periods and consequently additional profits in future periods. There are a number of situations in which it is useful to know how large these future profits will be.

The manager of the Accu-Time Watch Company has estimated, using the regression analysis described in Chapter 3, that the demand function for Accu-Time watches is given by the following:

$$Q_{w,t} = 50{,}015 - 436P_{w,t} + 23I_t + 4177a_{t-1} + 1546a_{t-2} + 389a_{t-3}$$

where $Q_{w,t}$ equals the quantity of Accu-Time watches sold in year t, $P_{w,t}$ equals the price of Accu-Time watches in year t, I_t equals income in year t, a_{t-1} equals the number of minutes of prime time television advertising in year $t-1$, a_{t-2} equals the number of minutes of prime time television in year $t-2$, and a_{t-3} equals the number of minutes of prime-time television advertising in period $t-3$. Some values of a_{t-1}, a_{t-2}, and a_{t-3} are given in Table 14.1. This lag structure is the result of experimentation that shows that advertising lagged 4, 5, or even more years does not significantly affect sales.

The manager wants to calculate the value in 1981 of profits due to advertising that occurred in 1978, 1979, and 1980. In 1981, advertising lagged 1 year (i.e., advertising in 1980) is estimated to produce 563,895 [= 4,177(135)] additional sales. Similarly, in 1981 advertising lagged 2 years (i.e., advertising in 1979) is calculated to yield 177,790 [= 1,546(115)] additional sales, and advertising lagged 3 years (i.e., advertising in 1978) is estimated to bring about

54,460 [= 389(140)] extra sales. Thus, the total additional sales in 1981 stemming from previous advertising equal

$$\Delta Q_{81} = 4{,}177(135) + 1{,}546(115) + 389(140)$$

$$= 563{,}895 + 177{,}790 + 54{,}460$$

$$= 796{,}145$$

Similar logic can be used to calculate the additional sales that are expected in 1982 as a result of advertising that occurred in 1979 and 1980. The anticipated additional sales in 1982 equal

$$\Delta Q_{82} = 1{,}546(135) + 389(115)$$

$$= 208{,}710 + 44{,}735$$

$$= 253{,}445$$

TABLE 14.1
MINUTES OF PRIME TIME
TELEVISION ADVERTISING

YEAR	CURRENT (a_t)	LAGGED 1 YEAR (a_{t-1})	LAGGED 2 YEARS (a_{t-2})	LAGGED 3 YEARS (a_{t-3})
1965	108	99	114	106
1966	115	108	99	114
1967	132	115	108	99
1968	124	132	115	108
1969	121	124	132	115
1970	101	121	124	132
1971	113	101	121	124
1972	94	113	101	121
1973	60	94	113	101
1974	75	60	94	113
1975	80	75	60	94
1976	126	80	75	60
1977	117	126	80	75
1978	140	117	126	80
1979	115	140	117	126
1980	135	115	140	117
1981		135	115	140
1982			135	115
1983				135

Finally, the additional sales that are expected in 1983 from advertising in 1980 equal

$$\Delta Q_{83} = 389(135)$$

$$= 52{,}515$$

But how much does the present value of profits as of 1981 rise as a result of these additional sales? If it costs $80 to make an Accu-Time watch that sells for $100, then each additional sale produces $20 in extra profits. The manager believes that this "profit per watch" will not change over time. Accordingly, the present value of additional profits at a 10 percent interest rate equals

$$PV\ (\Delta\Pi) = (P - MC_p)_{81}\Delta Q_{81} + \frac{(P - MC_p)_{82}\Delta Q_{82}}{1 + r} + \frac{(P - MC_p)_{83}\Delta Q_{83}}{(1 + r)^2}$$

$$= 20(796{,}145) + \frac{20(253{,}445)}{1.10} + \frac{20(52{,}515)}{(1.10)^2}$$

$$= 15{,}922{,}900 + 4{,}608{,}091 + 868{,}017$$

$$= \$21{,}399{,}008$$

Consequently, advertising in 1978–1980 is estimated to produce $21,399,008 worth of higher profits in 1981, 1982, and 1983. This information can be used by banks in determining whether or not to lend money to the Accu-Time Watch Company and also can be used by potential buyers in determining a reasonable value for the company.

GOODWILL   Many consumers will return to a particular store if they have been treated well there in the past or if they trust the store to deal with them reputably. Customers return to a store because of the goodwill that they feel toward it. These return visits—and their associated profits—are the product of previous expenditures on goodwill-producing policies such as no-questions-asked refunds, cheerful personnel, and product quality control.

The manager can ascertain the present value of the additional profits due to the goodwill that is felt toward his store in much the same way as he calculates the profits associated with advertising capital, which was just described. The value of the goodwill that is felt toward a firm is part of that firm's correctly calculated net worth. This information therefore is useful to the firm's potential creditors and to potential investors in the firm.

FIRM-SPECIFIC HUMAN CAPITAL   Another, often unmeasured, component of a firm's net worth is related to the firm's co-ownership of firm-specific human capital. In Chapter 9, we saw that the employee and the firm will *share* in paying for the cost of firm-specific human capital. This is because under any other arrangement either the owner or the employee has no incentive to continue the employee's attachment to the firm, and investment in firm-specific human capital is more beneficial the longer the employee stays with the firm.

Let's now consider a $10,000 investment in firm-specific human capital that yields an 8 percent annual return. If the firm pays for one-quarter of the cost, it does so expecting to receive one-quarter of the annual return, or $200 per year. There are a number of points that can be made regarding accounting for the amount of firm-specific human capital that the firm co-owns.

The firm's expected annual return on its investment ($200) is very much a part of the cost of employing this worker after the investment has been made. If the manager sets input levels so that the employee's annual earnings (wt_w) equal the value of the annual marginal product that she produces $(MR)(MP_L)$, then the employee's addition to current total revenue equals the employee's addition to current total costs. The employee is not producing enough additional total revenue to also cover the required return on the firm's investment in the employee's firm-specific skills. Profits are maximized when

$$(MR)(MP_L) = wt_w + 200$$

That is, the value of the marginal product equals the employee's earnings *plus* the implicit return to the firm on its investment in the employee's skills. The accounting department can help to remind the manager that there is an implicit return that needs to be taken into account.

Keeping track of the amount of firm-specific capital in a business generates additional information about the business's net worth. In the above example, the firm that has already made the $2,500 investment in the employee's firm-specific skills did so expecting that employee to bring in a $200 net return each year. The future stream of $200 annual net returns is part of the company's net worth at some point in time.

Finally, information about the net returns that a firm can expect to receive in future years from an employee can guide personnel decisions. A manager needs to be aware when he decides whether or not to keep an employee whether the firm would be precluded from receiving a sizable return on its investment in that employee's firm-specific human capital if the employee left the firm.

14.5

TRANSFER PRICING

The firm's long-run average cost curve is thought to be positively sloped at high levels of output due to managerial diseconomies of large scale. This means that as the firm gets larger, the managerial skills and abilities in the firm become strained. Some loss of control may occur, and errors can invade the decision-making process at the top levels. Top executives become too far removed from serious operational problems. Moreover, the layers of bureaucratic hierarchy slow down the decision-making process. Generally, the managerial function simply is performed less efficiently. Since this decline in efficiency raises per unit costs, it has an adverse effect on profit. Consequently, there is an incentive for someone to devise a way around this loss in efficiency. The response has been to decentralize the large firm.

In a decentralized firm, operating authority is given to territorial divisions or product line divisions. A central staff is retained for policy analysis and advice, but it is not supposed to provide operating direction. The operating divisions are set up as separate profit centers. Each profit center will be under the direction of a manager whose performance is evaluated by her division's profit and loss statement. The manager's salary and bonus will depend upon her division's performance.

The purpose of decentralization is to increase the profit for the entire firm by making the managerial function more efficient. But the rewards for each division's manager depend upon her division's performance. This may create a conflict between what is good for one profit center and what is good for the firm as a whole. For example, suppose that the Tubby Tire Company makes and distributes automobile tires. The profits of the production division will depend to some extent upon the transfer price that it charges the distribution division for the tires that it produces. But the higher the transfer price, the higher the costs of the distribution division. An inappropriate transfer price may maximize the production division's profits but will result in decisions of the distribution division that reduce the total profits of Tubby Tire. Consequently, the firm should use a transfer price that maximizes profits of the firm as a whole.

MAXIMUM PROFITS   If the Tubby Tire Company has some market power, then the demand for its tires can be described by D in Figure 14.4. The associated marginal revenue is denoted by MR. For convenience, we have assumed that the marginal cost of producing tires MC_p is constant, as is the marginal cost of distributing the tires MC_D. Tubby Tire's marginal cost of production and distribution MC is given by the sum of the two components

FIGURE 14.4   Tubby Tire Company
maximizes profit by selling Q_0 units at price
P_0.

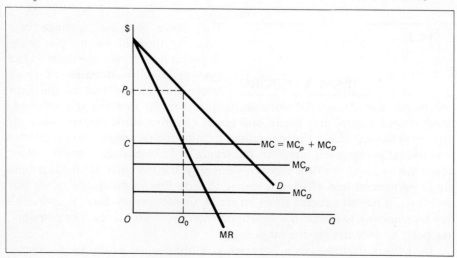

$$MC = MC_p + MC_D$$

For the firm as a whole, profits are maximized by producing where marginal cost MC equals marginal revenue MR. In this case, an output of Q_0 tires should be produced and distributed at a price of P_0. Profits will be equal to

$$\Pi = \Pi_P + \Pi_D$$

We shall see that a divisionalized Tubby Tire Company may run into problems in achieving these maximum profits.

DIVISIONAL PROFIT MAXIMIZATION   Suppose that the tires produced must be sold as Tubby Tires through the distribution division. Similarly, suppose that the distribution division can only buy Tubby Tires. The production manager must find the demand for her tires. In Figure 14.5, we have subtracted the marginal distribution costs MC_D from the marginal revenue curve MR and labeled it d. This is the distribution division's demand curve for the Tubby Tire production division's output. Let's see why.

The distribution division will maximize its profits by distributing where the sum of its marginal cost MC_D and the transfer price it pays for tires is equal to marginal revenue MR:

$$MR = MC_D + P_T$$

where P_T represents the transfer price. If we subtract the marginal distribution costs MC_D from marginal revenue, we will have the maximum transfer price that the distribution division will pay for various quantities of tires:

$$MR - MC_D = P_T$$

FIGURE 14.5   If each division maximizes its profit, Q_T tires are sold at price P_1, resulting in lower profit for Tubby Tire.

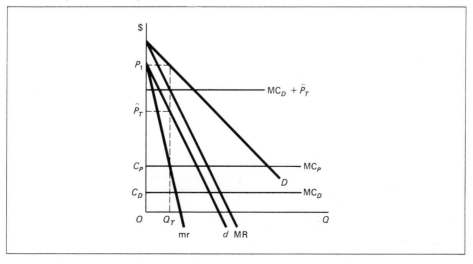

Thus, this is the derived demand for tires from the production division (labeled d in Figure 14.5).

The manager of the production division will attempt to maximize her division's profits by equating the marginal revenue mr associated with the derived demand d to her marginal production costs MC_P. As a result, she produces Q_T tires and charges a transfer price of $\hat{P}_T$, as shown in Figure 14.5. The distribution division's marginal cost curve is the sum of MC_D and $\hat{P}_T$. Divisional profit maximization leads the distribution manager to distribute Q_T tires and charge price P_1.

Tubby Tire's profit will be equal to the sum of the divisional profits:

$$\Pi = \Pi_P + \Pi_D$$

These profits are easily calculated. For production, the profits are

$$\Pi_P = (\hat{P}_T - C_P)Q_T$$

For distribution, the profits are

$$\Pi_D = (P_1 - C_D - \hat{P}_T)Q_T$$

The total profits are

$$\Pi = (P_1 - C_D - \hat{P}_T)Q_T + (\hat{P}_T - C_P)Q_T = (P_1 - C_D - C_P)Q_T$$

A careful study of Figure 14.5 reveals that profits are reduced as a result of divisionalization. We can see this because the firm is operating where marginal revenue is equal to $MC_D + \hat{P}_T$, which is higher than $MC_D + MC_P$. Consequently, too few Tubby Tires are being sold and too high a price is being charged to maximize overall firm profits.

Question What is the optimal transfer price in this case?

Answer The manager of the production division should be instructed to charge a transfer price equal to the marginal cost of producing the tires. If $P_T = MC_P$, then the distribution division will equate marginal revenue to $MC_D + MC_P$ and Tubby Tire will have the profits shown in Figure 14.4:

$$\Pi = (P_0 - MC_p - MC_D)Q_0 \tag{14.3}$$

This solution causes something of a problem. Specifically, the distribution manager looks like a hero while the production manager looks as if she contributed very little. Common sense suggests that this is deceptive. In fact, both managers contributed to the overall profit. The economic reason why the production manager's performance looks relatively bad is that she set the transfer price as though she were a perfect competitor. The Tubby Tire top executives will have to take this into account when determining the rewards for the two managers. The accounting department can provide a valuable service to all decision makers by providing precise cost data so that the correct transfer prices can be used for the maximization of overall firm profits.

In addition, the accounting department can show the top executives that the location of the profit is arbitrary. One profit-maximizing solution to the transfer pricing problem was for the production manager to set her price at marginal cost while the distribution manager set his price to maximize his division's profit. We could solve the problem a different way by asking the distribution manager to act as a perfect competitor and set his price at marginal cost. If the production manager is allowed to maximize her division's profit, Tubby Tire will experience the same profits under both solutions. To see this we must examine the influence that this will have upon the derived demand. In Figure 14.6, we have subtracted the marginal distribution costs from demand curve D. The resulting curve, labeled d, is the derived demand for tires by the distribution division. Since the distribution manager must charge a price equal to the sum of the marginal distribution costs and the transfer price, derived demand d represents the maximum price that the distribution division can pay for various quantities of tires.

The production manager maximized profit by equating MC_p and mr, the curve marginal to derived demand d. A careful examination of Figure 14.6 reveals that she will produce Q_0 tires and sell them for P_T, which is equal to $P_0 - MC_D$. Thus the distribution manager will distribute Q_0 tires at price P_0. Profit at the production stage is $(P_T - MC_P)Q_0$. Note, however, that $P_T = P_0 - MC_D$. By substituting for P_T, we see that profit at the production stage is $(P_0 - MC_D - MC_P)Q_0$, which is the same as that shown in equation (14.3). Thus, Tubby Tires can maximize its profits this way, too.

FIGURE 14.6   If the distribution division sets prices competitively and the production division sets prices monopolistically, Tubby Tire will achieve maximum profits producing Q_0 tires.

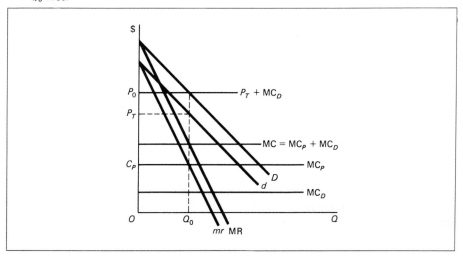

It is apparent that Tubby Tire's profits are the same whether (1) the production division acts as a competitive firm and the distribution division acts as a monopolist, or (2) the production division acts as a monopolist and the distribution division acts as a competitive firm. In the former solution, the distribution manager looks like a hero, and in the latter solution, the production manager looks like a heroine. Clearly, in a divisionalized firm, the location of the profits is arbitrary and should not affect material compensation. Nevertheless, one of these two solutions must be adopted if Tubby Tire is to maximize its profits. It is in this sense that the appropriate transfer price is necessary for company profits to be maximized. Transfer pricing arises in other situations, and in each of these the principle is clear: a transfer price must be chosen that will maximize the company's profit.

14.6 OPTIMAL METHOD OF DEPRECIATION: TAX CONSIDERATIONS

Suppose that the manager of XYZ, Ltd., is considering a $10,000 capital investment that has an economic life of 5 years. In calculating the profit each year, the accountants will deduct depreciation expense. Now, depreciation expense is an accounting artifact that is supposed to capture the use of productive services from fixed assets. It reflects the fact that these fixed assets wear out or become obsolete over time. On the basis of our earlier discussion of opportunity costs, it should be clear that the economically correct measure of depreciation must equal the difference between the asset's market value before and after its use. But depreciation is seldom measured this way in practice. Expediency and taxes on business income have more to do with the depreciation schedule than does economic analysis.

Depreciation expense is tax deductible. Consequently, an alert manager should examine the alternative methods of depreciation to determine which method should be used in the tax books so that the aftertax profits of the firm are maximized. The accounting department can be relied upon to prepare an analysis of the permissible alternatives. We shall consider only three methods of depreciation. The principles that are employed, however, carry over to any depreciation schedule that the Internal Revenue Service permits.

In Chapter 8, we examined the influence of taxation and depreciation expenses on the net-present-value calculations for an investment. Recall that the *aftertax* net present value of an investment can be written as

$$\text{NPV}_{\text{AT}} = \sum_{t=1}^{n} \frac{(1-T)R_t}{(1+r)^t} + \sum_{t=1}^{n} \frac{TD_t}{(1+r)^t} - I$$

Where T is the tax rate, R_t represents the net receipts before deducting depreciation at time t, r is the discount rate, D_t is the depreciation expense at time t, and I is the initial outlay. The first term on the right-hand side is the present value of the aftertax net receipts. The second term represents the present value of the tax shield, i.e., that portion of total receipts that is shielded from taxes due to the allowance of a depreciation expense. Whenever the sum of these two components exceeds the initial outlay, the investment should be made.

MAXIMIZING NET PRESENT VALUE   In order to maximize the net present value of a project after taxes, we can see that the accountant should select the depreciation schedule that maximizes the present value of the tax shield. Since we have taken the tax rate T to be a constant, maximizing the present value of the tax shield requires maximizing the present value of the stream of depreciation expenses. This can be seen by writing the second term above as

$$\sum_{t=1}^{n} \frac{TD_t}{(1+r)^t} = T \sum_{t=1}^{n} \frac{D_t}{(1+r)^t}$$

Question   What value for D_t will maximize the present value of the tax shield?

Answer   The accountant should depreciate the asset as quickly as possible. This means writing off the entire investment in the first year. In that case, D_1 will equal I and $D_2, \ldots, D_n$ will all equal zero. For obvious reasons, the Internal Revenue Service (IRS) will not permit this for most capital expenditures. As a result, the accountant will be forced to use the minimum number of years prescribed by the IRS for the asset class in question. But subject to that constraint, the accountant will attempt to accelerate the depreciation schedule as much as possible.

METHODS OF DEPRECIATION   We shall examine three methods of depreciation and determine which one will maximize the net present value of a specific project. In our opening example, XYZ, Ltd., can invest $10,000 in a project. Suppose that IRS will not permit a more rapid write-off than 5 years. Within that constraint, our accountant can select among the following depreciation schedules: straight line, sum of the year's digits, and double declining balance.

The easiest and most natural method of depreciating an asset is the straight-line method. It assumes a uniform reduction in the asset value over its prescribed life. In that case, depreciation in each year is the same and equals $1/n$ times the initial outlay where n is the number of years:

$$D_t = \frac{I}{n}$$

In our example, the accountant for XYZ, Ltd., would record depreciation as

$$D_t = \frac{\$10,000}{5} = \$2,000$$

in each year.

The sum of year's digits method is a depreciation method that accelerates the amounts written off. If the economic value of an asset falls more during the early years of its life than during the later years, this procedure makes some sense. A more likely reason for allowing this method is that it offers an investment incentive to business. In any event, our first step in devising this schedule is to calculate the sum of the year's digits for the investment life in question:

$$5 + 4 + 3 + 2 + 1 = 15$$

Then, the depreciation schedule is as follows:

$$D_1 = \left(\frac{5}{15}\right) I$$

$$D_2 = \left(\frac{4}{15}\right) I$$

$$D_3 = \left(\frac{3}{15}\right) I$$

$$D_4 = \left(\frac{2}{15}\right) I$$

$$D_5 = \left(\frac{1}{15}\right) I$$

For our investment of $10,000, the yearly depreciation expenses are shown in Table 14.2. Although the pattern is quite different from that generated by the straight-line method, the totals are the same. We can see clearly that using the sum of the year's digits method permits larger deductions in the first 2 years and smaller deductions in the last 2 years.

Finally, the double-declining-balance method is another method of accelerated depreciation. The logic for the depreciation formula is not obvious, but its purpose is to permit larger deductions in the early years than in later years. The double-declining-balance method accelerates the straight-line schedule. Instead of deducting $(1/n)I$ in the first year, the firm can deduct

TABLE 14.2
ALTERNATIVE DEPRECIATION SCHEDULES

YEAR	STRAIGHT LINE	SUM OF YEAR'S DIGITS	DOUBLE DECLINING BALANCE
1	$ 2,000	$ 3,333	$ 4,000
2	2,000	2,667	2,400
3	2,000	2,000	1,440
4	2,000	1,333	864
5	2,000	667	1,296
Total	$10,000	$10,000	$10,000

$(2/n)I$. In subsequent years, it continues to deduct $2/n$ times the undepreciated balance. In the final year, however, to bring the asset value to zero, the firm simply deducts the remaining undepreciated value of the asset. For our example, the stream of deductions for depreciation is as follows:[2]

$$D_1 = \frac{2}{5}(\$10,000) = \$4,000$$

$$D_2 = \frac{2}{5}(\$10,000 - 4,000) = 2,400$$

$$D_3 = \frac{2}{5}(\$10,000 - 4,000 - 2,400) = 1,440$$

$$D_4 = \frac{2}{5}(\$10,000 - 4,000 - 2,400 - 1,440) = 864$$

$$D_5 = \$10,000 - 4,000 - 2,400 - 1,440 - 864 = 1,296$$

This schedule is also summarized in Table 14.2, which can be used to compare the streams of depreciation expenses.

In order to select the optimal depreciation schedule, XYZ, Ltd.'s accountant must calculate the present value of the streams of depreciation costs shown in Table 14.2. The optimal method is the one that maximizes the present value of this stream. For the straight-line method, the present value at a discount rate of 12 percent is given by

$$\sum_{t=1}^{5} \frac{D_t}{(1+r)^t} = \frac{\$2,000}{1.12} + \frac{\$2,000}{1.25} + \frac{\$2,000}{1.40} + \frac{\$2,000}{1.57} + \frac{\$2,000}{1.76} = \$7,225$$

For the sum of the year's digits method, the present value is

$$\sum_{t=1}^{5} \frac{D_t}{(1+r)^t} = \frac{\$3,333}{1.12} + \frac{\$2,667}{1.25} + \frac{\$2,000}{1.40} + \frac{1,333}{1.57} + \frac{\$667}{1.76} = \$7,766$$

Finally, the double-declining-balance method yields a present value of

$$\sum_{t=1}^{5} \frac{D_t}{(1+r)^t} = \frac{\$4,000}{1.12} + \frac{\$2,400}{1.25} + \frac{\$1,440}{1.40} + \frac{\$864}{1.57} + \frac{\$1,296}{1.76} = \$7,807$$

It is clear that in this instance, the double-declining-balance method will maximize the present value of the depreciation expenses. This, in turn, will maximize the tax shield and thereby maximize the aftertax net present value of the investment option.

---

[2]More formally, the formula is given by

$$D_t = \frac{2}{n}\left(I - \sum_{i=1}^{t} D_{i-1}\right)$$

where $D_0 = 0$. In the final year, $D_n = I - \sum_{t=1}^{n-1} D_t$.

14.7

AUDITING AND SAMPLE SIZES

Auditing involves the formal examination and verification of financial records. Because of their expertise, accountants usually perform the audit function. In some instances, every financial record must be audited. In other cases, however, a manager can accept a fairly close approximation. When this is the case, the accountants can sample the financial records. Since the cost of an audit is a function of the number of records audited, there is an optimal sample size that minimizes the cost of achieving a given degree of accuracy. An example will make these suggestions more concrete.

Suppose a bank manager has received a number of complaints about discrepancies in savings account balances. He knows that these complaints may be due to innocent errors on the part of bank employees. But he also knows that someone may be embezzling funds by tampering with relatively inactive accounts. This possibility cannot be ignored. One way of determining the percentage of all accounts with incorrect balances would be to contact every account holder and verify the balance. Needless to say, this would be a formidable job in terms of time and expense. In any event, the manager's internal auditors convince him that he can get close to the actual truth by sampling these accounts.

On the basis of his previous experience, the bank manager can accept a 5 percent error rate as being accidental. If the error rate exceeds 5 percent, he will infer that someone is embezzling money. Since this determination would lead to a major investigation at significant expense in terms of money and employee morale, the bank manager demands a high degree of precision and a small probability that the results are due to chance. Consequently, the auditor suggests sampling a large enough number of the accounts such that the bank manager can be 99 percent confident that the results are not due to chance and that the error is estimated to within 1% of the true error rate.

The formula for required sample size n is

$$n = \frac{Z^2_{\alpha/2}pq}{B^2}$$

where $Z_{\alpha/2}$ represents the value of the standard normal variate with an area of $\alpha/2$ to its right, α is the confidence level, p is the proportion of errors, q is the proportion of correct balances, and B is the bound put on the precision of the estimated error rate.[3] The table value for $Z_{\alpha/2}$ where α is set at 0.01 is 2.575. Since a more or less normal error rate is 5 percent, we can let p be .05 and, therefore, q will be .95. The manager requested that the estimated error rate be within 1 percent of the true error rate, so we let B equal .01. Substituting these values into the formula reveals that some 3,150 accounts will have to be

---

[3]For this and many other excellent discussions of business problems, see James T. McClave and P. George Benson, *Statistics for Business and Economics*, San Francisco: Dellen Publishing Company, 1979.

sampled:

$$n = \frac{(2.575)^2(.05)(.95)}{(.01)^2} = 3,149.5$$

According to the auditors, account balance verification will cost $2 per account sampled. Thus, this effort will cost $6,300. The manager must decide whether this expenditure is appropriate in light of the information that it will provide on the possibility of an embezzler's being at work.

The manager should investigate the effects of changing the values of certain parameters of his problem. For example, if he requires that the estimated error rate be within one-half of 1 percent of the actual error rate, he will find that the required sample goes to 12,598:

$$n = \frac{(2.575)^2(.05)(.95)}{(.005)^2} = 12,598$$

The cost of achieving this added degree of precision is given by quadrupling the total expense of performing the necessary audit.

In contrast, if the manager were willing to accept a higher probability that the observed results were due to chance, the Z value changes. For example, if the degree of confidence (that the estimated error rate is within 1 percent of the true error rate) is reduced to 95%, the table value for $Z_{\alpha/2}$ is 1.96. Then the required sample size falls to 1,825:

$$n = \frac{(1.96)^2(.05)(.95)}{(.01)^2} = 1,824.8$$

which would cost $3,650.

In Table 14.3, we display the effects of changing α and B in the sampling

---

TABLE 14.3
REQUIRED SAMPLE SIZE*

α/B	.02	.01	.005
.10	321	1285	5141
.05	456	1825	7299
.01	787	3150	12598

*On the basis of the following formula:

$$n = \frac{Z_{\alpha/2}^2 pq}{B^2}$$

and the following normal variate table values:

$Z_{.05} = 1.645$

$Z_{.025} = 1.96$

$Z_{.005} = 2.575$

formula. The manager can easily translate these changes in the sample size to changes in auditing costs. His decision in selecting the appropriate values for α and B must depend upon the relative costs and benefits of greater precision and greater statistical confidence.

14.8

SUMMARY

In this chapter, we examined a few managerial decisions that involve accounting concepts and services to one degree or another. The break-even analysis traditionally performed by accountants has several shortcomings. It may be a satisfactory decision tool for marginal decisions where the assumed linearity of the cost and revenue functions is not a serious distortion. For more important decisions, however, the traditional linearity must be modified to reflect the true underlying cost and demand conditions.

The appropriate measurement of costs requires a recognition of implicit, as well as explicit, costs. We have examined the opportunity cost concept as it pertains to the firm's use of owned assets as well as to assets that are currently purchased and consumed immediately. The opportunity cost concept is crucial to sound business decisions and its importance cannot be overemphasized. We have extended this discussion to the controversy over the use of historical or replacement costs in decision making. Our conclusion on this score was that replacement costs provide the appropriate information for managerial decisions.

In the day-to-day business world, it is easy to lose track of many of the firm's intangible assets such as advertising, capital, goodwill, firm-specific human capital, and so on. We saw that keeping records on the value of these assets makes it possible to more precisely estimate the firm's net worth, which helps to raise money and to properly allocate inputs.

In a divisionalized firm, one division's output becomes an input for another division. There is a problem in accurately valuing the input as it is transferred from one division to the next. Any disputes between divisions should be resolved in such a way that the firm's overall profits are maximized. This will usually require that only one division exploit its market power.

Our discussion of depreciation was couched in terms of maximizing the tax savings. In doing this, the manager selects the depreciation schedule that maximizes the present value of after-tax profits.

Finally, we examined the costs of obtaining various degrees of precision from an audit by altering the sample size. The usual rule of optimization applies: precision should be increased until the marginal cost of increasing precision equals the marginal benefits.

IMPORTANT NEW TERMS

Historical cost

Replacement cost

Advertising capital

Goodwill

Transfer price

PROBLEMS

14.1 A building contractor recently offered to sell a new house for $50,000. He told a prospective customer that he would have to charge $55,000 for an identical house if he were to build it today. This, he explained, was due to rising materials costs. Has the builder priced this house correctly?

14.2 Suppose the Fine Jewelry Company purchased a supply of gold at $600 per ounce. Now, the pendants are priced at $800 and still yield a profit of $100 each. If the price of gold falls back to $200 per ounce, Fine Jewelry's FIFO method of inventory will lead the manager to continue pricing the pendants at $800. What is apt to happen to the firm's business?

14.3 The Regal Pizza Company has fixed costs of $100,000 per month and variable costs of $1.50 per frozen pizza produced. If Regal Pizza sells its frozen pizzas for $3.50 each, how many must be sold in order to break even?

14.4 Suppose that Pete's Pool Parlor purchased half a dozen pool tables for $600 apiece. They are expected to last 4 years and have a scrap value of $100 each. Calculate the pattern of depreciation for each method discussed in the text.

14.5 The Zippy Delivery Service pays a corporate profits tax of 48 percent. It owns 10 delivery trucks that could be rented to other firms for $100 per month. One of the employees pointed out that this implicit cost was not reported for tax purposes. Was Zippy Delivery Service paying too much tax? Explain.

14.6 Investigators attempt to ascertain whether or not there has been any embezzlement using the following two-stage procedure: (a) a sample of records is audited, and (b) if warranted by the information yielded from the audit, a major investigation is undertaken. Evaluate: A reduction in the cost of a major investigation will cause the optimal sample size of the audit to increase.

REFERENCES

Bell, Albert L.: "Break-Even Charts versus Marginal Graphs: A Case of Costs and Profits versus Resource Allocation," *Management Accounting*, vol. 50, February 1969, pp. 32–35.

Ferguson, C. E., and John R. Gould: *Micoeconomic Theory*, 4th ed., Homewood, Illinois: Richard D. Irwin, 1975, chap. 7

Hirshleifer, Jack: "On the Economics of Transfer Pricing," *Journal of Business*, vol. 29, July 1956, pp. 172–184.

Levy, Haim, and Marshall Sarnat: *Capital Investment and Financial Decisions*, London: Prentice-Hall International, Inc., 1978, chap 6.

McClave, James T., and P. George Benson: *Statistics for Business and Economics*, San Francisco: Dellen Publishing Company, 1979.

FOUR

RELAXATION OF PROFIT MAXIMIZATION

15 ALTER-NATIVE MANAGE-RIAL GOALS

Up to this point, we have analyzed managerial behavior on the assumption that the manager tries to maximize the firm's profits. This focus has been intentional because we believe that the profit motive drives most managerial behavior. Nonetheless, in this chapter, we shall relax that assumption and examine the consequences for some managerial decisions. We do this for several reasons. First, some influential economists have suggested that the goal of profits may not explain managerial behavior because each manager has private interests of his own. We shall examine some of the more commonly suggested alternative objectives and derive the implications for the firm. Second, not all firms are established for the pursuit of profit. There are nonprofit firms that still must be managed. For example, most hospitals, universities, and charitable organizations are not organized according to the profit motive. Nonetheless, managerial decisions must be made with respect to the employment of people and other inputs. We shall investigate the relevance of optimization in a nonprofit setting.

15.1

SALES REVENUE MAXIMIZATION

An unswerving pursuit of maximum profits is in the interest of the firm's owners. But the modern corporation is characterized by diffused ownership. Each corporation has a multitude of stockholders, and there is a suspicion that this diffusion of ownership puts the firm in the hands of its management. The owners lose effective control over the firm's activities. As a result, the manager has a certain degree of freedom to maximize her own utility at the expense of the firm. Since the manager's own interests influence her decisions, we must abandon maximization of profit as the manager's goal and search for an alternative.

A persuasive argument has been made for sales revenue maximization.[1] On the basis of his consulting experience, Baumol noted that top management seemed more concerned with sales revenue than with profits. We should wonder why this is the case. Several reasons have been advanced for the manager's focus upon sales.

First, and foremost, the manager may feel that her salary is determined more by the volume of sales than by the bottom line, i.e., profits. The empirical evidence, however, suggests that sales are not more important than profits in determining the manager's compensation. For example, Lewellen and

---

[1] William J. Baumol, *Business Behavior, Value and Growth*, rev. ed., New York: Harcourt, Brace and World, Inc., 1967. A mathematical treatment of this model is contained in Section 15A.1 of the mathematical appendix to this chapter.

Huntsman examined the determinants of the top executive's total compensation for 50 of the top 94 firms in the *Fortune* 500.[2] While they found that profit had a significant and positive effect on compensation, sales revenue was unimportant. In another study, Masson examined the determinants of the compensation of the top three to five executives in 39 firms in three industries; he discovered that sales revenue was unimportant but that stock market return was quite important in determining executive compensation.[3] He also found some evidence that executives may actually be paid not to sacrifice stock market return for sales revenue. Since the stock market appears to capitalize profits, managers seem to be rewarded for maximizing the present value of profits. Nevertheless, if a manager *believes* that sales revenue is more important than profit in determining her compensation, her decisions will reflect this belief.

Second, sales revenue is a more visible symbol to outsiders than profit. As a result, a manager can obtain more prestige from being in charge of a large operation than from putting an extra dollar of profit in the stockholders' pockets.

Third, a manager may feel more secure with a stable "satisfactory" profit performance than with fluctuating profits. The manager may try to provide the owners with satisfactory profits while avoiding large risks.

Question   The manager of ABC, Inc., heard that sales revenue was the key to success. He maximized sales revenue but lost his job. What went wrong?

Answer   A manager cannot simply maximize sales revenue without regard to costs, for stockholders expect a reasonable return on their investment. In order to offer a *satisfactory* performance, he should have maximized sales revenue subject to a minimum profit constraint. This minimum profit is a matter of judgment. Apparently, the profit that was generated by maximizing sales revenue was too low to be satisfactory to the owners.

The expectations of the stockholders will determine a minimum profit constraint that an alert manager will incorporate into the objective function. Thus, a manager considering sales revenue maximization will be successful if he instead maximizes sales revenue subject to the minimum profit constraint. This is shown in Figure 15.1. We analyze this decision process with total curves rather than with marginal and average curves.

Total revenue and total cost are labeled TR and TC, respectively. The difference between total revenue and total cost is defined to be profit and is labeled Π. In this case, the minimum profit constraint is designated as Π_0. Our manager's problem is to decide what output to produce. If he were going

[2]Wilbur G. Lewellen and Blaine Huntsman, "Managerial Pay and Corporate Performance," *American Economic Review,* vol. 60, September 1970, pp. 710–720.

[3]For an extensive discussion, see Robert T. Masson, "Executive Motivations, Earnings, and Consequent Equity Performance," *Journal of Political Economy,* vol. 79, December 1971, pp. 1278–1292.

to maximize profits, he would have the firm produce Q_1. If he wanted to simply maximize sales revenue, he would select Q_2. Notice, however, that if he sells Q_2 units of output, he will have profits of only Π_2, which is less than Π_0. Thus, he would fall short of the minimum acceptable profit.

Question   Given the revenue and cost functions depicted in Figure 15.1 and the minimum profit constraint Π_0, what output should the manager select to maximize sales revenue subject to the profit constraint?

Answer   All outputs between Q_4 and Q_3 will generate enough profit to satisfy the minimum profit constraint. Thus, we simply have to search among all of these output levels to find the one that provides the greatest sales revenue. In this case, we see that Q_3 satisfies the profit constraint and also generates a larger sales revenue than any other output level that satisfies the profit constraint. Consequently, our manager should produce Q_3 units of output.

When a manager substitutes constrained sales revenue for profit as the firm's objective, the firm's price and output are generally altered. This raises some questions about some of the firm's other decisions. As an example, consider the following question

Question   Since the XYZ Company's manager is attempting to maximize sales revenue rather than profits, there is no need to minimize costs any longer. Thus, we should expect a decrease in efficiency. Is this true?

Answer   This assertion is not true. Look at the profit functions in Figure

FIGURE 15.1   Equilibrium of the sales revenue-maximizing firm.

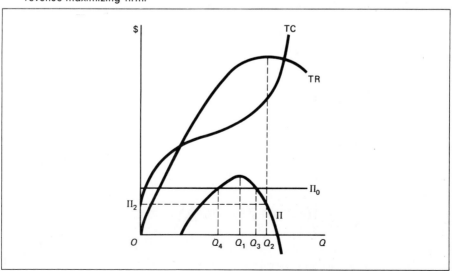

15.2. The curve labeled Π_1 represents the various levels of profit when the firm employs its inputs as efficiently as it can. When cost inefficiencies creep in, the total cost function rises and the profit function falls to Π_2. Given the minimum profit constraint, Π_0, we can see that the maximum output falls from Q_1 to Q_2. A quick glance at the total revenue function reveals that sales revenue is lower at Q_2 than at Q_1. Thus, cost inefficiency is not consistent with the goal of maximizing sales revenue subject to a minimum profit constraint. The manager has an incentive to minimize the cost of producing any particular output level.

15.2

EXPENSE PREFERENCE

When a manager has some discretion in the goals that he is to pursue, we should expect him to maximize his own utility. In addition to salary, which he can spend on most commodities, the manager may be interested in intangible things like power, prestige, and status. Consequently, he will obtain satisfaction from visible symbols of power, prestige, and status. This leads to the notion of "expense preference." In other words, a manager will get satisfaction from particular types of expenditures because these expenditures provide visible symbols. For example, the size of a manager's staff can be an important indicator of power and a symbol of professional success. As a result, a manager obtains satisfaction from expenditures on staff; that is, he has an expense preference for staff.[4]

---

[4]This model is based upon Oliver Williamson, "Managerial Discretion and Business Behavior," *American Economic Review*, vol. 53, December 1963, pp. 1032—1057

FIGURE 15.2 The effect of cost inefficiency upon the optimal output of a sales revenue maximizer.

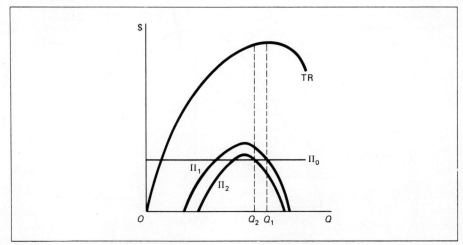

As in the sales revenue maximization model, the interests of the stock-holders cannot be ignored totally. In this model, we define the minimum profit Π_0 as that amount that will not result in large stock sales or a vote to fire the top management. Once the minimum profit is earned, any additional profit can be used to increase the manager's satisfaction. Thus, this discretionary profit is equal to actual profit minus the minimum profit:

$$\Pi_D = \Pi - \Pi_0$$

Since the discretionary profit can be used for a variety of purposes, a manager gets more satisfaction from greater discretionary profit.

We have already indicated that the number of staff may be important to the manager. If this is so, his utility function can be written as

$$U = U(S, \Pi_D)$$

where S denotes number of staff. An increase in either staff or discretionary profit will make the manager better off. We saw in Chapter 2 that this implies that indifference curves are negatively sloped; some sample indifference curves are depicted in Figure 15.3. As usual, combinations on U_1 provide less satisfaction than those on U_2.

The manager is constrained to choose a combination of discretionary profit and staff that is attainable. Attainable combinations of discretionary profit and staff are determined by the firm's profit function, which depends upon the demand and cost functions. The demand price is assumed to fall as the quantity of the commodity produced increases: $P = P(Q)$. The firm's discretionary profit (Π_D) equals total revenue $[P(Q)Q]$ less expenditures on staff (P_sS) less expenditures on other productive inputs (P_xX) less minimum profit (Π_0)

$$\Pi_D = P(Q)Q - P_sS - P_xX - \Pi_0$$

where P_s equals the price of a staff member, X equals the quantity of other

FIGURE 15.3   Indifference curves for a manager with expense preference.

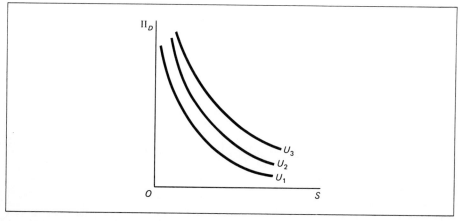

productive inputs, and P_x equals the price of X. Output is related to the number of staff and the quantity of other productive inputs by the production function

$$Q = Q(S,X)$$

For any given size of staff (S) the quantity of other productive inputs can be varied until discretionary profit (Π_D) is maximized for that particular staff size. The resulting relationship between discretionary profit and staff size is given in Figure 15.4.

The manager cannot select staff expenditures less than S_2 or more than S_3. If he were to do so, the discretionary profits would be negative. This would mean that the minimum profits would not be earned. Thus, he will select staff expenditures between S_2 and S_3. If he were to select S_1, then the discretionary profits would be maximized as would total profits.

In Figure 15.5, we have put the manager's indifference map on top of the discretionary profit function. The highest indifference curve attainable given the discretionary profit function is U_3. Notice that U_3 is just tangent to the curve Π_D, which gives the attainable combinations of Π_D and S, at point Z. Thus, the utility-maximizing level of staff expenditure is S_4 and the corresponding level of discretionary profit is Π_{D2}. It is readily apparent that this level of staff expenditure exceeds the profit-maximizing level. Consequently, the level of discretionary profit is less than the maximum. The manager has exercised his discretion and traded off some profit for staff. As we learned earlier, he does this because a larger staff is a visible symbol of power, status, or prestige and because of this a larger staff provides utility.

Question   Some managers have an expense preference for their own children. That is, they are willing to forgo some discretionary profit to have one or more of their children working with them. Analyze the effect of this

FIGURE 15.4 Discretionary profit: actual profit minus minimum profit.

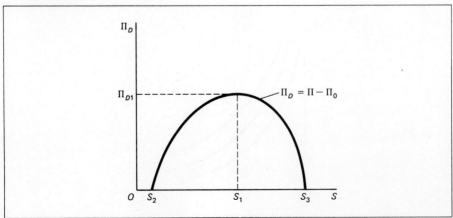

expense preference on the salaries that managers' children receive. How might the owners try to reduce the loss in profits that results?

Answer   We saw in Chapter 5 that a firm operating in a competitive labor market maximizes profit by increasing or decreasing the quantity of a particular type of labor until the value of that labor's marginal product $[(MR)(MP_i)]$ equals the wage rate of that labor (W_i). A manager with an expense preference for his own children would be willing to pay one of his children not only that child's contribution to the firm's total revenue $[(MR)(MP_i)]$ but also the value that the manager places on the child's working with him. Consequently, a manager's child is likely to be paid a higher salary than other comparably skilled workers. This practice obviously is costly to the firm's owners. They can increase their profits by prohibiting managers from employing their own children or by closely monitoring the salaries of managers' children.

Another form of expense preference is found when an employer discriminates against certain employees.[5] Just as a manager who wants his sons or daughters to work with him would be willing to pay a premium above their contribution to the firm's total revenue to bring them into his firm, a manager who discriminates against blacks, for instance, would be willing to hire a black only if the black costs the firm *sufficiently less* than the black's contribution to the firm's total revenue $[(MR)(MP)]$. Accordingly, managers who discriminate against blacks are willing to employ blacks only if the blacks are paid sufficiently less than equally productive whites. How much less this amount is will depend on the extent of the manager's discrimination.

---

[5]The analysis of discrimination that follows draws on Gary S. Becker, *The Economics of Discrimination*, Chicago: University of Chicago Press, 1971.

FIGURE 15.5   Utility maximization for a manager with expense preference.

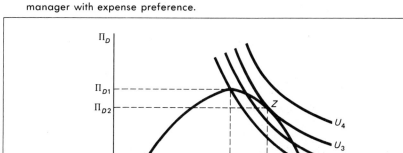

Managers differ in the extent of their discrimination. Indeed, many managers do not discriminate at all! These nondiscriminating managers would be willing to pay equally qualified blacks and whites the same wage and would outbid the discriminating managers for blacks. As a result, blacks first would seek employment with nondiscriminating managers.

The market demand curve for blacks thus can be thought of as a schedule that orders managers in terms of their preferences for discrimination. A representative market demand curve for blacks is labeled D in Figure 15.6. The ratio of the wage rate of blacks to the wage rate of equally skilled whites (W_b/W_w) is given on the vertical axis, and the number of blacks is found on the horizontal axis. The horizontal segment of the demand curve represents the demand for blacks by nondiscriminating employers; in this segment, blacks are paid the same wage rate as whites. The downward sloping segment of D represents the demand for blacks by discriminating managers. These managers are induced to employ blacks only when black wage rates fall below white wage rates. As we move down D, the preferences for discrimination become stronger.

Equilibrium in the market for black labor occurs where supply curve S_0 intersects demand curve D. At this point, L_0 blacks are employed and are paid the same wage rate as equally skilled whites. The fact that some managers discriminate against blacks has not affected black wage rates because there are enough managers who do not discriminate for all working blacks to be employed by nondiscriminating managers.

It is, however, possible for discrimination to affect wage rates. In Figure 15.7, supply curve S_1 intersects demand curve D in the downward sloping segment of the demand curve. As a result, L_1 blacks are employed and receive a wage rate equal to eight-tenths of the wage rate of comparable whites. In this case, discrimination results in lower wage rates for blacks because there

FIGURE 15.6 Discrimination against blacks does not lead to lower wages for blacks, because there are enough managers who do not discriminate.

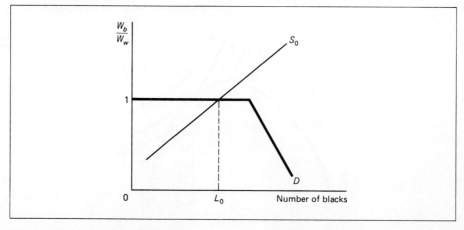

are not enough nondiscriminating managers to employ all of the blacks who desire employment at equal wage rates. Thus, we can see that discrimination must be *relatively* prevalent if it is to have an impact on wages.

In equilibrium, blacks are employed by the nondiscriminating managers and by managers with a slight preference for discrimination. These managers employ only blacks. Nondiscriminating managers, for instance, do not care whom they employ and can reduce their costs if they employ only blacks. On the other hand, managers with a strong preference for discrimination employ only whites and consequently experience higher costs. Once again, indulging an expense preference costs the firm money. This analysis of the effects of discrimination can be readily applied to discrimination against other groups (e.g., women or Jews).

15.3

INCENTIVE SCHEMES

The two preceding sections pose a difficult problem. Assuming that a decision maker cannot be monitored very closely, how can she be prevented from substituting her personal goals for the interests of the firm's owners? The owners are concerned with the value of the firm as measured by its stock market value. In contrast, the firm's manager is concerned with the firm's value only to the extent that it affects her utility. This fact provides the key to a partial solution: to the greatest extent possible, make the manager's well-being a function of the value of the firm. The question then becomes, How does one accomplish this?

From our earlier discussion, we know that the manager wants to maximize her utility. Her utility is a function of her consumption of items purchased in the market—food, clothing, housing, and so on—as well as the

FIGURE 15.7   Discrimination against blacks leads to lower wages for blacks, because there are too few managers who do not discriminate.

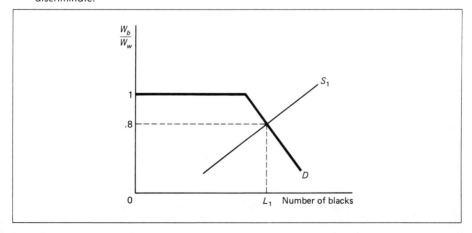

prestige, status, and power that she enjoys. Because the manager's income is used to purchase items in the market, the firm's owners need only concern themselves with the manager's income and the prestige, status, and power that she enjoys. The firm's owners must deal with the possibility that in order to get a sense of power or prestige, the manager may make decisions on behalf of the firm that sacrifice the firm's value for her own interests. To counter this tendency, the basis for the manager's monetary compensation should be designed to emphasize factors that increase the firm's value.

We observe that the compensation plans for top management in many actual firms do, indeed, depend upon the firm's performance. Top managers receive a salary that will be paid regardless of firm performance short of bankruptcy. But the manager's salary increase is often a function of the firm's profit. In addition, an important component of a manager's total compensation is her annual bonus. For some executives, the bonus may equal or exceed the salary. Generally, the size of a manager's bonus depends crucially upon the firm's performance. Finally, the manager's wealth is influenced by firm value through the stock options available plus the role that the firm's stock plays in the executive's pension fund.

As a result, we can see that when the manager trades a dollar of profit for an extra dollar of staff, she bears part of the cost. By making a larger fraction of total compensation depend upon the firm's profits, we can increase the cost to the manager of substituting her preferences for the interests of the firm. In other words, these efforts raise the price to the manager of the visible symbols of power, prestige, and status.

Nevertheless, these efforts often are not 100 percent effective. There are several reasons why this is so. First, the firm's owners do not benefit from a better allocation of the firm's resources unless they receive part of the additional profit that results. This means that the manager receives only part of any additional profit that she produces. Consequently, she does not bear the full cost of expenditures on staff and so on and the price to her of the visible symbols of power and prestige is lower than it would be if she bore the full cost. Second, the manager is willing to forgo *some* income in order to obtain visible symbols of additional prestige or power, and unless the price to the manager of the visible symbols of power, prestige, and status is sufficiently high, she will choose an output level that does not maximize the firm's profit.

15.4

A MODEL OF A NONPROFIT INSTITUTION

By law, a nonprofit firm is not allowed to keep any profit that it generates. Any profit earned in one period must be used to provide additional output in future periods. In exchange for giving up the opportunity to retain profits, nonprofit firms are given certain tax advantages, notably the ability of donors to treat gifts to nonprofit firms as tax deductions. Consequently, firms that have the opportunity of receiving gifts (e.g., universities, hospitals, research organizations, churches, charities) may find it worthwhile to operate as nonprofit firms.

Also, in many industries the cost of becoming a nonprofit firm may not be very substantial. Recall that positive profits are earned either in the short run by being able to take advantage of changing times or in the long run by having superior entrepreneurial or managerial talent. As a result, firms in stable industries that are characterized by little variation in entrepreneurial skills have little to lose from becoming nonprofit firms.

Most nonprofit firms compete with other nonprofit firms for donations and grants that help to maintain these institutions. Because potential donors are interested in achieving the greatest possible impact with their donations, nonprofit firms will compete for donations by providing services efficiently. That means minimizing the cost of any combination of quality and quantity of service that is provided. Moreover, if customers pay for the services that nonprofit firms provide, competition among nonprofit firms for customers will force nonprofit firms to provide services at lowest cost. For example, Princeton University would attract few students if it charged $2,000 more per year for tuition than Harvard or Yale. It would lose students to Harvard, Yale, and other universities offering the same kind of education that Princeton provides.

Nonprofit firms are not allowed to keep any profits they make, and creditors presumably do not let them operate at a loss. Thus, we will assume that the manager operates where total revenue equals total cost. In other words, production occurs somewhere along the average cost curve. But just where?

An example will help to make our discussion more concrete. Suppose our nonprofit institution is a hospital. Consider the minimum permissible quality level that still provides accreditation. There will be an average cost curve relating per unit costs to various quantities of service at the fixed quality level. This is shown as AC_1 in Figure 15.8. If the hospital produces Q_1 units of quantity at price P_1, another hospital with the same cost curves could

FIGURE 15.8 Competition for gifts and for customers will force the nonprofit firm to operate at the minimum point on its average cost curve.

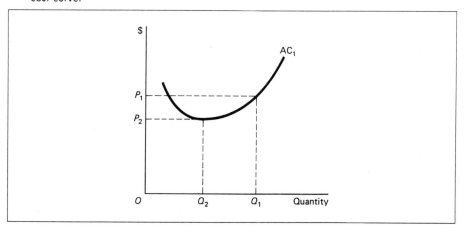

produce Q_2 units of quantity at price P_2. The lower price offered by the second hospital would attract customers and donors away from the first hospital, and this would lead each hospital to produce Q_2 units at price P_2. Competition from other nonprofit institutions therefore causes each institution to produce at the minimum point on its average cost curve.

This analysis suggests that competition will determine the quantity of any given quality of service that a nonprofit firm will produce. Yet the firm must decide at what quality level it will produce. Some administrators may be better suited to directing a research hospital that specializes in exotic cures, while other administrators may be better suited to directing a hospital that mass produces common treatments. The administrators in the first group could underbid other administrators in the provision of high-quality care, while the administrators in the second group could underbid others in the provision of less intensive treatment. Any given quality care will be provided by the most efficient firms in that quality level.

Some nonprofit firms may not face competition from other nonprofit firms. In Figure 15.9, the nonprofit firm with average cost curve AC_1 faces demand curve D. There is only one solution at which the quantity supplied equals the quantity demanded and zero profits are being made. This occurs where the demand curve intersects the average cost curve. In Figure 15.9, this solution implies that Q_0 units will be supplied at a price equal to P_0.

15.5

SUMMARY

In this chapter, we examined several departures from the model of profit maximization.

A realization that diffusion of ownership may result in marginal discretion led us to consider possible managerial goals. In each instance—

FIGURE 15.9   Without competition, nonprofit firms often operate where the average cost curve intersects the demand curve.

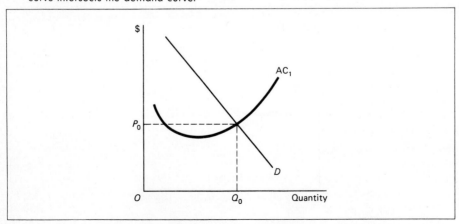

sales revenue maximization, preference for large staff, preference to hire certain employees—the manager's decisions further his goals at the expense of the firm's profits. The firm's owners are able to, and often do, temper this misallocation by paying the manager not to pursue his own goals. For a number of reasons, however, this policy is not completely effective.

We also examined the behavior of nonprofit firms. We saw that many nonprofit firms are not completely free to do what they want to do. Competition for donors and for customers constrains them to produce their output efficiently and to operate at the minimum-cost positions on their average cost curves.

PROBLEMS

15.1 For the firm that maximizes sales revenue subject to the minimum profit constraint, price will be higher than for the profit-maximizing firm. Discuss.

15.2 Suppose that managers feel the same way about discriminating against women as they feel about discriminating against blacks. Are women or blacks more likely to experience lower wage rates as a result of this discrimination?

15.3 The president of General Motors owns 1 percent of the stock of GM. Evaluate: Because he owns such a small fraction of GM's stock, he has very little incentive to maximize GM's profits.

15.4 Answer true, false, or undecided: Because nonprofit firms have no profit incentive, they are operated inefficiently. Does it matter to your answer whether the nonprofit firm is the only firm in the industry?

15.5 Over time, personal income tax rates have risen. Analyze the impact of this change on the demand for the services provided by nonprofit firms.

15.6 Family partnerships are more likely to succeed than partnerships among nonrelated persons. Evaluate: Therefore, owners should encourage their managers to hire their (the managers') relatives.

REFERENCES

Baumol, William J.: *Business Behavior, Value and Growth,* New York: Harcourt, Brace & World, Inc., 1967.

Becker, Gary S.: *The Economics of Discrimination,* Chicago: University of Chicago Press, 1971.

Lewellen, Wilbur G., and Blaine Huntsman: "Managerial Pay and Corporate Performance," *American Economic Review,* vol. 60, September 1970, 710–720.

Masson, Robert T.: "Executive Motivations, Earnings, and Consequent Equity Performance," *Journal of Political Economy*, vol. 79, December 1971, 1278–1292.

Williamson, Oliver: "Managerial Discretion and Business Behavior," *American Economic Review*, vol. 53, December 1963, 1032–1057.

MATHEMATICAL APPENDIX

15A.1

SALES REVENUE MAXIMIZATION

The firm's manager wants to maximize sales revenue PQ subject to the constraint that actual profit must equal or exceed some minimum satisfactory profit Π_0. Thus, the lagrangian expression is

$$L = PQ + \lambda[PQ - C(Q) - \Pi_0] \tag{A15.1}$$

where $C(Q)$ is the firm's cost function and λ is the Lagrange multiplier. The first-order conditions for a constrained optimum require that the first partial derivatives of (A15.1) vanish:

$$\frac{\partial L}{\partial Q} = P + Q\frac{dP}{dQ} + \lambda\left[P + Q\frac{dP}{dQ} - C'(Q)\right] = 0 \tag{A15.2}$$

$$\frac{\partial L}{\partial \lambda} = PQ - C(Q) - \Pi_o = 0 \tag{A15.3}$$

Algebraic manipulation of (A15.2) reveals that optimality requires that

$$C'(Q) = \text{MR}\left(1 + \frac{1}{\lambda}\right)$$

If λ is positive, this means that the optimal output is found where marginal cost $C'(Q)$ exceeds marginal revenue. This output will be larger than the profit-maximizing output.

APPENDIX: PRINCIPLES OF OPTIMIZATION

Throughout this book we shall be concerned with problems of optimization, that is, the maximization or minimization of one thing or another. There are good reasons for believing that the vast majority of firm managers maximize profit. Other managers, however, may maximize prestige, market share, total revenue, or some other objective. Whatever their objective, all managers are constrained to one extent or another by the utility-maximizing behavior of their employees and customers. Furthermore, managers usually must minimize the cost of producing any given level of output.

The maximization or minimization of a particular objective can be done quite mechanically. For example, a profit-maximizing firm could compute total revenue and total cost at each conceivable output level and then search for the particular output at which profit is maximized. This, however, is a very tedious task. It is often easier to use elementary concepts from calculus to find the quantity at which profits are maximized. For the same reason, calculus is often beneficial in other maximization or minimization problems.

In this appendix, we do not intend to make mathematicians out of business students. We simply intend to provide a few principles of optimization. For those readers who follow the mathematical development in the text, these principles will be used so often that they will soon become quite familiar. At this level, we are not concerned with proofs and mathematical rigor. We are concerned with understanding and familiarity.

A.1

LINES, CURVES, AND FUNCTIONS

LINES Every line can be characterized by its steepness and by its location. In particular, each linear relationship between X and Y can be written as

$$Y = a + bX \tag{A.1}$$

which is the slope-intercept formula for a straight line. When $X = 0$, $Y = a$. Thus, parameter a denotes the location of the line on the Y axis; it is the Y intercept. Three lines are shown in Figure A.1. Since lines CD and EF intercept the Y axis at the same point, both have the same value for a, which is 6. Line GH intercepts the Y axis at a lower point, 4.

Associated with each line is a steepness. We measure the steepness of a line by the slope.

DEFINITION ▶   The *slope* of a line is the change in the height of the line per unit moved to the right.

Consider line CD. The equation for this line is

$$Y = 6 - \frac{1}{2}X$$

From this equation, it follows that $Y = 4$ when $X = 4$. If we were to increase X by one unit to 5, Y would change to

$$Y = 6 - \frac{1}{2}5 = \frac{7}{2}$$

Thus, we see that a 1-unit increase in X brings about a $1/2$-unit fall in Y. Accordingly, $-1/2$ equals the slope of the line. More generally, b in equation (A.1) represents the slope of the line. Lines CD and GH have the same negative slope; consequently, they are parallel. Line EF, on the other hand, has a positive slope.

FUNCTIONS   For each line, an equation of the form

$$Y = a + bX$$

assigns a value to Y for each value of X. The equation is the rule which associates values of Y with values of X. A function is a particular rule which assigns values to one variable based on the values of another variable. It is conventional to call X the independent variable and Y the dependent variable in the equations we have written. We call Y dependent because its value is determined by the value of X given the functional relationship. For example, the general functional form is

$$Y = f(X)$$

where the value of Y is determined by the value that X assumes. In the case of line CD

$$f(X) = 6 - \frac{1}{2}X$$

FIGURE A.1   Each line is described by its slope and intercept.

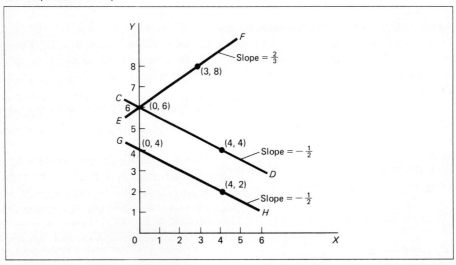

The function takes an X equal to 0 and transforms it to a Y equal to 6. Similarly, the function takes an X equal to 6 and transforms it to a Y equal to 3. The line

$$Y = 6 + \frac{2}{3}X$$

could also be expressed as

$$Y = g(X)$$

where

$$g(X) = 6 + \frac{2}{3}X$$

Functions $f(X)$ and $g(X)$ describe different relations between X and Y.

CURVES Functions need not always be linear. Some examples of nonlinear functions are

$$Y = a + bX + cX^2$$
$$Y = a + bX + X^2 + \cdots + mX^n$$
$$Y = a + b \log X$$

One such nonlinear function is graphed in Figure A.2. This curve has a different slope at each point. Since the slope is changing as the value for X changes, it does not appear to be a simple matter to determine the slope. But we can use the fact that the slope of the curve at point A is equal to the slope of line BC, which is tangent to (or just touching) the curve at A. This tangency procedure may be used to obtain the slope of the curve at all other points.

We may now proceed to find the values of X at which Y is minimized or

FIGURE A.2 Y is maximized locally at D and is minimized locally at E.

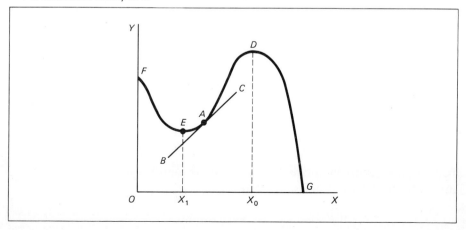

maximized. A point at which either a minimum or a maximum occurs is called an "extremum." The reader will notice that at point A the slope of the curve is positive. This means that a small increase in X will lead to an increase in Y. A person interested in maximizing Y will increase X and, in fact, will continue to increase X as long as the slope is positive. Only when the slope of the curve is equal to zero does an infinitesimal change in X have no effect on Y. To maximize Y, X is increased from a point such as A, where the curve is positively sloped, until the slope of the curve equals zero. In Figure A.2, Y is maximized at point D, where $X = X_0$. Increasing X beyond X_0 leads to decreases in Y, for in this region the curve is negatively sloped.

In this particular case, Y is maximized at point D where the slope of the curve equals zero. Unfortunately, Y is not necessarily maximized at *any* point at which the slope of the curve equals zero. This can be seen in Figure A.2, at point E. Although the slope is also zero at point E, it is clear that point E represents the lowest value of Y in the area immediately around point E. Why, then, is Y minimized at point E when it is maximized at point D? At E, the slope is increasing; at values of X just below X_1, the slope of the function is negative, while at values of X just above X_1, the slope of the function is positive. This means that either an increase or a decrease in X from X_1 will bring about an increase in Y. At point D, on the other hand, where Y is maximized, the slope is decreasing. Because the slope is negative at values of X slightly greater than X_0, increasing X past X_0 results in a fall in Y. Similarly, a decrease in X from X_0 will also cause Y to fall. Let us summarize our findings: (1) to *maximize* Y the slope of the function must equal zero *and* be decreasing; (2) to *minimize* Y the slope must equal zero *and* be increasing.

Frequently, the numbers that X and Y may take on are bounded by physical limitations or by economic common sense. It does not make sense, for example, to talk about using negative quantities of labor or to talk about producing negative quantit'es of output. When X and/or Y are bounded, additional work is required to find the minimum or maximum of Y. Let us suppose that neither X nor Y can be negative. It is therefore possible that a minimum or maximum value of Y is found either where X equals zero (point F) or where Y equals zero (point G). Only by comparing the values of Y at points D, E, F, and G can the minimum and maximum values of Y be found. It is clear from examining Figure A.2 that Y is maximized at point D, an interior point, and is minimized at point G, a boundary point. Quite often, however, a consideration of boundary points (e.g., points F and G) does not alter the conclusion that the function is maximized or minimized where the slope is zero.

The functions that have been discussed so far have related one variable to another variable. Some relationships are too complicated for the bivariate relationships that we have been considering. For instance, the quantity of steak demanded depends on income, the price of chicken, and the price of ham, as well as on the price of steak. This is a multivariate relationship. A multivariate function can be written as

$$Y = f(X, A, \ldots, U, V)$$

where $X, A, \ldots, U,$ and V are variables affecting Y. Some examples of multivariate functions are

$$Y = a + bX + cZ$$

$$Y = a + bX + cZ + eZ^2 + fXZ$$

$$Y = a + bX + cZ + dF$$

More will be said about multivariate functions in the next section.

A.2

DERIVATIVES

Let's return to simple functions of the form

$$Y = f(X)$$

For these functions, the derivative of Y with respect to X is quite simply the slope of the curve at the point being considered. It is a convention that we write the derivative of Y with respect to X as

$$\frac{dY}{dX} = \frac{df(X)}{dX} = f'(X)$$

All these symbols represent the derivative of Y with respect to X.

SIMPLE DERIVATIVES   It is beyond the scope of this appendix to teach the fundamentals of calculus. As we have noted, the derivative of a function is the slope of that function. With this in mind, we shall turn to some rules of differentiation that provide a lot of help in finding the slopes of different functions. These rules should be memorized and trusted to do their job.

Rule 1   If $Y = aX^b$, $\dfrac{dY}{dX} = abX^{b-1}$.

Example 1: If $Y = 3X^{7/3}$, then $a = 3$ and $b = \dfrac{7}{3}$.

Thus, $\dfrac{dY}{dX} = 3\,(7/3)\,X^{7/3-1} = 7X^{4/3}$.

There are two special cases of the rule:

Rule 1a: If $Y = aX$, then

$$\frac{dY}{dX} = aX^0 = a$$

because of the mathematical convention that X^0 equals 1.

Example 1a: If $Y = 0.8X$, then $\dfrac{dY}{dX} = 0.8$.

Rule 1b: If $Y = a$, $\dfrac{dY}{dX} = 0$.

Example 1b: If $Y = 6$, $\dfrac{dY}{dX} = 0$.

Rule 2 If $Y = U + V$ where U and V are functions of X, then

$$\frac{dY}{dX} = \frac{dU}{dX} + \frac{dV}{dX}$$

Example 2: Suppose $Y = 6X + 4X^2$. Then $U = 6X$ and $V = 4X^2$. Consequently,

$$\frac{dY}{dX} = 6 + 8X$$

because $\dfrac{dU}{dX} = 6$ and $\dfrac{dV}{dX} = 8X$.

Rule 3 If $Y = UV$ where U and V are functions of X, then

$$\frac{dY}{dX} = U\frac{dV}{dX} + V\frac{dU}{dX}$$

Example 3: Suppose $Y = (6X^3 + 2)(4X^2 + X)$. Then $U = (6X^3 + 2)$ and $V = (4X^2 + X)$. Since

$$\frac{dU}{dX} = 18X^2 \text{ and } \frac{dV}{dX} = 8X + 1,$$

$$\frac{dY}{dX} = (6X^3 + 2)(8X + 1) + (4X^2 + X)18X^2$$

$$= 120X^4 + 24X^3 + 16X + 2$$

Rule 4 If $Y = \dfrac{U}{V}$ where U and V are functions of X. Then

$$\frac{dY}{dX} = \frac{V\dfrac{dU}{dX} - U\dfrac{dV}{dX}}{V^2}$$

Example 4: Suppose $Y = \dfrac{2X + 3}{6X + 1}$. Then $U = 2X + 3$ and $V = 6X + 1$. Since

$$\frac{dU}{dX} = 2 \text{ and } \frac{dV}{dX} = 6, \text{ we have}$$

$$\frac{dY}{dX} = \frac{(6X + 1)2 - (2X + 3)6}{(6X + 1)^2}$$

$$= \frac{-16}{(6X + 1)^2}$$

Rule 5 If $Y = f(V)$ and V is a function of X, then

$$\frac{dY}{dX} = \frac{dY}{dV}\frac{dV}{dX}$$

Example 5: Suppose $Y = V^2$ and $V = 6X^2 + 3X$. Then

$\dfrac{dY}{dX} = 2V$ and $\dfrac{dV}{dX} = 12X + 3$. Consequently,

$$\frac{dY}{dX} = 2(6X^2 + 3X)(12X + 3)$$

Rule 6   If $Y = \ln U$, where ln denotes the natural logarithm and U is a function of X, then

$$\frac{dY}{dX} = \frac{1}{U}\frac{dU}{dX}$$

Example 6: Suppose $Y = \ln(3X^2 + 2)$. Then $U = 3X^2 + 2$ and $\dfrac{dU}{dX} = 6X$. As a result, $\dfrac{dY}{dX} = 6X/(3X^2 + 2)$.

We can now use these rules to find the slope of a particular function. Consider the function given by the following equation:

$$Y = \frac{1}{6}(X^3 - 6X^2 + 9X + 6).$$

This function is graphed in Figure A.3, and it is fairly obvious that the slope of the function changes as one changes the value of X. We can determine the slope at any point by evaluating the derivative at that point. First, we know by applying rule 2 that the derivative is given by

$$\frac{dY}{dX} = \frac{1}{6}(3X^2 - 12X + 9)$$

Suppose that we want to find the slope of the function at $X = 0$. Then we substitute 0 for X into the general form given above:

FIGURE A.3   A particular function.

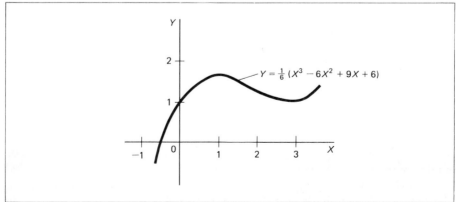

$$\left.\frac{dY}{dX}\right|_{X=0} = \frac{1}{6}(3 \cdot 0^2 - 12 \cdot 0 + 9)$$

$$= \frac{9}{6}$$

Thus, the slope of the function at $X = 0$ is $^3/_2$. Similarly, the slope of the function at $X = 1$ is zero:

$$\left.\frac{dY}{dX}\right|_{X=1} = \frac{1}{6}(3 \cdot 1^2 - 12 \cdot 1 + 9)$$

$$= 0$$

As a last example, consider the slope of the function at $X = 2$:

$$\left.\frac{dY}{dX}\right|_{X=2} = \frac{1}{6}(3 \cdot 2^2 - 12 \cdot 2 + 9)$$

$$= \frac{1}{6}(12 - 24 + 9)$$

$$= -\frac{1}{2}$$

PARTIAL DERIVATIVES   When Y is a function of several variables, differentiation is a somewhat more complicated process. The concepts, however, are relatively unaltered and the mechanics remain simple. To see what is meant by partial differentiation, let us first consider an example. Suppose that the height of a mountain (H) is a function of the number of feet north of San Francisco (N) and of the number of feet east of San Francisco (E). Then we may write:

$$H = f(N, E)$$

If a mountain climber proceeds north 1 foot, while maintaining his easterly position, the height of the mountain changes. The change in the height that results from moving north one step, keeping the number of feet east constant, is called the partial derivative of H with respect to N and is written as

$$\frac{\partial H}{\partial N} = \frac{\partial f(N, E)}{\partial N}$$

In Figure A.4, we have a stylized drawing of our mountain. The mountain climber is located at point P. If he maintains his easterly position, he can only move along the north-south path labeled APB on the mountain. The partial derivative of height with respect to the number of feet north represents the slope of the north-south path at the climber's position P.

The mountain climber could just as easily have moved one step east, keeping his northerly position unchanged. The change in height would be given by the slope of the east-west path on the mountain, which is labeled CPD, at the climber's original position. The slope of that path is the partial derivative of height with respect to the number of feet east:

$$\frac{\partial H}{\partial E} = \frac{\partial f(N, E)}{\partial E}$$

The partial derivative thus is defined to be a change in the value of the function as one variable changes and as all other variables in the function are held constant. These other variables are treated as constants. Consider the function

$$Y = 4X_1^2 + 7X_1X_2 + 5X_2^2$$

Since we treat X_2 as a constant to find the partial derivative of Y with respect to X_1,

$$\frac{\partial Y}{\partial X_1} = 8X_1 + 7X_2$$

Similarly, if we treat X_1 as a constant, we can obtain the partial derivative of Y with respect to X_2, which is

$$\frac{\partial Y}{\partial X_2} = 7X_1 + 10X_2$$

A.3

MAXIMIZATION AND MINIMIZATION WITH CALCULUS

This elementary knowledge of calculus now makes it possible to explicitly derive points of maximization and of minimization. Consider the maximization of a firm's profit.

Profit (Π) equals total revenue (TR) less total cost. If the firm receives \$4 for

FIGURE A.4   The partial derivative at P of height with respect to feet north is given by the slope of the north-south path APB.

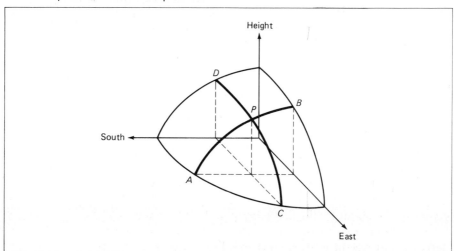

each unit produced, no matter how many, then $4Q$ is the total revenue received from sales of Q units. Let total cost equal

$$TC = Q + .015Q^2$$

Now profit is given by

$$\Pi = 4Q - (Q + .015Q^2)$$

$$= 3Q - .015Q^2$$

The profit function is graphed in panel (*a*) of Figure A.5.

We have shown that if boundary points are unimportant, then the slope must equal zero for a function to be maximized. The slope of the profit function is the derivative of profit with respect to output, which is

$$\frac{d\Pi}{dQ} = 3 - .03Q \qquad\qquad\qquad (A.2)$$

This derivative, plotted in panel (*b*) of Figure A.5, can be interpreted as the rate of change in profit as output rises. Accordingly, profit is maximized where the derivative equals zero.

$$\frac{d\Pi}{dQ} = 3 - .03Q = 0$$

or

$$3 = .03Q$$

or

$$100 = Q$$

When output is less than 100, the derivative of the profit function is positive. This indicates that profit can be increased by raising production. When output is greater than 100, the derivative of the profit function is negative; in this region, a decrease in output increases profit. Profit is thus maximized, rather than minimized, at an output level of 100. Profit is maximized at $Q = 100$ because the slope of the profit function is positive at smaller output levels and is negative at larger output levels; the slope of the profit function falls as output rises. This can also be seen by examining equation (A.2), the equation for the slope of the profit function. This equation is a straight line with a slope of $-.03$.

$$\frac{d}{dQ}\frac{d\Pi}{dQ} = -.03$$

Note how simple a process it has become to find the point at which profit is maximized. Set the first derivative of the profit function equal to zero and find possible solutions. Then verify that the derivative decreases as quantity increases. The check to be sure that the derivative decreases as output increases is nearly always unnecessary.

The conditions for maximizing or minimizing a function of several variables are similar to the conditions for maximizing or minimizing a function of one variable. To find an extremum (i.e., a maximum or minimum), the slope of a function of one variable is set equal to zero. If the slope is decreasing (increasing), setting the slope equal to zero guarantees that a higher (lower) value of the function cannot be found by making small changes in the independent variable. To find an extremum in a multivariate function, we also want to be sure that a small change in any of the independent variables will not bring about a more desirable value of the function. This requires that

FIGURE A.5 Profit is maximized by producing 100 units.

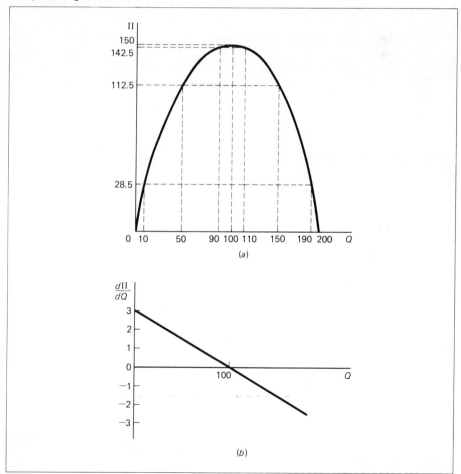

the partial derivatives of the function with respect to *each* independent variable be set equal to zero. An example will help to clarify this.

Once again consider a profit-maximizing firm. Let total cost be written as

$$TC = 10Q + 96A$$

where A is the minutes of radio advertising. In this example, the manager is able to increase the price the firm receives by increasing the amount of advertising that the firm undertakes or by reducing the quantity that the firm sells. As a result, the demand function is given by

$$P = 100 - .1Q + .2A$$

Total revenue, which is $P \cdot Q$, can be written as

$$PQ = 100Q - .1Q^2 + .2AQ$$

The firm wishes to maximize profit, which is the difference between total revenue and total cost:

$$\Pi = 100Q - .1Q^2 + .2AQ - 10Q - 96A$$

and is maximized by setting the partial derivatives of profit with respect to quantity (Q) and with respect to minutes of advertising (A) equal to zero. To get the partial derivative with respect to quantity, A is treated as a constant:

$$\frac{\partial \Pi}{\partial Q} = 100 - 2(.1)Q + .2A - 10 = 0 \qquad \text{(A.3)}$$

Likewise, Q is treated as a constant in order to obtain the partial derivative of profit with respect to minutes of advertising:

$$\frac{\partial \Pi}{\partial A} = .2Q - 96 = 0 \qquad \text{(A.4)}$$

Both equations (A.3) and (A.4) must be satisfied to maximize profits. Values of Q and A must be found which satisfy both equations simultaneously. In this instance, this is not a difficult task. From equation (A.4), we find that $Q = 480$. Substituting this value into equation (A.3), we get

$$100 - .2(480) + .2A - 10 = 0$$

$$.2A = 6$$

$$A = 30$$

Thus, to maximize profit, the firm must produce 480 units and buy 30 minutes of radio time. Given the quantity and the amount of advertising, we can substitute into the demand function to determine that the firm receives

$$P = 100 - .1(480) + .2(30)$$

$$= 100 - 48 + 6$$

$$= 58$$

for each unit that it produces. Substituting into the profit function reveals that profit equals

$$\Pi = PQ - 10Q - 96A$$

$$= 58(480) - 10(480) - 96(30)$$

$$= 27,840 - 4,800 - 2,880$$

$$= 20,160$$

How can the manager be sure that profit is maximized at these values and not minimized? We sould first note that in almost every real world problem of this nature, the solution will be a point of profit maximization. In addition, common sense suggests that a profit of $20,160 could not be a *minimum* because these profits could easily be reduced by giving away the 480 units. Nevertheless, by calculating profit at several points in the region of the solution, the manager can assure herself that the solution maximizes profit. For instance, at $A = 25$ and $Q = 520$, $P = 53$ and profit equals 19,960.

A.4

CONSTRAINED OPTIMIZATION AND LAGRANGE MULTIPLIERS

In many maximization decisions, there is at least one constraint which must be satisfied. For one example, consumers maximize their utility or happiness subject to the constraint that their expenditures may not exceed their income. As another example, some department managers are charged with minimizing cost subject to the constraint that output equal some assigned number. Finally, firms that produce durable goods operate under the constraint that over the long run the sum of monthly outputs must equal the sum of monthly sales.

There are two equivalent ways to incorporate constraints into the maximization or minimization process: (1) the use of substitution, and (2) the use of Lagrange multipliers. While substitution is somewhat easier to understand than Lagrange multipliers, Lagrange multipliers are often easier to use in practice than substitution.

SUBSTITUTION   Once again, an example will help to clarify the discussion. Consider a profit-maximizing firm that faces the following relationship between the price it charges (P) and the quantity it can sell (Q):

$$P = 200 - .15Q$$

Output is produced in two plants. In plant 1, total cost equals

$$2Q_1 + .005Q_1^2$$

where $Q_1 = $ output of plant 1. In plant 2, total cost equals

$$3.25Q_2 + .0025Q_2^2$$

where $Q_2 =$ output of plant 2. The manager wishes to maximize profit (Π), the difference between total revenue (PQ), and the total cost in both plants.

$$\Pi = PQ - 2Q_1 - .005Q_1^2 - 3.25Q_2 - .0025Q_2^2$$

$$= 200Q - .15Q^2 - 2Q_1 - .005Q_1^2 - 3.25Q_2 - .0025Q_2^2 \tag{A.5}$$

The constraint facing the firm is that the number of units sold (Q) must equal the number of units produced in the two plants ($Q_1 + Q_2$).

$$Q = Q_1 + Q_2 \tag{A.6}$$

How can this constraint be incorporated into the profit-maximization problem?

The substitution solution involves using constraint (A.6) to eliminate Q in equation (A.5). Thus,

$$\Pi = 200(Q_1 + Q_2) - .15(Q_1 + Q_2)^2 - 2Q_1 - .005Q_1^2 - 3.25Q_2 - .0025Q_2^2 \tag{A.7}$$

Any solution to equation (A.7) will satisfy the constraint that total output must equal sales. Profit can now be maximized by taking the partial derivatives with respect to Q_1 and Q_2, setting them equal to zero, and solving for Q_1 and Q_2:

$$\frac{\partial \Pi}{\partial Q_1} = 200 - .3(Q_1 + Q_2) - 2 - .01Q_1 = 0 \tag{A.8}$$

$$\frac{\partial \Pi}{\partial Q_2} = 200 - .3(Q_1 + Q_2) - 3.25 - .005Q_2 = 0 \tag{A.9}$$

Equation (A.8) can be rewritten to read

$$200 - .3(Q_1 + Q_2) = 2 + .01Q_1 \tag{A.10}$$

Similarly, equation (A.9) can be rewritten to read

$$200 - .3(Q_1 + Q_2) = 3.25 + .005Q_2 \tag{A.11}$$

Together, equations (A.10) and (A.11) imply that

$$200 - .3(Q_1 + Q_2) = 2 + .01Q_1 = 3.25 + .005Q_2$$

The latter equality can be rewritten as

$$.01Q_1 = 1.25 + .005Q_2$$

$$Q_1 = 125 + .5Q_2$$

This result can then be used to eliminate Q_1 from equation (A.8). Combining terms, we can write equation (A.8) as

$$198 - .31Q_1 - .3Q_2 = 0$$

Substituting for Q_1, we get

$$198 - .31(125 + .5Q_2) - .3Q_2 = 0$$

$198 - 38.75 - .155Q_2 - .3Q_2 = 0$

$159.25 = .455Q_2$

$350 = Q_2$

Using this value for Q_2, we can solve for Q_1:

$Q_1 = 125 + .5Q_2$

$= 125 + .5(350)$

$= 300$

The firm maximizes profit by producing 300 units in plant 1 and 350 units in plant 2. The 650 units of output are sold at a price of \$102.50 each. We leave it to the reader to find the maximum profit by substituting these values into the profit function.

ALTERNATIVE METHOD   Lagrange multipliers can also be used to find the profit-maximizing quantities. Let us once again consider the manager who wishes to maximize profit, as expressed by equation (A.5), subject to the constraint found in equation (A.6). We can form an objective function which incorporates this constraint by writing the so-called lagrangian function

$$L = 200Q - .15Q^2 - 2Q_1 - .005Q_i^2 - 3.25Q_2 - .0025Q_2^2 + \lambda(Q_1 + Q_2 - Q)$$
$$(A.12)$$

The symbol λ is called a Lagrange multiplier. We want to be sure that the constraint is satisfied no matter what value λ takes on. For this to occur, $Q_1 + Q_2 - Q$ must always equal zero. As we will soon see, this requirement is satisfied if we treat λ as a variable. There are consequently four variables $(Q_1, Q_2, Q,$ and $\lambda)$ which can be altered to increase profit.

Profit is maximized by setting the partial derivatives with respect to Q_1, Q_2, Q, and λ equal to zero and simultaneously solving for these four variables. The necessary conditions for profit maximization are

$$\frac{\partial L}{\partial Q} = 200 - .3Q - \lambda = 0 \tag{A.13}$$

$$\frac{\partial L}{\partial Q_1} = \lambda - 2 - .01Q_1 = 0 \tag{A.14}$$

$$\frac{\partial L}{\partial Q_2} = \lambda - 3.25 - .005Q_2 = 0 \tag{A.15}$$

$$\frac{\partial L}{\partial \lambda} = Q_1 + Q_2 - Q = 0 \tag{A.16}$$

The last condition (A.16) *guarantees* that the constraint $(Q = Q_1 + Q_2)$ is satisfied. If we solve the first three conditions (A.13)–(A.15) for λ, we have

$$\lambda = 200 - .3Q = 2 + .01Q_1 = 3.25 + .005Q_2$$

We may use the final condition to write

$$\lambda = 200 - .3(Q_1 + Q_2) = 2 + .01Q_1 = 3.25 + .005Q_2 \qquad (A.17)$$

But the last two equalities in equation (A.17) are the same equalities that were obtained using the method of substitution. This means that the two methods have the same solution, which is

$$Q_1 = 300$$

$$Q_2 = 350$$

$$Q = 650$$

Using equation (A.17), the method of Lagrange multipliers also tells us that the Lagrange multiplier λ equals 5.

The Lagrange multiplier λ has an economic interpretation. It is equal to the increase in total cost that results from producing 1 more unit in plant 1 $(2 + .01Q_1)$ and is equal to the increase in total cost associated with producing 1 more unit in plant 2 $(3.25 + .005Q_2)$. It is also equal to the increase in total revenue that results from selling 1 more unit *as well as* the increase in total cost from producing in plant 1 *or* in plant 2. Profit maximization evidently requires that these all be equal.

PROBLEMS

A.1 If $Y = 3 + 4X + 5X^2$, find dY/dX.

A.2 If $Y = (6X + 3)(3X^2 - 1)$, find dY/dX.

A.3 If $Y = (2X^2 + 3X + 7)/(2X - 4)$, find dY/dX.

A.4 If $Y = 8 + 3X$, find the value of X that minimizes Y.

A.5 If $Y = 6 + 300X - X^2$, find the extremum. Is this a minimum or a maximum?

A.6 If $Y = \frac{1}{3}X^3 - 75X^2 + 5000X$, find the values of X where $dY/dX = 0$. Are these points at which Y is minimized or maximized?

A.7 If $Q = L^\alpha K^{1-\alpha}$, find $\partial Q/\partial L$ and $\partial Q/\partial K$. Are there simple expressions for these partial derivatives?

A.8 Maximize $Q = L^{3/4}K^{1/4}$ subject to the constraint that $1{,}000 = 5L + 10K$.

A.9 Find the profit-maximizing quantity if total revenue $= 10Q$ and total cost equals $Q + .3Q^2$. Profit equals total revenue minus total cost.

A.10 If $Y = X^2 - 10X - 6XZ + 10Z^2 + 10Z + 53$, find the values of X and Z at which $\partial Y/\partial X = 0$ and $\partial Y/\partial Z = 0$.

REFERENCES

Chiang, Alpha C.: *Fundamental Methods of Mathematical Economics*, New York: McGraw-Hill Book Company, 1967.

Silberberg, Eugene: *The Structure of Economics*, New York: McGraw-Hill Book Company, 1978.

TABLES

TABLE 1

FUTURE VALUE* OF $1

PERIODS (YEARS)	1%	2%	3%	4%	5%	6%	7%	8%	9%	10%
1	1.010	1.020	1.030	1.040	1.050	1.060	1.070	1.080	1.090	1.100
2	1.020	1.040	1.061	1.082	1.102	1.124	1.145	1.166	1.188	1.200
3	1.030	1.061	1.093	1.125	1.158	1.191	1.225	1.260	1.295	1.331
4	1.041	1.082	1.126	1.170	1.216	1.262	1.311	1.360	1.412	1.464
5	1.051	1.104	1.159	1.217	1.276	1.338	1.403	1.469	1.539	1.611
6	1.062	1.126	1.194	1.265	1.340	1.419	1.501	1.587	1.677	1.772
7	1.072	1.149	1.230	1.316	1.407	1.504	1.606	1.714	1.828	1.949
8	1.083	1.172	1.267	1.369	1.477	1.594	1.718	1.851	1.993	2.144
9	1.094	1.195	1.305	1.423	1.551	1.689	1.838	1.999	2.172	2.358
10	1.105	1.219	1.344	1.480	1.629	1.791	1.967	2.159	2.367	2.594
11	1.116	1.243	1.384	1.539	1.710	1.898	2.105	2.332	2.580	2.853
12	1.127	1.268	1.426	1.601	1.796	2.012	2.252	2.518	2.813	3.138
13	1.138	1.294	1.469	1.665	1.886	2.133	2.410	2.720	3.066	3.452
14	1.149	1.319	1.513	1.732	1.980	2.261	2.579	2.937	3.342	3.797
15	1.161	1.346	1.558	1.801	2.079	2.397	2.759	3.172	3.642	4.177
16	1.173	1.373	1.605	1.873	2.183	2.540	2.952	3.426	3.970	4.595
17	1.184	1.400	1.653	1.948	2.292	2.693	3.159	3.700	4.328	5.054
18	1.196	1.428	1.702	2.026	2.407	2.854	3.380	3.996	4.717	5.560
19	1.208	1.457	1.754	2.107	2.527	3.026	3.617	4.316	5.142	6.116
20	1.220	1.486	1.806	2.191	2.653	3.207	3.870	4.661	5.604	6.727
21	1.232	1.516	1.860	2.279	2.786	3.400	4.141	5.034	6.109	7.400
22	1.245	1.546	1.916	2.370	2.925	3.604	4.430	5.437	6.659	8.140
23	1.257	1.577	1.974	2.465	3.072	3.820	4.741	5.871	7.258	8.954
24	1.270	1.608	2.033	2.563	3.225	4.049	5.072	6.341	7.911	9.850
25	1.282	1.641	2.094	2.666	3.386	4.292	5.427	6.848	8.623	10.835

*FV $= 1 \cdot (1 + r)^t$

11%	12%	13%	14%	15%	16%	17%	18%	19%	20%
1.110	1.120	1.130	1.140	1.150	1.160	1.170	1.180	1.190	1.200
1.232	1.254	1.277	1.300	1.322	1.346	1.369	1.392	1.416	1.490
1.368	1.405	1.443	1.482	1.521	1.561	1.602	1.643	1.685	1.728
1.518	1.574	1.630	1.689	1.749	1.811	1.874	1.939	2.005	2.074
1.685	1.762	1.842	1.925	2.011	2.100	2.192	2.228	2.386	2.488
1.870	1.974	2.082	2.195	2.313	2.436	2.565	2.700	2.840	2.986
2.076	2.211	2.353	2.502	2.660	2.826	3.001	3.185	3.379	3.583
2.305	2.476	2.658	2.853	3.059	3.278	3.511	3.759	4.021	4.300
2.558	2.773	3.004	3.252	3.518	3.803	4.108	4.435	4.785	5.160
2.839	3.106	3.395	3.707	4.046	4.411	4.807	5.234	5.695	6.192
3.152	3.479	3.836	4.226	4.652	5.117	5.624	6.176	6.777	7.430
3.498	3.896	4.335	4.818	5.350	5.936	6.580	7.288	8.064	8.916
3.883	4.363	4.898	5.492	6.153	6.886	7.699	8.599	9.596	10.699
4.310	4.887	5.535	6.261	7.076	7.988	9.007	10.147	11.420	12.839
4.785	5.474	6.254	7.138	8.137	9.266	10.539	11.974	13.590	15.407
5.311	6.130	7.067	8.137	9.358	10.748	12.330	14.129	16.172	18.488
5.895	6.866	7.986	9.276	10.761	12.468	14.426	16.672	19.244	22.186
6.544	7.690	9.024	10.575	12.375	14.463	16.879	19.673	22.901	26.623
7.263	8.613	10.197	12.056	14.232	16.777	19.748	23.214	27.252	31.948
8.062	9.646	11.523	13.743	16.367	19.461	23.106	27.393	32.429	38.338
8.949	10.804	13.021	15.668	18.822	22.574	27.034	32.324	38.591	46.005
9.934	12.100	14.714	17.861	21.645	26.186	31.629	38.142	45.923	55.206
11.026	13.552	16.627	20.362	24.891	30.376	37.006	45.008	54.649	66.247
12.239	15.179	18.788	23.212	28.625	35.236	43.297	53.109	65.032	79.497
13.585	17.000	21.231	26.462	32.919	40.874	50.658	62.669	77.388	95.396

TABLE 2

PRESENT VALUE* OF $1

PERIODS (YEARS)	1%	2%	3%	4%	5%	6%	7%	8%	9%	10%
1	0.990	0.980	0.971	0.962	0.952	0.943	0.935	0.926	0.917	0.909
2	0.980	0.961	0.943	0.925	0.907	0.890	0.873	0.857	0.842	0.826
3	0.971	0.942	0.915	0.889	0.864	0.840	0.816	0.794	0.772	0.751
4	0.961	0.924	0.888	0.855	0.823	0.792	0.763	0.735	0.708	0.683
5	0.951	0.906	0.863	0.822	0.784	0.747	0.713	0.681	0.650	0.621
6	0.942	0.888	0.837	0.790	0.746	0.705	0.666	0.630	0.596	0.564
7	0.933	0.871	0.813	0.760	0.711	0.665	0.623	0.583	0.547	0.513
8	0.923	0.853	0.789	0.731	0.677	0.627	0.582	0.540	0.502	0.467
9	0.914	0.837	0.766	0.703	0.645	0.592	0.544	0.500	0.460	0.424
10	0.905	0.820	0.744	0.676	0.614	0.558	0.508	0.463	0.422	0.386
11	0.896	0.804	0.722	0.650	0.585	0.527	0.475	0.429	0.388	0.350
12	0.887	0.788	0.701	0.625	0.557	0.497	0.444	0.397	0.356	0.319
13	0.879	0.773	0.681	0.601	0.530	0.469	0.415	0.368	0.326	0.290
14	0.870	0.758	0.661	0.577	0.505	0.442	0.388	0.340	0.299	0.263
15	0.861	0.743	0.642	0.555	0.481	0.417	0.362	0.315	0.275	0.239
16	0.853	0.728	0.623	0.534	0.458	0.394	0.339	0.292	0.252	0.218
17	0.844	0.714	0.605	0.513	0.436	0.371	0.317	0.270	0.231	0.198
18	0.836	0.700	0.587	0.494	0.416	0.350	0.296	0.250	0.212	0.180
19	0.828	0.686	0.570	0.475	0.396	0.331	0.277	0.232	0.194	0.164
20	0.820	0.673	0.554	0.456	0.377	0.312	0.258	0.215	0.178	0.149
21	0.811	0.660	0.538	0.439	0.359	0.294	0.242	0.199	0.164	0.135
22	0.803	0.647	0.522	0.422	0.342	0.278	0.226	0.184	0.150	0.123
23	0.795	0.634	0.507	0.406	0.326	0.262	0.211	0.170	0.138	0.112
24	0.788	0.622	0.492	0.390	0.310	0.247	0.197	0.158	0.126	0.102
25	0.780	0.610	0.478	0.375	0.295	0.233	0.184	0.146	0.116	0.092
26	0.772	0.598	0.464	0.361	0.281	0.220	0.172	0.135	0.106	0.084
27	0.764	0.586	0.450	0.347	0.268	0.207	0.161	0.125	0.098	0.076
28	0.757	0.574	0.437	0.333	0.255	0.196	0.150	0.116	0.090	0.069
29	0.749	0.563	0.424	0.321	0.243	0.185	0.141	0.107	0.082	0.063
30	0.742	0.552	0.412	0.308	0.231	0.174	0.131	0.099	0.075	0.057
40	0.672	0.453	0.307	0.208	0.142	0.097	0.067	0.046	0.032	0.022
50	0.608	0.372	0.228	0.141	0.087	0.054	0.034	0.021	0.013	0.009

*PV $= 1/(1 + r)^t$

11%	12%	13%	14%	15%	16%	17%	18%	19%	20%
0.901	0.893	0.885	0.877	0.870	0.862	0.855	0.847	0.840	0.833
0.812	0.797	0.783	0.769	0.756	0.743	0.731	0.718	0.706	0.694
0.731	0.712	0.693	0.675	0.658	0.641	0.624	0.609	0.593	0.579
0.659	0.636	0.613	0.592	0.572	0.552	0.534	0.516	0.499	0.482
0.593	0.567	0.543	0.519	0.497	0.496	0.456	0.437	0.419	0.402
0.535	0.507	0.480	0.456	0.432	0.410	0.390	0.370	0.352	0.335
0.482	0.452	0.425	0.400	0.376	0.354	0.333	0.314	0.296	0.279
0.434	0.404	0.376	0.351	0.327	0.305	0.285	0.266	0.249	0.233
0.391	0.361	0.333	0.308	0.284	0.263	0.243	0.225	0.209	0.194
0.352	0.322	0.295	0.270	0.247	0.227	0.208	0.191	0.176	0.162
0.317	0.287	0.261	0.237	0.215	0.195	0.178	0.162	0.148	0.135
0.286	0.257	0.231	0.208	0.187	0.168	0.152	0.137	0.124	0.112
0.258	0.229	0.204	0.182	0.163	0.145	0.130	0.116	0.104	0.093
0.232	0.205	0.181	0.160	0.141	0.125	0.111	0.099	0.088	0.078
0.209	0.183	0.160	0.140	0.123	0.108	0.095	0.084	0.074	0.065
0.188	0.163	0.141	0.123	0.107	0.093	0.081	0.071	0.062	0.054
0.170	0.146	0.125	0.108	0.093	0.080	0.069	0.060	0.052	0.045
0.153	0.130	0.111	0.095	0.081	0.069	0.059	0.051	0.044	0.038
0.138	1.116	0.098	0.083	0.070	0.060	0.051	0.043	0.037	0.031
0.124	0.104	0.087	0.073	0.061	0.051	0.043	0.037	0.031	0.026
0.112	0.093	0.077	0.064	0.053	0.044	0.037	0.031	0.026	0.022
0.101	0.083	0.068	0.056	0.046	0.038	0.032	0.026	0.022	0.018
0.091	0.074	0.060	0.049	0.040	0.033	0.027	0.022	0.018	0.015
0.082	0.066	0.053	0.043	0.035	0.028	0.023	0.019	0.015	0.013
0.074	0.059	0.047	0.038	0.030	0.024	0.020	0.016	0.013	0.010
0.066	0.053	0.042	0.033	0.026	0.021	0.017	0.014	0.011	0.009
0.060	0.047	0.037	0.029	0.023	0.018	0.014	0.011	0.009	0.007
0.054	0.042	0.033	0.026	0.020	0.016	0.012	0.010	0.008	0.006
0.048	0.037	0.029	0.022	0.017	0.014	0.011	0.008	0.006	0.005
0.044	0.033	0.026	0.020	0.015	0.012	0.009	0.007	0.005	0.004
0.015	0.011	0.008	0.005	0.004	0.003	0.002	0.001	0.001	0.001
0.005	0.003	0.002	0.001	0.001	0.001	0.000	0.000	0.000	0.000

GLOSSARY

ADVERTISING CAPITAL   The stock of information that individuals have as a result of advertising.

ARBITRAGE   The simultaneous buying and selling of the same good in different markets in order to profit from the existing difference in prices between the markets.

AVERAGE COST   Total cost divided by output.

BIVARIATE REGRESSION   The estimate of the line that best describes the relationship between two variables.

BUDGET LINE   A set of points representing various combinations of commodities that can be purchased with the same amount of money income.

CANVASS   To scrutinize, as in going from store to store in search of low prices.

CAPITAL BUDGETING   The allocation of a firm's investment funds to specific projects.

CARTEL   A group of firms that have agreed to limit production in order to enhance the group's total profits.

CERTAINTY EQUIVALENT   The certain return that provides the same utility as a given random return.

COMPARATIVE ADVANTAGE   An advantage relative to others in an overall allocation.

COMPETITIVE MARKET   A market in which neither the buyer of a good nor the seller of a good behaves as if he or she can affect the price of the good being transacted.

COMPLEMENT   Two goods are said to be complements when a rise in the relative price of one good leads to a fall in the consumption of the other good.

CONSTANT RETURNS TO SCALE   When a change in all inputs by a common percentage changes output by the same percentage.

COST MINIMIZATION   Finding the input combination that produces a given level of output at lowest cost.

CROSS-SECTIONAL DATA   Information obtained from different individuals, cities, etc., at a particular time.

DEMAND CURVE   A curve relating the optimal quantities purchased by the individual to the various market prices of the commodity for given levels of money income and other prices.

DEMAND FUNCTION   A function that expresses the relationship between the quantity demanded of a specific good and income and various prices.

ECONOMIC RENT   The additional earnings beyond the earnings that would be necessary to keep a person in a job; the difference between total revenue and total cost.

EFFICIENCY FRONTIER   A function in mean-variance space that separates attainable from unattainable combinations of risk and return.

ELASTICITY OF DEMAND   (See price elasticity.)

ELASTICITY OF SUBSTITUTION   The percentage change in the capital-labor ratio required to change the marginal rate of technical substitution by 1 percent.

EXPANSION PATH   For any given input prices, the set of all cost minimizing combinations of inputs.

EXPECTED UTILITY   A general objective function for a decision maker facing a risky situation.

EXPERIENCE GOOD   A good that has one or more important characteristics that can only be determined by consuming the commodity.

EXPLICIT COSTS   Out-of-pocket expenditures.

FALSE ADVERTISING   The provision of incorrect information through advertising.

FIRM   An organization that converts inputs into goods and services that it sells.

FIRM-SPECIFIC HUMAN CAPITAL   Those skills that can only be used in a particular firm.

FIXED INPUT   An input with costs which are inversely related to the duration of use.

FIXED PROPORTIONS PRODUCTION FUNCTION   A production function in which the ratio of capital to labor does not depend on the price of labor or the price of capital.

FRANCHISE   A retailer or distributor with the authorization to sell a particular company's product.

GENERAL HUMAN CAPITAL   Those skills that can be used in a number of firms.

GOODWILL   The prestige and friendly relations built up by a firm with its customers.

GROUP (OR TEAM) PRODUCTION   The output of a team.

HISTORICAL COST   A cost that was incurred in purchasing an item.

IMPLICIT COSTS   Opportunity costs associated with using resources that are owned by the firm (e.g., building, car, time of the owner).

INDIFFERENCE CURVE   The set of points representing various combinations of commodities that provide a consumer with the same level of satisfaction.

INFERIOR GOOD   A good whose consumption decreases as income rises.

INFORMED BUYERS   Buyers who are aware of a seller's existence.

INSPECTION GOOD   A good whose relevant characteristics can be determined by a potential buyer's inspection prior to purchase.

INTERNAL RATE OF RETURN   The discount rate that makes the net present value of a project equal to zero.

ISOCOST   A line that describes the combinations of inputs that can be purchased for a given sum of money.

ISOQUANT   A curve that shows all the combinations of inputs that will produce a specific level of output.

LEARNING BY DOING   The additional productivity that comes from experience with a process or model.

LEVERAGE   The introduction of fixed interest-bearing debt into the capital structure of a firm in an effort to increase the return to the firm's shareholders.

LONG RUN   A period of time during which the quantities of all inputs are adjusted (if necessary).

MALFEASANCE   The performance of some act which is unlawful or which one has specifically contracted not to perform.

MANAGERIAL ECONOMICS   The application of microeconomic principles to business problems by the manager of a firm.

MARGINAL COST   The change in total cost that results from a unit increase in output.

MARGINAL FACTOR COST   The increase in the total expenditures on a factor accompanying a 1-unit increase in the employment of that factor.

MARGINAL PRODUCT   The change in output that results from a 1-unit increase in the input.

MARGINAL RATE OF SUBSTITUTION   The maximum rate at which a consumer is willing to substitute one commodity for another while maintaining a constant level of satisfaction or utility.

MARGINAL RATE OF TECHNICAL SUBSTITUTION OF CAPITAL FOR LABOR   The decrease in capital that results from a 1-unit increase in labor when output is held constant.

MARGINAL REVENUE   Change in total revenue resulting from selling 1 more unit.

MARKET INSURANCE   The reduction through the market of the firm's losses in the event of misfortune.

MEAN   Average value.

MONOPOLY   A market in which a single firm *produces* a *commodity* for which there are no close substitutes.

MONOPSONY   A market in which a single firm *purchases* an *input* for which there are no close substitutes.

MULTIVARIATE REGRESSION   The estimate of the line that best describes the relationship between one variable and several other variables.

NORMAL GOOD   A good whose consumption increases as income rises.

PORTFOLIO   A combination of securities usually designed to reduce the risk associated with the income provided.

PRESENT VALUE   The value today.

PRICE DISCRIMINATION   The charging, by a monopolist, of different prices for the same good, where the price differences are not the result of cost differences.

PRICE ELASTICITY   Minus the percentage change in the quantity demanded divided by the percentage change in the product's price.

PRIVATE BRAND   A uniform product that is sold under at least two brand names.

PRODUCTION FUNCTION   A function describing the relationship between a group of inputs and the maximum amount of output that can be produced from the inputs.

PROFIT   Total revenue less total cost.

PROFIT MAXIMIZATION   Finding the resource allocation that produces the highest profit.

R^2 (or COEFFICIENT OF DETERMINATION)   Proportion of the variation in the dependent variable (e.g., quantity demanded) that is explained by variation in the independent variable (e.g., prices, income).

REPLACEMENT COST   The cost of replacing an item with a physically identical item.

RISK   A situation in which the specific outcome of a random experiment is unknown, although the decision maker does know the probability associated with each outcome.

RISK AVERSION   Preference for certain income over uncertain income with the same expected income.

RISK-FREE ASSET   An asset that has zero variance in its rate of return.

RISK LOVER   One who prefers uncertain income over certain income with the same expected income.

RISK NEUTRALITY   Indifference between certain income and uncertain income with the same expected income.

SELF-INSURANCE   The reduction, through the firm's own efforts, of the firm's losses in the event of misfortune (e.g., the installation of a sprinkler system).

SELF-PROTECTION   The reduction, through the firm's own efforts, of the probability of a misfortune (e.g., the installation of a safe).

SHORT RUN   A period of time during which the manager does not vary at least one input because of the expense associated with such alteration.

STANDARD DEVIATION   Square root of the variance.

SUBSTITUTE   Two goods are said to be substitutes when a rise in the relative price of one good leads to an increase in the consumption of the other good.

SUPPLY CURVE   A curve showing the maximum amount supplied per unit time at different prices, all other things being equal.

TIME SERIES DATA   Information that follows behavior over time.

TOTAL COST   The sum of all the costs incurred in the production of a good or service.

TOTAL REVENUE   Total income received by a firm or industry in payment for its product(s).

TRANSACTION COST   The cost associated with the transaction itself, e.g., the cost of finding a buyer, the cost of negotiating a contract.

TRANSFER PRICE   The price at which a good is exchanged from one division of a firm to another.

UNCERTAINTY   A situation where the probabilities of the possible outcomes to a random experiment are not known by the decision maker.

VARIABLE INPUT   An input with costs which are independent of the duration of use.

VARIABLE PROPORTIONS PRODUCTION FUNCTION   A production
function in which the ratio of capital to labor does depend on the price of
labor and the price of capital.

VARIANCE   Average squared deviation from the mean.

INDEX